A TREASURY

of
Quips
Quotes
&Anecdotes

for Preachers and Teachers

ANTHONY CASTLE

XXIII
TWENTY-THIRD PUBLICATIONS
Mystic, CT 06355

Dedicated to my colleagues
Annette Hayes and Keir Page
in appreciation for their
devoted commitment
to Religious Education

First published in the United Kingdom in 1997 under the title
More Quotes and Anecdotes by
KEVIN MAYHEW LTD
Maypole Farm
Rectory Road
Buxhall
Stowmarket
Suffolk, IP30 0SZ, U.K.

Second North American Printing 2000

Reprinted under license in the USA by
TWENTY-THIRD PUBLICATIONS/BAYARD
185 Willow Street
P.O. Box 180
Mystic, CT 06355
(860) 536-2611
(800) 321-0411

ISBN 0-89622-920-3
Library of Congress Catalog Card Number 97-62562
Printed in the U.S.A.

CONTENTS

INTRODUCTION

In the past few years the pastoral and catechetical value of a good story has been rediscovered and the art of storytelling itself is experiencing a sort of renaissance. When stories are linked with the liturgical year, they are all the more effective because they help homilists, teachers, catechists, and indeed all believers, apply the gospel message to the everyday circumstances of life.

In this collection you will find numerous stories, but you will also discover an abundance of quips and quotes, brief and not-so-brief statements from people as diverse as Pope John Paul II, Ralph Waldo Emerson, Abraham Lincoln, Teilhard de Chardin, Alice in Wonderland, and Christina Rossetti. All are intended to help preachers, teachers and all searchers and believers to make connections between what they do on Sunday and how they live their daily lives.

These offerings are drawn from all over the world and from almost every century, and all are arranged into themes suggested by the liturgical calendar for all three cycles. Note that Appendix Two lists all of the Readings for Years A, B, and C and their corresponding themes. There is also a subject index and an index of sources.

It is our hope that this book will help, guide, and delight all of you who have the inestimable privilege of publicly proclaiming Christ's gospel as preachers, teachers, and catechists. We hope too that it will inspire and motivate those of you who simply want to read these pages for personal prayer, reflection, and enjoyment.

A1
THE VALUE OF TIME

'You know *the time* has come.'
Romans 13:11

QUOTATIONS

Time never takes time off.
St Augustine of Hippo

Time surveyed in its wholeness is Eternity.
Josiah Royce

Time heals what reason cannot.
Seneca

Time is the deposit each one has in the bank of God and no one knows the balance.
Ralph W. Sockman

Time is a three-fold present: the present as we experience it, the past as a present memory and the future as a present expectation.
St Augustine of Hippo

It is magnificent to grow old, if one keeps young.
Harry Emerson Fosdick

The morning hour has gold in its hand.
Benjamin Franklin

In rivers, the water that you touch is the last of what has passed and the first of that which comes: so with present time.
Leonardo da Vinci

The voice of Time cries to man, 'Advance'. Time is for his advancement and improvement, for his greater worth, his greater happiness, his better life.
Charles Dickens

This time, like all other times, is a very good one, if we but know what to do with it.
Ralph W. Emerson

We live in deeds, not years; in thoughts, not breaths;
in feelings, not in figures on a dial.
We should count time by heart throbs: he most lives
who thinks most, feels the noblest, acts the best.
Philip James Bailey

'The core of our being is drawn like a stone to the quiet depths of each moment where God awaits us with eternal longing.'
Thomas Merton

Time is
– too slow for those who wait,
– too swift for those who fear,
– too long for those who grieve,
– too short for those who rejoice; but for those who love,
   time is eternity.
Henry Van Dyke

Make a careful use of your fragments of time. It is wonderful how much can be got through by these means. A great deal of study, or writing, or other work, can be done by a resolute will in odd quarters of hours, and very often we can get no more. Nothing is more commonly said than that if you want something done, you will have a much better chance of getting it done by a busy man than by an idle one, and this simply because the former has learnt the secret of economising his time.
Bishop Walsham How

HUMOUR

'I've got ten pairs of trainers; one for every day of the week'
Samantha Fox

WORD PICTURES

A hunter in India with a sling had come to the end of his stones and wanted one to sling at a bird on a tree. He saw some fine stones lying near, and took up a handful to hurl one by one with his sling. Without very much success, however, for the bird flew gaily off, and the stones fell into the river, only one remaining of the handful he had taken. He was going to throw it away, but seeing it was pretty, he saved it as a plaything for his little daughter. On the way home, he met a diamond merchant, and showed him the stone. The merchant saw at once that it was a diamond, and offered a large sum for it. The hunter started lamenting his bad fortune, and on being asked why he was so disconsolate, he explained that it was because he had not realised the value of the stones he had thrown into the river. Had he but saved them, a fortune might have been his. They were now lost to him forever. So is every day of life precious – it can never be recovered.
Anon

'Listen to the exhortation of the Dawn!
Look to this day . . .
for yesterday is but a dream,
and tomorrow is only a vision:
but today, well-lived, makes
every yesterday a dream of happiness,
and every tomorrow a vision of hope.
Look well therefore to this day!
Such is the salutation of the dawn!'
Sanskrit poem

For a long time it seemed to me that real life was about to begin, but there was always some obstacle in the way. Something had to be got through first, some unfinished business; time still to be served, a debt to be paid. Then life would begin. At last it dawned on me that these obstacles were my life.
Catholic Digest

Take time to work – it is the price of success.
Take time to think – it is the source of power.
Take time to play – it is the secret of perpetual youth.
Take time to read – it is the foundation of wisdom.
Take time to be friendly – it is the road to happiness.
Take time to dream – it is hitching your wagon to a star.
Take time to love and be loved – it is the privilege of the Gods.
Take time to look around – the day is too short to be selfish.
Take time to laugh – it is the music of the soul.
Irish saying

I would pick more daisies
If I had my life over, I'd dare to make
   more mistakes next time!
I'd relax, I'd limber up, I would be
   sillier than I have been this trip!
I would take fewer things seriously,
   take more chances, take more trips.
I'd climb more mountains, and swim more rivers.
I would eat more ice-cream and less beans,
   and would, perhaps have more actual troubles,
   but I'd have fewer imaginary ones.
You see, I'm one of those people who lived seriously,
   sanely, hour after hour, day after day.
Oh I've had my moments, and if I had to do it over again,
   I'd have more of them.
In fact, I'd try to have nothing else, just moments,
   one after another instead of living
   so many years ahead of each day.
I've been one of those persons who never goes anywhere without
   a thermometer, hot water bottle, rain coat and parachute.
If I had to do it again, I would travel lighter, this trip.
If I had my life over I would start going barefoot
   earlier in the Spring, and stay that way later into Autumn.
I would go to more dances, I would ride more merry-go-rounds.
I would pick more daisies.
Margaret Wilkinson

Lord Nelson used to say that he owed everything he had done in life to the fact that he was always there a quarter of an hour before the time, rather than a quarter of an hour late.

There are two days in every week about which we should not worry, two days which should be kept free from fear and apprehension.

One of these days is Yesterday with its mistakes and cares, its faults and blunders, its aches and pains. Yesterday has passed forever beyond our control.

All the money in the world cannot bring back Yesterday. We cannot undo a single act we performed; we cannot erase a single word we said. Yesterday is gone.

The other day we should not worry about is Tomorrow with its possible adversities, its burdens, its large promise and poor performance. Tomorrow is also beyond our immediate control.

Tomorrow's sun will rise, either in splendour or behind a mask of clouds – but it will rise. Until it does, we have no stake in Tomorrow, for it is yet unborn.

This leaves only one day – Today. Any man can fight the battles of just one day. It is only when you and I add the burdens of those two awful eternities – Yesterday and Tomorrow – that we break down.

It is not the experience of Today that drives men mad – it is remorse or bitterness for something which happened Yesterday and the dread of what Tomorrow may bring.
Anon

USEFUL TEXTS

Time:
> Appropriate, for different events, *Eccles. 3:1-8*
> Of Christ's return, *Matt. 24:36*
> Right, to respond to the Gospel, *Mark 1:15*
> Should be carefully used, *Eph. 5:16*

See also: A19 Patience
     B25 Quiet-time for prayer
     C34 The value of little things

A2
INTEGRITY

'Integrity is the loincloth round his waist.'
Isaiah 11:5

QUOTATIONS

God wants the heart.
The Talmud

A man of integrity, sincerity, and good nature can never be concealed, for his character is wrought into his countenance.
Marcus Aurelius

My worth to God in public is what I am in private.
Oswald Chambers

Never esteem anything as of advantage to you that makes you break your word or lose your self-respect.
Marcus Aurelius

The measure of a man's real character is what he would do if he knew he would never be found out.
Thomas Macaulay

When he has no lust, no hatred, a man walks safely among the things of lust and hatred.
The Bhagavad Gita

The freedom to communicate also requires in a Christian community not only a response of integrity but one of love.
Jack Dominian

Power is never good unless he be good who has it. A good name is better than wealth. No sword can slay it; no rope can bind it.
King Alfred

No Mirabeau, Napoleon, Burns, Cromwell, no man adequate to do anything, but is first of all in right earnest about it; what I call a sincere man. I should say sincerity, a deep, great, genuine sincerity, is the first characteristic of all men in any way heroic. A little man may have it; it is competent to all men that God has made; but a great man cannot be without it.
Thomas Carlyle

A sweet attractive kind of grace,
a full assurance borne by looks,
continual comfort in a face,
the lineaments of Gospel books.
A friend's description of Sir Philip Sidney

I am not bound to win,
    but I am bound to be true.
I am not bound to succeed,
    but I am bound to live up to the light I have.
I must stand with anybody that stands right,
    stand with him while he is right,
and part with him when he goes wrong.
Abraham Lincoln

PROVERBS

If you hear that a mountain has moved, believe; but if you hear that a man has changed his character, believe it not.
Islamic proverb

HUMOUR

Live so that the preacher can tell the truth at your funeral.
K. Bechstrom

Some years ago, a young businessman, who had risen to a position of importance, fell in love with a well-known and highly respected actress. For many months he was constantly in her company, escorting her to all 'the right places'. Eventually he decided to marry the young lady.

Before doing so, however, he hired a private detective to investigate her. The task was assigned to a special agent, who had no knowledge of the identity of his client.

Finally, the agent's report was sent to him. It read: 'Miss – – has an excellent reputation. Her past is spotless, her associates beyond reproach. The only hint of scandal is that in recent months she has been seen in the company of a businessman of doubtful reputation.'
P.F.

WORD PICTURES

Bishop Taylor Smith relates that during one of his voyages business was done on the ship between the soldiers and the natives at Aden. One native, ignorant of the value of English coins, sent back too much change to one of the soldiers, who promptly returned it. The native, realising that he was in error, but not knowing how, sent back more change. The soldier returned the surplus money. 'You're a silly fool,' exclaimed an onlooker to him. 'Do you think so, sir?' asked Tommy. 'I was not going to sell my character for the sake of a few coppers.'
Anon

Pseudo-goodness will prefer routine duty to courage and creativity. In the end it will be content with established procedures and safe formulas, while turning a blind eye to the greatest enormities of injustice and uncharity. Such are the routines of piety that sacrifice everything else to preserve the comforts of the past, however inadequate and shameful they may be in the present. Meditation, in such a case, becomes a factory for alibis and instead of struggling with the sense of falsity and inauthenticity in oneself, it battles against the exigencies of the present with platitudes minted in the previous century. If necessary it also fabricates condemnations and denunciations of those who risk new ideas and new solutions.
Thomas Merton

'There are, indeed, two types of human beings: the pharisees and the publicans,' said the Master after reading the parable of Jesus. 'How does one recognise the pharisees?'
'Simple. They are the ones who do the classifying!' said the Master.
Anthony de Mello

If

If you can keep your head when all about you
    Are losing theirs and blaming it on you,
If you can trust yourself when all men doubt you,
    But make allowances for their doubting you;
If you can wait and not be tired by waiting
    Or being lied about, don't deal in lies,
Or being hated, don't give way to hating,
    And yet don't look too good, nor talk too wise:

If you can dream – and not make dreams your master;
    If you can think – and not make thoughts your aim;
If you can meet with Triumph and Disaster
    And treat those two imposters just the same;
If you can bear to hear the truth you've spoken
    Twisted by knaves to make a trap for fools,
Or watch the things you gave your life to, broken,
    And stoop and build 'em up with worn-out tools:

If you can make one heap of all your winnings
    And risk it on one turn of pitch-and-toss,
And lose, and start again at your beginnings
    And never breathe a word about your loss;
If you can force your heart and nerve and sinew
    To serve your turn long after they are gone,
And so hold on when there is nothing in you
    Except the Will which says to them: 'Hold on!'

If you can talk with crowds and keep your virtue,
    Or walk with Kings – nor lose the common touch,
If neither foes nor loving friends can hurt you,
    If all men count with you, but none too much;
If you can fill the unforgiving minute
    With sixty second's worth of distance run –
Yours is the Earth and everything that's in it,
    And – what is more – you'll be a Man, my Son!
Rudyard Kipling

USEFUL TEXTS

Integrity:
  In trials, *Job 2:9*
  As guide, *Prov. 11:3*
  As protection, *Ps. 25:21*

See also: B19 Conscience
           B20 Growth to maturity
           B26 The whole person
           C23 Zeal for what is right

A3
PERSEVERANCE

'Happy are those who do not lose faith in me.'
Matthew 11:6

QUOTATIONS

Patient endurance attaineth to all things.
Saint Teresa of Avila

Never say die!
Charles Dickens

By perseverance the snail reached the ark.
Charles H. Spurgeon

Great works are performed not by strength but by perseverance.
Samuel Johnson

Never give in! Never give in! Never, Never, Never, Never, Never,
– in anything great or small, large or petty – never give in except
to convictions of honour and good sense.
Winston Churchill

Perseverance is not a long race; it is many short races one after
another.
Walter Elliott

That man is perfect in faith who can come to God in the utter
dearth of his feelings and desires, without a glow or an aspiration,
with the weight of low thoughts, failures, neglects and wandering
forgetfulness, and say to him, 'Thou art my refuge'.
George Macdonald

PROVERBS

What can't be cured must be endured.
English proverb

Don't listen to anyone who tells you that you can't do this or that. That's nonsense. Make up your mind, you'll never use crutches or a stick, then have a go at everything. Go to school, join in all the games you can. Go anywhere you want to. But never, never let them persuade you that things are too difficult or impossible.
Sir Douglas Bader to a 14-year-old boy who lost a leg in a car crash.

WORD PICTURES

An old preacher was asked to define Christian perseverance. He answered: 'It means, firstly, to take hold; secondly, to hold on; thirdly and lastly, to never leave go.'

M. Louis Bleriot, the famous airman who was first to cross the Channel in an aeroplane of his own designing, only achieved his object through marvellous perseverance. Ten machines were built and wrecked, but still he did not give up; it was with his eleventh aeroplane that he finally, on 25 July 1909, flew the Channel in 37 minutes. And even then he was badly lame with a scalded foot, which would have prevented most men from attempting the adventure.
Anon

The story of how Sir Ronald Ross discovered which of the two thousand species of mosquitoes that exist was the carrier of the malaria parasite, is a perfect example of perseverance. Ross dissected mosquito after mosquito, each one of which cost him two or three hours of intense peering through his microscope, until he had done many hundreds . . . (working until, as he said), 'The screws of my microscope were rusted with sweat from my forehead and hands, and its last remaining eye-piece was cracked! . . .

By August, 1897 he had some thirty promising mosquitoes, all bred from larvae and fed on malaria patients. He dissected one from another, until he had come to the last three, but still he had not traced the parasite in the mosquito body. When he looked at his last three insects on the morning of 20 August, he saw that one had died; then he decided to look at the last but one, although his eyesight was already very tired. He took the stomach out and searched the remainder of the body and again found nothing. He could scarcely bring himself to look at the numerous cells of the stomach-tissue, which under the microscope looked like a collection of flagstones. He had done it a thousand times before, without convincing result.

'But,' he said' 'the Angel of Fate fortunately laid his hand on my head . . .' He looked, and looked again. He saw a circular object which could not be one of the cells of the stomach-tissue of the mosquito. In it were black granules exactly like those seen in the malaria parasite. If these were malaria granules, then they had got into the walls of the mosquito's stomach. He laughed, and shouted for his assistant, but he had gone for his siesta . . .

He made careful notes and drawings, went home for tea and slept soundly for an hour. He awoke and it occurred to him that if the cells he had seen were indeed a stage of the developing parasite, those in his last remaining mosquito should have grown during the night. On the next morning he arrived at the hospital in intense excitement. He examined his last specimen with a shaking hand. There indeed were the peculiar cells, and they were much bigger!

The basic problem was solved at last. He had discovered that the species of mosquito which carried the parasite was the *Anopheles*, and he had found that the parasite lives in or on the wall of its stomach, and can be recognised at once by its characteristic dark pigment. From this point, the elucidation of the details of the complete life-history and mode of transmission was primarily a matter of technical skill and patience. On the same evening he scribbled:

This day designing God
    hath put into my hand
a wondrous thing. And God
    be praised. At his command
I have found thy secret deeds.
    O million-murdering Death!
I know that this little thing
    a million men will save –
Oh death, where is thy sting?
    Thy victory, O grave?
J. G. *Crowther*

13

Accidents happen so easily; and once they have happened nothing can undo them, no matter how we may regret that they have befallen.

A small boy, born on 4 January, 1809, was the victim of such an accident when he was only three years old. His father, a harness-maker in a village near Paris, had been boring holes in leather with an awl but had put down his tool for a moment. It was Louis' chance to try it for himself but, instead of making a hole in the leather, he succeeded in making a hole in his eye. For days he was in pain. Then infection spread to the other eye and that was the last young Louis ever saw. For the rest of his life he was blind. For many that might have been the end of a useful life.

But as soon as he was old enough, he was sent to a school for the blind in Paris, where he was taught to read by touching large raised letters with his fingers. Louis was so successful that he soon found himself teaching others to read by the same method.

But it was not easy. Some people just could not do it. Louis Braille determined to invent another method by which blind people could read. He worked and persevered for many a long hour to try to perfect an alphabet for the blind. When he was twenty years old he succeeded.

The Braille alphabet consists of groups of raised dots, which can be recognised by touching them with the finger-tips. Braille requires much more space than ordinary print and is expensive but it has proved a blessing to thousands of blind people who are enabled to read without using their eyes.

Anon

USEFUL TEXTS

Perseverance:
  In practising forgiveness, *Matt. 18:21-22*
  Until the end, *Mark 13:13*
  In doing good, *Gal. 6:9*
  In prayer, *Eph. 6:18*

See also: A19 Patience
           B49 Coping with doubt
           C30 Increase our faith
           C35 Hope

A4
EMMANUEL – MARY'S CHILD

'The maiden is with child and will give birth
to a son whom she will call Emmanuel.'
Isaiah, 7:14

QUOTATIONS

The Word of God became man that you also may learn from a
man how a man becomes a God.
St Clement of Alexandria

On account of him there have come to be many Christs in the
world, even all who, like him, loved righteousness and hated iniquity.
Origen

In order that the body of Christ might be shown to be a real body,
he was born of a woman; but in order that his Godhead might be
made clear he was born of a virgin.
St Thomas Aquinas

We know that the Word assumed a body from a virgin, and
through a new creation, put on our old nature. We know that he
was a man, formed from the same substance as we are. If he were
not of the same nature as ourselves, his command to imitate him
as a master would be a futile one.
St Hippolytus

HUMOUR

A nativity play was to be performed in the church hall and a
country vicar went to town to get a streamer for display.
Unfortunately he forgot the measurements so he wired his wife for
details. The telegraph clerk at the other end nearly had a fit when
the reply message was received. It read: 'Unto us a Child is Born
– seven feet six by one foot three.'

Dialogue from a church nativity play, written, directed and acted by a class of nine-year-olds, opens with the scene at the inn. Joseph and Mary ask for a room overlooking Bethlehem.

Innkeeper: Can't you see the 'No Vacancy' sign?

Joseph: Yes, but can't you see that my wife is expecting a baby any minute?

Innkeeper: Well, that's not my fault.

Joseph: Well it's not mine either!

WORD PICTURES

It is unbelievable that men could take a word like 'Bethlehem', so glorious and beautiful, and make out of it a synonym for confusion and disorder. Yet this is what happened. St Mary of Bethlehem was founded as a hospital in England in 1247. Two centuries later it was turned into a hospital for the insane. The noise and confusion of that institution became known throughout the country. The original name, through contraction and corruption, was changed to Bedlam.

Anon

In the house alongside the City Road chapel, made forever memorable by the preaching of John Wesley, they show you the room where Wesley died, on a March day in 1791. Sometime before his death, he had been trying vainly to make those who stood by his bed understand what he would say. He kept silent for a few moments and then, gathering all his strength, uttered in a clear, loud voice those words which have become a watchword of the Church he founded, 'The best of all – God is with us.'

Clarence E. Macartney

Night had fallen and the only light was from the flickering flames of a pile of burning sticks. They lit up the faces of the Zulu menfolk sitting round the fire on their mats and sent their shadows dancing on the low, beehive-shaped huts that encircled them.

There were young men there, just returned to the homestead. They had tales to tell of strangers in the land.

'Not like the ones who came before with weapons that spat fire and screeching pebbles. These strangers pay respect to their chiefs, they have comforting words for the sufferer, care for the sick.

And all the time they speak about a wonderful one they call the saviour of all men.

Born in a stable, he was. Important though, because kings came looking for him with gifts of gold. They speak with power, like our old men reciting the tribal history.'

Old Shaka, named after a famous chief, had been taking it all in. The party dispersed. He crouched down through the low entrance into his hut, spread his mat on the foot of the tree trunk which was the centrepost of the hut, lay down and lowered the back of his head on the wooden headrest. Shaka slipped into sleep and the talk of the evening moulded his dreams.

'Gold,' he mused in his dream, 'I have no gold. But my staff is precious, with its knob carved like the head of a Zulu chief. And powerful. It could beat down many an enemy.'

To the child in the stable he offered his staff.

The child said: 'All power is given me in heaven and on earth. I come not to strike men down but to love and redeem them. You are kind, Shaka, but keep your staff.'

His next most precious possession was a blanket. Off he went to offer that.

But the child said: 'Birds have their nests, but the son of man will have no place to rest, no comfort.' Smiling, he gave back the blanket.

Shaka had no other treasures. 'I know what,' he said. In his dream he put on his warrior's feathered head-dress and took his shield. 'When there is war,' he said, 'I serve my chief. I will be your warrior in war.'

But the child said: 'My kingdom is not of this world. If it were, my Father would give me an army of a thousand angels.'

Shaka woke up. He took his staff, and walked into the dawn.

It was deep in the night when he came at last to a big hut of a place with light glowing inside. It was full of people, his tribespeople. A tin hurricane lamp hung from a beam.

17

Leaning on his staff, his fingers twined round the Zulu chief knob, there was little Shaka understood at that Christmas midnight Mass.

The long catechumenate was to make everything clear and at baptism Shaka was named Noel. 'Comes from Emmanuel,' the missionary explained, 'which means, God with us.'

And Shaka understood. The child was the Prince of Peace and the kingdom was within.

William Burridge

USEFUL TEXTS

Emmanuel:
>   Observance of God's coming in flesh, *1 Tim. 3:16*
>   Observance of Christ's birth, *Matt. 1:18-21*

See also: A37 Christ the King
           B4   Mary – Handmaid of God
           B8   The Word
           B46 Christ the Sacrament of God
           C45 The Divinity of Christ

A5
ONE FOR ANOTHER – UNSELFISHNESS

'You are my servant in whom I shall be glorified.'
Isaiah, 49:3

QUOTATIONS

Real unselfishness consists in sharing the interests of others.
George Santayana

The secret of being loved is in being lovely; and the secret of being
lovely is in being unselfish.
Josiah Holland

They that deny themselves for Christ shall enjoy themselves in Christ.
John Mason

Watch your habits; the selfish life and the self-indulgent life
polarises around them.
Paul Campbell

Self-love is more ingenious than the most ingenious man in the
world.
Francois de la Rochefoucauld

Living in our selfishness means stopping at human limits and
preventing our transformation into divine love.
Carlo Carretto

The most satisfying thing in life is to have been able to give a large
part of oneself to others.
Teilhard de Chardin

You give but little when you give of your possessions. It is when
you give of yourself that you truly give.
Kahlil Gibran

WORD PICTURES

On the tomb of the British philanthropist, John Howard, in St Paul's is this inscription:

'He who lives for others treads an open but unfrequented path to immortality.'

Two-year-old Sharon and her friend Michael, who was nearly four, were playing happily in the garden. Suddenly their mums, who were enjoying a quiet cup of coffee in the kitchen, were disturbed by a great commotion. Rushing to the window they saw both children trying to jam themselves, at the same time, on the seat of the one and only tricycle. After much shouting and screeching both managed to squeeze on, but neither could move! When their mums got to them Sharon was sobbing and Michael was stoutly and loudly proclaiming, 'If one of us got off I could ride it properly.'

It was resolved that they would take turns. Michael had the first short ride up the concrete garden path, pursued after less than thirty seconds by Sharon, calling, 'Me turn, me turn.'
A.P.C.

Two little boys, one leading his smaller sister, were going through the woods. They came to a tree that had fallen across the creek and formed a natural bridge. The first little fellow bounded over, and, turning, said, 'Come on, it's easy.' But the other gripped his little sister's hand a little tighter, and shrank back, saying, 'I could manage it, but she might fall.' Many members of churches will not deny themselves some pet indulgence for the sake of someone weaker than themselves.
Anon

It is said of the great artist Michelangelo that when at work he wore over his forehead, fastened on his cap, a lighted candle, so that no shadow of himself might fall upon the marble or the canvas. We need to take exceeding care that no shadow of ourselves, our personal ambitions, our self-seeking, falls upon that which we are doing for Christ.
F. L. McKean

In Pompeii the body of a crippled boy was found with his foot lame. Round his body was a woman's arm, bejewelled. The great stream of fire suddenly issuing from the volcano had driven a terror-stricken crowd for refuge. The woman had evidently taken pity on the cripple. Only the arm outstretched to save was saved itself.
S. D. Gordon

In the cold mountainous regions of North India, where it is very cold, travellers are helped to keep warm in this way. They take a small vessel, put burning coal in it, and cover it up. They weave strings around it and, wrapping it with cloth, carry it under their arms. Three men were travelling thus towards the sacred place of Amarnath. One of them saw several others suffering with cold, and, taking the fire out of his vessel lit a fire so that everyone could get warm. So everyone left the place alive. When they had all to walk in the dark the second man of the party took out the fire in his vessel and lit a torch with it, and helped them all to walk along in safety. The third man of the party mocked them and said: 'You are fools. You have wasted your fire for the sake of others.' 'Show us your fire,' they said to him. When he broke open his vessel there was no fire, but only ashes and coal. With his fire one had given warmth and another had given light. But the third man was selfish and kept the fire to himself, and it was no use even to him.

In the same way, it is God's will that the fire of the Holy Spirit which we receive should give warmth and light to others and help them to be saved.
Sadhu Sindar Singh

USEFUL TEXTS
Unselfishness, Examples of:
Abraham, *Gen. 13:8-9*
David, *1 Chr. 21:17*
Paul, *1 Cor. 9:12-22*
Christ, *Mark 6:30-34*
See also: A33 Love your neighbour
            B41 Generosity
            B47 Dying to self
            C34 The value of little things

A6
LIGHT OF THE WORLD

'The Lord is my light and my help.'
Psalm 27

QUOTATIONS

Light, even though it passes through pollution, is not polluted.
St Augustine of Hippo

The first creature of God, in the works of the days, was the light
of sense, the last was the light of reason.
Francis Bacon

Before the eyes of men let duly shine thy light.
But ever let thy life's best part be out of sight.
R. C. Trench

Jesus Christ, the Lord, is our true life, and apart from him we are
only ghosts, masquerading as human beings lacking substance.
St Ignatius of Antioch

The light everlasting unto the blind is not, but is born in the eye
that has vision.
H. W. Longfellow

And the Lord said: 'I am the light, and the holder is your heart.'
St Mechtild of Magdeburg

It is written, 'For God is light' – not the light seen by these eyes
of ours, but that which the heart sees upon hearing of the words,
'he is truth'.
St Augustine of Hippo

When you walk towards the light, the shadow of your burden falls
behind you.
Kahlil Gibran

PROVERBS

There is more light than can be seen through a window.
Russian proverb

WORD PICTURES

John Ruskin once sat with a friend in the dusk of an evening and watched a lamplighter, torch in hand, lighting the street lights on a distant hill. Very soon the man's form was no longer distinguishable in the distance, but everywhere he went he left a light burning brightly. 'There,' said Ruskin, 'that is what I mean by a real Christian. You can trace his course by the light that he leaves burning.'
Carl Knudsen

A man was flying his single-engine airplane towards a small country airport. It was late in the day, and before he could get the plane into position to land, dusk fell and he could not see the hazy field below. He had no lights on his plane and there was no one on duty at the airport. He began circling, but the darkness deepened, and for two hours he flew that plane around and around, knowing that he would certainly crash when his fuel was expended.

Then a miracle occurred. Someone on the ground heard his engine and realised his plight. A man drove his car back and forth on the runway, to show where the airstrip was and then shone the headlights from the far end of the strip to guide the pilot to a safe landing.

Christ is the light and the way for our lives. There is safety in the lighted area of his path for us. But disaster lies in the darkness to the left or the right.
James Dobson

It is said that Tennyson was walking one day in a beautiful garden where many flowers were blooming. A friend who accompanied him said: 'Mr Tennyson, you speak so often of Jesus. Will you tell me what Christ really means to you?' Tennyson stopped, thought a moment; then, pointing down to a beautiful flower, said: 'What the sun is to that flower, Jesus Christ is to my soul.'
Anon

The keeper of the lighthouse at Calais was talking of the brightness of his lantern, which can be seen ten leagues at sea. A visitor said to him, 'What if one of the lights should chance to go out?' 'Never! Impossible!' he cried, horrified at the thought. 'Sir,' said he pointing to the ocean, 'yonder, where nothing can be seen, there are ships going to all parts of the world. If tonight one of my burners went out, within six months would come a letter, perhaps from India, perhaps from America, perhaps from some place I never heard of, saying, "Such a night, at such an hour, the light of Calais burned dim, the watchman neglected his post, and vessels were in danger." Ah, sir, sometimes in the dark nights, in stormy weather, I look out to sea, and feel as if the eyes of the whole world were looking at my light. Go out? Burn dim? Never!'
D. Williamson

USEFUL TEXTS

Light, Descriptive of:
   God, *1 John 1:5*
   Jesus Christ, *John 8:12*
   Christians, *Matt. 5:14*
   Christian life, *1 John 1:7; 2:9-10*

See also: A37 Christ the King
           B4   Mary – Handmaid of God
           B8   The Word
           B46 Christ the Sacrament of God

A7
Poor in Spirit

'How happy are the poor in spirit;
theirs is the kingdom of heaven.'
Matthew 5:3

Quotations

The man who is poor in spirit is the man who has realised that
things mean nothing and that God means everything.
William Barclay

Being poor in spirit means, above all, being unrestrained by what
is called fashion, it means freedom.
Carlo Carretto

'Poor in spirit' refers, not precisely to humility, but to an attitude
of dependance on God and detachment from earthly supports.
Ronald Knox

Poverty is not material. It is a beatitude. 'Blessed are the poor in
spirit.' It is a way of being, thinking and loving. It is a gift of the
Spirit. Poverty is detachment, and freedom, and above all, truth.
Carlo Carretto

It is a good thing to have money and it is a good thing to have the
things that money will buy. It is good too to check up once in a while
and make sure you haven't lost the things that money can't buy.
George Horace Lorimer

Proverbs

He is not poor that hath little, but he that desireth much.
English proverb

Word Pictures

Once some robbers came into the monastery and said to one of
the elders: 'We have come to take away everything that is in your

cell.' And he said: 'My sons, take all you want.' So they took everything they could find in the cell and started off. But they left behind a little bag that was hidden in the cell. The elder picked it up and followed after them, crying out: 'My sons, take this, you forgot it in the cell!' Amazed at the patience of the elder, they brought everything back into his cell and did penance, saying: 'This one really is a man of God!'
Tales of the Desert Fathers

Rabbi Moshe Leib of Sasou once gave his last coin to a man of evil reputation. His students reproached him for it. Whereupon he replied: 'Shall I be more particular than God, who gave the coin to me?'
Hasidic story

What really matters is to be 'poor in spirit'; and some of those noble and princely saints who lived amongst outward riches managed to be among the most truly 'poor' for the love of Christ. St Francis of Assisi lived in actual poverty; St Elizabeth of Hungary lived in a rich palace, and yet she had the same spirit. When about thirteen years old St Elizabeth became a member of St Francis's Third Order. Cardinal Ugolino, the friend of St Francis, was also a friend of Elizabeth's, and she must have asked him to get her some little thing belonging to the holy Founder, for Ugolino asked St Francis to do as Elias had done for his disciple and leave her his cloak – 'as she is full of your spirit', he said. St Francis, delighted to hear of this dear little Lady Poverty, sent her his cloak. It remained St Elizabeth's greatest treasure. When she was dying she left it to one of her friends, saying: 'Despise it not because it is old and patched and worn: it is the most precious jewel that I ever possessed', and she told how she always put it on when she wished to pray for some special grace, and how she was always heard.
F. H. Drinkwater

In AD 258 the Emperor Valerian issued an edict that all bishops, priests and deacons should at once be arrested and put on trial. The Pope, Sixtus II, was one of the first to be seized. He had entrusted the treasury of the Church to the deacon Laurence, with instructions to distribute everything to the widows and orphans, which Laurence did, even selling the sacred vessels.

As the Pope was being taken to execution Laurence followed him in tears.

'Where are you hurrying to, holy Father? And what have I done – why are you going to the sacrifice without your deacon? I have done your command with the treasures of the Church.'

'I am not leaving you, my son. You will follow me in three days.'

Laurence was soon arrested. The Prefect demanded that he should produce the treasures of the Church.

'The Church is indeed rich,' said Laurence. 'I will show you the treasures but give me a little time to gather them.' Time was given, and Laurence went over the city seeking the widows and orphans and lame and aged whom the Church supported. He gathered them all together in rows in front of the church, then went and brought the Prefect. 'Here are the Church's treasures!'

The enraged Prefect promised Laurence a slow and painful death, and he was chained to a gridiron over a slow fire. So great was his desire of God that he seemed not to feel the torment. After some time he said to the Prefect: 'Let my body be turned now, one side is roasted enough.' He was turned by the Prefect's order, and soon he said: 'Now it's done enough – all ready to be served.' He then prayed for the conversion of Rome, that through Rome the world might come to the Faith: and lifting his eyes to heaven gave up his spirit.

F. H. Drinkwater

USEFUL TEXTS

Poor People:
> Protection of, *Isa. 14:30*
> Blessings on, *Luke 6:20*
> Among believers, *Rev. 2:9*
> Provision for, *Ps. 68:10*

See also: A11 God's loving Providence
             C21 Rise above materialism
             C25 Humility
             C29 Not through luxury

A8
THE LIGHT OF EXAMPLE

'Your light must shine in the sight of others.'
Matthew 5:16

QUOTATIONS

Few things are harder to put up with than the annoyance of a good example.
Mark Twain

Example is not the main thing in influencing others – it is the only thing.
Albert Schweitzer

People seldom improve when they have no other model but themselves to copy.
Oliver Goldsmith

It would scarcely be necessary to expand doctrine if our lives were radiant enough. If we behaved like true Christians, there would be no pagans.
Pope John XXIII

Men will not attend to what we say, but examine into what we do; and will say, 'Do you first obey your own words, and then exhort others.' This is the great battle, this is the unanswerable demonstration, which is made by our acts.
St John Chrysostom

The tree is made manifest by its fruit; so they who profess themselves to be Christians are known by what they do. For Christianity is not the work of an outward profession; but shows itself in the power of faith, if a man be found faithful unto the end. It is better for a man to hold his peace, and be; than to say he is a Christian and not to be.
St Ignatius of Antioch

PROVERBS

A child's life is like a piece of paper on which every passer-by leaves a mark.
Chinese proverb

Not the cry, but the flight of the wild duck, leads the flock to fly and follow.
Chinese proverb

WORD PICTURES

An American teacher was employed in Japan on the understanding that during school hours he should not utter a word on the subject of Christianity. The engagement was faithfully kept, and he lived before his students the Christian life, but never spoke of it to them. Not a word was said to influence the young men committed to his care. But so beautiful was his character, and so blameless his example, that forty of the students, unknown to him, met in a grove and signed a secret covenant to abandon idolatry. Twenty-five of them entered the Kyoto Christian Training School, and some of them are now preaching the Gospel which their teacher had unconsciously commended.
Anon

The example of my grandfather Verus taught me to be candid and to control my temper. By the memory of my father's character I learnt to be modest and manly. My mother taught me regard for religion, to be generous and open-handed, and neither to do an ill turn to anyone nor even to think of it. She bred me also to a plain and inexpensive way of living.

From my adoptive father I learnt a smooth and inoffensive temper, and a great proof against vanity and the impression of pomp and power; I learnt that it was the part of a prince to check flattery, to have his exchequer well furnished, to be frugal in his expenses, not to worship the gods of superstition, but to be reserved, vigilant, and well poised.
Marcus Aurelius

There is a beautiful incident in the life of St Vincent de Paul (1576-1660) which illustrates his character. Soon after he was ordained priest, as he was voyaging from Toulouse to Narbonne, the ship in which he was sailing was attacked by Barbary pirates; there was a fierce fight, many were killed, and Vincent and others were taken prisoners and carried to Tunis, where they were sold as slaves.

Vincent was first bought by a fisherman, then again sold to a chemist, and finally to a farmer – an Italian who had been a Christian, but had gone back to heathenism. The young priest probably made an excellent servant, doing his duty cheerfully and wholeheartedly as a slave, for we learn that, as time passed, the spiritual life and fine character of Vincent must have so impressed his master that he returned to the Church and together the master and slave escaped back to France.
P.F.

A troubled mother one day came to Gandhi along with her daughter and explained to him that her daughter was in the habit of eating far more sweet food than was good for her. Please, she asked, would Gandhi speak to the girl and persuade her to give up this harmful habit? Gandhi sat for a while in silence and then said: 'Bring your daughter back in three weeks' time, and then I will speak to her.' The mother went away as she was told and then came back after three weeks. This time Gandhi quietly took the daughter aside and in a few simple words pointed out to her the harmful effects of indulging in sweet food; he urged her to abandon the habit. Thanking Gandhi for giving her daughter such good advice, the mother then said to him in a puzzled voice: 'Still, I would like to know, Gandhi-ji, why you did not just say these words to my daughter three weeks ago when I first brought her to you?' 'But,' explained Gandhi in reply: 'Three weeks ago I myself was still addicted to eating sweet foods.'
Donald Nichol

USEFUL TEXTS

Example:
  I have given, *John 13:15*
  Of Christ, *1 Peter 2:21*
  Of Believers, *1 Tim. 4:12*

See also: A9 Relationships
          A33 Love your neighbour
          B24 Go tell everyone

A9
RELATIONSHIPS

'All you need is "Yes" if you mean yes, "No" if you mean no.'
Matthew 5:37

QUOTATIONS

The hope of the future lies not in better human inventions, but in better human relations.
Victor Kitchen

Loving relationships are a family's best protection against the challenges of the world.
Bernie Wietre

The essence of the ethics of Jesus is not law, but a relationship of persons to God.
Arthur Michael Ramsey

Nothing is a greater impediment to being in good terms with others than being ill at ease with yourself.
Honoré de Balzac

To be needed in other human lives – is there anything greater or more beautiful in this world.
David Grayson

He who would do good to another, must do it in minute particulars. General good is the plea of the scoundrel, hypocrite and flatterer.
William Blake

To reflect that another human being, if at a distance of ten thousand years from the year 1883, would enjoy one hour's more life, in the sense of fullness of life, in consequence of anything I had done in my little span, would be to me a peace of the soul.
Richard Jefferies

WORD PICTURES

Rupert Brooke, the poet, paid 'a dirty little boy' sixpence to wave to him from Liverpool quay as he set forth on a voyage to the United States. It was just the expression of a longing for friendliness in a lonely hour.

People think there are circumstances when one may deal with human beings without love, but no such circumstances ever exist. Inanimate objects may be dealt with without love: we may fell trees, bake bricks, hammer iron without love. But human beings cannot be handled without love, any more than bees can be handled without care. That is the nature of bees. If you handle bees carelessly you will harm the bees and yourself as well. And so it is with people. And it cannot be otherwise, because mutual love is the fundamental law of human life.
Leo Tolstoy

God is to be found in cancer as in everything else. If he is not, then he is not the God of the Psalmist who said 'if I go down to hell, thou art there also', let alone of the Christian who knows God most deeply in the Cross. And I have discovered this experience to be one full of grace and truth.

I cannot say how grateful I am for all the love and kindness and goodness it has disclosed which I am sure was always there but which it has taken this to bring home. Above all, I would say it is relationships, both within the family and outside, which it has deepened and opened up. It has been a time of giving and receiving grace upon grace.
John Robinson

Kevin, a ten-year-old from the country, came to spend the Easter holidays with his aunt, who lived in the London suburb of Wimbledon. Curious to explore not only her large garden but also an overgrown path at the back, he heard odd noises coming from a shed in a neighbour's garden. When he asked his aunt about the noise she told him that she thought her unmarried lady neighbour kept chickens. Kevin had been brought up on a chicken farm and knew immediately that what he had heard was not 'chicken-noise'. He went back through a hole in the fence to investigate. The neighbouring garden was very overgrown but with a clear path running from the house to the old shed. The shed door was padlocked and the window was blacked out but there was a large sort of letter-box slit in the door. First checking that no one was watching, Kevin peeped through the 'letter-box'. It was covered on the inside by a piece of hanging material but a powerful stench caught Kevin's nose. Just as he was about to turn away the cover was lifted and a pair of wild staring eyes appeared at the slit. Kevin gave a startled scream and bolted out of the garden back to his aunt's. He ran straight into her. He was so upset that he blurted out just what he had seen. His aunt called the police.

The dignified maiden lady was very indignant at first when the police asked to inspect her garden shed. When they insisted, her resistance collapsed and she gave them a key. On opening the shed door a sight met the eyes of the two constables that they are never likely to forget. Cowering in a darkened corner from the bright light, and the strange intruders, was a naked figure of what seemed to be a strange animal. It was on all fours and had long black hair. There was fear in the wild eyes and 'it' made strange little noises. The police officers, taken aback by the sight and the stench, closed the door again and radioed for assistance.

The nine-year-old boy was taken into very special care. He had been in the shed for seven years, since the age of two, when the woman, fearing the discovery of her secret illegitimate child, had incarcerated him in the shed. Besides the filth, long hair and nails, his back was bent in such a way that he would never be able to learn to walk upright. Terrified at the presence of other people, he could not communicate but merely express emotions by grunts. He had never known any caring relationships and there was no hope of a return to full human existence.

A. P. Castle

Important words
The six most important words . . .
I made a mistake.
The five most important words . . .
you did a good job.

The four most important words . . .
what is your opinion?
The three most important words . . .
if you please.
The two most important words . . .
thank you.
The one most important word . . .
we.
Anon

The meeting
As I went up and he came down, my little six-year boy,
upon the stairs we met and kissed, I and my tender Joy.
O fond and true, as lovers do, we kissed and clasped and parted;
and I went up and he went down, refreshed and happy-hearted.

What need was there for any words, his face against my face?
And in the silence heart to heart spoke for a little space
of tender things and thoughts on wings and secrets none discovers;
and I went up and he went down, a pair of happy lovers.

His clinging arms about my neck, what need was there for words?
O little heart that beat so fast like any fluttering bird's!
'I love,' his silence said, 'I love,' my silence answered duly;
and I went up and he went down comforted wonderfully.
Katherine Tynan

USEFUL TEXTS

Relationships:
    Of believers with one another, *1 Cor. 12:12-14*
    Agreement necessary in, *Amos 3:3*
    A continuing relationship, *Prov. 17:17*

See also: A33 Love your neighbour
             B6   The family
             B30 Married love
             B52 God is Love
             C10 Love your enemies
             C19 Friendship

A10
SEEKING PERFECTION

'You must be perfect, just as your heavenly Father is perfect.'
Matthew 5:48

QUOTATIONS

God did not make men perfect. He made them pilgrims after perfection.
Henry Ward Beecher

If every year we would root out one vice we should sooner become perfect men.
Thomas à Kempis

Self-reverence, self-knowledge, self-control, these three alone lead life to sovereign power.
Alfred, Lord Tennyson

Ideals are like stars – we never reach them but we chart our course by them.
Carl Schurz

It is right to be contented with what we have but never with what we are.
J. Mackintosh

To come to possess all, desire to possess nothing.
St John of the Cross

The noble love of Jesus impels a man to do great things, and stirs him up to be always longing for what is more perfect.
Thomas à Kempis

Perfection does not lie in not seeing the world, but in not tasting or relishing it.
St Francis of Sales

The divine nature is perfection; and to be nearest to the divine nature is to be nearest to perfection.
Xenophon

Perfection does not consist of macerating or killing the body, but in killing our perverse self-will.
St Catherine of Siena

He who would fully and feelingly understand the words of Christ, must study to make his whole life conformable to that of Christ.
Thomas à Kempis

WORD PICTURES

I understand more and more how true Daddy's words were when he said, 'All children must look after their own upbringing.' Parents can only give good advice or put them on the right paths, but the final forming of a person's character lies in his own hands.
The Diary of Anne Frank

A group of boys were trying to see who could make the straightest track across a snowy field. Only one of them succeeded in making a path which was almost perfectly straight. When asked how he managed to do it, he said, 'It was easy, I just kept my eyes fixed on the lightning rod on top of the barn at the end of the field – while the rest of you kept looking at your feet.'

The great sculptor, Michelangelo, was at work on one of his statues when a friend called on him, and said, 'I can't see any difference in the statue since I came here a week ago. Have you not been doing any work all the week?' 'Yes,' said the sculptor, 'I have retouched this part, softened this feature, strengthened this muscle, and put more life into that limb.' 'But those are only trifles,' said the friend. 'True,' said Michelangelo, 'but trifles make perfection, and perfection is no trifle.'

A root set in the finest soil, in the best climate, and blessed with all that sun and air and rain can do for it, is not in so sure a way

of its growth to perfection, as every man may be, whose spirit aspires after all that which God is ready and infinitely desirous to give him. For the sun meets not the springing bud that stretches towards him with half that certainty, as God, the source of all good, communicates himself to the soul that longs to partake of him.
William Law

In my unforgettable college days, a boy who played next to me in the college orchestra never made a mistake. Not once was he called down by the professor. But one day this lad ceased to be a member of the orchestra, and the professor told us why that boy never made a mistake. He did not play loud enough for anyone to hear him. It is human to err. Any man who is playing his God-given part in life may make a mistake, may do some wrong, he may be a victim of circumstances. The important thing is not the mistake he makes, but his reaction to that mistake and the circumstances surrounding it.
P. Fontaine

It is the mark of the soul that is sensitive to the love of God ever to seek the glory of God in its fulfilment of every commandment, and to delight in its own abasement, since to God, on account of his greatness, belongs glory, and to man belongs abasement whereby we become members of the household of God. If we do that, we too will rejoice, like Saint John the Baptist, in the glory of the Lord, and begin to say increasingly: 'He must increase, but I must decrease.'
Diadochus of Photike

USEFUL TEXTS
Perfection:
  Growing towards, *Heb. 6:1*
  Limit of, *Ps. 119:96*
  Prayer for, *2 Cor. 13:9*
  Requirements for, *Matt. 19:21*

See also: A20 The Kingdom of God
          A22 Seeking God
          B26 The whole person
          C47 The indwelling spirit

A11
GOD'S LOVING PROVIDENCE

'Surely life means more than food, and the body more
than clothing! Look at the birds in the sky.'
Matthew 6:26

QUOTATIONS

God tempers the wind to the shorn lamb.
Laurence Sterne

Providence is the care God takes of all existing things.
John of Damascus

Providence has at all times been my only dependence, for all other
resources seem to have failed us.
George Washington

If you leap into a well, providence is not bound to fetch you out.
Thomas Fuller

There's a divinity that shapes our ends,
Rough-hew them how we will.
William Shakespeare

God looks forth from the high watch-towers of his providence; he
sees what suits each man, and applies to him that which suits him.
Boethius

Where the ray of God's light shall fall upon my path, there will I
walk and in his strength perform without inquietude the work
that his providence shall set me.
Francis Fenelon

I firmly believe in divine providence.
Without it, I think I should go crazy.
Without God the world would be a maze without a clue.
Woodrow Wilson

Adapt thyself to the things with which thy lot has been cast; and love the men with whom it is thy portion to live, and that with a sincere affection . . . No longer be either dissatisfied with thy present lot, or shrink from the future.
Marcus Antoninus

Looking back from this my seventieth year, it seems to me that every card in my working life has been dealt to me in such a manner that I had but to play it as it came.
Rudyard Kipling

For, if the providence of God does not preside over human affairs, there is no point in busying oneself about religion.
St Augustine of Hippo

'It were providence that put me here', says Ben Gunn, the castaway in *Treasure Island*. 'I've thought it all out in this 'ere lonely island, and I'm back on piety.'
Robert Louis Stevenson

HUMOUR

The story is told of the devout Irishman, who, when his house was caught in a great flood, climbed for safety to the roof. Along came a rescue launch and offered to take him off. 'No thanks,' he said, 'I believe God will save me.' The rescuers on the launch could not persuade him and went away. The water rose and covered the roof and the Irishman climbed onto the chimney. A helicopter arrived and lowered a crewman. 'No thanks,' Paddy said, 'I believe God will save me.' He drowned. On arrival in heaven he met God and asked, 'Why didn't you save me?' 'I don't know what went wrong,' God replied. 'I sent a launch and a helicopter!'
Anon

WORD PICTURES

I saw a delicate flower had grown up two feet high, between the horses' path and the wheel-track. An inch more to right or left had

sealed its fate, or an inch higher; and yet it lived to flourish as much as if it had a thousand acres of untrodden space around it, and never knew the danger it incurred. It did not borrow trouble, nor invite an evil fate by apprehending it.
Henry D. Thoreau

Confide ye aye in providence, for providence is kind,
and bear ye a' life's changes wi' a calm and tranquil mind;
tho' press'd and hemm'd on ev'ry side, ha'e faith and ye'll win
    through,
for ilka blade o' grass keps its ain drap o' dew.
James Ballantine

One evening when Luther saw a little bird perched on a tree, to roost there for the night, he said, 'This little bird has had its supper, and now it is getting ready to go to sleep here, quite secure and content, never troubling itself what its food will be, or where its lodging on the morrow. Like David, it "abides under the shadow of the Almighty". It sits on its little twig content, and lets God take care.'
Anon

Rabbi Bunam was once walking outside the city with some of his disciples. He bent, picked up a speck of sand, looked at it, and put it back exactly where he found it. 'He who does not believe', he said, 'that God wants this bit of sand to lie in this particular place, does not believe at all.'
Hasidic Story

In all your affairs, rely wholly on God's providence . . . Intimate little children, who with one hand hold fast to their father, and with the other hand gather strawberries along the hedges. So too, as you gather and handle the goods of this world with one hand, you must with the other always hold fast the hand of your heavenly Father, turning yourself towards him from time to time to see if your actions or occupations be pleasing to him. About all things, take heed that you never leave his hand or think to gather more or to gain some advantage. For should he forsake you, you will not be able to go a step further without falling to the ground. *St Francis of Sales*

USEFUL TEXTS

Providence:
   For believers, *Matt. 6:33; Matt. 10:28-31*
   For salvation, *Luke 2:10-11; 2 Pet. 3:9*
   For the earth, *Matt. 5:45*

See also: A7   Poor in Spirit
               A19 Patience
               B21 Trust in God
               C39 Doing God's will

A12
HOLY SCRIPTURE

'Everyone who listens to these words of mine and acts on
them will be like a sensible man who built his house on rocks.'
Matthew 7:24

QUOTATIONS

Lay hold on the Bible until the Bible lays hold on you.
William Houghton

Here is knowledge enough for me. Let me be a man of one book.
John Wesley

The man who is well grounded in the testimonies of the Scriptures
is the bulwark of the Church.
St Jerome

The Bible is an inexhaustible fountain of all truths. The existence
of the Bible is the greatest blessing which humanity ever
experienced.
Immanuel Kant

We need never tremble *for* the Word of God, though we may
tremble *at* it and the demands which it makes upon our faith and
courage.
William Robertson Smith

Its light is like the body of heaven in its clearness; its vastness like
the bosom of the sea; its variety like scenes of nature.
John H. Newman

I read my Bible to know what people ought to do and my
newspaper to know what they are doing.
John H. Newman

God the Father is the giver of Holy Scripture. God the Son is the theme of Holy Scripture; and God the Spirit is the author, authenticator and interpreter of Holy Scripture.
J. I. Packer

We must not only pause to reflect upon passages from the Bible, but upon 'slices of life' too, relating them together, and to the will of the Risen Christ for us.
Michel Quiost

If, as the apostle Paul says, Christ is the power of God and the wisdom of God, then he who is ignorant of the Scriptures is also ignorant of the power of God and his wisdom; ignorance of the Scriptures is ignorance of Christ.
St Jerome

HUMOUR

After hearing the story of Lot's wife in catechism class and how she looked back and turned into a pillar of salt, a little boy put his hand up and said, 'Please, Sister, when my mum was driving, she looked back and turned into a pillar box!'

A nearby clergyman preaching at the children's anniversary service, was stressing that the Bible is the best book – or the best book is the Bible. He then said to the children, 'Now, remember the three "Bs" – and if you meet me in the street I want you to be able to tell me that you've remembered my message.'

Lo and behold, a few days later, a little girl, about six years old, ran up to him in the street, saying, 'Oh, Vicar, Vicar, I can remember everything you told us last Sunday about those three WASPS.'
Jean Dawson

A Sunday school teacher asked her young class how Noah spent his time in the ark. When there was no response, she asked, 'Do you suppose he did a lot of fishing?'

'What,' piped up a six-year-old, 'with only two worms?'

A Sunday School class had just been hearing about the parable of the prodigal son. 'Now,' said the Sunday School teacher, 'who was not glad to know of the prodigal's return?' 'Please, sir,' replied one boy, 'the fatted calf!'

WORD PICTURES

One Susanah Hannokes, an elderly woman of Wingrove, near Aylesbury, was accused by her neighbour of bewitching her spinning wheel, so that she could not make it go round, and offered to make oath of it before a magistrate; on which the husband, to justify his wife, insisted upon her being tried by the church Bible, and that the accuser should be present. Accordingly, she was conducted to the parish church, where she was stripped of all her clothes to her shift, and weighed against the Bible; when, to the no small mortification of her accuser, she outweighed it, and was honourably acquitted of the charge.
Gentleman's Magazine, 1759

When Charles Dickens' youngest son was leaving home for Australia, his father gave the boy a New Testament, and explained why he had done so: 'Because it is the best book that ever was, or will be known in the world; and because it teaches you the best lesson by which any human creature can possibly be guided.'
Anon

So far as western Europe is concerned, the first book to be published with movable metal type was the so-called *Gutenberg Bible*, which came off the presses at Mainz around the year 1455.

It is also known as the 42 line Bible because each column had 42 lines. And yet another name for it is the *Mazorin Bible* because the first of the surviving copies of the original edition to be discovered in modern times – 1760 to be exact – was in the library founded by Cardinal Mazorin in Paris.

It is reckoned that the first edition of the *Gutenberg Bible* consisted of 120 copies on paper and 30 on vellum. Of these 48 survive, 12 of them vellum copies, and of the 12, three are in perfect condition. They are each valued at well over a million pounds.

The *Black Bible* won its place in history because the word 'not' was accidentally dropped from the seventh commandment, leaving it to read, 'Thou shalt commit adultery.' The offending printers, Richard Barker and Martin Lucas, who issued an edition of 1,000 copies in 1631, were fined £3,000.

A similar fine was imposed on printers in the same era for transcribing a famous verse of Psalm XIV thus: 'The fool hath said in his heart there is a God.' Naturally, their edition (all copies of which were suppressed) came to be known as the *Fool Bible*.

A negative also was omitted from the so-called *Unrighteous Bible*, printed at Cambridge in 1653. Here the 'not' slipped out of a verse in First Corinthians VI, so that it read 'Know ye not that the unrighteous shall inherit the Kingdom of God'?

The *Sin On Bible* was the first Bible printed in Ireland and dated 1716. In it, John V 14 has the misprint 'Sin on more' instead of the obvious admonition.

Anon

Bede passes at Ascensiontide
So until Ascensiontide he worked with his pupils to conclude his translation of St John's Gospel into the English tongue: but the Tuesday before Ascensiontide his sickness increased upon him. Nevertheless, he taught and bade his scholars work, saying cheerfully, 'Write with speed now, for I cannot tell how long I may last.'

The day broke (that is, Wednesday), and about the third hour the scribe said, 'There is yet a chapter wanting: It is hard for thee to continue vexing thyself.' 'That is easily done,' said he: 'take thy pen again and write quickly' and joyfully he dictated until the evening at the ninth hour.

'Dear Master,' said the boy, 'there is yet one sentence to be written.' He answered, 'Write it quickly.' Soon after the boy said, 'It is finished now.' 'Thou has well said. It is finished. Raise my head in thy arms and turn my face towards the holy spot where I was wont to pray, for I desire to sit facing it and call upon my Father.'

46

So they held him up on the pavement, and he chanted, 'Glory be to the Father, and to the Son and to the Holy Spirit.' Then, as he named the Holy Spirit, his spirit took leave, and departed to the heavenly kingdom.
Cuthbert, writing in the seventh century

Sixteen hundred years ago in a garden in Milan a young man from North Africa became a Christian believer. He had been searching for *something* for many years and had tried quite a few of the spiritual disciplines and therapies on offer. He had a girlfriend he'd abandoned – and a little son. He also had a ferocious mother who got at him for his fecklessness.

He managed to find a good job in a university, but his underlying depression weighed him down. As he sat in the garden with tears in his eyes he heard the sing-song voice of a child next door, chanting the Latin words: *'Tolle, lege . . . tolle, lege . . .'* ('Take, read'). In the end he took hold of a copy of the Scriptures and read: 'Arm yourself with the Lord Jesus Christ, and spend no more thought on nature's appetites'.

That conversion was a turning point in history, for the young man was Augustine, who became one of the greatest philosophers of the western world.

I am thinking of summer gardens because this time of year reminds me of the weeks I spent in the garden years ago trying to revise for exams. Bird song, cherry and magnolia blossom bring back a *frisson* of fear. Yet they also bring a sense of grace. Gardens in May were the places I learnt to learn. You see, I wasn't very attentive in class, but on my own, with a text, I would suddenly get the point – and my mind sang.

Without books, without reading, our understanding is uninformed, our judgements narrow . . . I sometimes think God would rather we were literate than that we were indiscriminately caring. Augustine found his true self through a child's cry and a challenging text. He met the living God on the page of a book, and it broke his heart and set him free.
Angela Tilby

It is possible to take scientific measurements of the Scriptures, to make a critical and searching analysis of their contents, and yet utterly miss their meaning and message.

A prisoner who was condemned to solitary confinement had the Authorised Version of the Bible as his only companion and studied it for several years. He gathered the following facts: it contained 3,586,489 letters; 773,692 words; 31,173 verses; 1,189 chapters; the word 'and' occurs 46,277 times; the middle verse is the eighth verse of the 118th Psalm; all the letters of the alphabet are found in the twenty-first verse of the eighth chapter of Ezra; the longest verse is Esther 8:9 and the shortest verse is John 11:35.

We are not told that the message of the Bible touched the prisoner's heart.
Walter D. Cavert

A limited facsimile edition of a medieval *Biblia Pauperum* (Bible of the Poor) is on sale at £2,600 a copy. Some pauper! Whatever happened to the option for the poor? The irony seems to have escaped the publishers, Faksimile Verlag of Lucerne in Switzerland, who go on about the exquisite miniatures, the red leather binding tooled in gold and the generally de luxe feel of their product. But the irony also seems to have escaped the fourteenth-century Dutch patron, probably royal, who caused this lavish book to be made in the first place.

The *Biblia Pauperum* was a popular aid to instruction in the later middle ages. It is uncertain how it got its name, for even at its simplest no one who was poor could have acquired one. Perhaps its popularity with the Mendicant Orders helped to fix the association with poverty. It consisted of pictures illustrative of the New Testament flanked by pictured episodes from the Old Testament held to be analogous or prophetic. There was a minimum of text. The pictures were typically pen and ink drawings or simple woodcuts of no pretensions.
The Tablet

USEFUL TEXTS

Holy Scripture:
    Given by God, *2 Tim. 3:16*
    Inspired by the Holy Spirit, *Acts 1:16; 2 Pet. 1:21*
    Called Sword of the Spirit, *Eph. 6:17*
    For instruction, *Rom. 15:4*
    Bears witness to Christ, *John 5:3a-40*

See also: B2 The Good News
           B9 Revelation
           B24 Go tell everyone
           C6 The Old Testament Law

A13
THE CHURCH IS FOR SINNERS

'Indeed I did not come to call the virtuous, but sinners.'
Matthew 9:13

QUOTATIONS

It does not take a perfect church to introduce a man to the perfect Christ.
Richard Woodsome

Every man may err, but not the whole gathered together; for the whole hath a promise.
R. H. Benson

Wherever we see the Word of God purely preached and heard, there a church of God exists, even if it swarms with many faults.
John Calvin

Since the Church, as much as heresy, is composed of men, sinful men, the Church's treasure has always been concealed among dross and even dirt.
Hans Kung

The great criticism of the Church today is that no one wants to persecute it: because there is nothing very much to persecute it about.
George McLeod

It is common for those that are farthest from God to boast themselves nearest to the Church.
Matthew Henry

The Church is the only institution in the world that has lower entrance requirements than those for getting on a bus.
William Laroe

Religion that is not embedded in the common life too soon degenerates into religiosity, and an inward-looking Church is a dying Church.
F. R. Barry

Every Church should be engaged in continuous self-reformation, scrutinising its traditions in the light of Scripture and where necessary, modifying them.
John R. W. Stott

God never intended his Church to be a refrigerator in which to preserve perishable piety. He intended it to be an incubator in which to hatch converts.
F. Lincicome

HUMOUR

A clergyman and one of his elderly parishioners were walking home from church one frosty day when the old gentleman slipped and fell flat on his back. The minister looked at him for a moment, and being assured that he was not hurt, said, 'Friend, sinners stand on slippery places.' The old gentleman looked up at him and said, 'I see they do, but I can't.'
Anon

WORD PICTURES

In her small book, *St Catherine of Siena*, Maisie Ward puts it very clearly. 'Too much awareness of the defects of Catholics (especially Catholics in high places) tends with most of us to dim our realisation of Christ working mightily through his Church . . . But with Catherine the appalling evils in the lives of so many ecclesiastics seemed only to highlight her vision of the glorious thing they were profaning.'
Frank Sheed

I have long thought that the real difference between the Catholic and Protestant view of Christianity is, or ought to be, this – that whereas we think of the Church as a sort of lucky bag which

51

contains good bargains and bad, people who will be lost as well as people who will be saved; real Protestantism ought always to think of the Church as an assembly of the elect. I do not understand how a Christian can square this latter view with our Lord's parables, but I see its attractiveness on logical grounds.
Ronald A. Knox

For a variety of reasons, people are drawn in more often by the warmth of relationship than the brilliance of apologetics. In fact, people are almost too vulnerable to community; if they feel loved, they will tend to believe anything. This situation is exploited to the fullest by a number of the fringe religious groups like the Unification Church of Sun Myung Moon. As Christians true to Christ we do care about emotional needs, but we must be careful not to manipulate people through it. It is fine that the world is drawn into our midst because they feel welcomed and cared for. But we must be as concerned for their minds as for their souls. We must offer not only love but excellent biblical teaching as well.
Rebecca Pippert

A minister was called to a certain church in America. He was warned that the congregation was dead, but nevertheless he regarded the call as a challenge and he decided to accept it. He soon discovered that the church was dead. No planning, no toil, no exhortation, no urging could kindle a spark of life or waken any response.

He told the congregation that they were dead, and that he proposed to carry out the funeral of the church. A day was fixed. Into the church there was brought a coffin; the church was decked with mourning wreaths.

The time of the 'burial service' came. The church was crowded as it had not been for years. The minister carried out the 'burial service'. Then, at the end, as a last token of respect, he invited the congregation to file past the open coffin. As they did so, they received a shock. The coffin was open and empty. But the bottom of the coffin was not wood; it was a mirror. As each man looked into the coffin of the dead church he saw – his own face.
William Barclay

USEFUL TEXTS

Church:
   The pillar of truth, *1 Tim. 3:15*
   Gifts of, *1 Cor. 12:27-30*
   Loved by Christ, *Eph. 5:25*

See also: A30 God's sinful people
            B17 The Church – Bride of Christ
            C12 The Church for all people
            C27 The Father who receives us back

A14
THE SUCCESSORS OF THE APOSTLES

'He summoned his twelve disciples, and gave them authority over unclean spirits, with power to cast them out and to cure all kinds of diseases and sickness.'
Matthew 10:1

QUOTATIONS

A bishop should die preaching.
John Jewel, Bishop of Salisbury, 1571

Whoever is sent by the Master to run his house, we ought to receive him as we would receive the Master himself. It is obvious, therefore, that we ought to regard the bishop as we would the Lord himself.
St Ignatius of Antioch

You can't be an other-worldly archbishop.
George Carey

The very conception of Israel or the Church as a flock involves the institution of pastoral rule and oversight; the flock must have shepherds who rule it and feed it under the ultimate supervision of the Chief Shepherd himself.
Alan Richardson

Nobody told me what a bishop is supposed to do – I had to work it out for myself.
George Carey

It is no accident that the symbol of a bishop is a crook, and the sign of an archbishop is a double-cross.
Dom Gregory Dix

I believe ministers should be assessed every five years to expose and deal with those who are incompetent, lazy or simply inept.

Bishops, too, should not hold jobs in freehold, but should be subject to evaluation.
George Carey

HUMOUR

A little girl, a vicar's daughter, saw a bishop in all his robes for the first time. She gazed at him in wonder for a moment, then smoothing the handsome stole that he was wearing said: 'And have you panties to match?'
Anon

Now hear an illusion: a mitre, you know,
is divided above, but united below.
If this you consider, our emblem is right,
the bishops divide, but the clergy unite.
Jonathan Swift

WORD PICTURES

When Christ had finished his work on earth, it is said, and had returned to heaven, the angel Gabriel met him.

'Lord,' said Gabriel, 'is it permitted to ask what plans you have made for carrying on your work on earth?'

'I have chosen twelve men, and some women,' said Christ. 'They will pass my message on till it reaches the whole world.'

'But,' said the angel, 'supposing these few people fail you – what other plans have you made?'

Christ smiled. 'I have no other plan,' he said. 'I am counting on them.'
Anon

I write to all the churches and I bid all men know that of my own free will I die for God, unless you should hinder me. I exhort you, be ye not of an unseasonable kindness to me. Let me be given to the wild beasts, for through them I can attain unto God. I am God's wheat, and I am ground by the teeth of wild beasts, that I may be found pure bread (of Christ). Rather entice the wild beasts, that they may become my sepulchre and may leave no part

of my body behind, so that I may not, when I am fallen asleep, be burdensome to anyone. Then shall I be truly a disciple of Jesus Christ, when the world shall not so much as see my body. Supplicate the Lord for me, that through these instruments I may be found a sacrifice to God. I do not enjoin you as Peter and Paul did. They were Apostles, I am a convict; they were free, but I am a slave to this very hour. Yet if I shall suffer, then am I a freed-man of Jesus Christ, and I shall rise free in Him. Now I am learning in my bonds to put away every desire.
St Ignatius of Antioch

St Alphege (d. 1012) as Bishop of Winchester, spent all his time looking after the poor, denying himself as much as possible to have more to give away. He was Archbishop of Canterbury when the Danes besieged and took the city. They treated the inhabitants with barbarity, despite St Alphege's fearless intercessions, and they imprisoned him on one of their boats on the Thames. When plague broke out the Danes asked his prayers, and when he prayed it ceased, but they still refused to release him without ransom, and he refused to ask for the money since it would have come from the goods of the Church and the poor. So the Danes ill-treated him with stoning and other torments, so badly that one of them in pity split his skull with his battle-axe. 'Jesu, receive me in peace and forgive them' were his last words.
F. H. Drinkwater

(The pagan Goths in eastern Europe attacked the Roman Empire many times in the fourth century, and among the hostages sent to Constantinople was a young Goth named Ulfilas. He became a Christian and determined to return to his people as a missionary.) ... When he was thirty Ulfilas was made a bishop and was allowed to go back as a missionary to his own people. Perhaps some of the new friends he had made in Constantinople thought it was a pity he should give up his chance of becoming famous as a great scholar, choosing instead to live among the wild folk in the 'barbarian' land. We can picture them saying: 'You'll be nobody when you get back there; whereas here you are known to be clever and you can take part in all the learned debates and read all the books you like in the great libraries.' But Ulfilas knew he had found a great treasure in the imperial city, and he did not want to stay to enjoy it by himself but to share it with the people at home whom he loved.

The Goths could neither read nor write. Stories and songs lived on from generation to generation because they could be spoken or sung, but nothing could be written down. Of course they could not read the Greek Bible which belonged to Ulfilas, for they did not understand the foreign language which he had learned in Constantinople. Yet Ulfilas knew that if they were to become strong and faithful Christians they must be able to read the Bible for themselves. 'Somehow I must translate the Bible into the language of my people', he thought to himself. But there was not even a proper alphabet he could use. There was only a primitive one made from Runic letters which he himself had learnt when he was a boy . . . These 'runes' were strange letters formed from straight lines and angles, and Ulfilas knew that they were far too clumsy for his great work. So he set to work and made a new alphabet based chiefly on the Greek.

Having made the alphabet Ulfilas began his long task of translating the Bible into Gothic. He was very thankful that he had learnt both Greek and Latin in Constantinople, for now he could use his knowledge to bring the good news of Christ right into the homes of his people. Ulfilas was the first missionary to translate the Bible into a language which had never been written down. It was a great task and he could only do it in his spare time, for most of his days were spent in teaching the people and in training Gothic missionaries. It was not at all an easy or straightforward piece of work to do. There were many words in the Bible for which there was no Gothic word because they stood for things or actions which belonged to a civilised people, and so the savage Goths would not understand them. When he tried to think of a Gothic word for 'mammon' (St Matthew 6:24) he remembered that for his people wealth meant not money but cattle and made it from part of the word meaning 'hoard of treasure' or 'mammon'. As he thought of the Christian Goths who had only just learned to live at peace instead of constantly fighting, he decided to leave out of the Gothic Bible the books of Samuel and Kings with their stories of battle in case they should awaken the love of war among the new Christians.

The new Bible grew bit by bit until at last it was finished. Then it was carried by Gothic missionaries, traders and warriors from village to village and from camp to camp. Far and wide it spread into their homes in distant places which Ulfilas himself could never have reached with the Christian message.
Phyllis Garlick

USEFUL TEXTS
Bishops:
 Qualifications, *1 Tim. 3:1-7; Titus 1:6-9*
 Responsibilities, *1 Thess. 5:14; Heb. 13:17*
 Duties, *Acts 20:17; 28-30*

See also: A24 Papacy
    A45 The Priesthood
    B13 Authority

A15
SIN

'Sin entered the world through one man,
and through sin death.'
Romans 5:12

QUOTATIONS

Sin is always a crime against the Father's love.
Archimandrite Sophrony

All sins are attempts to fill voids.
Simone Weil

There is no man but knows more evil of himself than of any other.
Thomas Wilson

We are sinners, but we do not know how great. He alone knows
who died for our sins.
John Henry

Almost all our faults are more pardonable than the methods we
think up to hide them.
La Rochefoucauld

It is astonishing how soon the whole conscience begins to unravel,
if a single stitch drops; one little sin indulged makes a hole you
could put your head through.
Charles Buxton

For wickedness is nothing else than the withdrawal of goodness,
just as darkness is nothing else than the withdrawal of light.
St John of Damascus

Sin is not hurtful because it is forbidden but sin is forbidden
because it is hurtful.
Benjamin Franklin

Learn from the mistakes of others. You can't live long enough to make them all yourself.
Anon

Should we all confess our sins to one another we would all laugh at one another for our lack of originality.
Kahlil Gibran

So true is it that every sin is voluntary, that, unless it be voluntary, it is not sin at all.
St Augustine of Hippo

God loves us in our sin, and *through* our sin, and goes on loving us, looking for a response.
Donald Coggan

Pride is the ground in which all the other sins grow, and the parent from which all the other sins come.
William Barclay

For if we never fell, we should not know how feeble and how wretched we are of ourself, and also we should not fully know that marvellous love of our Maker.
Julian of Norwich

A dreadful matter is sin, and disorder of life is the soul's worst sickness . . . sin is evil of man's choosing, springing from free-will.
St Cyril of Jerusalem

Let us remember for our consolation that we never perceive our sins till we begin to cure them.
François Fenelon

The devil makes many disciples by preaching against sin. He convinces them of the great evil of sin, induces an emotional crisis which persuades them that God ignores their sins, and after that

he lets them spend the rest of their lives meditating on the intense sinfulness and evident reprobation of other men.
Thomas Merton

PROVERBS

Habits are first cobwebs, then cables.
Spanish proverb

He does not cleanse himself of his sins who denies them.
Latin proverb

Every sin brings its punishment with it.
English proverb

To fall into sin is human, but to remain in sin is devilish.
German proverb

HUMOUR

Priest, having finished his sermon:
   'Will the person who took all the cabbages from the church garden last evening kindly come and remove the stumps as we have no further use for them.'

During a conversation with a kindly old priest, the young man asked:
   'Is it really such a sin to sleep with a girl?'
   'Oh, no,' replied the priest, 'but you, young man – you don't sleep.'

An Anglican vicar noticed that an Evangelical neighbour was having some success with posters displaying slogans exhorting this and that, and decided to follow suit.
   After much thought he devised a winner:
   'IF YOU'RE TIRED OF SIN, STEP IN.'
   Imagine the poor man's chagrin when the next day he saw written below his text:
   'BUT IF YOU ARE NOT, PHONE PADDINGTON 04655.'

WORD PICTURES

Chrysostom, the eloquent Church Father, had incurred the anger of Emperor Arcadius. Enraged, the emperor consulted with his counsellors as to the best method of punishing the powerful preacher. 'Confiscate his property!' said one. 'Whom will that harm?' asked his majesty. 'Not Chrysostom, but only the poor, to whom he gives all he has.' – 'Cast him into prison!' said a second. 'What would be the use? He would glory in his chains.' – 'Well, then kill him!' said another. 'How would that help? It would only open the gates of heaven to him.'

Finally, one wiser than the rest proposed: 'There is only one thing in the world that Chrysostom fears. He is afraid to sin. We must make him sin!'

On the slope of Long's Peak in Colorado lies the ruins of a gigantic tree. Naturalists tell us it stood for some four hundred years. It was a seedling when Columbus landed at San Salvador and half-grown when the Pilgrims landed by Plymouth Rock. During the course of its long life it was struck by lightning fourteen times, and the innumerable avalanches and storms of four centuries thundered past it. It survived them all. At the end, however, an army of beetles attacked the tree and levelled it to the ground. The insects ate their way through the bark and gradually destroyed the inner strength of the tree by their incessant attacks. A forest giant which age had not withered, nor lightning blasted, nor storms subdued, fell at last to beetles so small that a man could crush them between his fingers and his thumb.
Roy A. Burkhart

A night in the nick costs 30 per cent more than a night in a Mayfair hotel. Average cost of a night's detention in a police cell: £289. Price of a night at London's Dorchester: £215.

When Mahmoud, the conqueror of India, had captured the city of Gujarat he proceeded, as was his custom, to destroy the idols. There was one fifteen feet high which the priests earnestly besought

him to spare. He declined and, seizing a hammer, struck it a blow, when down fell a shower of gems, pearls and diamonds. Let us not spare our idols. We enrich ourselves by destroying them.
Anon

Two men once visited a holy man to ask his advice.
'We have done wrong actions,' they said, 'and our consciences are troubled. What must we do to be forgiven?' 'Tell me of your wrongdoing, my sons,' said the old man. The first man said, 'I committed a great and grievous sin.' 'I have done a number of wrong things,' said the second man, 'but they are all quite small, and not at all important.'
'Go,' said the holy man, 'and bring me a stone for each misdeed.'
The first man staggered back with an enormous boulder. The second cheerfully brought a bag of small pebbles. 'Now,' said the holy man, 'go and put them back where you found them.'
The first man shouldered his great rock again, and staggered back to the place from which he had brought it. But the second man could only remember where a very few of his pebbles had lain. He came back, saying that the task was too difficult.
'Sins are like these stones,' said the old man. 'If a man has committed a great sin, it lies like a heavy stone on his conscience; yet if he is truly sorry, he is forgiven and the load of guilt is taken away. But if a man is constantly doing small things that he knows to be wrong, he does not feel any great load of guilt, and so he is not sorry, and remains a sinner. So you see, my sons, it is as important to avoid little sins as big ones.'
Slav folk tale

USEFUL TEXTS
Sin:
>   Consequences of, *Exod. 20:5; Prov. 14:11; Rom. 5:12*
>   Forgiveness of, *Exod. 24:7; Matt. 26:28*
>   God's displeasure in, *Gen. 6:6; Deut. 25:16; Ps. 5:4*

See also: A13 The Church is for sinners
           A30 God's sinful people
           A38 Original Sin
           C37 Temptation

A16
The Saints

'Anyone who welcomes a prophet because he is a prophet
will have a prophet's reward.'
Matthew 10:41

Quotations

From silly devotions and sour-faced saints, Good Lord deliver us.
St Teresa of Avila

The simplest and most effective way to sanctity is to disappear
into the background of ordinary everyday routine.
Thomas Merton

To most, even good people, God is a belief. To the saints he is an
embrace.
Francis Thompson

To live in the world today as becomes a true Christian calls for a
profound spirit of faith, and a power of endurance such as is
proper to martyrs.
Pope Pius XII

The life of a saint is a struggle from one end to the other, the
greatest saint is the one who at the end is the most vanquished.
Paul Claudel

The Blessed Francis (of Assisi), fearing that the people might take
too much notice of this astonishing miracle, began saying funny
things to make them laugh.
John R. H. Moorman

God creates out of nothing. Wonderful, you say. Yes to be sure, but
he does what is still more wonderful: He makes saints out of sinners.
Sören Kierkegaard

The healing of the world is in its nameless saints. Each separate star seems nothing, but a myriad scattered stars break up the night, and make it beautiful.
Bayard Taylor

If you become holy, it is because God has made you so. You will not know it anyway.
Cardinal Basil Hume

We need heralds of the gospel who are experts in humanity, who know the depth of the human heart, who can share the joys and hopes, the agonies and distress of the people but who are at the same time contemplatives who have fallen in love with God. For this we need saints today.
Pope John Paul's address to the European Bishops, October 1984

PROVERBS

Things are going well for me, like for a saint in this world.
Yiddish proverb

The saint who works no miracles has few pilgrims.
English proverb

HUMOUR

A footballer died and arrived at the gates of heaven where a figure all in white awaited him. 'Now,' said the gatekeeper, 'before you enter here, is there anything that happened to you on earth upon which you would like your mind set at rest?' The footballer thought for a moment and then said, 'There is one matter. I belonged to the famous St Mirren Club and one cup final when we were playing the Rangers, I scored a goal which I am sure was off-side. It won us the match and the cup, but I've always been troubled about it.' 'Oh,' replied the gatekeeper, 'we know all about that goal up here, it was perfectly right, so you can banish all your doubts.' 'Oh, thank you, St Peter,' said the footballer. He replied, 'But I'm not St Peter, you know.' 'Then who are you?' asked the footballer. 'St Mirren,' came the reply.
Anon

WORD PICTURES

The story goes that a little girl was with her family in a party being shown around one of our great cathedrals. As the guide was explaining an historic tomb nearby, the girl was staring at a great stained glass window through which the summer sun was streaming, bathing the cathedral floor in colour. As the group was about to move on she asked the guide in a shrill clear voice, 'Who are those people in the pretty window.' 'Those are the saints,' the man replied.

That night as she was undressing for bed she told her mother, 'I know who the saints are.'

'Do you dear?' replied her mother. 'Who are they?' 'They're the people who let the light shine through.'

Anon

For courageously preaching that Nazism was contrary to Christianity, Fr Jakob Gapp, an Austrian Marianist priest, was beheaded.

He had started to denounce the Nazi regime shortly after the invasion of Austria in 1938. Because of the danger he was in his Religious superiors moved him first to France and then to Spain. However the Gestapo, the Nazi secret police, were out to get him. Two undercover agents claiming to convert to Catholicism, lured the priest back into France, where he was arrested for treason and sent to Berlin.

He was interrogated, tried and condemned to death. On 13th August 1943 he was beheaded at the Berlin-Ploetzensee Prison and his body was given to a medical institute for experimentation. He has no tomb.

P.F.

Popular religious pictures first emerged in the 15th century in the monasteries of Germany and Burgundy. With the great improvements in printing which were achieved in the following century, they became widespread. The main centre of production was Antwerp, and some idea of the vast scale of it can be deduced from the stock which the widow of a printer sold to an Italian merchant of such wares in 1666. There were 68,947 prints on parchment, an equal number on paper, and some 12,000 in colour. The fervour of the Counter-Reformation encouraged the popularity of these images, which did much to spread the cult of Jesuit saints such as Ignatius, Aloysius Gonzaga and Francis Xavier.

A similar combination of religious revivalism and technological innovation brought about a second great flowering of popular religious imagery, and this was the subject of the Paris exhibition, entitled *'L'Image de la Piete en France 1814-1914*. Reaction against the French revolution stimulated a religious revival, complicated though it was by the emphasis on the alliance between throne and altar. Meanwhile, the invention of lithography, and the application of the steam engine to processes of printing, made possible the proliferation of pious imagery on an undreamt-of scale. By 1860 firms such as Turgis, which marketed 430 different subjects and 75 patterns on First Communion cards, had branches in New York, and were supplying the British market. The precise effect of these images on theological belief, or devotional practice, is difficult to estimate, but they certainly helped promote and publicise new cults: of the Sacred Heart, of the Immaculate Conception, of Our Lady of Lourdes, of the Cure d'Ars and of the Little Flower.
The Tablet

USEFUL TEXTS

Saint:
    Called by God, *Rom. 1:7; 1 Cor. 1:2*
    Any member of God's family, *Eph. 2:19*
    Immorality not fitting, *Eph. 5:3*
    God will not forsake, *Ps. 37:28*

See also: A10 Seeking perfection
            B26 The whole person
            B51 One with Christ
            C8   God's messengers

A17
GENTLENESS

'Learn from me, for I am gentle and humble in heart.'
Matthew 11:30

QUOTATIONS

Gentleness is invincible.
Marcus Aurelius

Gently deal with souls untaught.
St Aidan

The gentle mind by gentle deeds is known.
Edmund Spenser

Your gentleness shall force more than your force move us to gentleness.
Shakespeare

If you would reap praise, sow the seeds, gentle words and helpful deeds.
Benjamin Franklin

If someone, in hatred, were to pluck out my left eye, I think I could look kindly at him with my right eye. If he plucked that one out too, I would still have my heart with which to love him.
St Francis of Sales

I can make a Lord, but only the Almighty can make a gentleman.
King James I

It is almost a definition of a gentleman to say he is one who never inflicts.
John Henry Newman

PROVERB

What is it to be a gentleman? The first to thank and the last to complain.
Serbian proverb

WORD PICTURES

I always remember one incident that was told to me. A group of young priests wanted to make a pilgrimage to the Holy Land and greatly longed to have speech with the great Scripture scholar, Père Lagrange. They travelled by a French boat where they had the privilege of an altar for saying Mass. After going on the boat, a rather poorly dressed gentle friar from the steerage came along, and asked them politely if he might say Mass the next morning. Rather unwillingly they agreed, telling him that he might say Mass after they had said theirs. Morning after morning he came humbly to say his Mass and then went back to the steerage.

When the young priests arrived at St Étienne to call on the great master it was the grubby little friar from the steerage that they found to be Lagrange.

Vincent McNabb

It was winter, and Martin was riding with his regiment through the snow and slush into the city of Amiens. Crowds had gathered to watch the soldiers coming in, worn and weary, with sodden equipment, perishing with cold, in spite of thick, warm military cloaks and uniform. As they pass through the city gate a young officer dismounts. He has seen among the crowd a poor man, well-nigh naked, blue with cold, holding out a trembling hand for alms to buy bread. The officer flings off his cloak, and, having drawn his sword, he cut the cloak in two – gently and courteously he wraps one half of it round the shivering shoulders of the beggar. . . . Perhaps a great laugh goes up as the crowd see the surprised old beggar-man decked out in the smart purple-blue cloak, and Martin, laughing with the rest, wraps the other half round himself, remounts and rides on. That night, as he lay asleep in his billet, he saw a vision. He saw the half of a military cloak. And he heard a voice which bade him look well at it, and asked him if he had seen the cloak before. And as he looked upon it he expected to see beneath it the features of his shivering friend at the city gate, but he saw the figure of no beggar-man, but the strong and gracious face and form of Jesus himself. And as in adoring silence

69

Martin listened for the voice to speak again, the laughing crowd of peasants seemed to change into groups of the heavenly host . . .
J. A. Bouquet

At which time of George Herbert's coming alone to Bemerton, there came to him a poor old woman, with an intent to acquaint him with her necessitous condition, as also, with some troubles of her mind; but after she had spoken some few words to him she was surpriz'd with a fear, and that begot a shortness of breath, so that the spirits and speech fail'd her; which he perceiving, did so compassionate her, and was so humble, that he took her by the hand, and said, Speak good Mother, be not afraid to speak to me; for I am a man that will hear you with patience; and will relieve your necessities too, if I be able; and this I will do willingly, and therefore, Mother, be not afraid to acquaint me with what you desire. After which comfortable speech, he again took her by the hand, made her sit down by him, and understanding she was of his parish, he told her, he would be acquainted with her and take her into his care: and having with patience heard and understood her wants (and it is some relief for a poor body to be but hear'd with patience) he like a Christian clergyman comforted her by his meek behaviour and counsel; but because that cost him nothing, he reliev'd her with money too, and so sent her home with a chearful heart, praising God, and praying for him. Thus worthy, and thus lowly, was Mr George Herbert in his own eyes: and thus lovely in the eyes of others.
Izaak Walton

USEFUL TEXTS
Gentleness:
    A characteristic God likes, *1 Pet. 3:4*
    Of Christ, *2 Cor. 10:1*
    Deal with others in, *1 Cor. 4:21*

See also: A19 Patience
            B41 Generosity
            C18 Compassion
            C46 Loving kindness

A18
Balance in Nature

'It was not for any fault on the part of creation that it was made unable to attain its purpose, it was made so by God.'
Romans 8:20

Quotations

Nature is the art of God.
Dante

Nature never breaks her own laws.
Leonardo da Vinci

Nature is not governed except by obeying her.
Francis Bacon

Let us permit nature to have her way: She understands her business better than we do.
Michel de Montaigne

When I du see the may in bloom, I ain't afeard to ask the Almighty for eternal life.
Old Wiltshire Countryman

Nature is the living, visible garment of God.
Goethe

God's holy life would not be manifested without nature, but be only in an eternal stillness.
Jacob Boehme

An ecologist wants to clean up the world; an environmentalist wants you to clean up your garden.
Bill Copeland

The ground is holy, being even as it came from the Creator. Keep it, guard it, care for it, and for it keeps man, guards man, cares for man. Destroy it and man is destroyed.
Alan Paton

I have a great faith in the kindliness of nature, and I feel sure that whatever happens to this battered old cage of mine, the little bird inside will be all right.
George Meredith

HUMOUR

A country parson was congratulating one of his flock on the success with which he had transformed a plot of waste land into a beautiful garden. 'It is indeed wonderful,' he said, 'what man can achieve with the help of Almighty God.'

'Yes, sir,' was the reply, 'but you should have seen the place when only the Almighty was looking after it.'
K. Edwards

Two men met on a mountain peak. 'I came here because I love adventure, and I have an insatiable curiosity,' said one. 'I like to see the sunrise from new surroundings, and I like to tread where no man has trod before. I like to embrace the universe and admire the beauty of nature from the height and silence of mountain peaks. What about you?'

'I came because my daughter is learning to play the piano, and my wife is learning to sing.'
Harvest Magazine

A tree's a tree. How many more do you need to look at?
Ronald Regan

WORD PICTURES

Gerry Carr, member of Skylab 4 crew, on viewing earth from space: 'I would look at the earth's horizon and see the earth's atmosphere. It is very beautiful. It is blue and white, gold and orange. But it is so thin and fragile. That atmosphere is all that keeps earth habitable,

but it's no thicker than the skin on an orange – no, thinner than that, like the skin on an apple. There's no way to explain how clearly you can see the fragility of the earth. You have to have been there.'
Molly Ivins

In a Spanish park posted on a tree are these words:
I am a tree. You who would pass by me and would raise your hand against me, remember that I am the heat of your hearth on cold nights; the friendly shade screening you from summer heat; the source of refreshing draughts; the beam of your house; the board of your table; the bed on which you lie; the timber of your boat; the handle of your hoe; the wood of your cradle; and the shell of your coffin. Harm me not.
Anon

A very old Chinaman was busy in his orchard when the ruler of that district happened to pass. 'You are very old, surely,' said the ruler.
'I have lived one hundred years,' replied the old man.
'Indeed?' the ruler was impressed. 'But are you not planting fruit trees?'
'I am,' said the old man.
'My friend,' murmured the ruler, 'surely you do not hope to live long enough to gather the fruit from these saplings? and if not, why make your back ache?'
'It is as you say,' the gardener replied. 'But sire, when I came into this world I found many good things awaiting me. I would like to think that when I pass on there will be good things waiting for others.'
Anon

The most blessed father Francis was journeying through the valley of Spoleto, and came to a spot near Bevagna where a very great number of birds of different sorts were gathered together; doves, rooks and those other birds that are called jackdaws.
When he saw them, being a man of the most fervent temper and also very tender and affectionate towards all the lower and irrational creatures, Francis, the most blessed servant of God, left

his companions in the way and ran eagerly towards the birds. When he was come close to them and saw that they were awaiting him, he gave them his accustomed greeting. But, not a little surprised that the birds did not fly away (as they are wont to do), he was filled with exceeding joy and humbly begged them to hear the word of God. After saying many things to them he added:

'My brother birds, much ought you to praise your Creator, and ever to love him who has given you feathers for clothing, wings for flight, and all that you had need of. God has made you noble among his creatures, for he has given you a habitation in the purity of the air, and, whereas you neither sow nor reap, he himself doth still protect and govern you without any care of your own.'

On this (as he himself and the brethren who had been with him used to say) those little birds rejoicing in wondrous fashion, after their nature, began to stretch out their necks, to spread their wings, to open their beaks and gaze on him. And then he went to and fro amidst them, touching their heads and bodies with his tunic. At length he blessed them, and, having made the sign of the cross, gave them leave to fly away to another place.

Thomas of Celano, 1225

In the last fifty years, the earth has been destroyed and devastated more than in all the millions of years behind us. . . . If we want to live we have to do something immediately. . . . Let us always have the eyes of St Francis to see God in everything. And the heart St Francis had, to call all that is alive, all that can be developed or restored, our sisters and brothers.

Cardinal Arns of Brazil

Chico had a lot of faith in God, and the Church always supported him. People hid him in church when enemies were after him. God helps people. When Chico died I was filled with despair. But God comforted me and inspired me to work alongside others to carry on Chico's work. They killed him, but they didn't kill his ideas. We continue his battle.

Wife of Chico Mendes

Once I needlessly killed a fly. The poor thing crawled on the ground, hurt and mangled, and for three whole days I wept over my cruelty to a living creature, and to this day the incident remains in my memory.

Somehow it happened that some bats bred on the balcony of the storeroom where I was, and I poured boiling water over them, and once again I shed many tears on this account, and since then I have never harmed any living creature.

One day, going from the Monastery to Old Russikon-on-the-Hill, I saw a dead snake on my path which had been chopped into pieces, and each piece writhed convulsively, and I was filled with pity for every living creature, every suffering thing in creation, and I wept bitterly before God.

The Spirit of God teaches the soul to love every living thing so that she would have no harm come to even a green leaf on a tree, or trample underfoot a flower of the field. Thus the Spirit of God teaches love towards all, and the soul feels compassion for every being, loves even her enemies and pities even devils because they have fallen away from the good.
St Silouan

There are people who attach themselves to animals, and stroke and fondle and talk to them; and have forsaken the love of God, and because of this that love between brothers for which Christ died in great suffering gets lost. It is silly to do this. Feed animals and cattle, and do not beat them – in this consists man's duty of kindness towards them; but to become attached, to love, caress and talk to them – that is folly for the soul.

The soul that has come to know the Lord ever stands before Him in love and awe – how then can she at the same time love, stroke and talk to cattle, cats or dogs? To do so means that we have forgotten Christ's commandment to love God with all our hearts, with all our souls, with all our minds.
St Silouan

People read documents from a particular perspective. I came to read *Veritatis Splendor*, the papal encyclical on the foundations of

75

morality, with questions prompted by almost two decades of involvement with environmental issues. . . . Given what is at stake, I was saddened that despite its length – 179 pages – *Veritatis Splendor* was silent on environmental issues. . . . The encyclical deals with the universal and unchanging nature of moral norms and restates that particular moral acts like homicide, genocide, abortion and euthanasia are intrinsically evil. There is, however, no mention of the morality of biocide or geocide, the poisoning of the air, water and soil, nor the irreversible destruction of the rain forests. The morality of sexual, political and economic matters is discussed and clear norms enunciated. The perspective is exclusively God-centred and human-centred. It would appear that the drafters of the encyclical are blind to the moral implications of environmental destruction.
Sean McDonagh

USEFUL TEXTS
Earth:
   Created by God, *Gen. 1:1*
   To be inhabited, *Isa. 45:13*
   As God's footstool, *Isa. 66:1*

See also: B32 The Wonders of God
            B39 Creation
            B42 Signs of the times
            C34 The value of little things

A19
PATIENCE

'Do you want us to go and weed it out?' But he said, 'No, because when you weed out the darnel, you might pull up the wheat with it. Let them both grow till the harvest'.
Matthew 13:28

QUOTATIONS

He that has patience may encompass anything.
Rabelais

Beware the fury of a patient man.
John Dryden

Everything comes if a man will only wait.
Benjamin Disraeli

The virtue of patience is the one which most assures us of perfection.
St Francis of Sales

Patience is needed with everyone, but first of all with ourselves.
St Francis of Sales

Faith takes up the cross, love binds it to the soul, patience bears it to the end.
Bonard

These things that a man cannot amend in himself or in others, he ought to suffer patiently, until God order things otherwise.
Thomas à Kempis

Prompt to move, but firm to wait – knowing things rashly sought are rarely found.
William Wordsworth

'Rest in the Lord, wait patiently on him and he will give thee thy heart's desire.' The more central this thought becomes, the less difficult you will find its outward expression, that is to say, long-suffering and gentleness in all the encounters of everyday life.
Evelyn Underhill

PROVERBS

Patience conquers the devil.
German proverb

One moment of patience may ward off great distaste, one moment of impatience may ruin a whole life.
Chinese proverb

WORD PICTURES

There is a story of a man who prayed earnestly one morning for grace to overcome his besetting sin of impatience. A little later he missed a train by half a minute and spent an hour stamping up and down the station platform in furious vexation. Five minutes before the next train came in he suddenly realised that here had been the answer to his prayer. He had been given an hour to practise the virtue of patience; he had missed the opportunity and wasted the hour.
Bernard Hodgson

The Chinese tell of one of their countrymen, a student, who, disheartened by the difficulties in his way, threw down his book in despair. Seeing a woman rubbing a crowbar on a stone, he enquired the reason, and was told that she wanted a needle, and thought she would rub down a crowbar till she got it small enough. Provoked by this example of patience to 'try again' he resumed his studies and became a famous scholar.

On one occasion when Mahomet and his friend Ali were together, they met a man who, imagining some ill-treatment, began abusing Ali.

Ali bore the insults for a long time, but at last lost his patience

and returned railing for railing. When Mahomet heard this, he walked away, and left the two disputants to settle their differences as best they could. When, later on, Ali met Mahomet, he asked reproachfully, 'Why did you go away like that and leave me to bear such insults alone?' and Mahomet replied, 'My friend! while that rude man was insulting you so cruelly and you kept silent, there were ten angels guarding you and answering him: but as soon as you began returning his insults they left you, and I also came away.'
A Moslem Tradition

USEFUL TEXTS

Patience:
  Waiting for the Lord, *Ps. 130:5*
  Need for, *Heb. 10:36*
  Holy Spirit gives, *Gal. 5:22*
  Produced by suffering, *Rom. 5:3*

See also: A11 God's loving Providence
           B21 Trust in God
           C39 Doing God's will

A20
The Kingdom of God

'A disciple of the kingdom of heaven is like a householder
who brings out from the storeroom things both new and old.'
Matthew 13:52

Quotations

The kingdom of God is not realm but reign; not domain but
dominion.
W. N. Clarke

To accept his kingdom and to enter in brings blessedness, because
the best conceivable thing is that we should be in obedience to the
Will of God.
C. H. Dodd

If man lost his liberty, he would be disqualified for membership in
the kingdom of God. Not even God could build a society of love
out of puppets or robots.
Kirby Page

This life, this kingdom of God, this simplicity of absolute existence,
is hard to enter. How hard? As hard as the master of salvation
could find words to express the hardness.
George Macdonald

The highest type of prayer has for its object not any material
benefit, but the enlightenment and amendment of our wills, the
elevation of all humanity, and the coming of the kingdom.
Oliver Lodge

According to the saying of our Lord and Saviour, the kingdom of
God does not come in such a way as to be seen. No one will say,
'Look, here it is!' or, 'There it is': because the kingdom of God is
within us. The word is very near us; it is on our lips and in our

heart. It is clear from this that when a man prays that God's kingdom may come, he is praying as he should, for the kingdom of God which is within him, that it may rise, flourish and reach its full growth.
Origen

WORD PICTURES

A Russian youth who had become a conscientious objector to war through the reading of Tolstoy and the New Testament was brought before a magistrate. With the strength of conviction he told the judge of the life which loves its enemies, which does good to those who despitefully use it, which overcomes evil with good, and which refuses war.

'Yes,' said the judge, 'I understand. But you must be realistic. These laws you are talking about are the laws of the kingdom of God; and it has not come yet.'

The young man straightened, and said, 'Sir, I recognise that it has not come for you, nor yet for Russia or the world. But the kingdom of God has come for me! I cannot go on hating and killing as though it had not come.'
Neil H. Swanson

'Where are you going, your Royal Highness?'
'Wherever the king goes.'
'But do you know exactly where the king is going?'
'He has told me in a general way, but I'm not anxious to know, I only want to go with him.'
'So, your Majesty, you have no idea about this journey?'
'No, I have no idea except that it will be in the company of my dear lord and husband.'
'Your husband is going to Egypt, and stopping at Acre, and many other places. Don't you mean to go there too, your Majesty?'
'No, not really. All I want is to be near my king. It is quite unimportant to me where he goes, except in so far as he will be there. I'm not so much going as following him. I don't want to make this journey, but the king's presence is enough for me.'
St Francis of Sales

There is an old legend about a holy old monk named Cassianus. Weary of men's wickedness, he knelt alone in church praying to be taken to a better world. He fell into ecstasy with his eyes fixed on the large crucifix over the altar, and saw the five wounds on the figure begin to shine white like diamonds; then from each wound fell drops, not of blood, but of sparkling crystal water, falling faster and faster till it formed a stream down the altar and the altar-steps and down the middle of the church and out at the main door.

The shining water lighted up the dark church and was so beautiful that the sight of it filled the monk with joy. He heard a voice at his side say: 'The living waters of grace, which I won for men by my death on the cross,' and turned and saw our Lord himself standing.

Our Lord then said: 'Come with me,' and they went through a little door to the top of the church-tower, and the monk could see all the town, streets and houses and people, spread out below. He saw the stream of living water flowing through the streets, into houses, seeking out all the people. Some people knelt down to drink from it, and he could see their souls within them become radiant like the water; he shouted to tell the other people to drink too, but he saw that nobody heard him. He asked: 'Who are these happy ones, Lord?' 'These are the souls in whom God reigns by his grace, so that they do his Will.'

Then our Lord said again: 'Come with me,' and in a moment they stood outside the closed gate of heaven, looking down from a balcony upon the earth far below. There the monk saw all the cities and countries of mankind and the rivers of living water flowing through them, and everywhere souls in a state of grace, here few and there many, shining like stars and lighting up the darkness of the earth; and sometimes he was terrified to see some of the stars go out, and sometimes he rejoiced when a new group of stars suddenly shone forth. Our Lord said, 'It is the kingdom of God come upon earth', and the monk felt that he could go on looking at the sight for ever.

Then our Lord said, 'Now Cassianus, you shall choose for yourself. You may go into heaven straightaway by this gate, or you may go back to earth for seven years more to work and pray for the kingdom of God. Which will you choose?' He fell at our Lord's feet, 'Dear Lord, let me go back to earth for seven years.' Thereupon he came out of his ecstasy in church, and worked and prayed constantly to get men to live for the glory of God. His favourite prayer was the 'Our Father', and whenever he came to the words, 'thy kingdom come', he would stop and say them slowly over again for hours at a time. He died after seven years, with the same words on his lips.

The kingdom of God means that God lives and reigns in the hearts of men by his grace.

F. H. Drinkwater

USEFUL TEXTS

The Kingdom:
>   Of God, *1 Chr. 29:11; Ps. 22:28*
>   Of Christ, *Matt. 16:28; 2 Pet. 1:11*
>   Of the world, *Rev. 11:15*

See also: A31   Heaven
>   B17   The Church – Bride of Christ
>   B51   One with Christ
>   C39   Doing God's will

A21
FEEDING THE HUNGRY

'Give them something to eat yourselves.'
Matthew 14:16

QUOTATIONS

The road to Jericho today, the road to the Good Samaritan runs through every under-developed country.
Michel Quoist

We must live simply, that others may simply live. We must re-think our priorities, and strip down our life-style to be a witness to true Christian living.
Pauline Webb

Beware of invoking the fear of Communism as an excuse for avoiding a change in the structures which confine millions of the sons of God in a sub-human condition.
Helder Camera

The war against hunger is truly mankind's war of liberation.
John F. Kennedy

I'm not interested in the bloody system! Why has he no food? Why is he starving to death?
Bob Geldof

The hungry hare has no frontiers and doesn't follow ideologies. The hungry hare goes where it finds food. And the other hares do not block its passage with tanks.
Lech Walesa

In a consumer society there are inevitably two kinds of slaves; the prisoners of addiction and the prisoners of envy.
Ivan Ilich

The Catholic who is not a revolutionary is living in mortal sin.
Camillo Torres

The Church and the Jesuits have made an option for the poor.
This is the option Jesus made; the option the prophets like Isaiah
and Micah made. That doesn't make the Church Communist.
That makes the Church simply Christian.
*Fr Jon Sobrino SJ, speaking on television following the murder of
his six brother Jesuits in El Salvador.*

The poverty of the poor is not a summons to alleviate their plight
with acts of generosity, but rather a compelling obligation to fashion
an entirely different social order.
Gustavo Gutierrez

PROVERBS

Hungry bellies have no ears.
English proverb

Hunger and cold deliver a man up to his enemy.
English proverb

HUMOUR

A little Japanese boy called at the house of a retired gentleman
and offered some picture postcards for sale at 10p each.

'What are you going to do with the money?' he asked him.

'I am raising one million pounds for the earthquake relief,' he
answered, gravely, and he was so tiny and the sum he named was
so large that the gentleman had to laugh.

'One million pounds?' he cried. 'Do you expect to raise it all by
yourself?'

'No, sir,' he replied gravely. 'There's another little boy helping me.'

WORD PICTURES

During a persistent famine in 980, Ethelwold, Bishop of Winchester,
sold the gold and silver vessels of his cathedral church in order to

relieve the poor, saying, 'There is no reason that the senseless temples of God should abound in riches, and the living temples of the Holy Ghost starve for hunger.'

St Vincent de Paul, as a small boy, used to work with the shepherds. When he was twelve years old (it was 1588, year of the Spanish Armada) he was sent to do some work for a neighbouring farmer, and started back home the proud possessor of thirty sous, the first money he had ever earned. He was thinking that he would not spend them, but lay them aside to begin some savings. But on the road he met with a poor man, whose rags and misery moved him to such pity that he took out the thirty sous and gave him the lot. Then he went on, lighter in pocket and still lighter in heart.
F. H. Drinkwater

Victor Hugo, in *Ninety-Three*, tells the story of a French mother who, after the Revolution, had been driven from her home with her two children. She had wandered through the woods and fields for several days. She and her two children had lived on roots and leaves. On the third morning they had hidden in some bushes on the approach of two soldiers, a captain and a sergeant. The captain ordered the sergeant to find out what was stirring in the bushes; he prodded the mother and her two children out. They were brought to the captain's side, and he saw in an instant that they were starving; he gave them a long loaf of brown French bread. The mother took it eagerly, like a famished animal, broke it into two pieces, giving one piece to one child and the other to the second child. The sergeant looked up to the captain and said, 'Is it because the mother is not hungry?' The captain replied, 'No, sergeant, it is because she is a mother!'
Homiletic Review

If Mother Teresa of Calcutta – one of those women who are not afraid to descend, following Christ, to all the dimensions of humanity, to all the situations of man in the modern world – were present here, she would tell us that along the streets of Calcutta, and other cities in the world, men are dying of hunger.

The consumer approach to life does not take into consideration the whole truth about man – not the historical truth nor the social, interior and metaphysical truth. It is rather a flight from this truth. It does not take into consideration the whole truth about man.

Man is created for happiness. Yes, but man's happiness is not to be identified with pleasure. The consumer-orientated man loses, in this pursuit of pleasure, the full dimension of his humanity and loses awareness of the deepest meaning of life. Such orientation of progress kills in man, therefore, what is most deeply and most essentially human.

Pope John Paul II

USEFUL TEXTS

Food:
> Provided by God, *Gen. 1:29-30*
> For strength, *Ps. 104:15*
> To abstain from, *Gen. 2:16-17*
> Christ provided, *Matt. 14:19-20*

See also: A33 Love your neighbour
           B15 Jesus, friend of outcasts
           C21 Rise above materialism
           C29 Not through luxury

A22
Seeking God

'After the fire there came the sound of a gentle breeze.'
1 Kings 19:12

Quotations

God enters by a private door into every individual.
Ralph Waldo Emerson

He alone is God who never can be sought in vain, even when he
cannot be found.
St Bernard of Clairvaux

Art thou looking for God, seeking God with a view to thy personal
good, thy personal profit? Then in truth thou art not seeking God.
Meister Eckhart

I hurry wherever I am beckoned, in search of what can bring men
together in the name of the essential.
Helder Camara

'O thou Great Chief, light a candle in my heart that I may see
what is therein and sweep the rubbish from thy dwelling place.'
African Child's Prayer

There is one approach to an infinite realm where God might be.
There is one door that opens to the holy of holies. The search
must *begin* in your own bosom.
Rufus Jones

My only task is to be what I am, a man seeking God in silence and
solitude with respect for the demands and realities of his own
vocation, and fully aware that others too are seeking the truth in
their own way.
Thomas Merton

Oh, who will give me a voice that I may cry aloud to the whole world that God, the all-highest is in the deepest abyss within us and is waiting for us to return to him.
Hans Denck

PROVERBS
Search yourself and you will find God.
Kurdish proverb

Many millions search for God and find him in their hearts.
Sikh proverb

Those who roam to other lands in pilgrimage to find the God that dwells within them are like a shepherd who searches his own flock for the sheep he has under his arm.
Telugu proverb

WORD PICTURES
'The patriotic Archbishop of Canterbury found it advisable . . .'
    'Found what?' said the Duck.
    'Found it,' the Mouse replied rather crossly. 'Of course you know what "it" means.'
    'I know what "it" means well enough when I find a thing,' said the Duck:
    'It's generally a frog or a worm. The question is: what did the Archbishop find?'
Alice in Wonderland

Six hundred and thirteen commandments were given to Moses . . .
Then David came and reduced them to eleven. Then came Isaiah, and reduced them to six. Then came Michah, and reduced them to three. Then came Isaiah came again, and reduced them to two, as it is said, 'Keep ye judgement and do righteousness.' Then came Amos, and reduced them to one, as it is said, 'Seek you me and live.'
Rabbi Samlai

USEFUL TEXTS

Characteristics of God:
  Omnipresence, *Ps. 139:7-12*
  Omniscience, *Amos 9:2-3*
  Omnipotence, *Jer. 32:17, 27*

Manifestations of God:
  Voice of, *Deut. 5:22-26*
  Glory of, *Exod. 40:34-35*
  In Jesus, *John 14:9*

See also: A10 Seeking perfection
           B28 The Father who draws us to himself
           C16 Come follow me
           C38 Discerning God's will

A23
MERCY

'My salvation will come and my integrity be manifest.'
Isaiah 56:1

QUOTATIONS

If we refuse mercy here, we shall have justice in eternity.
Jeremy Taylor

God gives his wrath by weight, but his mercy without measure.
Thomas Fuller

We implore the mercy of God, not that he may leave us in peace
in the midst of our vices, but that he deliver us from them.
Blaise Pascal

Our faults are like a grain of sand beside the great mountain of the
mercies of God.
St John Vianney

Whoever falls from God's right hand is caught into his left.
Edwin Markham

With thee 'tis one to behold and to pity. Accordingly, thy mercy
followeth every man so long as he liveth. Withersoever he goeth,
even as thy glance never quitteth any.
Nicholas of Cusa

There's a wideness in God's mercy
like the wideness of the sea,
there's a kindness in his justice,
which is more than liberty.
Frederick W. Faber

PROVERBS

The Goddess of Mercy has a thousand hands – and needs them all.
Japanese proverb

If God were not willing to forgive sin, heaven would be empty.
German proverb

WORD PICTURES

A Cromwellian of the Civil War, meeting a Cavalier in heaven, was surprised at his old enemy's presence there, and asked him how it had come about. The Royalist answered:
Between the saddle and the ground
I mercy sought and mercy found.
Anon

A notable instance of mercy shown to enemies occurred in Swiss history, when, in 1318, the town of Solothurn was being besieged by the Emperor Leopold. The river Rare, near which the town stands, was much swollen at the time, and a bridge that the beleaguered forces had thrown across was carried away by the flood, and their men were being drowned in numbers.
Then the Solothurners, forgetting all injuries, rushed out with boats to save their enemies. Leopold was so touched by this magnanimity that he at once raised the siege, and presented the town with a beautiful banner.
Anon

A boy was sent by his teacher to the principal of the school for doing something wrong. After hearing the facts the principal took out a blank book and wrote down the boy's name, observing as he did so: 'You have not been sent to me before. Now, I don't know you: you may be a good boy, for all I know. Good boys sometimes make mistakes. Now I'll just make a note in pencil that you were sent to me today, and I will also note why you were sent. But you see I am making this memorandum in pencil, and I am not bearing on very hard. And if you are not sent to me again this year, I shall erase this from my book and no one will ever

know anything about it.' It was a lesson in mercy the boy never forgot.
Anon

When John Sebastian Bach sought to give musical expression to the very kernel of Christian truth, he turned to the Mass for his words. The B minor Mass opens with the poignant cry of the whole chorus and orchestra, *Kyrie Eleison, Lord have mercy*, and in the fugue which follows all the voices and instruments independently take up the theme; there are no other words, simply *Kyrie Eleison*. No one who has ever heard it can doubt that in that universal cry for mercy we are led to the threshold of our religion. Nor is it merely a preliminary; the sense of utter human unworthiness is the permanent ground-base through which the melody of the gospel of the mercy of God sounds in our ears, so that the suitable epitaph for a Christian is composed of two words only: 'Jesu, mercy'. This is far more impressive, far more Christian, than a catalogue of virtues, or of benevolent actions, or of intellectual achievements.
Anon

USEFUL TEXTS
Mercy:
    Characteristic of God, *Lam. 3:22-23*
    God showed in salvation, *Titus 3:4-5*
    To characterise believers, *Matt. 5:7; Luke 6:36*

See also: A17 Gentleness
             C14 Forgiveness
             C18 Compassion
             C46 Loving kindness

A24
PAPACY

'You are Peter and on this rock I will build my Church.'
Matthew 16:18

PROVERBS

Where the Pope is, Rome is.
Italian proverb

HUMOUR

Pope Elopes, was the headline attributed to a Miss Dorothy Parker, who won the most sensational conceivable newspaper headline with it in an Algonquin Round Table contest.

When I met Pope Paul VI, he mentioned that he had read *The Power and the Glory*. I told him that it had been condemned by the Holy Office.
 'Who condemned it?'
 'Cardinal Pissardo.'
 He repeated the name with a wry smile and added, 'Mr Greene, some parts of your books are certain to offend some Catholics, but you should pay no attention to that.'
Graham Greene

The tea manufacturers wanted a new advertising gimmick, so the senior creative man at their advertising agency decided to go to Rome to see if he could persuade the Pope to make a TV commercial.
 The Pope gave the ad man an audience and he made his request. 'We'll give you £100,000 for a ten-second commercial. All you have to do is say: "Give us this day our daily tea".'
 'I'm sorry,' replied the Pope, 'but I cannot do as you request.'
 '£500,000,' offered the ad man.
 'I'm afraid not,' said the Pope, solemnly.

'All right, £1,000,000. And that's the very last offer.'

But still the Pope refused to make the commercial and the ad man left. On the way home the ad man turned to his secretary and said: 'That's odd. I mean, the Pope refusing to do a commercial for tea. I wonder how much the bread people are giving him.'

Anon

WORD PICTURES

There have been sixteen Popes named Gregory, the first and greatest of them, often referred to as Gregory the Great, is remembered by the Church on 12 March. He was born of well-to-do parents in Rome, where, for some years he was an important magistrate. He showed a great interest in monasteries and gave large sums of money for starting a new monastery in Rome and several others in Sicily. When he was about thirty-five, Gregory decided to become a monk himself and, some years later, was chosen to be Pope, the first monk ever to hold that high office. For fourteen years as Pope, he worked to make the Church stonger and he wrote many books and letters about religious matters.

For one thing he is particularly remembered by the people of Britain. In the days before he became Pope, it is said that he was walking through Rome when he noticed some slave children who were up for sale. Being attracted by their fair hair and skin, he asked where they had come from. 'They are Angles,' was the reply. 'Not Angles, but Angels,' was Gregory's comment.

He vowed to set off himself in order to teach the English people about Christ but he was not permitted to do so. But he never forgot and, once he had become Pope, he sent Augustine and other monks to teach the English.

Though Gregory was a great man, he remembered the words of Jesus that the greatest must be the servant of all and so he called himself 'the servant of the servants of God' – a title used by all Popes since then.

Rowland Purton

The one and only English Pope, Nicholas Breakspeare, was born at Langley, Herts, about 1100. While still a youngster he felt drawn to becoming a monk, and applied for admission to the famous abbey of St Albans. For some reason or other the abbot refused to accept him and young Nicholas turned away, disappointed.

Packing his few belongings into a bundle he stepped off along the road to the coast. Here he managed somehow to get a passage; and before long he was swinging along the roads of France. His hike finished up at Arles – for the monks of St Rufus admitted him to their number.

Though handicapped by being a stranger and a simple country lad, he had actually been chosen abbot of these French monks before he was thirty-seven. Once in power he asserted his authority by a thorough revision of the Abbey's discipline. A section of the monks resented this, and applied to Rome for his removal. But Nicholas Breakspeare, knowing he was in the right, decided to go straight to the Holy Father. He promptly took to the road, and in due course arrived in Rome; there, his sound arguments and energetic personality won over the Pope to his side.

After various other jobs he was sent on an important mission to Norway and Sweden, where the Church was not yet fully organised, and where troubles with heathen tribes and quarrels between princes needed a firm control. Nicholas succeeded not only in his political and ecclesiastical undertakings, but also in winning the friendship of these fierce Northerners – whom, as an Englishman, he must have understood better than a French or Italian legate would have done. Such a good father did he show himself, whether to monks of the south or fierce warriors of the north, that in 1154, he was chosen to be the 'Spiritual Father of all Christians' and ruled the Church for some six years as Adrian IV.
F. H. Drinkwater

In the course of two thousand years, these words 'You are Peter' have been spoken 264 times to the ears and conscience of a fragile and sinful man. Two hundred and sixty-four times a new Peter was set at the side of the first one to be the foundation stone of the Church. The last in time, it was to me that the promise of Caeserea Philippi was repeated, and it is in the office of Peter that I am in your midst. With what message?

The same one that Peter proclaimed. Peter, ardent but fearful, the friend, the renegade, the penitent, had just received the Holy Spirit. And with the force of the Spirit he proclaims to a Jerusalem full of pilgrims: 'God has made this Jesus, whom you crucified both Lord and Christ.'

All that Peter will say up to the last confession on the hill of the Vatican, which crowns that of Caesarea Philippi, is reduced to this sentence: All that the Successor of Peter must say is perhaps contained in these simple words: 'God made him Lord.' Fundamentally, it is what the Pope feels: The sweet and urgent duty of proclaiming, wherever he passes, with the power and fervour of one who announces good news.
Pope John Paul II

On the face of it, there is little obvious connection between Tipperary, lust, and the present Holy Father. But I will try to explain.

One of the First World War's most famous marching songs came not from Germany or France, from Scotland or Ireland, but from Cockneyland. It was based on the love of an English soldier for the girl he has left behind in 'Tipperary'. Even when he was far away, his heart remained 'right there'.

'Tipperary' was the nickname given by the Tommies to the red-light district which then lurked just east of the lower part of London's Shaftesbury Avenue. Hence its juxtaposition, in the song, with Piccadilly and Leicester Square.

The song, in other words, has nothing to do with that part of Ireland famous for its lush green pastures, fabulous glens and 'fair golden vale'. Recently, however, the Pope received an Irish pilgrimage in a special audience at Castel Gandolfo. As always, John Paul rose to the occasion and provoked a joyous, holiday mood. So much so that part of the group struck up with 'It's a long way to Tipperary'.

The Pope put his arms round the shoulders of the singers and at the end of their song asked, 'Who or what is Tipperary?' He was delighted to be told that it was a county in Ireland and beamed at the image of the soldier longing to return to the faithful wife, and no doubt many bambini, who were waiting for him when the war was over.

Perhaps it was just as well he was not told the true provenance of 'Tipperary' in this context.

Urbanus

USEFUL TEXTS

Peter:
    Called by Christ, *Matt. 4:18-20*
    Walked on water, *Matt. 14:22-23*
    Confessed Jesus as Christ, *Matt. 16:13-18*
    Denied knowing Jesus, *Matt. 26:69-75*
    Witnessed empty tomb, *John 20:1-9, etc*

See also: A14 The successors of the Apostles
           B13 Authority
           B17 The Church – Bride of Christ
           C44 Feed my sheep

A25
COURAGE

'Jesus began to make it clear to his disciples that he was
destined to suffer grievously at the hands of the elders.'
Matthew 16:21

QUOTATIONS

Fortune never helps the man whose courage fails. *Sophocles*

Fear can keep a man out of danger, but courage can support him
in it. *Thomas Fuller*

Success is never final and failure never fatal. It's courage that counts.
Anon

In sport, in courage, and the sight of heaven, all men meet on
equal terms. *Winston S. Churchill*

Courage consists not in blindly overlooking danger, but in seeing
it and conquering. *Jean Paul Richter*

Have plenty of courage. God is stronger than the devil. We are
on the winning side. *John Chapman*

The bravest thing – the courage we desire and prize – is not the
courage to die decently, but to live manfully. *Thomas Carlyle*

PROVERBS

To a brave heart nothing is impossible. *French proverb*

It is better to live one day as a lion than a hundred years as a sheep.
Italian proverb

WORD PICTURES

A story is told of a Breton priest who, in the early days of the
German occupation, complied with the Vichy directive to instruct

99

his flock in the attitude towards the invader by outlining the legal minimum. That done, he devoted his sermon to a denunciation of Nazi paganism, aggression and injustice, declaring: 'No true peace can live without liberty, otherwise it means only tyranny, hatred and revolt'. Having spoken his mind he left the pulpit, saying first to his congregation: 'If anyone among you wishes to report me to the Germans, tell them they will find me in my presbytery.'
Hugh Martin

Fathers Peto and Elstowe, two men who had dared to speak out bravely as to Henry VIII's misdeeds, were summoned before the King's Council to receive a reprimand. Lord Essex told them they deserved to be sewn into a sack and thrown into the Thames. 'Threaten such things to rich and dainty folk, who have their hope in this world,' answered Elstowe, gallantly. 'We fear them not: with thanks to God, we know the way to heaven to be as ready by water as by land.' Men of such metal might be broken, but they could not be bent. The two offenders were hopelessly unrepentant and impracticable and Lord Essex decided it was necessary to banish them.
Anon

In whatever arena of life one may meet the challenge of courage, whatever may be the sacrifices he faces if he follows his conscience – the loss of his friends, his fortune, his contentment, even the esteem of his fellow men – each man must decide for himself the course he will follow. The stories of past courage can define that ingredient – they can teach, they can offer hope, they can provide inspiration. But they cannot supply courage itself. For this each man must look into his own soul.
John F. Kennedy

A more remarkable example of Christian courage has rarely been presented than that shown by Mrs S. J. Brooks, the telephone operator of Folsom, New Mexico, in 1908, who, when warned by a resident of the hills to flee for her life from the flood speeding to engulf the valley, rejected the opportunity to save herself and employed the hour that intervened between the warning received and her own death by drowning, in calling up subscribers by telephone and acquainting them of their danger. More than forty families have acknowledged their lives saved through the magnificent courage of one frail woman, whose lifeless body, with the telephone headpiece still adjusted to her ears, was found twelve miles down the canyon.

Anon

Hilary started life just like any other child, healthy and strong. She grew up to be very good at games and dancing. She became a PE and Dance teacher. Then quite suddenly a terrible disease struck. Hilary could feel and hear everything, but she couldn't move. She couldn't move her mouth or her eyelids. She couldn't sing; she couldn't talk; she couldn't make a sound. Because she couldn't chew or eat, she was fed through tubes and kept alive with a breathing machine. The only thing she could move was the big toe of her right foot. Her big toe would give a tiny flicker, 1/16th of an inch, less than 2mm, when she wanted it to. The only other thing Hilary could do was hear.

But Hilary didn't just give up and die. For ten years she carried on speaking and smiling, praying and helping – through her big toe. At first she had to spell the words out but, after three years, science came to help Hilary and she got a Possum machine. This meant she was able to operate a whole range of switches – turn on the radio, and, most important of all, operate a typewriter. Letters poured from her; she wrote poems and articles. She worked so hard for handicapped people that in 1973 the Queen wrote to her to tell her that she had been awarded the MBE for her brave work for others.

A.P.C.

USEFUL TEXTS

Courage:
  Call to, *Deut. 31:7; Ps. 27:14*
  Paul testified to having, *2 Cor. 5:6-8*

See also: B35 The Grace of God
          C13 Coping with grief
          C41 Starting afresh

A26
THE SACRAMENT OF PENANCE

'Whatever you bind on earth
shall be considered bound in heaven;
whatever you loose on earth
shall be considered loosed in heaven.'
Matthew 18:18

QUOTATIONS

The life of Christ was massively a ministry of reconciliation.
J. D. Crichton

The Church has water and tears, the water of baptism and the
tears of repentance.
St Ambrose

The confession of evil works is the first beginning of good works.
St Augustine of Hippo

For him who confesses, shams are over and realities have begun.
James S. Knowles

The Church is the sacrament-sign of the ministry of forgiveness
and reconciliation and that penance is in the here and now the
sacrament of the forgiving and reconciling Church.
J. D. Crichton

The grace of the remission of sins is assured to the penitent
because Christ prays with the Church for the sinner.
E. H. Schillebeeckx

The sacrament of penance is no longer seen as an isolated and
exclusive means of obtaining forgiveness of one's sins, but as the
source and summit of a whole Christian life of conversion.
Mark Searle

Proverb

Open confession is good for the soul.
Scottish proverb

Humour

Gerry went to confession and told the priest he'd taken bits of wood from work. The priest said 'How much?' Gerry replied, 'Not much, Father, just enough to make a garage at the back of the house.' 'Now, Gerry, you know that's not right and for your penance I want you to make the Stations of the Cross.' 'What size do you want them, Father, so as I get the right wood?'

Maria was eighty-two years old and one day she went to confession and said: 'Father, I have sinned. I have committed adultery with a seventeen-year-old gardener.'
   'When was this?' asked the priest.
   'Fifty years ago – but I just felt like recalling pleasant experiences this week.'
Anon

Word pictures

There is an Oriental story of a sultan who failed to waken one morning at the hour of prayer. The devil waked him up and told him to get up and pray. 'Who are you?' asked the sultan. 'Never mind. My act is good, is it not?' replied the devil. 'No matter who does the good action, so long as it is good.' 'Yes, but I think you are Satan and you must have some bad motive,' the sultan persisted. 'You are the tempter; that's your business, and I wish to know why you want me to get up and pray.' 'Well,' said the devil, 'if you had slept and forgotten your prayers, you would have been sorry for it afterwards, and penitent; but if you go on as now, and do not neglect a single prayer for ten years, you will be so satisfied with yourself that it will be worse for you than if you had missed one and repented of it. God loves your fault mixed with penitence more than your virtue seasoned with pride.'
Anon

People who scoff at regular confession make me think of Jonathan Swift's servant. After spending the night at an inn, Swift asked for his boots in the morning and saw them brought in covered in dust. 'Why didn't you clean them?' he asked. 'I thought there was no point,' said the servant. 'After a few miles on the road, they'll be covered in dust again, whatever I do.' 'Quite right, now go and get the horses ready; we're leaving.' Soon afterwards the horses came out of the stable and Swift was ready for the journey. 'But we can't leave without breakfast!' cried the servant. 'There's no point,' replied Swift. 'After a few miles on the road you'll be hungry again!'

After confession the soul will grow dirty again, people say. Very likely. But to keep it clean in the meantime can't fail to be a good idea. Not only because confession takes away the dust of sin, but because it gives us a special strength to avoid it, and makes firmer our friendship with God.
Pope John Paul I

A King of Prussia once visited a convict prison and, interviewing the prisoners one by one asked each of them for what crime they had been sentenced. They all declared themselves innocent of any misdeed whatsoever, except one man who owned up to the evil he had done, and said that he deserved what he was getting. The king ordered his immediate release, 'For,' said he, 'this man obviously has no business here among all these innocent people.'

If we want our sins forgiven the first step is to acknowledge that we have committed them and need to seek reconciliation.
Anon

If any word needs to be given back its original meaning it is the word 'repentance'. It must be rescued from the musty, dusty, old-fashioned feel that it has for so many that makes them dismiss it as part of an 'olde-worlde' expression of the faith that has now been superseded.

The word, 'repentance' as used in the New Testament comes not from the Greek word 'metanoia', but from the Hebrew word 'shub'. It means to return, to return home, then to return to our only true home which is God. Unlike the Greek word 'metanoia',

the Hebrew word 'shub' means an inner turning, not just the mind but of the heart and of the whole person. This about turn is always begun by God, who calls us back home and continually sustains us on the journey, so long as we are open to his grace.
David Torkington

An English priest, on holiday in Italy, found himself travelling north up the motorway from Siena to Florence at the same moment as a gun battle was being fought on the hard shoulder of the south-bound carriageway. As he saw a man fall to the ground bleeding, gun in hand, he hastily muttered a conditional absolution. It appears, however, that for his ministration to have been efficacious he would have had to zoom into the fast lane and manoeuvre himself within closer range of the dying man, for on his return to England he was told by a learned colleague that his absolution would not have taken, because he was more than twenty paces away.
The Tablet

USEFUL TEXTS

Reconciliation:
   To God, *Rom. 5:10-11*
   To brother, *Matt. 5:23-24; Matt. 18:15-17*

See also: A27 As we forgive those
              B16 Christ heals and forgives
              C14 Forgiveness
              C40 Reconciliation

A27
AS WE FORGIVE THOSE

'Not seven, I tell you, but seventy-seven times.'
Matthew 18:22

QUOTATIONS

The Church should be the society of the forgiven and the forgiving.
William G. Spencer

The man who is truly forgiven and knows it, is a man who forgives.
Martyn Lloyd-Jones

There's no point in burying a hatchet if you're going to put up a marker on the site.
Sydney Harris

He that cannot forgive others breaks the bridge over which he must pass himself: for every man has need to be forgiven.
Thomas Fuller

Only one petition in the Lord's Prayer has any condition attached to it; it is the petition for forgiveness.
William Temple

Better by far that you should forgive and smile than that you should remember and be sad.
Christina Rossetti

In taking revenge, a man is but even with his enemy; but in passing it over, he is superior – for it is a prince's part to pardon.
Francis Bacon

PROVERBS

The noblest vengeance is to forgive.
English proverb

WORD PICTURES

(Corrie ten Boom was arrested by the Gestapo at the end of February 1944 and sent to Ravensbruck Concentration Camp.) Suddenly Corrie caught sight of him in the congregation at Munich – the former SS man who had been their guard at Ravensbruck camp. Somehow she managed to go on speaking, but scenes of horror and anguish from those past days crowded into her mind. It was not for herself she cared – she remembered her poor sister, Betsie, ill, frail, yet made to strip while those mocking guards examined their helpless prisoners. Now the leader of them was here in church.

After the service he came up the church towards her, smiling broadly and with outstretched hand. 'Thank you for your message,' he said, 'Jesus has washed my sins away.' Corrie looked at him unable to lift her hand from her side. She had preached forgiveness, but how could she show it to the very person who had humiliated and hurt her beloved sister? For a long moment she paused, then prayed silently, 'Lord Jesus, forgive me and help me to forgive him.' But still she could neither smile nor raise her hand – it seemed bound to her side. 'Give me your forgiveness,' she prayed, 'I cannot forgive him on my own.'

As she took his hand, Corrie felt an amazing current passing from herself to him and love filled her heart. So, she concluded, 'I discovered that when God tells us to love our enemies, he gives, along with the command, the love itself.'
Corrie ten Boom

In the second century, a priest of Antioch, named Sulpicius, had steadfastly refused to sacrifice to the gods, even under torture, and was being led away to be beheaded. On the way, a Christian named Nicephorus ran up to him. He had quarrelled bitterly with Sulpicius and now sought reconciliation. 'Martyr of Christ!' he said, on his knees, 'Forgive me, for I have wronged thee.'

Sulpicius refused to speak to him, even at the place of execution. But when the moment came to kneel under the executioner's sword, he turned pale. 'No, no! I will obey the Emperor. I will sacrifice to the gods.' Again Nicephorus ran up

to him and implored him not to lose his martyr's crown at this last
moment. In vain, Sulpicius went off to sacrifice. 'Then I will take
his place,' said Nicephorus. 'Tell the Prefect I am a Christian.'

So Nicephorus won the martyr's crown and Supicius turned
coward, and all the Christians said it was because he would not
forgive.

F. H. Drinkwater

USEFUL TEXTS

Forgiveness:
  Of enemies, *Luke 6:27*
  Among believers, *Eph. 4:32*
  Of sin, by God, *Ps. 130:4*
  Of sin, by Christ, *Acts 10:43*

See also: A26 Sacrament of Penance
            B16 Christ heals and forgives
            C14 Forgiveness
            C40 Reconciliation

A28
WORK

'Call the workers and pay them their wages,
starting with the last arrivals and ending with the first.'
Matthew 20:8

QUOTATIONS

Work is love made visible.
Kahlil Gilbran

Thou, O God, dost sell us all good things at the price of labour.
Leonardo da Vinci

God give me work till my life shall end, and life till my work is done.
Wilfred Holtby

He who sees how action may be rest and rest action, he is wisest among his kind; he has the truth. He does well acting or resting.
Hindu saying

One becomes more interested in a job of work after the first impulse to drop it has become overcome.
Fulton J. Sheen

I am glad to think I am not bound to make the world go right, but only to discover and to do with cheerful heart the work that God appoints.
Jean Ingelow

This is the fundamental evil of industrialism. It has depersonalised work. It made the work the least interesting, because the least personal part of his life. It has created a state of things in which nothing is expected from work, but the pay for doing it, and all the happiness of living is relegated to the time when we are not working.
Eric Gill

Love your work. Love the people with whom you work. From love and goodness will spring also your joy and your satisfaction.
Pope John Paul II

Do the work that's nearest,
though 'tis dull at whiles,
helping when you meet them
lame dogs over stiles.
Charles Kingsley

PROVERBS

A man grows most tired by standing still.
Chinese proverb

Hats off to the past; coats off to the future.
American proverb

HUMOUR

Lady: 'Well, do you want a meal badly enough to be willing to work for it?'
Tramp: 'Oh, no lady, I'm just hungry – not desperate!'

'Work is the curse of the drinking classes.'
William Spooner

Navvy: 'I dug this hole where I was told to, and the following day I put the earth back as per instructions. But it won't all go back in. What'll I do?'
Irish Foreman (after mature consideration): 'There's only one thing to do – you'll have to dig the hole deeper.'

'Has your husband got another job yet,' Mrs Murphy? 'Sure and he has, Mrs O'Hara. It's hard work, and it's killing him – but, thanks be, it's permanent!'

An exasperated mother to her naughty children: 'Well, as a punishment, I won't let you play with your train set tomorrow.'

'It doesn't matter,' the nine-year-old retorted, 'we were going on strike anyway.'

Blank was a planter, and he was singularly blessed in the possession of a glass eye. Even a man with false teeth is in a pretty strong position with really unsophisticated natives. They simply can't understand how a man can take out his teeth and snap them at people.

Blank was an indolent old devil, and much preferred dozing on a shady veranda to supervising his copracutters in the broiling sun. So he used to put his eye out on a log so that it would watch them work. The natives worked like Trojans under the baleful eye of the master. But one day the planter awoke to find the work undone and his labourers asleep in the sun. Astonished and indignant, he strode to the log where he had left his eye. It was covered with a jam-tin.'

A. J. Marshall

WORD PICTURES

You may have heard the story of a visitor to a quarry who asked the men who were toiling there what they were doing. 'Can't you see I'm breaking stone?' said one gruffly. 'I'm making a living for my wife and family,' said the second. The third man had a greater vision. 'I'm helping to build a cathedral,' he replied with a glowing smile.

Professor Morse exhibited his telegraphic invention before the United States Congress in 1837, but had to struggle on scanty means till 1843. On the last night of Congress, it voted a substantial sum for the enterprise. The daughter of the Commissioner of Patents brought the news early in the morning to the despondent Morse, and was promised by him the first message over the wires. The first telegram in the world ran: 'What hath God wrought.'

In Westminster Abbey there are two magnificent statues carved in the time of Henry III. One is of Our Lady, and the other of the

111

Angel of the Annunciation. They have come down to us, still beautiful, carved by a man whose very name is unknown. The work is entered on the old wages roll as 'two figures dressed by the job,' and the man received something less than three pounds for the work. Such masons as those old English workmen would be content to do any work they were given; at one time, it may be the carving of some beautiful statue, such as the glorious angels, swinging censers, high up in the transepts of Westminster Abbey, which were carved by John of St Albans. Or they would, when that was finished, go on with the ordinary stone laying. It was the work, the building, which mattered, not their own importance.

Over the Medical School of the old St Bartholomew's Hospital are carved these words: 'Whatever thy hand findeth to do, do it with all thy might.' That was the spirit of Rahere, who founded this great hospital, in 1133, and that is the secret of the measure of its successful work during more than 800 years.
P.F.

USEFUL TEXTS
Physical Work:
    Forbidden on the Sabbath, *Exod. 23:12*
    Be diligent in, *Eccles. 9:10; Col. 3:23; 1 Thess. 4:11*
    Illustrated by parables, *Matt. 21:28; Matt. 25:21*
    With God's help, *Rom. 8:26; 1 Cor. 3:6-9*

See also: A1 The value of time
            A18 Balance in nature
            A36 Using talents
            A39 The glory of God

A29
TRUE OBEDIENCE

'He became as human beings are; and being in
every way like a human being, he was humbler yet,
even to accepting death, death on a cross.'
Philippians 2:7

QUOTATIONS

Obedience is the courtesy due to kings.
Alfred, Lord Tennyson

In a rational creature, obedience is, as it were, the mother and
guardian of all virtues.
St Augustine of Hippo

Thirty years of our Lord's life are hidden in these words of the
Gospel: 'He was subject unto them.'
Jacques B. Bossuet

God sets the soul long, weary, impossible tasks, yet is satisfied by
the first sincere proof that obedience is intended, and takes the
burden away forthwith.
Coventry Patmore

When we choose deliberately to obey him, then, with all his almighty
power, he will tax the remotest star and the last grain of sand to
assist us.
Oswald Chambers

Can we want obedience then to him, or possibly his love desert,
who form'd us from the dust!
John Milton

Every duty, even the least duty, involves the whole principle of
obedience. And little duties make the will dutiful, that is supply
and prompt to obey. Little obediences lead to great.
Henry E. Manning

The world would be darker than it is if every human spirit, so soon as it became obedient, did not become the Lord's candle. A poor, meager, starved, bruised life, if only it keeps the true human quality and does not become inhuman and if it is obedient to God in its blind, dull, half-conscious way, becomes a light.
Phillips Brooks

HUMOUR

Mother announced that in future a prize would be given every Saturday to the member of the family who had been the most obedient.

'Oh, but, Mummy,' chorused the children, 'that wouldn't be fair. Daddy would win every time!'

WORD PICTURES

Brother Masseo has said that he was present with the Blessed Francis when he preached to the birds. Rapt in devotion, Francis once found by the roadside a large flock of birds, to whom he turned aside to preach, as he had done before to another lot. But when the birds saw him approaching, they all flew away at the very sight of him. Then he came back and began to accuse himself most bitterly, saying, 'What effrontery you have, you impudent son of Peter Bernardone!' – and this because he had expected irrational creatures to obey him as if he, not God, were their creator.
John R. H. Moorham

Occasionally I meet someone who seems to have a secret, some special knowledge that sets that person apart. Such a person was Ruby Free. I met her when she was conducting a Holy Land tour. 'She must have a secret,' I said to myself enviously. 'How else can she accomplish so much, so easily?' She was a good listener, a troubleshooter, an organiser, a mother-hen to all 72 of us, plus her own two children; yet she was never tired, never out of sorts.

Then, back home, I visited Ruby. And I think I discovered her secret. There it was, a two-word motto over her sink: 'YES, LORD.'
Rosa Cornelia Veal

Centuries ago, in one of the Egyptian monasteries, a man came and asked to be admitted. The abbot told him that the chief rule was obedience, and the man promised to be patient on all occasions, even under excessive provocation. It chanced that the abbot was holding a dried-up willow-wand in his hand; he forthwith fixed the dead stick into the earth and told the newcomer that he was to water it until, against all the rules of nature, it should once again become green.

Obediently the new monk walked two miles every day to the River Nile to bring back a vessel of water on his shoulders and water the dry stick. A year passed by, and he was still faithful to his task, though very weary. Another year, and still he toiled on. Well into the third year he was still trudging to the river and back, still watering the stick, when suddenly one day it burst into life.

This story is related in the *Dialogues of Sulpicius Serverus*, on the authority of an acquaintance named Postumianus who had travelled in the East. 'I myself,' said the latter, 'have beheld the green bush – the former dead stick – which flourishes to this day in the atrium of the monastery. Its waving green foliage is a living witness to the mighty virtues of obedience and faith.

F. H. Drinkwater

There was once a farmer in Spain who had three sons and a daughter. One day the farmer became very ill and a passing traveller told his family that he could only be saved by the water of life.

'Where do we get that from?' said Alonso, the eldest son.

'From a well on a mountain top which is three days hard riding away from here,' said the stranger.

So Alonso set off. After three days riding he came to the mountain. An old man sat at the bottom of it.

'I suppose you've come for some of the water of life,' said the old man.

'Yes, I have,' said Alonso.

'Well you get it from a well up there,' said the old man, nodding towards the mountain top. 'But let me give you some advice. As you climb you will find that many of the stones shout and jeer and mock you. Don't look at them or touch them whatever you do.'

'Hmmm,' thought Alonso, 'that sounds ridiculously easy.'

He began climbing the mountain. Immediately stones began to jeer at him and call him names. He paid no attention until one in particular began to shout: 'You're a boaster, Alonso, always bragging and boasting.' When he heard this, Alonso was furious, perhaps because this insult was rather near the truth. Angrily he turned towards the stone and . . . immediately turned into a stone himself.

Two weeks later the second son Carlo set out, to get the water of life and to find his brother. He found the mountain, and the old man, and received exactly the same warning. Soon he was climbing up the mountain. He ignored the cries of the stones . . . until suddenly he thought he heard his brother's voice. He looked to see where it was coming from . . . and was immediately turned into a stone.

A week later the third son, Alfredo, was on the mountain. Having heard the old man's warning he was singing and whistling to drown the sounds of the stones' voices. Suddenly he tripped, and as he fell he thought he heard a voice he recognised. He turned to look . . . and was turned into a stone.

The old farmer was by now very weak and in a last desperate effort to save his life, Maria, his daughter, set off to find the water of life. When she had heard the old man of the mountain's warning she set off up the path her brothers had already taken. Now Maria knew that her father's life depended on her getting the water, so no matter what the stones shouted she kept her eyes fixed on the well up ahead. Eventually she reached it and filled her goatskin full of the precious liquid. As she did so a drop fell on a stone nearby, and immediately it turned into a man. At once Maria felt she must help here too, and at that moment the cries of the stones all stopped. Sprinkling a drop on each large stone Maria began to move slowly down the mountain. Behind her there gathered an ever-increasing crowd of men and women, including her brothers.

Finally she reached the bottom, with just enough of the water of life to take home to her father. With the whole crowd cheering and thanking her, Maria and her brothers set off for home. When they arrived it needed only a few drops of the water to restore her father to good health.

Adapted from an old Spanish legend.

USEFUL TEXTS

Obedience:

    To God, *1 Sam. 15:22*
    To Christ, *2 Cor. 10:5*
    To the covenant, *Exod. 24:7*
    To the Gospel, *2 Thess. 1:8, 1 Pet. 4:17*

See also: A14 The successors of the Apostles
             A32 Civic duty
             B13 Authority
             B31 The commandments of life
             C25 Humility

A30
GOD'S SINFUL PEOPLE

'He looked for justice but found bloodshed,
for righteousness but heard cries of distress.'
Isaiah 5:7

QUOTATIONS

There is no social evil, no form of injustice whether of the feudal or
the capitalist order which has not been sanctified in some way or
other by religious sentiment and thereby rendered more impervious
to change.
Reinhold Niebuhr

The rich man in his castle,
the poor man at his gate,
God made them high or lowly,
and ordered their estate.
Cecil Frances Alexander

I live in a country [South Africa in the days of apartheid] where
most of the white citizens would claim to be Christians, would feel
it to be their supreme duty to preserve their Christian civilisation,
and sometimes, in moments of stress, would call it 'White
civilisation'. Many of them believe that God placed them in
southern Africa to carry out a 'civilising mission'. Most of them
hold firmly to the belief that this civilising mission can only be
carried out by the separation from one another of all racial groups.
Alan Paton

The white man came to Africa with the Bible and taught the black
man to pray. The trouble was that when the black man opened his
eyes he found that the land had been taken over by the white man.
What they should have done was to ban the Bible, since the Bible
taught the inevitability of God's righteousness.
Desmond Tutu

Shame on the cant and hypocrisy of those who can teach virtue, preach righteousness, and pray blessings for those only with skins coloured like our own.
C. Lenox Remond

Lost is a place, too.
Christine Crawford

Do not be afraid to refuse words, acts and attitudes which are not in conformity with Christian ideals. Be courageous in rejecting what destroys your innocence or damages the freshness of your love of Christ.
Pope John Paul II

WORD PICTURES

At the beginning of the fifth century when Rome was officially a Christian society, blood sports were still held in the Colosseum for the amusement of the crowds. They came to an end when a Christian hermit called Telemachus jumped into the arena and threw himself between the fighting gladiators. He urged them, in the name of Christ, to stop their fighting, but one of them struck him with his sword and Telemachus fell dead in the sand. The crowd of eighty thousand spectators which, until that moment, had been howling and jeering at his interference with the games, was shamed into silence. Such blood sports were never held again in Rome.

John Newton (the author of 'How sweet the name of Jesus sounds' and other well-known hymns) was converted to Christianity in 1748, but for six years after that he was the master of a slave ship. As with many other Christians at that time, it was only slowly that it dawned on him that slavery was evil and was incompatible with the teachings of Christ. However, from then on he was a staunch supporter of the anti-slavery movement which brought about the abolition of the slave trade throughout the British Empire in 1807 – the year of Newton's death.

The Church is not a clean, well-lighted place where everything runs smoothly and actions automatically match ideals. It is, in the words of the Gospel, a field of cockle and wheat growing up together and beyond human power to separate. The enthusiast will always be running up against rigidity of mind, narrowness of vision, stoniness of heart; no great development in the Church has ever received a fair wind from the start. The lover of good order, of uniformity and discipline will always be confounded by a spirit that blows where it will, by the sheer complexity of human situations and individuals, by prophets and visionaries and nonconformists who cannot be regulated like alarm-clocks. Whether one aches for a Church of inspired wholehearted enthusiasts or a Church where everyone sings perfectly in tune, one aches in vain. It will always be untidy and riddled with contradictions. It will always have a dark side as well as a bright. Its hidden life will always be more enriching and reassuring than its public demeanour. It is, after all, the People of God. And people are imperfect and contradictory. To know it we have only to look at ourselves.
John F. X. Harriott

There are always those who are anxious to explain away the divine nature of the Church. They examine its history, analyse its political position, assess the sociological factors, keep in mind the psychological need that human beings have for the religious, and pronounce that the phenomenon of the Christian Church is completely explicable without recourse to any suggestion of a divine character. And, of course, in one sense they are correct. But they need to remember that the divine origin of the Church is not to be sought in some way distinct from its human character. It is as human as the man who founded it, but as he was also divine, so is his Church. But there remains the vital qualification. In him divinity and humanity are united in a relationship of perfect harmony. Not so the Church. Christians have still to strive for and grow into that share in his life which God has granted them in Christ, but which their sinning compromises and obscures. Here is that teaching expounded by Vatican II: the Church is 'at the same time holy and always in need of being purified' (*Lumen Gentium*, 8). It is not

some ideal institution. It is a community of sinful people who have been given the means to become saints. And so we bear those magnificent qualities – one, holy, catholic and apostolic – while at times we still hedge on the truth and behave immorally.
Roderick Strange

Religion is a messy, untidy place where we try to join together two realities which don't fit easily and never will – this world and kingdom come, your prayer life and your sex life, retreats and rosaries with the rates bill, your see-through soul with the sauce and sausages you had for breakfast. My father was a tailor who stitched different cloths together. I try to stitch different worlds together, but I'll never be as successful. After all, how would you run an organisation when you ought to give all you have to the poor? How do you chair meetings when everyone has to do what is right and follow the conscience, yet all be bound by a majority vote? After a lifetime as a minister you've impressed a few adolescents or some people who are vulnerable because they're in hospital or in love. What sort of a business is that?

That's why we are tempted to cut corners and take refuge in politics or tribalism, but we don't succeed in making them pious – they just make us nasty.
Rabbi Lionel Blue

People are called to absorb evil, not to retaliate. To turn the other cheek, to walk the extra mile, to forgive not seven times but seventy times seven, not to harbour resentment, to look always for the beam in their own eyes, not to judge others and to love everyone. This is a call to absorb the world's evil. It is a radical departure from the Old Testament idea of revenge. 'An eye for an eye and a tooth for a tooth' is a recipe for perpetuating evil. The Christian, by contrast, absorbs, or should absorb, evil into him or herself by not letting it determine his or her reactions. The power of love is the power to stop evil in its tracks. This is, of course, incredibly demanding. Our natural human reaction is to 'get even', to seek revenge. A rejection of this path is not easy, but it is the only way of overcoming the cycle of past pride, selfishness, arrogance and jealousy.
Peter Vardy

USEFUL TEXTS

God's sinful people:
    Isa. 1:11-17; 58:1-12
    Ezek. 34:1-10
    Amos 5:21-24
    Jas. 2:1-7

See also: A13 The Church is for sinners
            A15 Sin
            A34 Hypocrisy and ambition
            A38 Original sin

A31
HEAVEN

'The Lord of hosts will remove the mourning veil covering all
peoples, and the shroud enwrapping all nations,
he will destroy Death for ever.'
Isaiah 25:7

QUOTATIONS

Heaven is the soul finding its own perfect personality in God.
Philip Brooks

Then I saw that there was a way to hell, even from the gates of
heaven.
John Bunyan

Hell is in heaven and heaven is in hell. But angels see only the
light, and devils only the darkness.
Jacob Boehme

Blessed are they that are homesick for they shall come at last to
their father's house.
Jean Paul Richter

The road to heaven is made up of resolutions, made, broken, and
renewed.
Anon

PROVERBS

He who looks only at heaven may easily break his nose on earth.
Czech proverb

Help your brother's boat across and your own will reach the shore.
Hindu proverb

Guard well thy thoughts, for thoughts are heard in heaven.
French proverb

Humour

Heaven for climate, hell for company.
J. M. Barrie

'Mummy,' asked a little girl, 'do men ever go to heaven?' 'Why, yes, of course, my dear,' answered her mother. 'Why do you ask?'

'Because I've never seen angels with whiskers.'

'Well,' replied the mother, 'some men do go to heaven, but they only get there by a close shave!'

Anon

The Irish have a story of an Irishman who appeared before St Peter expecting admission, and when his ledger showed pages and pages of heavy debit entries, said that the books had been badly kept, for he knew he had once given twopence to a beggar. St Peter, after much flipping over of the pages, found it so indeed; but was twopence sufficient to outweigh all these? Then the Irishman said he had a friend called Patrick. If they would have the common politeness to call him he would make it all right. St Patrick was summoned, looked at the ledger, and he and St Peter exchanged doubtful glances.

'What are we to do with this countryman of yours?' asked St Peter. 'You see how it is.'

'Yes,' said St Patrick, 'I see how it is. Give him back his twopence!'

Anon

Religious Education teacher: 'Now, children, I've just described all the pleasures of heaven. Hands up all those who want to go there?'

All the children put their hands up, except for Debbie.

Religious Education teacher: 'Debbie, why don't you want to go to heaven?'

Debbie (tearfully): 'I'd like to go, miss, but me mum said I had to come straight home after school.'

Anon

Word pictures

If we think of all the best and most glorious moments in our lives, the perfection of what we experience always seems just beyond our reach. As with striking a succession of matches to light a dark room, those moments invariably seem to flicker and fade. Heaven will be like turning on the full light. The perfection will be there for us to enjoy, undefiled, unflickering and unfading. 'And the city had no need of sun or moon to shine upon it, for the glory of God is its light . . .' (Revelation 21:23) Here is the summit of all our highest hopes and dreams.

In one sense, the Christian is not preparing for death. Essentially he is preparing for life, abundant life in all its fullness.
David Watson

A little girl was walking with her father along a country road. The night was clear, and the child was enthralled by the splendour of the sky, all lit up with twinkling stars from one end to the other. After moments of reflection she suddenly looked up to her father and said: 'Daddy, I was just thinking, if the wrong side of heaven is so beautiful, how wonderful the right side must be!'
Anon

A few years ago an Anglican clergyman, who was editing an extremely evangelical religious paper, published Vachel Lindsay's remarkable and astounding poem, *General William Booth Enters Heaven*. It is a lurid and quite sensational description of the tumultuous welcome which General Booth received in heaven from the criminals, fornicators, drunkards, and prostitutes who had been saved through the Salvation Army. There was a frightful row over the publication, and the perplexed and surprised clergyman was nearly thrown out of his editorial chair. The evangelical readers of this paper evidently did not like to think that heaven was inhabited by saved sots and converted harlots. They thought it was a respectable colony of blameless and well-to-do Plymouth Brethren. One of these days they will get the surprise of their lives.
British Weekly

That reminds me of the legend of the wealthy lady who became inordinately proud of her fine mansion and landscaped garden. She was an avowed materialist. Her faithful old gardener looked

at everything so differently. Despite his poverty, he saw the world as a wonderful place, full of beautiful, simple things – the flowers he tended, the birds who serenaded him at work, the delicacy of scudding clouds. From his pittance he was always ready to help where he could. The lady died, and as she looked around heaven for her rightful abode she was directed to a mean, tumble-down shack. 'I think you've made a mistake,' she said, 'I've always been used to something really worthy. I had a charming house – sixteen rooms – luxurious, the best that money could buy. But this!' Then, spotting a delightful dwelling close by, nearing completion, she brightened. 'Ah, now, what about that one? That's the sort of place I'd like.' 'Sorry, Ma'am, you can't have that; we're getting that ready for your gardener when he comes.' 'My gardener? But he's only used to a tiny cottage; why couldn't you prepare one like that for me?' And the celestial housing officer replied, 'Impossible, ma'am, it's right out of our hands; we can only build with the materials sent up by the future occupant. He's sent us magnificent material, always. Yours was a bit sub-standard you must admit.'
Winifred Eastment

When Thomas More was committed to the Tower, one of Aesop's Fables came to his mind. In it, Jupiter had invited 'all the poor worms of the earth for a solemn feast'. Every worm came except the snail. When asked why she was absent, the snail replied that she loved no place as much as her own house. Waxing angry, Jupiter decreed that the snail should carry her house on her back always, to which Thomas More added, 'and so she has ever done since, so they say.'

This snail led Thomas More to those Christians who 'by the foolish affection which they have set, like the snail, upon their own houses here on earth, cannot, for the lothness of leaving that house, find it in their hearts to go with good will to the great feast that God prepares in heaven and, of his goodness, so graciously calls them to.'
Bernard Bassett

Let me tell you the story of a Korean general. He died and was judged and assigned to paradise, but when he came up before St Peter he thought of something he would like to do. He wanted to peep into hell for a moment, just to have an idea of it. 'Right you are,' said St Peter.

So the general peeped in at the door of hell and saw an enormous hall. In it were a number of long tables with bowls of rice on them – well flavoured, smelling delicious, inviting. The guests were sitting there hungrily, opposite one another, each with a bowl of rice. What was happening? The guests all had chopsticks, but these were so long that, however hard they tried, not a grain of rice could they get into their mouths. And this was their torment, this was hell. 'I've seen it, that's quite enough for me,' said the general and went back to the gates of heaven, where he went in.

Inside, he saw the same hall, the same tables, the same rice and the same long chopsticks. But the guests were cheerful, all of them smiling and laughing. Each one, having put the food onto his chopsticks, held it out to the mouth of his companion opposite and so they managed to eat perfectly well. Thinking of others instead of oneself had solved the problem and transformed hell into heaven.

Pope John Paul I

USEFUL TEXTS

Heaven, Characteristics of:
    No death, *Luke 20:36*
    No pain, *Rev. 21:4*
    No corruption, *1 Cor. 15:42, 50*
    Joy, *Luke 15:7*
    Peace, *Luke 16:25*
    Glory, *Rom. 8:17-18*

See also: A20 The Kingdom of God
            B3   Joy in Christ
            B51 One with Christ
            C48 One in us

A32
CIVIC DUTY

'Give back to Caesar what belongs to Caesar –
and to God what belongs to God.'
Matthew 22:21

QUOTATIONS

Every duty we omit obscures some truth we should have known.
John Ruskin

Democracy is the worst form of government under the sun –
except for all the rest.
Winston Churchill

Civilisation is always in danger when those who have never
learned to obey are given the right to command.
Fulton J. Sheen

Maybe civilisation is dying; but it still exists and meanwhile we have
our choice: we can either rain more blows on it, or try to redeem it.
Saul Bellow

The right, practical divinity is this: Believe in Christ, and do your
duty in that state of life to which God has called you.
Martin Luther

We are justified, from the point of view of exegesis, in regarding
the democratic conception of the State as an expansion of the
thought of the New Testament.
Karl Barth

Those who gain no experience are those who shirk the King's
highway for fear of encountering the duty seated by the roadside.
George Macdonald

Whatever makes men good Christians makes them good citizens.
Webster

Do your duty, and do not trouble yourself whether it is in the cold
or by a good fire.
Marcus Aurelius

Bishops and Christians generally should beware of simply following
politicians. A politician has an excuse for compromising, but it
seems to me a Christian Bishop has not.
Archbishop Roberts

WORD PICTURES

Asked what he thought about Western civilization, Mahatma
Gandhi answered, 'I think it would be a good idea.'

When my father visited me he never asked, 'How's business?' or
even 'How are the children?' He'd pull cuttings out of his pockets
and say angrily, 'Did you see that editorial in this morning's
paper? Let's answer it!' My father was involved in mankind, and
that is why he lived into his eighties. A man is like a tree; he dies
on top first.
Harry Golden

There is a legend of a monk, to whom in his cell the Lord
vouchsafed to appear in a vision. The vision of Christ brought
great peace and joy to his heart. Scarcely had he been thus
favoured when the bell was heard, which summoned him to the
duty of distributing loaves of bread to the poor. Oh, what a
sacrifice to leave the glorious vision for the dull routine of duty!
But when he returned to his cell, what were his surprise and joy
to find the vision of the Lord as before, and to be met with the
greeting. 'Hadst thou tarried, I would have departed.'

We have all laughed at the reputed story of Pat Murphy at the
battle of Trafalgar, whose version of the battle was as follows:
'Lord Nelson came on deck and said 'Is Pat Murphy on board?'

And I said, 'Here I am, me Lord.' Then said his lordship, 'Let the battle proceed.'

And yet, while this was written for a joke, there is more to it than we are apt to think. For if it had not been for the Pat Murphys, or John Joneses or Tom Smiths and others who were on hand doing their duty, there would have been no victories for Nelsons, Wellingtons, Napoleons or Grants who now live in history as great commanders

A. W. Graham

The Great Wall of China was a gigantic structure, costing immense expenditure and labour, and when finished it seemed a superb way to gain security, but within a few years of its building it was breached three times by the enemy. Only note, it was breached, not by breaking down the wall but by bribing the gate-keepers. It was the human element that failed; what collapsed was character, proving insufficient to make the great structure men had built really work. A like fate awaits all those who, absorbed in political tasks, forget the spiritual foundations.

Anon

The final words of Archbishop Oscar Romero
'He who wants to avoid danger, will lose his life, but, whoever devotes himself through love of Christ to the service of others will live on like the grain of wheat which dies, but only appears to die. If it did not die it would remain alone.

'We are surprised by those people who think that Christians should not get involved in the affairs of this world. In fact, the opposite is the case. The face of this world, tainted by sin, will pass away but God teaches us that a new home and a new world is being prepared in which justice will reign, and its happiness will surpass the human heart's desire for peace.

'However, the hope of a new world must not deaden but rather increase our concern to improve this world where the new human family is taking shape and which can, in some way, be a dim prefiguring of the new age.

'Although we must distinguish carefully between temporal

progress and growth of the kingdom of Christ, the first nevertheless has a lot to do with the kingdom of God in so far as it can contribute to improving society . . . Through this Holy Mass, this Eucharist, which is in fact an act of faith, the voice of anger and hate is transformed through Christian faith into the body of the Lord which is offered up for the redemption of the world, as the wine in the chalice is transformed into the blood which was the price of our salvation.

'May this body which was offered up and this blood which was shed for mankind, give us strength to offer ourselves in suffering and in sorrow, just as Christ did, not for himself but in order to give our people true concepts of justice and peace.'

Then the shots rang out, and Archbishop Romero fell dead.

USEFUL TEXTS

Citizenship:
　Obligations, *Rom 13:1-7; 1 Pet. 13-17*
　Punishment for neglect, *Ezra 7:26*
　Jesus discussed, *Matt. 17:24-27; 22:17-21*

See also:　A29　True obedience
　　　　　B14　Freedom to serve
　　　　　B33　Faith and good works
　　　　　B34　Human rights

A33

LOVE YOUR NEIGHBOUR

'The second commandment resembles it:
You must love your neighbour as yourself.'
Matthew 22:39

QUOTATIONS

A loving heart is the truest wisdom.
Charles Dickens

It is as important to see others as they see themselves as to see
ourselves as others see us.
Antoine Bibesco

Oh, Great Spirit, help me never to judge another until I have
walked two weeks in his moccasins.
Sioux Indian prayer

Every neighbour, even though he be hateful in himself, becomes
lovable to the full-grown 'I' if he, too, is a child of God.
Fulton J. Sheen

Believe nothing against another but on good authority; nor report
what may hurt another, unless it be a greater hurt to conceal it.
William Penn

Imagine thyself always to be the servant of all, and look upon all
as if they were Christ our Lord in person; and so shalt thou do him
honour and reverence.
St Teresa of Avila

To yield reverence to another, to hold ourselves and our lives at
his disposal is the noblest state in which a man can live in this
world.
John Ruskin

If we gain our brother, we gain God; if we upset our brother, we sin against Christ.
St Anthony of Padua

Welfare is for a purpose. Christian love is for a person.
Mother Teresa of Calcutta

PROVERBS

A hedge between, keeps friendship green.
English proverb

The camel never sees its own hump, but its neighbour's hump is ever before its eyes.
Arab proverb

HUMOUR

My nephew Shawn, aged 5 (now 27, and father of Rhianne aged four months) had not long started school. My sister Vicki had just picked him up and was waiting at the crowded bus stop.

'Mum,' he suddenly announced, 'I know what they call men who love each other.'

You can imagine the thoughts that flashed through her mind . . .

'Oh, yes . . .' she said bravely, looking nervously around the queue, 'what's that?'

'Christians,' Shawn replied knowledgeably.
Karen Margerison

A small boy from a poor family wrote to God for help. His letter, addressed simply 'To God', asked if he could send £50 to buy food and clothing badly needed for his family. He said his father was out of work and his mother was ill and they had no money.

A Post Office official intercepted the letter and read it. He decided to give it to the local Rotary Club. The Club investigated and found the family was indeed destitute. However, as they only had £40 in their benevolent fund they gave that.

Some weeks later the Post Office official noticed another letter

addressed 'To God'. He opened it and read: Dear God, thanks for the money you sent, but next time could you deal direct? Those Rotary blokes took a commission out of it.'
Anon

WORD PICTURES

Sadhu Sundar Singh and a friend were once travelling through the mountains of North India. Winter storms were howling round them, and soon they were caught in a blizzard, through which they battled with great difficulty. Presently, they saw a man lying by the roadside, apparently dead. The Sadhu wished to stay to give help, but his friend, protesting that the effort would be unavailing, passed on his way.

Displaying the spirit of the good Samaritan, the Sadhu chafed the hands and feet of the prostrate man, and finally lifted him on his back and trudged painfully through the snow. The warmth of the man's body, added to that of his own had a reviving and sustaining effect on both.

After a mile's further progress, they found another body lying by the wayside. It was the Sadhu's companion, frozen to death. He had not sufficient warmth alone to fight the storm.
Wilton Rix

A Persian poet has put it all in a single stanza:
   No one could tell me what my soul might be;
   I searched for God, and God eluded me;
   I sought my brother out, and found all three,
   my soul, my God, and all humanity.
Frank D. Adams

Tolstoy's story of *The Two Pilgrims* tells of two Russians who set out on pilgrimage to Jerusalem intent on being present at the solemn Easter festivities. One had his mind so set on the journey's end and object that he would stop for nothing and take thought for nothing but the journey. The other, passing through, found people to be helped at every turn and actually spent so much time and money along the way that he never reached the Holy City. But

LOVE YOUR NEIGHBOUR A33

something came to him from God which the other missed; and something came through him from God into the lives of men which the other failed to find in the great Easter celebration.
William P. Merrill

Aristides, a non-Christian, defended the Christians before the Emperor Hadrian, in the second century AD in the following words:
Christians love one another. They never fail to help widows; they save orphans from those who would hurt them. If a man has something, he gives freely to the man who has nothing. If they see a stranger, Christians take him home and are happy, as though he were a real brother. They don't consider themselves brothers in the usual sense, but brothers instead through the Spirit, in God. And if they hear that one of them is in jail or persecuted for professing the name of their redeemer, they all give him what he needs. . . . This is really a new kind of person. There is something divine in them.
Anon

One day I was going to the Serbian Monastery of Chilandar. Father Nikolai, cellarer (guest-master) of our Thebaidian Hermitage, joined me. It was night and we walked through the green forest. The way was pleasant, our conversation, too. We were discussing love for one's neighbour, and Father Nikolai told me of a remarkable instance.

In the south of Russia, near Rostov, an *artel* consisting of a score of men was at work. One of the gang, whose name was Andrei, was a bad character, so that it was not easy to live with him. But another, the youngest of them all, was a very good person who loved God and kept the Lord's commandments. His name was Nikolai. Now, after Andrei had brought a great deal of evil and unpleasantness on his comrades they thought to murder him, but young Nikolai would not agree at all and tried to persuade them not to attack Andrei. The *artel* would not listen to him, and killed Andrei. News of the murder spread round, finally reaching the ears of the police. Then Nikolai, seeing his comrades' misfortune, said to them, 'All of you have wives and children, whereas I am a single man on my own. So say that I did the murder, and I will say

135

the same. Penal servitude will not be hard for me but if you are sentenced, think how many people will suffer.' At first the others made no reply. They were ashamed before Nikolai who had tried to prevail on them not to kill, but in the end Nikolai persuaded them and they all agreed to say that Nikolai was the murderer.

The authorities – the public prosecutor, the investigators, the gendarmes – arrived on the spot, and the inquiry began into who had done the murder. 'I did,' declared Nikolai. The others were interrogated and they, too, said it was Nikolai. Nikolai had a gentle face and a humble disposition and he spoke softly and quietly. The investigators questioned him at length – they could not believe that such a gentle, quiet man could be a murderer; but the matter went to court in the usual way, and again everyone wondered that such a humble, kind man should have committed murder, and none of the judges was willing to believe it, although Nikolai insisted he was guilty. For a long time the court could not bring itself to pronounce sentence. Not a hand was lifted to sign the verdict. And again they questioned him, and the others, too, in order to get to the bottom of the mystery, adjuring him to tell the truth. At last he said that if they would not seek the real culprit, he would tell them the real story. The trial had brought out the fact that Andrei had been a bad man, and the public prosecutor and the judges agreed to stop the case if they knew the truth. And then not Nikolai but the others related what had really happened, and how Nikolai had arranged to take the guilt on himself so as to save them from punishment. The judges stopped the case, saying that Nikolai had not been proved guilty, and one of them even declared, 'Andrei was a wicked man and got what he deserved, whereas these are good people, let them live in peace.'

This story shows what a strong force is love for one's neighbour. The grace of God was in the heart of that young Nikolai, and was reflected in his face, and reacted on all the others.
St Silouan

There is an ancient legend about three men, who each carried two sacks – one behind and one in front. The first man, when asked what was in his, said; 'All my friends' kind deeds in the sack behind, where they are hidden from sight and soon forgotten; the sack in front carries all the unkind things my acquaintances do. These I turn out and study as I walk.' Consequently, he made little progress.

One day he met another man carrying two sacks, 'What have you there,' he asked. 'Why, my good deeds!' said Number Two. 'I keep all these before me, and continually take them out and air them.' 'What's in the other sack?' asked the first traveller. 'It seems heavy.' 'Merely my little mistakes. I always keep them on my back.'

Presently they met another man, who strangely enough, also carried two sacks. 'What is in your sacks?' they queried. 'Oh,' said the stranger, 'I have a goodly assortment and like showing them. This front sack is full of my friends' kind deeds.' 'It looks full; it must be heavy,' said the first man. 'There you are mistaken,' repeated the stranger; 'it is big, but not heavy. The weight is only such as sails are to a ship. Far from being a burden, it helps me onward.' 'Well, your sack behind you can be of very little use,' said Number Two; 'it seems empty, and has a great hole at the bottom.' 'That is on purpose,' said the stranger; 'I put all the evil I hear of others there, it falls through and is lost, so I have no weight to impede me.'

Anon

The first soldier saint of World War II may soon be canonised. In Italy squares, schools and streets are named after him; yet he is little known outside his native land.

Born in Naples, Salvo D'Aquisto at 18 enrolled in the Carabinieri, the oldest regiment in the Italian Army. He enjoyed the military life and on the outbreak of war he served for 18 months in North Africa, on active service. Tall, athletic and handsome, 'a true son of Southern Italy', Salvo had a girlfriend, Maria, and was devout in the practice of his Catholic Faith.

Italy changed sides in the War and Salvo, promoted to an NCO, was posted to a little village north of Rome. On Thursday 23rd September he went to confession, Mass and Holy Communion. His commanding officer was absent so Salvo was the senior officer in the village when a detachment of the German

SS arrived. Salvo went out to greet them but was struck and arrested.

The previous day the SS had occupied a medieval tower at nearby Palidoro; there had been an explosion that was later discovered to have been an accident. The SS, however, suspected sabotage. The SS commander rounded up 22 men of the village and threatened to kill them as a reprisal unless Salvo told him who was responsible for the explosion, which had killed one German and wounded two others.

The prisoners were forced to dig a ditch, which was to be their grave. Salvo kept calm and tried to reason with the SS commander. At 5 pm he had persuaded him to release the 22 men, only one, a 17 year old, who Salvo had been talking to while they dug the ditch, stayed to see what happened. Salvo had convinced the SS officer that if anyone was responsible, it must be his responsibility as officer in charge. Salvo was shot and buried in the ditch. He had said earlier in the day to the young man, 'you live once, you die once'.

A man of generosity, bravery and the highest Christian charity. 'No greater love can a man have than to lay down his life', the words of Jesus. His simple tomb is in the beautiful Santa Chiara church, Naples.

P.F.

USEFUL TEXTS

Love your neighbour:
    Love towards, *Rom. 13:9-10; Matt. 22:39*
    Speak the truth to, *Eph. 4:25*
    Urged to be good, *Luke 10:29-37*

See also: A9   Relationships
            B52 God is Love
            C10 Love your enemies
            C19 Friendship

Hypocrisy and Ambition

'Do not be guided by what the Pharisees do; since they do
not practise what they preach.'
Matthew 23:3

Quotations

Nothing is humbler than ambition when it is about to climb.
Benjamin Franklin

God's gift puts man's best dreams to shame.
Elizabeth Barrett Browning

At home he is a savage; abroad a saint.
Seneca

Ambition is pitiless; any merit that it cannot use it finds despicable.
Joseph Joubert

I hope you have not been leading a double life, pretending to be
wicked, and being really good all the time. That would be hypocrisy.
Oscar Wilde

An ill man is always ill, but he is worst of all when he pretends to
be a saint.
Francis Bacon

No bird soars too high if he soars with his own wings.
William Blake

I've never tolerated phoneyness in anyone and there's a lot of it at
Wimbledon.
John McEnroe

There are people who laugh to show their fine teeth; and there are
those who cry to show their good hearts.
Joseph Roux

If the Lord has willed that the value of our life should be altogether hidden in him, it would be ridiculous to seek anything else. The ambitious are the most ridiculous and the most wretched creatures on earth.
Pope John XXIII

There's not much practical Christianity in the man who lives on better terms with angels and seraphs than with his children, and neighbours.
Henry Ward Beecher

PROVERB

Every ambitious man is a captive and every covetous one is a pauper.
Arab proverb

WORD PICTURES

One day St Philip Neri was talking with a young student of the University, whose worldly prospects were very flattering, and whose ambition was great. St Philip asked him concerning his studies, and what was to be his career. 'I am now studying philosophy,' he replied, 'but I shall finish my philosophical course next year.' 'And then?' asked St Philip. 'Why, then I shall study the full course of Canon and Civil Law, and take my cap as a doctor.' 'And then?' said St Philip again. 'Then I shall practise as an Advocate, and make for myself a reputation.' 'And then?' asked the Saint once more. 'Then I shall marry, and succeed to the estates of my family, and become an Auditor of the Rota, and perhaps rise still higher.' 'And then?' still asked St Philip. 'Why, then I suppose I shall be satisfied with the position I have won, and shall be respected by my fellow-citizens; and, like everybody else, shall grow old, and die.' 'And then?' St Philip still enquired. The young man hesitated; his lips quivered and he flung himself at St Philip's feet. His ambitious dream had been dispelled by the two simple words of the Saint. He relinquished his legal studies, and hopes of promotion, and gave himself to the study of that Divine science by which he had been shown the vanity of human ambition and its projects.
P.F.

There is a legend of an Indian chief who was wont to try the strength of his youths by making them run in a single effort as far up the side of a mountain as each could reach by his own strength. On an appointed day, four left at daybreak. The first returned with a branch of spruce, indicating the height to which he had attained. The second bore a twig of pine. The third brought an Alpine shrub. But it was by the light of the moon that the fourth made his way back. Then he came, worn and exhausted, and his feet were torn by the rocks.

'What did you bring and how high did you ascend?' asked the chief.

'Sire,' he replied, 'where I went there was neither spruce nor pine to shelter me from the sun, nor flower to cheer my path, but only rocks and snow and barren land. My feet are torn, and I am exhausted, and I have come late, but –' and as a wonderful light came into his eyes, the young brave added: '– I saw the sea.'
Edward W. Bok

USEFUL TEXTS

Hypocrisy, Description of:
    Blindness, *Matt. 23:17-26*
    Unclean hearts, *Luke 11:39*
    Seeks self-acclaim, *Matt. 6:2-5*
    Ascribed to Pharisees, *Matt. 23:13-15; Luke 12:1*

See also: A2   Integrity
            A15 Sin
            A30 God's sinful people
            B26 The whole person
            B44 The dignity of the individual

A35
PREPARING FOR DEATH

'Stay awake, because you do not know either the
day or the hour.'
Matthew 25:13

QUOTATIONS

The fear of death is more to be dreaded than death.
Publilius Syrus

To die will be an awfully big adventure.
J. M. Barrie

This is the end – for me the beginning of life.
Dietrich Bonhoeffer

Each person is born to one possession which outvalues all the
others – his last breath.
Mark Twain

Death is the veil which those who live call Life; they sleep – and it
is lifted.
Percy B. Shelley

Heaven and earth are one, even as the way and the goal are one.
Guiseppe Mazzini

Loss is nothing else than change. Things are changed this way, it
is true, but they do not perish.
Marcus Aurelius

HUMOUR

An Irish priest, revisiting his old parish in the spring, observed a
very old man, who had been a member of his parish, approaching.

'Why, Pat,' he called delightedly, 'so you are still with us, I am glad to see. However do you manage it?'

'Well, Your Reverence,' replied the old man, ''tis this way. I find that if I don't doy in winter I don't doy any other time of the year.'
K. Edwards

A Scotsman, an Englishman, and an Irishman were discussing the best way to go. 'I'd like to crash in a car doin' 120 miles an hour,' said the Scot. 'Actually, I'd like to die in a 600-mile-an-hour plane crash,' put in the Englishman. After a moment's thought, the Irishman said, 'I'd like to be shot by a jealous husband!'
Anon

WORD PICTURES

They that love beyond the world cannot be separated by it. Death cannot kill what never dies. Nor can spirits ever be divided that love and live in the same divine principle; the root and record of their friendship.

Death is but crossing the world, as friends do the seas: they live in one another still. For they must needs be present, that love and live in that which is omnipresent. In this divine glass they see face to face; and their converse is free as well as pure.

This is the comfort of friends, that though they may be said to die, yet their friendship and society are, in the best sense, ever present, because immortal.
William Penn

When I was told that I had six months, or perhaps nine, to live, the first reaction was naturally of shock – though I also felt liberated, because, as in limited-over cricket, at least one knew the target one had to get. My second reaction was 'Gosh, six months is a long time. One can do a lot in that. How am I going to use it?'

The initial response is to give up doing things – and it certainly sifts out the inessentials. My reaction was to go through the diary cancelling engagements. But I soon realised that this was purely negative. In fact, 'preparing for death' is not the other-worldly, pious exercise stamped upon our minds by Victorian sentimentality, turning away from the things of earth for the things of 'heaven'. Rather, for the Christian, it is preparing for 'eternal life', which means real living, more abundant life, which is begun, continued but not ended now.

And this means it is about quality of life not quantity. How long it goes on here is purely secondary. So preparing for eternity means learning really to live, becoming more concerned with contributing to and enjoying what matters most – giving the most to life and getting the most from it, while it is on offer.
John Robinson

A little girl lay dying, and she was afraid. Her friend, the priest, came to see her, and after a little talk she told him she was frightened. 'Listen, my child,' he said. 'Supposing I said I wanted to take you in my arms, and carry you upstairs to a beautiful room at the top of the house, where you could see much farther from the windows, and be more comfortable altogether, would you mind?' 'Why, no,' answered the child, 'you could do anything you liked with me, because I know you love me, and I love you.'

'Well, what people call dying is rather like that; the Lord Jesus, your best friend, who loves you more than I ever could, when your time comes will take you in his arms, and carry you into one of his most beautiful many mansions; so you see you need not be afraid, need you?' And the child lay back on her pillows, content.
Anon

A camp doctor witnesses Bonhoeffer's execution at Flossenburg Concentration Camp.
Through the half-open door in one room of the huts I saw Pastor Bonhoeffer, before taking off his prison garb, kneeling on the floor praying fervently to his God. I was most deeply moved by the way this lovable man prayed, so devout and so certain that God heard his prayer. At the place of execution, he again said a short prayer and then climbed the steps of the gallows, brave and

composed. His death ensued after a few seconds. In the almost fifty years that I worked as a doctor, I have hardly ever seen a man die so entirely submissive to the will of God.
Eberhard Bethage

The cruel and inescapable fact of death, however, causes many people to consider carefully the meaning of their lives. When I was in New Zealand in 1973 I read this fascinating comment in a newspaper article by the Director of radiotherapy and radiology in that country.

> Cancer makes people start thinking about the quality of their lives. Everything they do has a keener edge on it and they get more out of life. In fact, some people never become completely human beings and really start living until they get cancer. We all know we are going to die some time, but cancer makes people face up to it. . . . They are going to go on living with a lot of extra enjoyment, just because they have faced the fear of death. Cancer patients aren't dying. They're living. I have never seen a suicide because of cancer.

Palmerston North Evening Standard

That has certainly been my own experience, and I am much more aware of the value of each day, and the importance of making good use of it. The quality of my life has far from diminished. Philosophers have always maintained that the key to life is coming to terms with death. No one can live well until they can die well. In the famous words of Samuel Johnson, 'When a man knows he is to be hanged in a fortnight, it concentrates his mind wonderfully!' Certainly all the great issues of life and death come into sharp focus when the future is known to be precarious.
David Watson

A story is told about Martin Luther. One morning, while discussing points of theology with a group of friends, he was asked: 'Father Luther, what would you do if you knew for sure that the Lord was coming tonight?' In his usual quick and impetuous manner, Luther

replied: 'I'd go out into my garden and plant an apple tree' –
meaning he'd go about his ordinary business.
Anon

USEFUL TEXTS

Mortality:

    Death, common experience, *Heb. 9:27*
    End of earthly life, *Eccles. 9:10*
    Consequence of sin, *Rom. 5:12*

See also: A42 Life after death
              B21 Trust in God
              B22 Death
              B23 Pastoral care of the sick
              B47 Dying to self

A36
Using Talents

'To one he gave five talents, to another two, to a third one;
each in proportion to his ability.'
Matthew 25:15

QUOTATIONS

No talent can survive the blight of neglect.
Edgar A. Whitney

It's a great talent to be able to conceal one's talent.
La Rochefoucauld

Envy comes from people's ignorance of, or lack of belief in, their
own gifts.
Jean Vanier

Usefulness is the rent we pay for living on the earth.
Robert Baden-Powell

Hide not your talents: they for use were made.
What's a sun-dial in the shade!
Benjamin Franklin

Hell is full of the talented, but heaven, of the energetic.
Fulton J. Sheen

We judge ourselves by what we feel capable of doing; others judge
us by what we have done.
H. W. Longfellow

Talents are best nurtured in solitude; character is best formed in
the stormy billows of the world.
Goethe

It is really a matter of how you play with the cards that you have been dealt.
Edward de Bono

Talent is God-given; be thankful. Conceit is self-given; be careful.
Thomas La Mance

WORD PICTURES

Every ship that goes to America got its chart from Columbus. Every novel is a debtor to Homer. Every carpenter who shaves with a foreplane borrows the genius of a forgotten inventor. Life is girt all round with . . . the contributions of men who have perished to add their point of light to our sky.
Ralph W. Emerson

Galileo was a man of many talents and he put them to good use. One day, in the cathedral at Pisa, he watched a lamp swinging to and fro. He noticed that, though the length of the swing became shorter, the length of time taken for each swing was exactly the same. From this discovery, the pendulum was shown to be an accurate method of measuring the time.

Galileo was eighteen at the time and keen to find true scientific facts. He discovered that, whilst some people welcomed his findings, others refused to believe him. As a young man, he angered the professors at the university by telling them that they were wrong. He borrowed an idea that had been invented by a Dutchman and from it made a strong telescope. He was amazed to find stars that had never been seen before; he found that the moon did not have a flat surface; and he discovered moons moving round the planet Jupiter. He was now sure that the earth moved round the sun and the moon round the earth.

Galileo was thrilled with his discoveries, but other people were not. Some church leaders were as blind as the professors had been. They said that Galileo had no right to teach things which they said were wrong. They left Galileo with no choice. To save his life, Galileo was forced to tell lies about his discoveries. He

died on 8 January 1642 having become blind in his old age and
unable to see the wonders of the heavens.
Rowland Purton

To raise money for the Church Tower, the Vicar of Grundisburgh,
England, gave 100 of his villagers a £1 coin each and they returned
six months later with 13 times that amount – considerably more
than the most enterprising servants in the parables, who only
doubled their money. 'It was a great success,' the vicar said last
week after a special harvest festival service in the thirteenth-
century church of St Mary's in Grundisburgh, Suffolk.

Villagers found many novel ways to reap where their vicar had
sown. 'Taking £1 apiece, they invested their talents in everything
from rabbit-breeding and shoe shining to lemonade-making. One
of the most enterprising was Mrs Helen Taylor, the local
hairdresser. She bought £1 worth of material to make pots at the
local college and, by reinvesting the profits to buy more material
eventually raised £93.50.

Mrs Ann Johnson spent her £1 on ingredients for two cakes. And
with the £6 profit on those, held a cream tea party in her garden –
making £43. Unlike the master in St Matthew, Chapter 25, the vicar
had no need to reproach any of his flock for burying their talent.
'One of our ladies put her £1 in a fruit machine,' he said. 'I suppose
I ought not to approve, but she did double the money!'
P.F.

USEFUL TEXTS

Gifts:
> Given to each, *1 Cor. 12:4-11*
> Comes from Father, *James 1:17*
> Good stewards of, *I Pet. 4:10*
> Of Holy Spirit, *Luke 11:13*

See also: A1   The value of time
           A28 Work
           A39 The Glory of God

A37
CHRIST THE KING

'For he must be king until he has put all his enemies under his feet and the last of the enemies to be destroyed is death.'
1 Corinthians 15:25

QUOTATIONS

The core of all that Jesus teaches about the kingdom is the immediate apprehension and acceptance of God as King in his own life.
T. W. Manson

How marvellous is this King who renounces all the signs of power, the instruments of dominion, force and arrogance, and wishes to reign only with the power of truth and love, with the power of interior conviction and sheer abandonment.
Pope John Paul II

WORD PICTURES

General Smuts stood deeply impressed before a beautiful allegorical picture at the Royal Academy. It was a painting by Herbert Schmalz, and showed the interior of a large church in France. Weary soldiers lie on straw on the floor. One of them has started up and leans on his unwounded arm, gazing intently at a vision. He sees the transfigured Christ, wearing a crown of thorns, and standing out from a background of radiant light, the reflection of which throws a touch of brightness on his wounded head. The title of the picture is 'The Silent Witness'. The General stood silent, drinking in the beauty and strength of the lesson. Then he turned to a complete stranger by his side and said, 'That is a most beautiful picture. It is the vision many a man has seen.'
D. Williamson

In Lloyd Douglas' book, *The Robe*, the slave, Demetrius, pushed his way through the crowd on Palm Sunday, trying to see who was the centre of attraction. He got close enough to look upon the face of Jesus. Later another slave asked, 'See him – close up?'

Demetrius nodded. 'Crazy?' Demetrius shook his head emphatically. 'King!' 'No,' muttered Demetrius, 'not a king.' 'What is he, then?' demanded the other slave. 'I don't know,' mumbled Demetrius, 'but he is something more than a king.'

A furious actor once gave this crisp bit of advice to a group of young actors: 'The king sits in every audience, play to the king'. And the King of kings stands in the midst of all the common things in life: play to the King.
Albert G. Butzer

Caesar entered Rome with his chariot drawn by six tawny lions; Pompey used elephants to pull his, while other Roman emperors came riding golden chariots led by six or eight magnificent stallions. Kaiser Wilhelm II had hoped to have the streets of Jerusalem widened so that he might enter in a gilded carriage; the best that could be done was to heighten the Jaffa Gate so that he could come in on horseback to the dedication of the Lutheran Church of the Redeemer.

Hitler wanted to parade triumphantly into Paris after its fall, but his adjutants discouraged him from doing so. However, his General von Bock, chief of Army Group B, reached the city before his troops, and took the salute of the first combat troops. Arches and columns, plaques and memorials have long heralded the historical entry of great conquerors and resplendent kings. With Jesus, it was a donkey, a little fanfare, but hardly a triumph. What was to be his triumph was what others would consider his defeat.
Anon

The donkey
When fishes flew and forests walked
    and figs grew upon thorn,
some moment when the moon was blood,
    then surely I was born;
with monstrous head and sickening cry
    and ears like errant wings,
the devil's walking parody,
    on all four-footed things.

The tattered outlaw of the earth,
  of ancient crooked will;
starve, scourge, deride me: I am dumb,
  I keep my secret still.
Fools! For I also had my hour;
  one far fierce hour and sweet:
there was a shout about my ears,
  and palms before my feet.
Gilbert K. Chesterton

Some children were at play in their playground one day, when a herald rode through the town, blowing a trumpet, and crying aloud, 'The King! The King passes by this road today. Make ready for the King!' The children stopped their play, and looked at one another. 'Did you hear that?' they said. 'The King is coming. He may look over the wall and see our playground; who knows? We must put it in order.'

The playground was sadly dirty, and in the corners were scraps of paper and broken toys, for these were careless children. But now, one brought a hoe, and another a rake, and a third ran to fetch the wheelbarrow from behind the garden gate. They laboured hard, till at length all was clean and tidy. 'Now it is clean!' they said; 'but we must make it pretty, too, for kings are used to fine things; maybe he would not notice mere cleanness, for he may have it all the time.'

Then one brought sweet rushes and strewed them on the ground; and others made garlands of oak leaves and fine tassels and hung them on the walls; and the littlest one pulled marigold buds and threw them all about the playground, 'to look like gold', he said. When all was done the playground was so beautiful that the children stood and looked at it, and clapped their hands with pleasure. 'Let us keep it always like this!' said the littlest one; and the others cried, 'Yes! Yes! That is what we will do.'

They waited all day for the coming of the King, but he never came; only, towards sunset, a man with travel-worn clothes, and a kind face passed along the road and stopped to look over the wall. 'What a pleasant place!' said the man. 'May I come in and rest, dear children?' The children brought him in gladly, and set him on the seat that they had made out of an old cask. They had covered it with the old red cloak to make it look like a throne, and it made a very good one.

'It is our playground!' they said. 'We made it pretty for the King, but he did not come, and now we mean to keep it so for ourselves.' 'That is good!' said the man. 'Because we think pretty and clean is nicer than ugly and dirty!' said another. 'That is better!' said the man. 'And for tired people to rest in!' said the littlest one. 'That is best of all!' said the man.

He sat and rested, and looked at the children with such kind eyes that they came about him, and told him all they knew; about the five puppies in the barn, and the thrush's nest with four blue eggs, and the shore where the gold shells grew; and the man nodded and understood all about it.

By and by he asked for a cup of water, and they brought it to him in the best cup, with the gold sprigs on it; then he thanked the children, and rose and went on his way; but before he went he laid his hand on their heads for a moment, and the touch went warm to their hearts.

The children stood by the wall and watched the man as he went slowly along. The sun was setting, and the light fell in long slanting rays across the road. 'He looks so tired!' said one of the children. 'But he was so kind!' said another. 'See!' said the littlest one. 'How the sun shines on his hair! It looks like a crown of gold.'
Laura E. Richards

USEFUL TEXTS

Christ the King:
  Kingdom of, *2 Pet. 1:11; Matt. 16:28*
  Born to be, *Matt. 2:2*
  'Are you?' *Matt. 27:11; Luke 23:3*
  Title over cross, *Luke 23:38*
  King of kings, *Rev. 17:14; Rev. 19:16*

See also: A4 Emmanuel – Mary's child
           A44 Meeting Christ in the sacraments
           B4 Mary – Handmaid of God
           B8 The Word

A38
ORIGINAL SIN

'Sin entered the world through one man,
and through sin death.'
Romans 5:12

QUOTATIONS

What history does is to uncover man's universal sin.
Herbert Butterfield

One of the most distressing signs of contemporary times is the
denial of guilt.
Fulton J. Sheen

The lack of wealth is easily repaired; but the poverty of the soul is
irreparable.
Montaigne

As Chesterton pointed out, the Fall of Man is only the banana-
skin joke carried to cosmic proportions.
Malcolm Muggeridge

The line separating good and evil passes not through states, nor
between classes, nor between political parties either – but right
through every human heart. Even in the best of hearts, there
remains a small corner of evil.
Alexander Solzhenitsyn

It is not enough to say
that one must be set free from sin . . .
It is possible to be possessed
by the idea of sin . . .
It is not only real sin which enslaves man,
but also possession by the idea of sin
which corrodes the whole life.
Nicolas Berdyaev

HUMOUR

'Teacher was telling us all about Adam and Eve today,' said a little girl to her mother. 'She said they lived ever so happily in the Garden of Eden till the servant arrived!'

Old lady to vicar who is leaving the parish: 'I'm sorry you're going, Vicar. We never knew what sin was until you came.'

A teacher asked her class of small children to make a crayon picture of the Old Testament story which they liked best. One small boy depicted a man in a top hat driving an old car. In the back seat were two passengers, both scantily dressed. 'It is a nice picture,' said the teacher, 'but what story does it tell?' The young artist seemed surprised at the question. 'Well,' he exclaimed, 'doesn't it say in the Bible that God drove Adam and Eve out of the Garden of Eden?'

WORD PICTURES

Lucy says to Charlie Brown:
    'You know what the whole trouble with you is, Charlie Brown?'
    'No; and I don't want to know! Leave me alone!'
    'The whole trouble with you is you won't listen to what the whole trouble with you is!'
Robert Short – The Gospel According to Peanuts

We were meant, as Adam and Eve before the fall, to walk through this world and commune with God. We should be able to see God in the raindrop, in the soft colours of the evening sunset, in the thunder and lightning, in snow and frost, in heat and cold. But we do not. We are not in touch with God's energetic love that assumes millions of concrete manifestations surrounding us at every moment, even though he is touching us with his millions of fingers.
John Maloney

For this state of sin in which the world finds itself, the word most frequently used in the Scriptures is *harmartia*, which means 'missing the mark'. And this is significant, for it presumes there is

a mark to miss. It presumes there is a state in which human beings could find themselves, or towards which they could be moving, but from which they have in fact gone astray. Thus, to call our negative experience of the human condition 'sin' is at the same time to say that there is hope for us. This is precisely the Good News, revealed in Jesus Christ and preached by the Church: that our condition is not irredeemable, that we need not 'miss the mark'. The ground of this hope is given by God himself. The Father has loved the world so much that he sent his only son to bring the world back to himself. The human race is 'off the mark' until it begins to do the works of God by the obedience of faith, submitting to God's plan for the world.
Mark Searle

In We and Our Children, *Mary Newland demonstrates how she explained Original Sin to her children.*
'Suppose God had given Adam a stack of money. "Now you are rich," he would have said. "Take good care of the money, don't lose it, because one day you will have a big family and they will need it. It will buy them food, and clothes, keep a roof over their head, and all these things will keep them happy and well. If you lose the money, your children will have a very hard time. They will be cold and hungry and naked, and have no home, all because of a wasted inheritance you might have left them."

'Now, suppose Adam paid no attention to God and instead wasted his money. He would have had none to pass on to his children. Even if it wasn't their fault, the inheritance would be gone. Nothing could bring it back. So they would suffer because of their father's wastefulness. God didn't give Adam money. He did give him sanctifying grace. That was the wealth Adam could have passed on to his children. But he lost it, and what he did not have he could not pass on. Because he disobeyed God by committing original sin . . .'
Mary Newland

USEFUL TEXTS

Sin:
　God displeased with, *Gen. 6:6; Deut. 25:16*
　Upright do not condone, *Gen. 39:9; Deut. 7:26*
　Consequences of, *Exod. 20:5; Rom. 5:12*
　Forgiveness of, *Exod. 34:7; Matt. 26:28*

A39
THE GLORY OF GOD

'He was transfigured; his face shone like the sun and his
clothes became as white as the light.'
Matthew 17:2

QUOTATIONS

The world is charged with the grandeur of God.
Gerard Manley Hopkins

Grace is but glory begun, and glory is but grace perfected.
Jonathan Edwards

By faith we know his existence; in glory we shall know his nature.
Blaise Pascal

We are his glory, when we follow his ways.
Florence Nightingale

God made the universe and all the creatures contained therein as
so many glasses wherein he might reflect his own glory.
John Smith

The excellency of God is magnified; he is not glorified in one, but
in numberless suns, not in one earth nor in one world, but in ten
hundred thousand of infinite globes.
Giordano Brune 1589

To lift up the hands in prayer gives God glory, but a man with a
dung-fork in his hand, a woman with a sloppail, give him glory too.
He is so great that all things give him glory if you mean they should.
Gerard Manley Hopkins

WORD PICTURES

There is a legend that St Jerome, who lived for many years in a
cave near Bethlehem, was visited by the Christ Child and talked

with him. One day Jerome asked: 'What may I give to thee, O Christ Child?'

But the Holy Child replied: 'I need nought but that thou should'st sing, "Glory to God in the highest, and on earth peace, goodwill."' But Jerome persisted: 'I would give thee gifts – money.' 'Nay,' repeated the Child, 'I need no money; give it to my poor, for my sake. Thus shalt thou be giving to me.'
Anon

When the good people of Beauvais were building their cathedral, that of Amiens, then just completed, had excited the admiration of all France; and the people of Beauvais, in their jealousy and determination to beat the people of Amiens, set to work to build a tower to their own cathedral as high as they possibly could. They built it so high that it tumbled down, and they were never able to finish their cathedral at all – it stands a wreck to this day. A tribute to their vain quest for glory.
Anon

You remember how in Raphael's great painting of Christ's Transfiguration, the whole story is depicted. Up above Christ is hovering in glory, lifted from earth and clothed in light and accompanied on each side by his saints. Down below, in the same picture, the father holds his frantic child, and the helpless disciples are gazing in despair at the struggles which their charms have wholly failed to touch. It is the peace of divine strength above; it is the tumult and dismay of human feebleness below. But what keeps the great picture from being a mere painted mockery is that the puzzled disciples in the foreground are pointing the distressed parents of the child up to the mountain where the form of Christ is seen. They have begun to get hold of the idea that what they could not do he could do. So they are on the way to the faith which he described to them when they came to him with their perplexity.
Philip Brooks

In 1828, the Anglican priest, William Broughton, was sent out to Australia as Archdeacon of that island continent, which was then part of the diocese of Calcutta! Eight years later he was made Australia's first Bishop, and his work and energy and spiritual leadership in carrying out his vast task were marvellous. There are many stories associated with that great man. Here is one example of them.

When the great gold rush came, although he was an already ageing man, Bishop Broughton joined himself to the amazing exodus, arrived at the diggings and collected a great crowd of miners for service on Sunday, when he told them that on the following Wednesday, at 6am, the building of their church was to begin.

At six o'clock precisely, the Bishop, attended by a large crowd was at the ground. He first delivered a truly great sermon, which concluded by saying that he would set them an example of what it meant that they should dig together for the honour and glory of God. Then being supplied with a pick, he began to open the ground where the north-east support of the building was to stand. The example was contagious; in a few minutes all who could obtain tools were digging, so that before 8.30am more than half the holes were dug to the required depth. By midday the carpenters were at work; by evening the church was apparent in outline; and in four day's time was furnished and ready for consecration.
Anon

USEFUL TEXTS

Glory of God:
  Exod. 24:15-17, 40:34; Luke 2:9; Acts 7:55
  Reflected in Christ, *John 1:14*
  Reflected in man, *1 Cor. 11:7*

See also: A20 The Kingdom of God
           B40 One God
           C31 Thanksgiving
           C39 Doing God's will

A40
THE EQUALITY OF WOMEN

'His disciples returned, and were surprised to find him
speaking to a woman.'
John 4:27

QUOTATIONS

The loveliest masterpiece of the heart of God is the heart of a mother.
St Thérèse of Lisieux

Man has his will, but woman has her way.
Oliver Wendell Hoemes

I'm not denying that women are foolish. God Almighty made 'em
to match the men.
George Eliot

Next to God, we are indebted to women, first for life itself, and
then for making it worth having.
Christian Bovee

When I say I know women, I mean I know that I don't know them.
William Makepeace Thackeray

The sum of all that makes a just man happy consists in the well
choosing of his wife.
Massinger

God himself dressed Eve's hair, that the first woman might better
please the first man.
Jewish legend

A woman, like the Koh-i-noor, amounts to the price that's put on
her.
Coventry Patmore

The history of women is the history of the worst form of tyranny the world has known. The tyranny of the weak over the strong. It is the only tyranny that lasts.
Oscar Wilde

PROVERB

Woman is the confusion of man.
English proverb

HUMOUR

Woman's irrationality was for ever proved when she took dietary advice from a talking snake.
N. Carigg

He then made woman and, since then, neither man, woman, nor anything else has rested.
Author unknown

Doctors have noted that women's feet are getting larger. Presumably that's because they are trying to fill men's shoes.
Chicago Tribune

Notice in a Nottinghamshire church hall: Will ladies responsible for making tea kindly empty teapots and kettles, then stand upside down in the sink.
The Daily Telegraph

'Women are to blame for all the lying men do – they will insist on continually asking questions.
Anon

There are certain things I believe a man should do at home, like bringing in the wood and coal, mending the car and setting the mousetrap. There's simply no equality when it comes to mice.
Barbara Cartland

When Winston Churchill was told that writers were declaring that, by the year 2100, women would be ruling the world, his rejoinder, with a twinkle, was just one word: 'Still?'
Anon

Who was that little girl I saw you with, Tommy?'
'I dunno, Daddy, I just pulled a bag of sweets out of my pocket –
an' there she was.'

Show me a woman whose husband has never complained of
anything, and I will canonise her at once.
Pope Sixtus V

Asked where he saw the role of women in society, James Thurber
declared: 'A woman's place is in the wrong.'

I went to church yesterday, Mothering Sunday, and, as the children
were going around giving the mums small posies of flowers, the
Minister stopped one small boy and said:
   'Now, where do you go when you want anything, and who do
you go to?'
   Expecting the small boy to reply, 'Mum', the Minister and the
rest of us were shaken when the answer came back, loud and clear,
'Sainsbury's'.
Mary Fawson

It was time for the children's sermon. So I called the kids forward to
the altar steps and told them a story about Jesus and his disciples.
Then I asked a perfectly natural question: 'When Jesus called the
disciples to be fishers of men, what bait did he tell them to use?' One
little boy leaned toward my microphone and confidently replied,
'Women'.
Anon

WORD PICTURES

William Caxton, the first English printer, wrote the following
foreword to the *Dictes and Sayings of the Philosophers*, which was
published in 1477:
   The women of this country are right good, pleasant, humble,
   discreet, sober, chaste, obedient to their husbands, true, secret,
   steadfast, ever busy, never idle, temperate in speaking and
   virtuous in all their works. Or at least they should be so.

A college English professor wrote the words 'Woman without her man is a savage' on the board, directing his students to punctuate it correctly. He found that the men looked at it one way and the women another:

Males – 'Woman, without her man, is a savage!'

Females – 'Woman! Without her, man is a savage!'

When the good Lord was creating mothers, he was into his sixth day of overtime when an angel appeared and said, 'You're doing a lot of fiddling around on this one.' And the Lord said, 'Have you read the specifications on this order? She has to be completely washable, but not plastic . . . have 180 movable parts – all replaceable . . . run on black coffee and left-overs . . . have a lap that disappears when she stands up . . . a kiss that can cure anything from a broken leg to a disappointed love affair . . . and six pairs of hands.'

The angel shook his head slowly and said, 'Six pairs of hands? No way.' 'It's not the hands that are causing me problems,' said the Lord. 'It's the three pairs of eyes that mothers have to have.' 'That's on the standard model?' asked the angel. The Lord nodded. 'One pair that sees through closed doors when she asks "What are you children doing in there?" when she already knows. Another in the back of her head that sees when she shouldn't but what she has to know. And, of course, the ones in front that can look at a child when he gets himself into trouble and say, "I understand and I love you", without so much as uttering a word.'

'Lord,' said the angel, touching his sleeve gently, 'go to bed. Tomorrow is another . . .' 'I can't,' said the Lord. 'I'm so close now. Already I have one who heals herself when she is sick, can feed a family of six on one pound of mince, and can get a nine year old to have a bath.'

The angel circled the model of a mother very slowly. 'It's too soft,' he sighed. 'But tough!' said the Lord excitedly. 'You cannot imagine what this mother can do or endure.' 'Can it think?' asked the angel. 'Not only think, but it can reason and compromise,' said the Creator.

Finally, the angel bent over and ran his finger across the cheek. 'There's a leak,' he pronounced. 'It's not a leak,' said the Lord.

'It's a tear.' 'What's it for?' 'It's for joy, sadness, disappointment, pain, loneliness and pride.' 'You are a genius,' said the angel. The Lord looked sombre. 'I didn't put it there.'
Anon

Woman was made from the rib of man.
She was not created from his head – to top him,
nor from his feet – to be stepped upon.

She was made from his side – to be equal to him;
from beneath his arm – to be protected by him;
near his heart – to be loved by him.
Anon

Oh! the gladness of a woman when she's glad!
Oh! the sadness of a woman when she's sad!
But the gladness of her gladness,
and the sadness of her sadness,
are nothing to her badness –
when she's bad!
Anon

One of the most familiar characters at Vatican II and subsequent synods was 'the lady with the buttons'. Few among those who remember her knew or could pronounce her delectable name: Frances Lee McGillicuddy. Having accredited herself as a journalist for the Brooklyn *Tablet*, she got in everywhere and would pounce upon unsuspecting bishops as they emerged from St Peter's, presenting them with lapel buttons inscribed with slogans of her own devising.

Her buttons became collectors' items. Here is a random selection. 'Ordain women – or stop baptising them.' 'Sexism is a heresy – *anathema sit*.' 'Jesus was a feminist' – an allusion to his treatment of women. 'Women: don't make coffee, make policy.' 'Trust in God, she will provide.' One bishop mistook the latter button for a holy medal, and unwittingly blessed it.
Anon

The Archbishop forgot to tell me that my predecessor as parish priest was a woman. I suppose he did not think it was all that important. After all, a high proportion of the poorest parishes in this macho subcontinent are run by women and eyelids have not noticeably batted.

Sister Dolores is not (yet), of course, a Catholic priest in the strict canonical sense of the word. She is always careful to omit the consecration when she presides over the Word and Communion service and her liturgies of reconciliation are not confused, as far as I can judge, with sacramental confession.

I have witnessed her performance at the bedside of a dying youth and I have seen her blend of fervour and sensitive reverence at the traditional Central American wake held on the nine consecutive days that follow a burial. During her eight years as *responsable* (her official title conferred by the Archbishop), she visited the families of this parish assiduously. She established a social programme that included three different co-operatives, a clinic for the poor and a day-centre for 30 undernourished children.

When priests meet (without their bishops) the wish is often expressed half-jokingly as, 'Roll on Vatican III for married priests and roll on Vatican IV for women priests'.
John Medcalf

USEFUL TEXTS

Woman:
    Creation of, *Gen. 1:27; 2:21-23*
    Devout, *1 Sam. 1:15; Luke 1:25*
    Heirs with Christ, *Gal. 3:26-29*

See also: B34 Human rights
            B44 The dignity of the individual
            C33 Equality

A41
SPIRITUAL BLINDNESS

'I only know that I was blind and now I can see.'
John 9:26

QUOTATIONS

Though blind men see no light, the sun doth shine.
Robert Southwell

There are too many people we just leave asleep.
Antoine Saint Exupéry

The greatest of all disorders is to think we are whole, and need no
help.
Thomas Wilson

What is it: is man only a blunder of God, or God only a blunder
of man?
Friedrick Nietzsche

If there is no God, and everything, therefore, is permitted, the
first thing permitted is despair.
François Mauriac

By denying the existence, or the providence of God, men may
shake off their ease, but not their yoke.
Thomas Hobbes

Let him who gropes painfully in darkness or uncertain light lay
this precept well to heart, 'Do the duty which lies nearest to thee,
which thou knowest to be a Duty! Thy second duty will already
have become clearer.
Thomas Carlyle

WORD PICTURES

In Rome, when the troops of Honorius had defeated Alaric (403), great games were held in victorious celebration, including the cruel gladiatorial shows (where men fought and killed one another), which even Christians attended. Telemachus, a monk, determined to show that Christian love could not tolerate this, travelled to Rome, obtained entrance to the amphitheatre, and when the fight began leapt over the barrier to part the gladiators.

The crowd of people in the vast building shouted with rage that they should be baulked of their amusement, and throwing stones and other missiles at Telemachus, he was soon pelted to death. But the sight of him lying dead cooled their rage and opened their eyes to their cruelty. The Emperor said his death was a martyrdom, and the people agreed to give up their gladiatorial shows.
F. H. Drinkwater

Phillips Brooks told the story of a backward African tribe that was given a sundial. The natives were so pleased with their gift and so wanted to impress their neighbours that they built a special hut over it! Many people are like that; they are so reverent about their religion that they only bring it out for weddings and funerals.
Anon

Golfers rightly fear the hazards of bunkers, yet few can avoid them completely. At some time our course in life will catch us in the adversity of a sand trap. The danger is that we may be unprepared to deal with the tough situations in life.

Arnold Palmer, the famous golf champion, said on one occasion that over the years he had watched hundreds of golfers practising. He had observed them meticulously practising putting – the short putts on the soft velvet grass – and he had watched them practise the swing down the fairway, but in all his lifetime and experience, he had never once seen a golfer practising how to get out of a bunker!
Anon

I knew an atheist novelist who used to say his prayers every night. That didn't alter anything. How he gave it to God in his books! What a dressing down, as one might say. A militant freethinker to whom I spoke of this raised his hands – with no evil intention, I assure you – to heaven: 'You're telling me nothing new,' that apostle of free thought sighed, 'they're all like that.' According to him, 80 per cent of our writers, if only they could avoid putting their names to it, would write and hail the name of God.
Albert Camus

Moved by the beauty around him, one of the disciples asked his master how he could help others to see and feel such riches. 'What you ask is difficult,' answered the old man. 'To see and feel beauty outside oneself, one must first be – and feel himself to be – beautiful.'

'Master, how do we know if someone is beautiful?' asked the disciple. 'And if one isn't beautiful, how does one become so?'

'Beauty is a part of love,' the master explained. 'It is being great enough to give and humble enough to receive. To help another discover beauty is to open one's spirit to noble and generous ideas. It is removing the egotistic blindfold that covers the mind and tearing off the bandages that shroud the heart.'
Emilio Rojas

USEFUL TEXTS

Spiritual blindness:
  Prov. 4:19; Matt. 6:23
Condition of:
  Jewish leaders, *Matt. 15:14; 23:19,24,26*
  Israel, *2 Cor. 3:14-16*
  Unbelievers, *2 Cor. 4:3-4*

See also: A22 Seeking God
           B49 Coping with doubt
           C26 The human condition

A42
LIFE AFTER DEATH

'I am the resurrection. If anyone believes in me,
even though he dies he will live, and whoever lives
and believes in me will never die!'
John 11:25

QUOTATIONS

Life is the childhood of our immortality.
Goethe

The only ultimate disaster that can befall us is to feel ourselves at
home on this earth.
Malcolm Muggeridge

The shortest life is the best if it leads us to the eternal.
St Frances of Sales

I know as much about the afterlife as you do – nothing. I must
wait and see.
William Inge

To believe in immortality is one thing, but it is needful to believe
in life.
Robert Louis Stevenson

What seems to be the riddle, the abyss of our human existence . . .
is the beginning of eternal life.
Karl Rahner

There is only one way I can get ready for immortality, and that is
to love this life. And live it bravely and cheerfully and as faithfully
as I can.
Henry van Dyke

Love is the most real thing in the world, and I therefore do not believe that any real love that I have either given or received will pass out of my life in the next world.
A. Maude Royden

I have desired to go
where springs not fail
O thou Lord, send my roots rain.
Gerard Manley Hopkins

Easter declares death is dead and done with. Yet few reply to its persuasion – deadness is so safe. Its badge is boredom; boredom is unlived life, security is the groove. The only difference between the groove and the grave is the depth.
Hugh Lavery

HUMOUR

One of my favourite stories is about the golfer who goes to hell and is astonished to find himself on the most beautiful golf course he has ever seen. A little horned caddy brings him the most magnificent and deadly golf clubs he has ever handled. He takes a few practice swings with the driver and it cuts the air with the authority of a practised sword. Power surges through his muscles. 'OK, caddy, put down a ball.' 'I'm sorry, sir. That's the hell of it. There are no balls!'
Eamon Andrews

Overheard from a practising Catholic outside a church, Palm Sunday
'See you at the Holy Week services.'
'No fear, they are much too morbid.'
P.F.

A rather stone-faced and cold, celibate clergyman dies and, soon after, one of his best friends also passed away.
 On arriving in the 'other place' the clergyman's friend was surprised to see the clergyman with two beautiful blonde ladies

sitting on his knee, and a gorgeous black-haired lady stroking his shoulders. All three were clearly trying to seduce him.

'I see you're being well treated,' said the friend. 'I didn't realise heaven was going to be so good.'

'I'm not enjoying myself,' replied the clergyman with a sour look, 'And this isn't heaven. We're in hell – and I'm these three ladies' punishment.'

Anon

A missionary who had been several years in India was returning home and brought with him a supply of chutney of which he had become fond. A fellow passenger was interested in the, to him, entirely new food and was invited to partake. He helped himself liberally, then with great emotion with the tears running down his face, enquired, 'You are a missionary, aren't you?' 'Yes,' was the reply. 'And I suppose you believe in hell fire?' 'That is so,' replied the missionary. 'Well, then,' said the victim, 'you are the first missionary I ever knew who carried samples around with him.'

Anon

WORD PICTURES

Over the triple doorways of the Cathedral of Milan are some carvings. One is of a beautiful wreath of roses, and underneath are these words: 'All that pleases is but for a moment.' Over another is a cross, and underneath: 'All that troubles is but for a moment.' But over the great central archway leading into the main aisle is the inscription: 'That only is important which is eternal.'

Cuthbert Johnson

Eternal life – there is no end to it! It is life without end. The government was trying to make a treaty with the Indians, and in one place put the word, 'forever'. The Indians did not like the word 'forever' and said, 'No, put it, "as long as water runs and grass grows".' The Indians could understand that.

Dwight L. Moody

172

Ancient British practices demanded that mourners had to carry branches of yew and throw them into the grave after the body had been committed. It was thought that they would shoot and they were thus regarded as symbolic of the resurrection of the body, as well as the immortality of the soul.
Don Lewis

Science . . . tells us that nothing in nature, not even the tiniest particle, can disappear without a trace. Nature does not know extinction. All it knows is transformation. . . . And everything science has taught me . . . strengthens my belief in the continuity of our spiritual existence after death. Nothing disappears without a trace.
Werner von Braun

I never think upon eternity without receiving great comfort. For I say to myself: how could my soul grasp the idea of everlastingness, if the two were not related in some way? But as soon as I feel how close the yearning of my heart follows upon the thought of eternity, my happiness becomes incomparably greater. For I am certain that, according to his nature, man can yearn only for that which can be attained. And so my yearning makes me certain that I shall reach eternity.
St Francis of Sales

USEFUL TEXTS

Life after death:
   Of the righteous, *Matt. 25:46*
   Gift of God, *Rom. 6:23*
   Promise of, *1 John 2:25*
   Through Jesus, *John 3:15*

See also: A31 Heaven
             B22 Death
             C35 Hope

A43
BELIEVING COMMUNITY

'These remained faithful to the teaching of the apostles, to the fellowship, to the breaking of bread and to the prayers.'
Acts 2:42

QUOTATIONS

The primary duty of the Church is to be the Christian community.
W. A. Wisser't Hooft

We need society, and we need solitude also, as we need summer and winter, day and night, exercise and rest.
Philip G. Hammerton

Our generation is remarkable . . . for the number of people who must believe something but do not know what.
Evelyn Underhill

Community life brings a painful revelation of our limitations, weaknesses and darkness, the unexpected discovery of the monsters within us is hard to accept.
Jean Vanier

What the indwelling spirit within us reveals is that our proper dignity as children of God consists in our functioning within the Body of Christ out of love to serve the whole community.
George A. Maloney

WORD PICTURES

An old Easter legend said that the gate of heaven was so narrow that one man walking alone could not pass through; two walking side by side, one of whom had helped the other, found easy entrance; and when ten men came, who had all been serving one another in love, they found the gate so wide that they saw no post on either side.
Charles R. Brown

A remark was made by a leading citizen of Chicago to the famous evangelist, D. L. Moody, who was visiting him in his own drawing room. 'I do not see,' said the man, 'that I cannot be just as good a Christian outside the Church as within it.' Moody said nothing but stepped to the brightly burning Christmas fire, and, picking up a blazing coal in the tongs, allowed it to burn by itself. In silence the two men watched it smoulder and go out. Next Sunday the man was in church.
Anon

Years ago I heard a parable of a man in hell who prayed earnestly to be released from torment. At last a voice said, 'Rescue will come,' and a carrot held by a slender thread was let down and he was told to grasp it. He did so, and seemingly thin though the thread was, it began to draw him up. But others, seeing his ascent, seized upon his asbestos garments that they also might be rescued, and the man kicked them off, crying, 'The thread will break!' and break it did, alas! And again the voice spoke: 'The thread was strong enough to save both you and your brothers, but it was not strong enough to save you alone.'
The Living Church

When Louis Agassiz was a boy in Switzerland, he and his little brother one day thought they would cross a frozen lake and join their father. The mother anxiously watched them from a window till at length they came to a crack in the ice more than a foot wide. Her heart failed her. She thought Louis can get over it well enough, but the little fellow will try to do so and will fall in. They were too far away to hear her call. As she watched in an agony of fear she saw Louis get down on the ice, his feet on one side of the crack and his hands on the other, like a bridge, and his little brother crept over him to the other side. So may brother bridge life's dangerous and difficult places for brother.
Myers

Nero punished with exquisite torture, a race of men detested for their evil practices, by vulgar appellation commonly called 'Christians'. The name was derived from Christ, who in the reign of Tiberius, suffered under Pontius Pilate, the procurator of Judea. By that event the sect, of which he was the founder, received a blow, which, for a time, checked the growth of a dangerous superstition; but it revived soon after, and spread with recruiting vigour, not only in Judea, the soil that gave it birth, and even in the city of Rome, the common sink into which everything infamous and abominable flows like a torrent from all quarters of the world.

Nero proceeded with his usual artifice. He found a set of profligate wretches who were induced to confess themselves guilty, and, on the evidence of such men, a number of Christians were convicted, not, indeed, upon clear evidence of their having set the city on fire, but rather on account of their sullen hatred of the whole human race. They were put to death with exquisite cruelty, and to their sufferings Nero added mockery and derision. Some were covered with the skins of wild beasts, and left to be devoured by dogs; others were nailed to the cross; numbers were burnt alive; and many, covered over with inflammable matter, were lighted up, when the day declined, to serve as torches during the night.

For the convenience of seeing this tragic spectacle, the emperor lent his own gardens. He added the sports of the circus, and assisted in person, sometimes driving a curricle, and occasionally mixing with the rabble in his coachman's dress. At length the cruelty of these proceedings filled every breast with compassion. Humanity relented in favour of the Christians. The manners of that people were, no doubt, of a pernicious tendency, and their crimes called for the hand of justice; but it was evident that they fell a sacrifice not for the public good, but to glut the rage and cruelty of one man only.
The Annals of Tacitus

On the other end of the telephone in London was a great friend of mine and all the Jesuits in El Salvador, a man who has shown great solidarity with our country and our Church. He began with these words: 'Something terrible has happened.' 'I know,' I replied, 'Ellacuría.' But I didn't know. He asked me if I was sitting

176

down and had something to write with. I said I had and then he told me what had happened. 'They have murdered Ignacio Ellacuría.' I remained silent and did not write anything, because I had already been afraid of this. But my friend went on: 'They have murdered Segundo Montes, Ignacio Martín-Baró, Amando López, Juan Ramón Moreno and Joaquín López y López.' My friend read the names slowly and each of them reverberated like a hammer blow that I received in total helplessness. I was writing them down hoping that the list would end after each name. But after each name came another, on to the end. The whole community, my whole community, had been murdered. In addition, two women had been murdered with them. They were living in a little house at the entrance to the University and because they were afraid of the situation they asked the fathers if they could spend the night in our house because they felt safer there. They were also mercilessly killed.
Jon Sobrino

USEFUL TEXTS
Church:
  Loved by Christ, *Eph. 5:25*
  Pillar of truth, *1 Tim. 3:15*
  Head of, *Eph. 1:22*
  Building of, *Matt. 16:18; Eph. 2:20-21*

See also: B17 The Church – Bride of Christ
           B36 The Family of God
           C12 The Church for all people

A44
MEETING CHRIST IN THE SACRAMENTS

'He took the bread and said the blessing; then he broke it
and handed it to them. And their eyes were opened
and they recognised him.'
Luke 24:30-31

QUOTATIONS

Each sacrament is the personal saving act of the risen Christ
himself, but realised in the visible form of an official act of the
Church.
E. Schillebeeckx

The meaning of each sacrament is derived from two things: its
reference to the paschal mystery and the particular situation of the
individual or community upon whom the sacramental celebration
focuses.
Mark Searle

For mankind there are two unique sacraments which disclose the
meaning and convey the experience of reality: they are the created
universe and the person of Jesus Christ.
Charles E. Raven

Men are called to be by grace all that Christ is by nature.
St Maximus

WORD PICTURES

Legend says that the Holy Grail, the cup Jesus is said to have used
at the Last Supper, was carried to Glastonbury, but owing to the
wickedness of those who guarded it, it was caught up into heaven,
and thereafter could only be seen by those whose lives were pure.
Sir Launfal set out on a brilliant summer morning to seek the
Grail. As he crossed the draw-bridge across the moat of his castle,
he saw a leper sitting in the dust, holding up his hand for alms. Sir

Launfal, with a look of disgust, threw a gold coin to him, but it fell to the ground. The leper saw the look and left the gold lying where it fell.

Years passed away, and Sir Launfal was given up as dead, when an old man was seen coming across the plain to the castle, limping and leaning heavily on a stick. He was dressed almost in rags and seemed very poor and ill and weary. As he drew near to the bridge, his eye fell on the leper, now very old but still begging. The old man, who was Sir Launfal himself, opened a worn-out wallet and took from it a crust of bread and a battered tin cup. He broke the crust in half, ate one piece, and gave the rest to the leper. Then he dipped the cup in the stream, gave the leper to drink and then drank himself. Even as he drank the form of the leper seemed to be transfigured, and –

The voice that was softer than silence said,
'Lo, it is I, be not afraid.
In many climes, without avail,
thou has spent thy life for the Holy Grail;
behold, it is here! The cup which thou
didst fill at the streamlet for me but now;
this crust is my body, broken for thee;
this water his blood that died on the tree;
the Holy Supper is kept, indeed,
in what so we share with another's need;
not what we give, but what we share,
for the gift without the giver is bare;
who gives himself with his alms feeds three,
himself, the hungering neighbour, and me.'
Adapted from Lowell's poem

A certain holy Cistercian, in a dream, was taken by his guardian angel and shown a vast plain peopled with many men and cities. On one side of the plain a copious spring of water gushed out from a hill-side, dividing into seven clear streams, which flowed down into the plain. At the other side of the plain another fountain rushed up from a dark cavern also spreading out into seven streams.

He watched the streams that came from the cavern, and saw that many people drank from them eagerly, for their waters were sweet to the taste; but soon after drinking these people were seized with violent pains and vomiting, and many died.

'That is the cavern of Self-will,' said the angel. 'And its seven poisonous streams are the seven deadly sins. Now look across the plain to where the seven rivers of life take their rise from the hill of Calvary.' The seven rivers of life were not so sweet to the taste, but they had wonderful properties, for the sick who drank them were being healed, the old were being made young again, the ugly becoming beautiful; and in some of the rivers the beholder could see the dead being brought to life again.

The vision filled the holy monk with grief for so many souls who were deceived by poisonous pleasures, and with a great desire to bring them all to the saving waters of life. He understood that these seven rivers were the seven sacraments which are the channels of Christ's grace to mankind.

F. H. Drinkwater

See also: A37 Christ the King
            B4   Mary – Handmaid of God
            B46 Christ the Sacrament of God
            B51 One with Christ
            C45 The Divinity of Christ

A45
THE PRIESTHOOD

'The Lord is my Shepherd there is nothing I shall want.'
Psalm 23

QUOTATIONS

The furnace of purification for the priest in the active ministry is charity for other men.
Thomas Merton

It is not a priest's business to impose his own ideas, but to aid the workings of grace.
Abbé Huvelin

He who goes up with fear comes down with honour.
Ancient inscription on a pulpit

No man preaches his sermon well to others if he doth not first preach it to his own heart.
John Owen

The clergy can be the greatest barrier to spiritual growth in the world.
Cardinal Suenens

Everyone who can preach the truth and does not preach it, incurs the judgement of God.
Justin Martyr

A constant danger with priests, even zealous priests, is that they become so immersed in the work of the Lord that they neglect the Lord of the work.
Pope John Paul II

HUMOUR

A little boy who was hoping to be a preacher, was horribly dismayed when his mother hold him he would have to be always good. 'What!' said he. 'Shall I have to be *always* good?' 'Yes,' said his mother, 'always good!' 'But, mother, shall I have to be always *very* good?' 'Yes, you will have to be always very good.' 'Then,' said the boy, after he had thought a bit: 'I think I shall be a *local* preacher.'
Anon

'My friends,' said a village churchwarden, addressing a meeting of parishioners, 'our dear Vicar, as you know, will shortly be leaving us to take up work in another parish, and I therefore propose we take up a collection to give him a little momentum.'
Anon

A train was journeying through the night and down the corridor went an American calling out, 'Is there a Roman Catholic priest on the train?' Meeting with no response, he traced his steps calling out this time, 'Is there an Anglican priest on the train?' He had almost reached the last carriage when a little man wearing a 'dog-collar' stepped out into the corridor and said, 'Excuse me, I heard you asking first for a Roman Catholic priest then for an Anglican priest. Can I be of any help? I'm a Nonconformist minister.' 'Not a hope in hell,' came the reply. 'I'm only trying to borrow a corkscrew!'
Anon

When a clergyman asked the British politician George Canning how he had enjoyed his sermon, Canning replied:
    'You were brief.'
    'Yes,' said the clergyman, 'you know I avoid being tedious.'
    'But you were tedious,' concluded Canning.
Anon

WORD PICTURES

St Francis of Assisi resisted all suggestions that he should be ordained priest, and in this way he taught all his followers how lofty and holy a dignity the priesthood is. Only with reluctance did he allow himself to be ordained deacon. One day he said to the friars: 'If I met an angel and a priest walking together I would salute the priest first and then the angel.' This puzzled some of the friars, no doubt because they knew priests who were evidently not so holy as angels. So St Francis explained: 'I would salute the priest first because the angel, although so great, is only Christ's servant, but the priest actually represents Jesus Christ.'

During the Spanish Civil War, July 1936, forty priests (of the Claretian Order) were being taken off in lorries to execution. They sang hymns, shouted in chorus 'Long live Christ the King'. A young man in lay dress stopped one of the lorries and joined himself to the condemned; he, too, was a priest who preferred to die with his brethren. At the place of execution one of the firing squad spoke apologetically to one of the martyrs, pointing to the habit he was wearing. 'We have to kill you because you wear these.' 'And we die joyfully,' was the reply, 'because we wear them.'
F. H. Drinkwater

'I have never forgotten a young Roman Catholic priest I met during the war years on a ship,' Mr Dale, the new URC incumbent said. 'I was a wireless operator and we used to talk during the night watch when I was on duty in the wireless room. He had spent 15 years in the heart of West Africa, one of the most disease-ridden areas and had Blackwater fever. He was a very sick man. We talked about our faith and I asked him what made him give up everything to work in a place like that. His answer was, "When God calls then one must answer." During the Congo revolution I thought of him when more than 300 missionaries of different denominations were killed.'
Evening Echo

Baddesley Clinton has been called one of only two almost perfect examples of moated medieval manors in the country. Certainly the house fits the description of one breathtaking escape, though as exact records were naturally not kept the location may never be proved.

The Jesuit Superior Fr Garnet and seven priests were at prayers early one morning and their horses were prepared for departure when a sudden shouting and knocking at the door announced that government searchers had arrived. The servant barred the door saying that her mistress was in bed, and the priests hid their boots and swords and everything else that would betray them, and even 'turned their beds and put them cold side up, to delude anyone who put a hand in to feel them,' before clambering down into a disused sewer which ran along the west wing. Here they stood for hours, ankle deep in water seeping in from the moat, listening to the tramping and battering above while the searchers ransacked the house. Its mistress 'with great courage and skill kept the search party from looking in the stable, where they would have found all the horses ready for the priests' departure.' The pursuivants gave up at last and rode away; and when they had gone so far that 'there was no danger of their turning back suddenly, as they sometimes do,' the priests climbed out and said Mass, with much thankfulness, before going their separate ways.
Catholic Herald

A poor thing was dying, a London butterfly, broken on the wheel. They used her and cast her aside. She was now dying – hardly out of her teens. She was a drug addict. I was called in. She was conscious but speechless. There was no hope, poor child. They used her and threw her aside as a sucked orange. I was almost tempted to hate my fellow men . . . I was sent by the Shepherd. I didn't care two straws whether she wanted me or didn't. God wanted her.
Vincent McNabb

USEFUL TEXTS
Priest:
Jesus as:
   Appointed by God, *Heb. 5:5*
   Appointed for ever, *Heb. 5:6*
   Intercessor, *Rom. 8:34*
   Able to sympathise, *Heb. 4:14*

Priesthood of:
   Aaron, *Exod. 28:1; Heb. 5:1-5*
   Melchizedek, *Gen. 14:18*
   Christ, *Heb. 4:14; Heb. 5:5-10*

See also: A14 The successors of the Apostles
          A46 Priesthood of the laity
          B13 Authority

A46
PRIESTHOOD OF THE LAITY

'You are a chosen race, a royal priesthood, a consecrated
nation, a people set apart, to sing the praises of God.'
1 Peter 2:9

QUOTATIONS

If the Church is the true people of God, it is impossible to
differentiate between 'Church' and 'Laity'. *Hans Kung*

Laypersons do not *belong* to the Church, nor do they *have a role*
in the Church. Rather, through baptism, they *are* Church.
Leonard Doohan

All the baptised form a priestly people, that is, they have to offer
God the spiritual sacrifice of their whole life, animated with a loving
faith, uniting it with Christ's unique Sacrifice. *Pope John Paul II*

The priesthood of all believers consists in the calling of the faithful
to witness to God and his will before the world and to offer up
their lives in the service of the world. *Hans Kung*

WORD PICTURES

Jesus, the Risen Lord over all the universe, the Pantocrator, by his
resurrection is inserted as a leaven inside of the entire material
cosmos. Yet he operates, he speaks, he touches, he loves the poor
and the destitute, he conquers sin and death empirically only
through his living members. Those who worthily have received his
body and blood and have received the outpoured Holy Spirit in
the Eucharist are to go out and celebrate the Eucharistic Liturgy
of the High Priest, Jesus Christ.
John Maloney

You who are the laypersons in the Church, and who possess faith,
the greatest of all resources – you have a unique opportunity and
crucial responsibility. Through your lives in the midst of your

daily activities in the world, you show the power that faith has to transform the world and to renew the family of man. Even though it is hidden and unnoticed, like the leaven or the salt of the earth spoken of in the Gospel, your role as laity is indispensable for the Church in the fulfillment of her mission from Christ.

This was clearly taught by the Fathers of the Second Vatican Council when they stated: 'The Church is not truly established and does not fully live, nor is she a perfect sign of Christ among people, unless there exists a laity worthy of the name, working alongside the hierarchy, for the Gospel cannot be deeply imprinted on the mentality, life and work of any people without the active presence of lay people.'
Ad Gentes, 21, Pope John Paul II

The essential gifts and functions of Church life belong to every baptised member. Each one is filled with the Holy Spirit and enlivened with God's gifts of faith, hope and charity. Within the Church there is a secondary vocational distinction but a primary and essential quality. After twenty-nine sections of the document on the Church, the Second Vatican Council states: 'Everything which has been said so far concerning the People of God applies equally to the laity, religious, and clergy' (C30:1). All are endowed with charisms for the upbuilding of the Church (see C 30:2), and all share in the threefold office of Christ: priestly, prophetical and royal. Among all the people of God there is a true equality (see C 30:1; 32:2), a genuine freedom (see C 37:1), a profound dignity (see C 37:3), a global responsibility (see 30:2; 33:2), a sense of vocation (see C 31), and a personal union with Christ and his mission. In fact, each one has a 'proper and indispensable role in the mission of the Church.'
Leonard Doohan

USEFUL TEXTS

Priesthood of Believers:
   1 Pet. 2:5; Rev. 1:6

See also: B10 Baptism
            B44 The dignity of the individual
            C49 Receive the Holy Spirit

A47
THE SPIRIT OF TRUTH

'The Father will give you another Advocate to be with you for
ever, that Spirit of truth whom the world can never receive.'
John 14: 16-17

QUOTATIONS

The truth is always the strongest argument.
Sophocles

All truth is precious, if not all divine.
William Cowper

Truth is often eclipsed but never extinguished.
Livy

Love the truth but pardon error.
Voltaire

Truth exists, only falsehood has to be invented.
Georges Braque

It is better that scandals arise than that truth be silenced.
St Gregory the Great

Truth is always narrow, but error goes off in all directions.
Paul E. Johnson

Let us lie low in the Lord's power, and learn that truth alone
makes rich and great.
Ralph Waldo Emerson

God is Truth. To be true, to hate every form of falsehood, to live
a brave, true, real life – that is to love God.
Frederick Robertson

It is written, 'For God is light' – not the light seen by these eyes of ours, but that which the heart sees upon hearing of the words 'He is Truth'.
St Augustine of Hippo

Indeed it is not in human nature to deceive others for any long time, without in a measure deceiving ourselves also.
John Henry Newman

Time and Truth are friends, although there are many moments hostile to truth.
Joseph Joubert

The thing from which the world suffers just now more than from any other evil is not the assertion of falsehoods, but endless and irrepressible repetition of half-truths.
G. K. Chesterton

The sin against the Holy Spirit is the sin against new life, against self-emergence, against the Holy fecund innerness of each person. It can be committed quite as easily against oneself as against another.
M. C. Richards

PROVERBS

Truth is God's daughter.
Spanish proverb

It's the deaf people that create the lies.
Irish proverb

When a man say him do not mind, then mind him.
African-American proverb

Speak the truth but leave immediately after.
Yugoslav proverb

HUMOUR

Little girl: 'Mummy, do all fairy tales begin with "Once upon a time . . ."?'
Mother: 'No, darling. Some start with, "Sorry I'm so late, dear, I was detained at the office."'

If you think fishermen are the biggest liars in the world, ask a jogger how far he runs every morning.
Larry Johnson

Clever is when you believe only half of what you hear. Brilliant is when you know which half to believe.
Orben

'Is that the Schonheimer residence?' – 'No, you must have dialled the wrong number.' – 'Are you sure?' – 'Have I ever lied to you before?'

Truth is a good dog; but beware of barking too close at the heels of an error, lest you get your brains kicked out.
Samuel Taylor Coleridge

A young man whose father had been hanged was faced with a Life Insurance proposal form. After the usual questions enquiring about any hereditary diseases there was one asking for the cause of death of his parents. He put: 'Mother died of pneumonia. Father was taking part in a public function when the platform gave way.'
Cecil Hunt

A lecturer in a theological college informed his class that the subject of his next lecture would be the sin of deceit and that, by way of preparation, he wished them all to read the 17th chapter of St Mark's Gospel. When the time came he asked how many members of his class had complied with his instructions. Every one of them raised a hand. 'Thank you,' said the lecturer. 'It is to people like you that today's lecture is especially addressed. There is no 17th chapter of Mark!'
K. Edwards

There is a story told about Cardinal Heenan in a book called *The R.C.s* The (apocryphal) story goes that he was once called as witness in a civil case. Counsel asked him, 'Would it be true to say, Archbishop, that you are the brains of the Catholic Church in Britain?' The Archbishop paused for a moment, then answered, 'Yes'. Later he told a friend, 'You know, I thought for a moment he had me there, then I realised that I was on oath.'
J. Vose

WORD PICTURES

No one possesses the truth, everyone is searching for it. . . . One does not possess the truth, and I need the truth of other seekers. This is my experience with the thousands of Algerians whose existence I share and whose questions are my questions.
Bishop Claverie of Oban, murdered by Muslim Extremists, August 1996

Lie not; but let thy heart be true to God.
Thy mouth to it, thy actions to them both;
cowards tell lies, and those that fear the rod;
the stormy working soul spits lies and froth.
Dare to be true. Nothing can need a lie:
a fault, which needs it most, grows two thereby.
George Herbert

When Abby Mann's film *Judgement at Nuremburg*, was scheduled for transmission on American television, the American Gas Association succeeded in having any mention of Nazi gas chambers removed from the script. And the American Florists' Association have threatened to remove their sponsorship of any drama serial in which bereaved characters talk about donation to charity being given in lieu of flowers!

In the book *The Assisi Underground*, a Franciscan priest admits that he had become 'a cheat and a liar' – all in the name of God. What had he done? During the final months of World War II the Germans had occupied much of northern Italy and had begun

191

rounding up all Italian Jews for transportation to the gas chambers in Germany. Almost daily frightened Jews knocked on the door of the Franciscan monastery seeking refuge. What was the priest to do? After earnest prayer, he took the hapless refugees in and kept them in secret quarters.

When SS officers knocked at the door of the monastery, as they did at frequent intervals, asking if any Jews had been there, the priest had to make a moral decision. He could tell the truth and turn his secret 'guests' over to their sworn enemies, thus ensuring their death by becoming partners in a fracture of the Fifth Commandment, or he could tell a lie, thus sparing their lives, but breaking the Eighth Commandment!

Anon

USEFUL TEXTS

Truth:
    Attribute of God, *Isa. 65:16*
    Spirit of, *John 15:26*
    Christ is, *John 14:6*
    Word of God is, *John 17:17*

See also: B53 Consecrated in Truth
          C47 The indwelling Spirit
          C49 Receive the Holy Spirit

A48
WORSHIP

'All these joined in continuous prayer, together with several
women, including Mary the mother of Jesus,
and with his brothers.'
Acts 1:14

QUOTATIONS

As soon as we are with God in faith and in love, we are in prayer.
François Fenelon

He who does not praise God while here on earth shall in eternity
be dumb.
John of Ruysbroeck

Begin the day with God, and 'tis probable 'twill end with him and
goodness.
Thomas Wilson

The praise of Christ expressed by the liturgy is effective in so far
as it continues to inform the humblest tasks.
Roger Schutz

Liturgy and evangelism are simply the inside and the outside of
the one act of 'proclaiming the Lord's death'.
John A. C. T. Robinson

The great danger is that liturgy creates a world of things over
against the secular, instead of a vision of the sacredness of the
secular.
Eric James

Is there anyone who, when in fear and trembling amid dangers,
did not find that to invoke the Name of Power at once brought
confidence and banished apprehension? Is there anyone who,

when tossed and fluctuating amid doubts, did not find that, when we invoked the Name of Clearness, there shone forth instant Certainty? You may make proof of it.
St Bernard of Clairvaux

'Sing to the Lord a new song,' the psalm tells us.
'I do sing!' you may reply.
You sing, of course you sing. I can hear you.
But make sure that your life sings the same tune as your mouth.
Sing with your voices.
Sing with your hearts.
Sing with your lips.
Sing with your lives.
Be yourselves what the words are about!
If you live good lives, you yourselves are
the songs of new life!
St Augustine of Hippo

Some people praise with their hands up like that – I do it sometimes but I'm a stubborn man – if everybody does it I keep my hands in my pockets and the other way round.
George Carey

WORD PICTURES

One of the beautiful things about the life of the Venerable Bede was his joy in worship. When quite a boy, about thirteen years of age, a great sickness passed over the monastery, and many of the monks lay sick and dying; and at last only two were left who could sing the daily offices – the abbot, Ceolfrid, and young Bede. Together they met – at midnight – and during the day – seven times in all – and sang the beautiful psalms and antiphones. Dull work it would seem for a young boy, perhaps. Yet Bede never tired of his acts of worship. When later he found his work in writing books and in teaching, he was never too busy to attend the services. 'The angels must not miss me among the brethren,' he would say, 'or they would ask, "Where is Bede?"'

It was a beautiful ending to such a life of worship that the last words of the blind old man as he sat in his bare little cell, dying, were the glad hymn, 'Glory to the Father, and to the Son, and to the Holy Ghost'. Bede knew something of the joy of worship.
Anon

Almost above the pulpit in the north clerestory in Exeter Cathedral is the Minstrels' Gallery, built in the twelfth century, where twelve angels are depicted playing on various instruments of music. Manchester Cathedral also has carved angels on the principals supporting the roof of the nave. On the north side the angels hold wind instruments, and on the south side stringed instruments. Lincoln Cathedral has its famous 'Angel Choir', so-called from the sculptured figures of angels playing on musical instruments, fifteen on either side.

The old builders would have us bear in mind that in our worship we are joining with that perfect worship of heaven, where the angels praise God eternally.
Anon

On one of the great trunk roads of India a missionary saw a woman measuring herself in prostrations along the ground – a familiar form of pilgrimage. Through dust, dirt and heat she moved onwards, lying down, marking the farthest point her hand could reach, and rising and starting again from that point to prostrate herself and reach forward again. She must have made seven or eight hundred prostrations to cover a mile. He asked where she was going and she named a shrine in the Himalayas, where from some cleft in a valley a burst of natural gas would, from time to time, leap and take fire in the air and vanish – a fleeting manifestation of God. It meant for her a journey of a thousand miles. Why was she going? *Uski darshan*, she said – two words and no more: 'Vision of him'.
Anon

When we make the sign of the cross we are doing something that takes us back to the earliest days of Christianity. The cross was a dreaded idea to the pagan world of Rome, but the Christian Church at once adopted it as a glorious boast, as we see from St Paul: Gal. 6:14, Phil. 2:8-9. It is thought that the custom of signing oneself with the cross, at any rate with a small cross on the forehead, goes back to the days of the Apostles. Certainly, before the year 200 we find the Christian writer Tertullian, in North Africa, writing as follows:

> When we go in or out, when we dress and put on our shoes, at the bath, at the table, when the lights are brought, when we go to bed, when we sit down, whatever it is that occupies us, we mark the forehead with the sign of the cross.

Anon

Once when St Francis was about to eat with Brother Leo, he was greatly delighted to hear a nightingale singing. So he suggested to his companion that they also should sing praise to God alternately with the bird. While Leo was pleading that he was no singer, Francis lifted up his voice and, phrase by phrase, sang his duet with the nightingale. Thus they continued from vespers to lauds, until the saint had to admit himself beaten by the bird. Thereupon the nightingale flew on to his hand, where he praised it to the skies and fed it. Then he gave it his blessing and it flew away.

John Moorman

There is a story of some monks in France who were popular for their loving sympathy and kind deeds; but not one of them could sing. Try as they would, the music in their services was a failure, and it became a great grief to them that only in their hearts could they 'make melody to the Lord'. One day a travelling monk, a great singer, asked for hospitality. Great was their joy, for now they could have him sing at their services, and they hoped to keep him with them always. But that night an angel came to the abbot in a dream. 'Why was there no music in your chapel tonight? We always listen for the beautiful music that rises in your services.' 'You must be mistaken!' cried the abbot. 'Usually we have no

music worth hearing; but tonight we had a trained singer with a wonderful voice, and he sang the service for us. For the first time in all these years our music was beautiful.' The angel smiled. 'And yet up in heaven we heard nothing,' he said softly.
Sunday Companion

USEFUL TEXTS

Worship:
    Of God, *Exod. 20:3; Deut. 5:7; Matt. 4:10*
    Of Christ, *John 9:38; Heb. 1:6; Rev. 5:8-9*
    Attitude in, *Lev. 10:3; Ps. 5:7; John 4:24*

See also: B25 Quiet – time for prayer
             B29 The Eucharist
             C32 Prayer

B1
WAITING ON THE LORD

'Stay awake, because you do not know when the master
of the house is coming.'
Mark 13:35

QUOTATIONS

Truthful soul, prepare thy heart for this Bridegroom, that he may
vouchsafe to come unto thee, and to dwell within thee.
Thomas à Kempis

But we like sentries are obliged to stand in starless nights, and
wait the appointed hour.
John Dryden

Let us pray so to live that no crisis-hour will find us unprepared.
C. Albright

To him that waits all things reveal themselves, provided that he
has the courage not to deny, in the darkness, what he has seen in
the light.
Coventry Patmore

Throughout the whole (New Testament) there runs the conviction
that the time looked forward to by the prophets has in fact arrived
in history with the advent of Jesus Christ. . . . The time of Jesus is
kairos – a time of opportunity. To embrace the opportunity means
salvation; to neglect it, disaster. There is no third course.
John Marsh

PROVERB

People count up the faults of those who keep them waiting.
French proverb

WORD PICTURES

In the not too distant past, a company would send to a shopkeeper about a week or so ahead, a card saying, 'Our Mr Smith will have the pleasure of waiting on you, on such and such a day.' The representative duly arrives and waits inside the shop for the buyer to be free. He comes expecting an order and promises to return if one is not forthcoming. So God wants us to wait upon him – come into his presence and expect an order from him.
Anon

Such were the elements fused in mankind, towards the eighth century of Rome, in the 192nd Olympiad and according to Jewish chronology, at the end of four thousand years from the creation.

It was, according to the first word which fell from the lips of Jesus, 'the fullness of time'. The empire, paganism, philosophy, official Judaism, all human forces had accomplished their evolution; the world was dying, enslaved by Roman policy, degraded and brought to despair by false religions, asking philosophers in vain for the secrets of life and virtue. Judaism itself was in the death-throe, faithless to its destiny. There was never a more critical moment; but God was over all, and among his elect people, humble souls prayed and hoped. Beyond Judaism, a vague expectation, to which poets, historians and the Sibylline books bear witness, was astir, and kept the world in suspense; such a presentiment as goes before all the great events of history.

The birth of Jesus was at hand.
Père Didon

'As unhappy as the man that has not seen the Advent Images.' This was an old Yorkshire saying. In the north of England it was the custom during Advent to dress two dolls, one to represent the Saviour, another the Virgin Mary. These images were paraded around the houses and a halfpenny was asked for from the people who saw them. This became known as the 'Vessel Cup', and was associated with the goodwill song:

God bless the master of this house,
the mistress also,
and all the little children
that round the table go.

These dolls were surrounded by evergreen leaves, and everybody to whom the 'Advent Image' was shown was allowed to take a leaf. This was carefully kept as it was believed to be a remedy for toothache.
Don Lewis

The truth of Christianity depends on two fundamental realities which we can never lose sight of; both are closely connected. The first reality is called 'God', the second one 'man'. Christianity arises from a special mutual relationship between God and man. In recent times there have been long discussions as to whether this relationship is God-centred or man-centred. There will never be a satisfactory answer to this question if we continue to consider the two terms of the question separately.

In fact Christianity is man-centred precisely because it is fully God-centred; and simultaneously it is God-centred, thanks to its being so unusually man-centred. It is just the mystery of the Incarnation, which, in itself, explains this relationship. It is for this reason that Christianity is not only a 'religion of advent', but Advent itself. Christianity lives out the mystery of God's real coming to man; this is the reality which gives it life.
Pope John Paul II

There is an even richer kind of waiting, a waiting which has a special point to it – waiting for the fulfilment of a process which has already begun. When we plant seeds in the garden we do not grudge the time spent waiting for flowers to appear; we know that time is needed for the seeds to ripen and the plants to grow.

The philosopher, the writer and the artist do not resent the time spent in apparently aimless brooding, when they know that a new idea is developing and taking shape. And, above all, the mother expecting a child knows that her time of waiting is not time wasted; she knows that the child within her is growing and coming close to the moment of birth. The people of Israel knew all these emotions during the long years they were asked to wait for the coming of the Saviour. They were sometimes bored, anxious, impatient, at other times full of the joy of anticipation. Only gradually did the form in which God would reveal himself take shape.

Only gradually did their expectation of a Messiah, a national hero, give way to the expectation of a universal liberator for all creation, Emmanuel: 'In those days ten men out of nations speaking every language will seize hold of the robe of a single Jew and say: We will go with you, for we have heard that God is with you.' (Zacc 8:23). Theirs was a creative waiting. The stage was being prepared for God's entrance. His people were being given time to grow and mature, fitted to receive the Saviour among men. Their faith put down roots, their hope became the impulse of their lives.
John Harriott

USEFUL TEXTS

Waiting:
    On the Lord, *Ps 27:14; Isa. 40:31*
    For the promise of God, *Acts 1:4*
    For guidance and teaching, *Ps. 25:5*
    For the Coming of Christ, *1 Cor. 1:7; 1 Thess. 1:10*

See also: A1 Value of time
           A22 Seeking God
           A35 Preparing for death
           B21 Trust in God
           C1 Liberation from fear
           C36 The Day of the Lord

B2
THE GOOD NEWS

'Go up on a high mountain, joyful messenger to Zion.
Shout with a loud voice, joyful messenger to Jerusalem.'
Isaiah 40:9

QUOTATIONS

The glory of the Gospel is that when the Church is absolutely
different from the world, she invariably attracts it.
Martyn Lloyd-Jones

Humble and self-forgetting we must be always but diffident and
apologetic about the Gospel never.
James S. Stewart

The preaching of the Gospel and its acceptance imply a social
revolution whereby the hungry are fed and justice becomes the
right of all.
Cardinal Suenans

Jesus alone is able to offer himself as the sufficient illustration of
his own doctrine.
Hensley Henson

We have no such proof that Caesar died in the Capital as we
possess that Christ suffered in the manner revealed in the
Gospels.
Dr Samuel Johnson

The strength to see the good side of things should be
characteristic of the Christian. If the Gospel really means 'good
news' then being a Christian means being a happy man, one who
spreads joy. 'Gloomy faces,' said St Philip Neri, 'aren't made for
the happy house of Paradise.'
Pope John Paul I

I wish those people who tell us that Christianity won't work would be kind enough to tell us what will. Moreover, how do they know that it won't? You cannot say anything is a failure until it has been tried. When was Christianity last tried? G. K. Chesterton stated an important truth when he wrote, 'Christianity has not been tried and found wanting: it has been found hard and not tried.'
S. J. Marriott

HUMOUR

One Sunday morning a minister had been telling his congregation that there was a sermon in every blade of grass. The following day, when he was cutting his grass in the vicarage garden, a parishioner who was passing called out: 'That's right, Vicar. Keep them short.'
Anon

WORD PICTURES

'I can't tell you just now what the moral of that is, but I shall remember it in a bit.' 'Perhaps it hasn't one,' Alice ventured to remark. 'Tut, tut, child!' said the Duchess. 'Everything's got a moral, if only you can find it.'
Lewis Carroll

It should never be forgotten that Christianity did not come into the world through the editorial page; it came through the news columns. It was a news event – front page, stop-the-press news. Something happened. 'The Word became flesh and dwelt among us.' The Gospel was first preached as news. Whenever it has been preached with power, it has been preached as news. Whenever it has dwindled down to mere advice, become merely editorial Christianity, it has evaporated into a cloud as vague as fog.
Halford E. Luccock

It was one of the dramatic days in the history of our islands when Paulinus came to the Court of King Edwin with the good news from Galilee (and with a gold and ivory comb from the Pope). The king declared that he would consider with his friends and counsellors, and if they were of his opinion they might all together be cleansed in Christ, the Fountain of Life. It is Bede who tells us what followed.

The king, holding a council with the wise men, asked of everyone in particular what he thought of the new doctrine, and the new worship that was preached. To which the chief of his own priests, Coifi, immediately answered:

'O king, consider what this is which is now preached to us; for I verily declare to you that the religion which we have hitherto professed has, as far as I can learn, no virtue in it. For none of your people has applied himself more diligently to the worship of our gods than I; and yet there are many who receive greater favours from you, and are more preferred than I, and are more prosperous in all their undertakings. Now, if the gods were good for anything, they would rather forward me, who have been more careful to serve them. It remains, therefore, that if upon examination you find those new doctrines better, we immediately receive them.'

Another of the king's chief men, approving of his words and exhortations, presently added:

'The present life of man, O king, seems to me, in comparison of that time which is unknown to us, like to the swift flight of a sparrow through the room wherein you sit at supper in winter, with your commanders and ministers, and a good fire in the midst, while the storms of rain and snow prevail abroad. The sparrow, flying in at one door and immediately out at another, while he is within is safe from the wintry storm; but after a short space of fair weather he immediately vanishes out of your sight, into the dark winter from which he had emerged. So this life of man appears for a short space, but of what went before, or what is to follow, we know nothing. If, therefore, this new doctrine contains something more certain, it seems justly to deserve to be followed.'

The king gave his licence to Paulinus to preach the Gospel, renouncing idolatry, declaring his own Faith in Christ.   *Anon*

It was a great day in a small mountain church in the Philippines, when twenty-three adults and young people confessed their faith in Christ by baptism.

At the conclusion of the service, a visitor, a Mr Taglucop, congratulated the minister. 'You must be exceedingly happy to have so many new believers enter the fellowship of your church today.' 'Of course I am, but I'm not the person most responsible for this group being ready for membership today. Seventeen of these twenty-three have come because one man visited their homes and prepared them for membership through prayer and Bible study. He's sitting back there on the last bench.'

Mr Taglucop went back to talk with this remarkable steward of the Gospel, and immediately noticed that one of the man's legs was several times normal size. Amazed that the man could have visited seventeen people whose homes were all in the steep mountain regions, he asked, 'How can you manage with that leg?' 'God gives me strength to drag it along,' was the simple reply.

'But I hid in these mountains during the last war,' protested Mr Taglucop, 'I know how steep the trails are.' The man replied: 'Then you know how God provides us with roots and saplings to pull ourselves along.' Mr Taglucop then advised the man to go to a hospital and have his leg treated before it was too late. When he heard that this treatment would take several months, the man shook his head. 'There is no time. You see there are seven more families in the mountains to whom I must first bring the gospel.' This earnest witness to the Good News died soon thereafter, on his way up a mountain to visit one of those homes.

B. H. Pearson

USEFUL TEXTS

Good News:
  Of Christ, *2 Cor. 2:12*
  Preached by Paul, *Acts 14:15*
  Of God, *Rom. 1:1*
  As Refreshment, *Prov. 15:30*

See also: B9 Revelation
           B12 On a mission
           B24 Go tell everyone
           C2 Joy of salvation

B3
JOY IN CHRIST

'Be happy at all times.'
1 Thessalonians 5:16

QUOTATIONS

Joy is the serious business of heaven.
C. S. Lewis

Sour godliness is the devil's religion.
John Wesley

Happiness is a wondrous commodity, the more you give, the more you have.
Voltaire

Contentment consists not in great wealth, but in few wants.
Epictetus

Fortify yourself with contentment, for this is an impregnable fortress.
Epictetus

No one has a right to consume happiness without producing it.
Helen Keller

The most evident sign of wisdom is continued cheerfulness.
Michel de Montaigne

Grief can take care of itself, but to get the full value of a joy you must have somebody to divide it with.
Mark Twain

Those who bring sunshine to the lives of others cannot keep it from themselves.
James M. Barrie

Happiness is a perfume you cannot pour on others without getting a few drops on yourself.
Ralph Waldo Emerson

The sweet mark of a Christian is not faith, or even love, but joy.
Samuel M. Shoemaker

Happiness is as a butterfly, which, when pursued, is always beyond our grasp, but which, if you will sit down quietly, may alight upon you.
Nathaniel Hawthorne

Joy is not the absence of pain. Joy is the awareness of God's loving presence within you.
John Catoir

HUMOUR

'There was a little Indian girl at school today,' announced my son proudly. 'Does she speak English?' I asked. 'No,' came the reply. 'But it doesn't matter because she laughs in English.'

A couple called a friend and sang 'Happy Birthday' into the telephone. When they had finished their off-key rendition they discovered they had the wrong number! 'Don't let it bother you,' said the stranger. 'You folks can sure use the practice.'

An Englishman, a Frenchman and a Russian were trying to define true happiness. 'True happiness,' said the Englishman, 'is when you return home tired after work and find a gin and tonic waiting for you.' 'You English have no romance,' countered the Frenchman. 'True happiness is when you go on a business trip, find a pretty girl who entertains you, and then you part without regrets.' 'You are both wrong,' concluded the Russian. 'Real true happiness is when you are home in bed at four o'clock in the morning and there is a hammering at the front door and there stand members of the Secret Police, who say to you, "Ivan Ivanovitch, you are under arrest", and you are able to reply, "Sorry, Ivan Ivanovitch lives next door!"'
Anon

There is a story of an Irishman who died suddenly and went up for divine judgement, feeling extremely uneasy. He didn't think he had done much good on earth! There was a queue ahead of him, so he settled down to look and listen. After consulting his big book, Christ said to the first man in the queue: 'I see here that I was hungry and you gave me to eat. Good man! Go on into heaven.' To the second he said: 'I was thirsty and you gave me to drink,' and to the third: 'I was in prison and you visited me.' And so it went on. As each man ahead of him was sent to heaven the Irishman examined his conscience and felt he had a great deal to fear. He'd never given anyone food or drink, he hadn't visited prisoners or the sick. Then his turn came. Trembling he watched Christ examining the book. Then Christ looked up and said: 'Well, there's not much written here, but you did do something: I was sad and discouraged and depressed: you came and told me funny stories, made me laugh and cheered me up. Get along to heaven!'

That joke makes the point that no form of charity should be neglected or undervalued.

Anon

WORD PICTURES

Mother Teresa tells of a young Maltese girl who joined her order. On the first day she was sent to the Home for the Dying. When she came down she was radiant. Mother Teresa asked why she was so happy. The girl said: 'Mother, I have held Christ in my hands for three hours.'

A company of pilgrims were on the road, all carrying a burden of some sort, yet bearing them cheerfully, and thinking more of the purpose of their journey than of its hardships, as they went along together singing. An angel joined the little band, and passing from one to another, threw into each of the burdens a couple of little white seeds. Soon the seeds began to sprout, until they became a pair of glorious wings which carried the traveller, burden and all, along the dusty road.

Later on, a similar party were travelling on the same road, with downcast faces, and greatly complaining of the heavy burdens

they carried. The angel passed again, but left with them no gift of wings. 'Why do you not give them wings?' he was asked. 'They look so downcast and gloomy, surely they need them more than the others.' 'I have only the seeds,' replied the angel, 'and the seeds will not grow unless they have the right soil. They will flourish only in cheerfulness and helpfulness, but will perish at once in that atmosphere of grumbling.'
Anon

There are two kinds of happiness for mortal men: there is that which is carnal and imperfect, and hangs on circumstances, and the health of the body and suchlike things; and there is that which is spiritually perfect, which hangs on nothing else than the doing of the will of God almighty.
R. H. Benson

There is a Jewish Rabbinic saying which has a wealth of truth in it: 'At the judgement day a man will be called to account for all the good things he might have enjoyed and did not enjoy.'

Incredibly, in the midst of fear and loneliness, I was filled with joy, for I knew without a vestige of doubt, that God was with me, and that nothing that they could do to me could change that. I knew too that, in some strange way, the pain which I had suffered was his gift, and that far from being a sign of his lack of care or wrath, it was an unmistakable sign of his love. In some mysterious way, I had been permitted to share in the mystery of life and death, of the Incarnation and the Cross.
Sheila Cassidy

The word happiness comes from the Greek, meaning 'without pining'. God pines for nothing because he is whole and complete in himself. He wants this for each of us. He made us in his image so that we would know true happiness. We do well to imitate our Maker by loving the lover within. This is the first step to a life of happiness and service.
John Catoir

There are nine requisites for contented living:
Health enough to make work a pleasure.
Wealth enough to support your needs.
Strength to battle with difficulties and overcome them.
Grace enough to confess your sins and forsake them.
Patience enough to toil until some good is accomplished.
Charity enough to see some good in your neighbour.
Love enough to move you to be useful and helpful to others.
Faith enough to make real the things of God.
Hope enough to remove all anxious fears concerning the future.
Johann Wolfgang von Goethe

Yesterday the *Daily Mail* told us that the average six-year-old laughs 300 times a day but most grown-ups do it only 47 times and some sad individuals laugh a mere six times a day. Evidently laughter is described medically as internal aerobics because it quickens the heart, expands circulation, works muscles, enhances oxygen intake and boosts the immune system so if you laugh a lot you're less likely to get flu.

In fact it sounds as therapeutic as a week in a health farm or a daily half-hour jog and it's effortless and free. Above all, laughter is infectious. It lifts the heart and cheers the day.

People don't laugh because their life is easy but because they're givers and survivors. Marti Caine used laughter to combat pain and occasionally terror.

'So many people in show business come from a deprived background,' she said, 'you've got to laugh or you'd go mad. Adversity breeds either comedy or bitterness.' When she was diagnosed in 1989 as having malignant lymphoma, she was told initially that her life expectancy was 18 months but she survived until 1995.

P.F.

USEFUL TEXTS

Joy:
    In the Holy Spirit, *Rom. 14:17*
    Of the Lord, *Neh. 8:10*
    In trials, *Jas. 1:2*
    When a sinner repents, *Luke 15:10*

See also: B51 One with Christ
           C2   Joy of salvation
           C47 The indwelling spirit

B4
MARY – HANDMAID OF GOD

'I am the handmaid of the Lord,' said Mary,
'Let what you have said be done to me.'
Luke 1:38

QUOTATIONS

To work a wonder, God would have her shown, at once, a Bud, and yet a Rose full-blown.
Robert Herrick

Mary's humble acceptance of the divine will is the starting point of the story of the redemption of the human race from sin.
Alan Richardson

The feast we call *Annunciatio Mariae*, when the angel came to Mary and brought her the message from God, may be fittingly called the feast of Christ's humanity, for then began our deliverance.
Martin Luther

Since God has revealed very little to us about Mary, men who know nothing of who and what she was only reveal themselves when they try to add something to what God has told us about her.
Thomas Merton

Mary is our pattern of Faith, both in the reception and in the study of Divine Truth. She does not think it enough to accept, she dwells upon it; not enough to possess, she uses it; not enough to assent, she develops it; not enough to submit the Reason, she reasons upon it; not indeed reasoning first, add believing afterwards, with Zacharius, yet first believing without reasoning, next from love and reverence, reasoning after believing.
John Henry Newman

HUMOUR

A Protestant clergyman was visiting an orphanage, and the children were each reciting their prayers for him to hear. One little boy who had previously been to a Catholic school, after finishing the Our Father began the Hail Mary. 'No, no!' said the clergyman. 'We don't want to hear about her – go on to the Creed.' The little boy did so, but stopped suddenly when he came to 'born of the . . .' and said: 'Here she comes again – what shall I do now, sir?' Indeed we cannot have Jesus without Mary.

WORD PICTURES

When Mary Immaculate, the finest and most fragrant flower of all creation, said in answer to the angel's greeting; 'Behold the handmaid of the Lord,' she accepted the honour of divine motherhood, which was in that moment realised within her. And we, born once in our father Adam, formerly the adopted sons of God but fallen from that high estate, are now once more brothers, adopted sons of the Father, restored to his adoption by the redemption which has already begun. At the foot of the Cross we shall all be children of Mary, with that same Jesus whom she has conceived today. From today onwards she will be Mother of God and our Mother too.
Pope John XXIII

I sing of a maiden
that is makeles;
King of all kings
to he son she ches.

He came al so still
there his mother was,
as dew in April
that falleth on the grass.

He came al so still
to his mother's bour
as dew in April
that falleth on the flour.

He came al so still
there his mother lay,
as dew in April
that falleth on the spray.

Mother and maiden
was never none but she;
well may such a lady
goddes mother be.
*From the Sloan MS. No one knows who wrote this fifteenth-century carol. (In the first verse, 'makeles' means 'matchless';
'ches' means 'chose'.)*

This is that blessed Mary, pre-elect God's Virgin.
Gone is a great while, and she
dwelt young in Nazareth of Galilee.
Unto God's will she brought devout respect,
profound simplicity of intellect,
and supreme patience. From her mother's knee
faithful and hopeful; wise in charity;
strong in grave peace; in pity circumspect.
So held she through her girlhood; as it were
an angel-watered lily, that near God
grows and is quiet. Till, one dawn at home
she woke in her white bed and had no fear
at all, yet wept till sunshine, and felt awed
because the fullness of the time was come.
Dante Gabriel Rossetti

USEFUL TEXTS

Mary:
    Mother of Jesus, *Matt. 1:1-16*
    Present at first miracle, *John 2:1-10*
    Present at crucifixion, *John 19: 25-26*
    Cared for by the disciple, *John 19:27*

See also: A4   Emmanuel – Mary's child
           A40 The equality of women
           B7   Mary, Mother of God

B5
A Saviour Is Born for Us

'Today in the town of David a Saviour has been born to you;
he is Christ the Lord.'
Luke 2:11

QUOTATIONS

For what greater thing is there than that God should become man?
St John of Damascus

That there was no room in the inn was symbolic of what was to
happen to Jesus. The only place where there was room for him
was on the Cross.
William Barclay

The shepherds did not go to Bethlehem seeking the birth of a
great man, or a famous teacher, or a national hero. They were
promised a saviour.
H. H. Brown

Verbally in Scripture, visually in sacrament, Jesus Christ is set
forth as the only Saviour of sinners.
John R. W. Stott

Since God is approaching man, it is not a degradation, but a
triumph of his love, that he should come so far down to meet him.
R. H. Benson

I think, therefore, that the purpose and cause of the Incarnation
was that he might illuminate the world by his wisdom and excite
it to the love of himself.
Peter Abelard

If we really know Christ as our Saviour, our hearts are broken and
cannot be hard, and we cannot refuse forgiveness.
Martin Lloyd-Jones

Jesus was born twice. The birth at Bethlehem was a birth into a life of weakness. The second time he was born from the grave – 'the first-born from the dead' – into the glory of heaven and the throne of God.
Andrew Murray

Christmas is a cosmic celebration of the beginning of something which we cannot adequately describe: it is a liturgy that sings of the new covenant between the God of eternity and man in history.
Pope Paul VI

The birthday of the Lord is the birthday of peace. As the Apostle says, 'He is our peace, who made us both one.' For whether we be Jew or Gentile, 'through him we both have access to the Father'.
St Leo the Great

May each Christmas, as it comes, find us more and more like him who at this time became a little child, for our sake; more simple-minded, more humble, more affectionate, more resigned, more happy, more full of God.
John Henry Newman

Wisdom unsearchable, God the invisible, Love indestructible, in frailty appears.
G. Kendrick

On this night, as we Christians have done every year for 20 centuries, we recall that God's reign is now in this world and that Christ has inaugurated the fulness of time. His birth attests that God is now marching with us in history, that we do not go alone, and that our aspiration for peace, for justice, for a reign of divine law, for something holy, is far from earth's realities. We can hope for it, not because we humans are able to construct that realm of happiness which God's holy words proclaim, but because the builder of a reign of justice, of love and of peace is already in the midst of us.
Oscar Romero

HUMOUR

My sister went to a nativity play where the little Virgin Mary
became exasperated with the little Lord Jesus and said fiercely:
'Stop your snivelling, Jesus.'

At another nativity, when asked, 'Is there any room at the inn?'
the child replied, 'Oh yes,' making the story of the stable quite
redundant.

Finally, at yet another nativity, in answer to: 'And what shall the
child be called?', the reply came back: 'Colin.'
Olive Miles

Small daughter: 'Mummy, how many more days is it before
Christmas?'
Mother: 'Not many. Why do you ask?'
Small daughter: 'I just wondered if it's near enough for me to start
being a good little girl.'

It was Christmas morning and the family were plodding home
from church through the snow, discussing the service. They all
seemed to have a bad word to say.

Dad thought the bells had been rung dreadfully; Mum thought
the hymns were badly chosen; the eldest son fell asleep during the
sermon and his twin sister could not agree with the prayers. All
except for the youngest boy who said: 'I don't know what you are
all complaining about; I thought it was a damn good show for 10p!'

A little girl was trying to persuade her father to come to her school
nativity play. 'I'm to be one of the three kings,' she said, 'and carry
the frankenstein.'

One Christmas Eve the British Ambassador in Washington
received a telephone call from the local radio station asking:
'What would you like for Christmas?' The ambassador thought
for a while and gave his answer. The next day, he heard the
announcer say: 'We have been running a poll on what foreign
ambassadors want for Christmas. The French Ambassador said, 'I
earnestly desire that the next year should be a year of peace in the

world.' The Russian ambassador hoped for a year of justice for all men. The German Ambassador wanted to see a greater sharing of wealth in the world. And the British Ambassador said: 'I would like a box of crystallised fruit."
Sunday Express

WORD PICTURES

One Christmas Eve a prosperous businessman was hurrying to a butcher shop before closing time. 'Buying your Christmas turkey?' a friend asked. 'No, hot dogs,' he answered.

Then he explained how, in the Depression, a bank failure suddenly wiped out his fortune. He faced Christmas with no job, no money for gifts and less than a dollar for food. He and his wife and small daughter said grace before dinner that year and then ate hot dogs – a whole kennel of them in fact. His wife had given each frankfurter toothpicks for legs and broom straws for tails and whiskers. Their child was enchanted and her infectious delight spread merriment among them all. After dinner they gave thanks again for the most loving and festive time they'd ever had. 'Now it's tradition,' the man said. 'Hot dogs for Christmas – to remind us of that happy day when we realised we still had one another and our God-given sense of humour.'
Anon

There used to be a custom of making at Christmas little images of paste, called 'Yule doughs', which were given by bakers to their customers. Originally these images were intended as representations of the child Jesus and the Virgin. The 'Yule doughs', however, have long since degenerated into puddings and mince pies made simply to be eaten.
Don Lewis

The Russians have for centuries told a legend about a young medieval prince, Alexis, who lived (as Russian princes commonly did) in a sumptuous palace, while all around, in filthy hovels, lived hundreds of poor peasants. The Prince was moved with compassion for these poor folk and determined to better their lot. So he began to visit them. But as he moved in and out among them he found that he'd got absolutely no point of contact with them. They treated him with enormous respect, almost worship; but he was never able to win their confidences, still less their affection, and he returned to the palace a defeated and disappointed young man.

Then one day a very different man came among the people. He was a rough-and-ready young doctor who also wanted to devote his life to serving the poor. He started by renting a filthy rat-ridden shack in one of the back streets. He made no pretence of being superior – his clothes (like theirs) were old and tattered and he lived simply on the plainest food, often without knowing where the next meal was coming from. He made no money from his profession because he treated most people free and gave away his medicines. Before long this young doctor had won the respect and affection of all those people as Prince Alexis had never succeeded in doing. He was one of them. And little by little he transformed the whole spirit of the place, settling quarrels, reconciling enemies, helping people to live decent lives.

No one ever guessed that this young doctor was in fact the Prince himself, who had abandoned his palace and gone down among his people to become one of them. That's just what God did on that first Christmas Day. He came right down side by side with us to help us to become the sort of beings he intends us to be.
John Williams

Archbishop Romero said in words that make us shiver to this day: 'I am glad, brothers and sisters, that they have murdered priests in this country, because it would be very sad if in a country where they are murdering the people so horrifically there were no priests among the victims. It is a sign that the Church has become truly incarnate in the problems of the people.'

These words, so brutal at first sight, are far-seeing. There can be neither faith nor Gospel without incarnation. And with a crucified people there can be no incarnation without the cross. Ignacio Ellacuría said many times that the specifically Christian task is to fight to eradicate sin by bearing its burden. This sin brings death, but taking it on gives credibility. By sharing in the cross of the

Salvadoreans the Church becomes Salvadorean and thus credible. And although in the short term this murder is a great loss, in the long term it is a great gain; we are building a Church that is really Christian and really Salvadorean. Christians have shown truly that they are Salvadoreans and thus that Salvadoreans can really be Christians. This is no small fruit of so much bloodshed in El Salvador . . .
Jon Sobrino

An Irish Christmas
Christmas was *the* special feast and preparation for it began in late November. Lime from their own kilns was slackened for the big whitewash job within and without. Even the loose stone walls got a lick. The Christmas *share* (cheer) was purchased soon after Aonach Mor na Nollag – the Christmas Fair – when perhaps, a pig or a calf was sold. The woman of the house, accompanied by her husband, took off to Geesala on the ass and cart if they had one, if not the pardoga (panniers) for their long day's shopping. When they arrived home late in the evening there were many helping hands willing to unload their purchases knowing the reward would be a few raisins or currants which were a novelty to us. After that the fruit had to be carefully hidden for very good reasons. We as children, particularly the girls, the boys rarely persevered, made our own spiritual contribution, a bouquet of 4,000 Hail Marys, or as we called it a Christmas crown for Mary. These were said over a period of twenty-five nights commencing on November 30th. Our parents kept tally of the score to make sure there were no shortcuts taken. They may often have been words without thought, but somehow I do feel that to heaven they did go. On Christmas Eve all joined in the final prayers. Christmas supper was to us a lavish meal. The fruits of the harvest, wheat, oats and potatoes were baked into bread in thanksgiving. And so we had white, currant and oatmeal bread as well as boxty for supper. My father would also have salted mackerel. He led us in prayer as we stood around the table for the special Christmas Grace.
Maire Ni Ghachain remembers her childhood 'Dubhloch'

Light looked down and beheld Darkness:
'Thither will I go,' said the Light.
Peace looked down and beheld War:
'Thither will I go,' said Peace.
Love looked down and beheld Hatred:
'Thither will I go,' said Love.
So came Light and shone.
So came Peace and gave rest.
So came Love and brought Life.
And the Word was made Flesh and dwelt among us.
Laurence Housman

USEFUL TEXTS

Saviour:
  Applied to Christ, *2 Tim. 1:10*
  Incarnation, *Matt. 1:18-21; John, 1:1-18*

See also: A4 Emmanuel – Mary's Child
           B3 Joy in Christ
           C2 Joy of salvation
           C7 The humanity of Christ

B6
The Family

'The Lord honours the father in his children, and
upholds the rights of a mother over her sons.'
Ecclesiasticus 3:2

Quotations

A happy family is but an earlier heaven.
John Bowring

A child is not a vase to be filled, but a fire to be lit.
Rabelais

Train up a child in the way you should have gone yourself.
Charles H. Spurgeon

Domestic happiness depends upon the ability to overlook.
Roy L. Smith

Few are born to do the great work of the world, but the work that
all can do is to make a small home circle brighter and better.
George Eliot

There is no law which lays it down that you must smile! But you
can make a gift of your smile; you can be the leaven of kindness in
your family.
John Paul II

That man will never be unwelcome to others who makes himself
agreeable to his own family.
Plautus

All happy families resemble one another; every unhappy family is
unhappy in its own way.
Leo Tolstoy

Every effort to make society sensitive to the importance of the family is a great service to humanity.
John Paul II

HUMOUR

One of the Puritan fathers, who imposed the strictest discipline on his family, greeted his daughter arriving late at the breakfast table:
    'Child of the Devil.'
To which she replied:
    'Good morning, Father.'

'So Carol, you're a housewife and a mother. And have you any children?'
Michael Barrymore

Teenager to mother: '"Wanting to make the world a better place to live in", and "cleaning up my room" are two different things!'
Leo Garel

A woman got on a bus with seven children. The conductor asked, 'Are these all yours, lady, or is it a picnic?'
    'They're all mine,' came the reply. 'And it's no picnic!'

The small boy had pestered his father with a number of questions that small boys usually do ask their fathers – 'Where, When, Why, What for', and so on. Finally, he asked, 'Daddy, what do they make asphalt roads of?' His father replied, 'That's the nine hundredth question you've asked me today. Do give me a little peace. What do you think would have happened to me if I had asked my father so many questions?' The boy thought about this and finally decided: 'You might perhaps have learned the answers to some of my questions.'

A proud parent called up the local newspaper and reported the birth of twins. The girl at the news desk didn't quite catch the message over the phone. 'Will you repeat that?' she asked. 'Not if I can help it,' was the reply.

There are questions no man can answer. And most of them are known to five-year-olds!

Dad volunteered to babysit one night so Mum could have an evening out. At bedtime he sent the youngsters upstairs to bed and settled down to look at the newspapers. One child kept creeping down the stairs, but Dad kept sending him back. At 9pm the doorbell rang; it was the next-door neighbour, Mrs Smith, asking whether her son was there. The father brusquely replied, 'No'. Just then a little head appeared over the bannister and a voice shouted, 'I'm here, Mum, but he won't let me go home!'
Anon

Overheard at a weekend Aids conference for parents.
Woman One: I have problems knowing what to give my teenager to eat.
Woman Two: I have no difficulty with that. I butter wafer biscuits and spread them with honey or cream cheese for breakfast. I give him wafers spread with various pastes or paté for lunch. For dinner he has wafers with slices of ham or salmon.
Woman One: You are a wonderful mother. So thoughtful. But why the wafers all the time?
Woman Two: Because only wafers will slide under the door.

WORD PICTURES

Tonight, 40 per cent of American children will go to sleep in homes where their fathers do not sleep. Divorcees in the US: 15.5 million.
The Week

The old trinity was of father, mother and child and is called the human family. The new is of child and mother and father and has the name of the Holy Family. It is in no way altered except in being entirely reversed; just as the world which it transformed was not in the least different, except in being turned upside down.
G. K. Chesterton

G. K. Chesterton used to tell how, when he was a boy, he had a toy theatre with cardboard characters. One of the characters was the figure of a man with a golden key. He had long since forgotten what character the cardboard figure actually stood for, but always he connected the man with the golden key with his father, because his father unlocked all kinds of wonderful things to him.
William Barclay

Once a little boy of five was left alone with his father at bedtime. It had never happened before. After some manoeuvring and a lot of fun, the father finally got the little fellow into his night clothes, and was about to lift him into bed when the child said, 'But Daddy, I have to say my prayers.' He knelt down beside his bed, joined his hands, raised his eyes to heaven and prayed: 'Now I lay me down to sleep, I pray the Lord my soul to keep; if I should die before I wake, I pray the Lord my soul to take.' That was his usual prayer, but tonight he looked up at his dad, then raised his eyes to heaven and prayed, 'Dear God, make me a great big good man, like my daddy, Amen.' In a moment he was in bed, and in five minutes asleep. And then the father knelt by his son's bedside and prayed, 'Dear Lord, make me a great big good man like my boy thinks I am.'
P. Fontaine

A humble Methodist itinerant minister was often discouraged. The work was hard. The compensation meagre. How many times he was tempted to give it up! Three daughters grew to young womanhood in that home. In course of time all three were married. One became the mother of a celebrated artist; one was the mother of Stanley Baldwin, Prime Minister; the other was the mother of Rudyard Kipling.
Anon

E. V. Lucas wrote a very lovely kind of parable. 'A mother lost her soldier son. The news came to her in dispatches from the war. He had fallen fighting nobly at the head of his regiment. She was inconsolable. "O that I might see him again," she prayed, "if only for five minutes – but to see him." An angel answered her prayer. "For five minutes," said the angel, "you will see him." "Quick, quick," said the mother, her tears turned to momentary joy. "Yes," said the angel, "but think a little. He was a grown man. There are thirty years to choose from. How would you like to see him?" And the mother paused and wondered. "Would you see him," said the angel, "as a soldier dying heroically at his post? Would you see him again as on that day at school when he stepped to the platform to receive the highest honour a boy could have?" The mother's eyes lit up. "Would you see him," said the angel, "as a babe at your breast?"

'And slowly the mother said, "No, I would have him for five minutes as he was one day when he ran in from the garden to ask my forgiveness for being naughty. He was so small and so unhappy, and the tears were making streaks down his face through the garden dust. And he flew into my arms with such force that he hurt me." The one thing that the mother wished above all to recapture was the moment when her son needed her. There is nothing more moving in life than to hear someone say, "I need you; I cannot do without you."'
William Barclay

USEFUL TEXTS

The Family,
Responsibilities within:
 Husbands, *Col. 3:19*
 Wives, *Col. 3:18; Prov. 31:11-15*
 Children, *Col. 3:20*
 Fathers, *Col. 3:21*
 Mothers, *Prov. 31:15, 27-28*

See also: A9 Relationships
    B30 Married love
    C5 The institution of marriage

B7
MARY, MOTHER OF GOD

'The shepherds found Mary and Joseph,
and the baby lying in the manger.'
Luke 2:16

QUOTATIONS

In order that the body of Christ might be shown to be a real body, he was born of a woman; but in order that his Godhead might be made clear he was born of a virgin.
St Thomas Aquinas

For truly she was full of grace, to whom it had been granted by divine gift that she first among women should offer the most glorious gift of virginity to God.
The Venerable Bede

Nor was Mary less than was befitting the Mother of Christ. When the apostles fled, she stood before the Cross and with reverent gaze beheld her son's wounds, for she waited not for her child's death, but the world's salvation.
St Ambrose

Born of the Father, Christ created his mother; formed as man in his mother, he glorified his Father. He, the son of Mary and the spouse of holy Church, has made the Church like to his mother, since he made it a mother for us and he kept it a virgin for himself. The Church, like Mary, has inviolate integrity and incorrupt fecundity. What Mary merited physically the Church has guarded spiritually, with the exception that Mary brought forth only one child while the Church has many children destined to be gathered into one body.
St Augustine of Hippo

Humour

Nina was captivated with the story of the nativity, birth and eventual death of Jesus on the cross, and was overjoyed when she was chosen to be an angel in the nativity play. She learnt her lines to perfection.

However, Nina is given to adding her own logic to every situation.

The nativity was well under way and when it was her turn to say her lines to Mary, she said: 'Don't worry, Mary, you will have a lovely baby and you will call him Jesus.'

She then added, 'But I wouldn't get too attached to him, 'cos he'll be dead by Easter.'
John Marshall

Word Pictures

The best statement I know of the place of Mary in the economy of our salvation and the reason for devotion to her, was made in a letter written in 1399 by Thomas Arundel, then Archbishop of Canterbury, to the bishop of London and his other suffragans:

> The contemplation of the great mystery of the Incarnation, in which the Eternal Word chose the holy and immaculate Virgin that from her womb he should clothe himself with flesh, has drawn all Christian nations to venerate her from whom came the first beginnings of our redemption. But we English, being the servants of her special inheritance, and her own Dowry, as we are commonly called, ought to surpass others in the fervour of our praises and devotions.

Gordon Albion

A painting about which we were unable to separate fact from legend was the 'Virgin and child' in the Paulin monastery at Czestochowa, in Southern Poland. A Polish reader living in Leicestershire asked us to confirm the following story about the painting, known as the 'Protector of Poland', and said to have been painted by one of Christ's apostles.

When Sweden invaded Poland in 1655, the Swedes tried to remove the painting in a horse-drawn wagon, but could not budge it an inch. Exasperated, two Swedish soldiers drew their swords and slashed at the Virgin's cheek. As soon as their swords touched the canvas, the soldiers fell dead. And nobody has since been able to cover up the scars.

Although unable to confirm it to the letter, we were happy to find that such a good story certainly was based on some fact. Admittedly Our Lady of Czestochowa, first said to have been painted by St Luke, is now believed to be the work of an unknown Italian artist in 1383. But the painting certainly took on a special significance after the heroic defence of the monastery in 1655, when the invading Swedes were defeated after a 70-day siege.

Following this miraculous victory, King Casimar of Poland proclaimed: 'To touch Our Lady of Czestochowa is to touch the very soul of Poland.' Whether by Swedish swords or not, the Virgin's cheek remains scarred, and every year thousands of pilgrims go to see it.
'Old Codgers'

We cannot fathom the depth of the love of the Mother of God, but this we know:
The greater the love, the greater the sufferings of the soul.
The fuller the love, the fuller the knowledge of God.
The more ardent the love, the more fervent the prayer.
The more perfect the love, the holier the life.
St Silouan

Here is a story about a monk called Barnabas. Barnabas was sad. All the monks in the monastery seemed to have such clever and useful things to do. It was September 8th and the monks wished to celebrate Our Lady's birthday each according to his particular talent. One illuminated a page of a breviary in vibrant blue, red, green and gold. Another spent many hours at his easel capturing the beauty of the surrounding landscape, another composed an exquisite poem telling her of his love and a fourth set it to music, so that all were astonished at its melody.

But alas, Barnabas was grieved because he had none of these talents and he did want to give Our Lady a present. Before he entered the monastery he had been a tumbler of great renown, but now his bones were old and set, but so compelling was his love for Our Lady, that his desire to give her a present overcame his fear that the cleverer monks might ridicule his poor performance. So Barnabas retired to the chapel and practised and practised until much of his old skill returned. His efforts exhausted him and at last he was forced to rest for a while. The perspiration was running down his head and face and soaking his habit. At this moment the other monks entered the chapel bringing their birthday gifts to lay before Our Lady's statue. To their consternation, she was not on her pedestal but had descended towards the one who had loved her most. She had accepted with delight his efforts to entertain her.

April O'Leary

See also: A4   Emmanuel – Mary's Child
            A40 The equality of women
            B4   Mary, handmaid of God
            C7   The humanity of Christ
            C45 The Divinity of Christ

B8
THE WORD

'In the beginning was the Word, the Word was with God,
and the Word was God. He was with God in the beginning.'
John 1:1

QUOTATIONS

God hath now sent his living oracle into the world to teach his
final will.
John Milton

Nature's self, which is the breath of God, or his pure Word by
miracle revealed.
William Wordsworth

I can know myself as a person only where I feel my existence
grounded in responsibility, and that means where I know myself
to be created by and in the Word of God.
Emil Brunner

What is there more natural, and yet more magnificent, what is easier
to conceive and more in accord with human reason, than the creator
descending into the primordial night to make light with a Word?
François de Chateaubriand

This Word, this Logos, which Greeks and Hebrews unite in
recognising as the controlling power of the whole universe, is no
longer unknown or dimly apprehended. The Light which in some
measure lightens every man has shone in its full splendour.
William Temple

The divine and creative Word was not uttered once for all, but it
receives perpetual utterance in the radiation of light, in the
movements of the stars, in the development of life, in the reason
and conscience of man.
William Temple

Eternal God! Thy Word is not all fulfilled; Thy thought . . . not all revealed. The ages that are past have but revealed to us some fragments of it.
Giuseppe Mazzini

The Word of God is not a sounding but a piercing Word, not pronounceable by the tongue but efficacious in the mind, not sensible to the ear but fascinating to the affection. His face is not an object possessing beauty of form but rather it is the source of all beauty and all form. It is not visible to the bodily eyes, but rejoices the eyes of the heart. And it is pleasing not because of the harmony of its colour but by reason of the ardour of the love it excites.
St Bernard of Clairvaux

As we grow in contemplating the Logos within and outside of ourselves throughout the entire material universe, we begin to experience the Logos as relational. He points to the Father and he points from the Father to us.
George A. Maloney

WORD PICTURES

The Emperor Napoleon I was reviewing some troops in Paris when, in giving an order, he thoughtlessly dropped the bridle upon his horse's neck. The animal instantly set off at a gallop, and the Emperor was obliged to cling to the saddle.

At this moment a common soldier of the line sprang before the horse, seized the bridle, and respectfully handed it to the Emperor. 'Much obliged to you, Captain,' said the chief, by this one word making the soldier an officer. The man caught the Emperor's meaning, believed him, and saluting, quickly responded, 'Of what regiment, sire?' Napoleon, charmed with his faith, replied, 'Of my Guards,' and galloped off.

Then the soldier laid down his gun, and instead of returning to his comrades, approached the group of staff officers. On seeing him, one of the Generals asked what he wanted there? 'I am Captain of the Guards,' said the soldier, proudly. 'You, mon ami

– you are mad to say so!' was the retort. 'He said it,' replied the soldier, pointing to the Emperor, who was still in sight. The General respectfully begged his pardon: the Emperor's word was enough.

If we thus took God at his word, how different our position would be.

Anon

It was because she received the Word of God both in her heart and in her body that the Blessed Virgin has a unique role in the mystery of the Word incarnate and in that of the Mystical Body. She is closely united with the Church, for which she is the model of faith, charity and perfect union with Christ. In this way, in answer to our devotion and our prayer, Mary, who in a way gathers and reflects in herself the highest aspirations of faith, calls the faithful to her Son and to his sacrifice, as well as to the love of the Father.

With the Virgin, the Church started her way through the history of this world two thousand years ago, in the Upper Room as Pentecost. Since then, the Church has traversed every stage of this way with her, the luminous sign of hope and comfort for the people of God.

Pope John Paul II

At the hour appointed by the laws of the human nature he had assumed, the Word of God, now made man, issues from the holy shrine, the immaculate womb of Mary. He makes his first appearance in this world in a manger, the cattle are there, chewing their straw, and all around are silence, poverty, simplicity and innocence. Angels' voices are heard in the sky, announcing peace, that peace which the new baby has brought to us. His first worshippers are Mary, his mother, and Joseph, thought to be his father, and after these some humble shepherds who have come down from the hills, led by angels' voices. Later on comes a caravan of distinguished persons guided from far, far away by a star; they offer precious gifts, full of a mysterious meaning. Everything that night at Bethlehem spoke a language that the whole world could understand.

Pondering this mystery every knee will bow in adoration before the crib. Everyone will look into the eyes of the divine infant which gaze far away, almost as if he could see one by one all the peoples of the earth one after the other, as if he were reviewing them all as they pass before him, recognising and identifying them all and greeting them with a smile: Jews, Romans, Greeks, Chinese, Indians, the peoples of Africa and of every region of the world, of every age of history, the most desolate, deserted lands, and the most remote, secret and unexplored; past, present and future ages.

Pope John XXIII

USEFUL TEXTS

The Word, *John 1:1; John 1:14*

See also: A4   Emmanuel – Mary's Child
            A37 Christ the King
            B4   Mary – Handmaid of God
            C45 The Divinity of Christ

B9
REVELATION

'It was by a revelation that I was given the
knowledge of the mystery.'
Ephesians 3:3

QUOTATIONS

To see the world in a grain of sand, and heaven in a wild flower.
Hold infinity in the palm of your hand, and eternity in an hour.
William Blake

Every act formed by charity is a revelation of God. Every word of
truth and love, every hand extended in kindness, echoes the inner
life of the Trinity.
Gabriel Moran

Knowing all things, therefore, and providing for what is profitable
for each one, he revealed that which it was to our profit to know,
but what we were unable to bear he kept secret.
St John of Damascus

Revelation is the act of communicating divine knowlege by the
Spirit to the mind. Inspiration is the act of the same Spirit,
controlling those who make the truth known.
Charles Hodge

In revelation, God is the agent as well as the object. It is not just
that men speak about God, or for God; God speaks for himself
and talks to us in person.
J. I. Packer

God hides nothing. His very work from the beginning is revelation
– a casting aside of veil after veil, a showing unto men of truth
after truth. On and on from fact divine he advances, until at
length in his son Jesus he unveils his very face.
George MacDonald

God always communicated his marvels using the language and experience of men. . . . These considerations, however, as you know, bring up the problem of the historical formation of the language of the Bible, which is connected in some way with the changes that took place during the long succession of centuries in the course of which the written word gave birth to the sacred Books.

But it is precisely here that there is asserted the paradox of the revealed proclamation and of the more specifically Christian proclamation according to which persons and events that are historically contingent become bearers of a transcendent and absolute message. The clay vessels may break, but the treasure they contain remains complete and incorruptible (cf 2 Cor. 4:7).
Pope John Paul II

Every truth without exception and whoever may utter it is from the Holy Spirit. The old pagan virtues were from God. Revelation has been made to many pagans.
St Thomas Aquinas

WORD PICTURES

In Cracow, a rabbi dreamt three times that an angel told him to go to Livovna. 'In front of the palace there, near a bridge,' the angel said, 'you will learn where a treasure is hidden.' The rabbi went to Livovna. When he arrived at the palace, he found a sentinel near the bridge, so he told him the dream. The sentinel replied: 'I, too, have had a dream. The angel told me to go to a rabbi's house in Cracow, where a treasure is buried in front of the fireplace.' Hearing this, the rabbi returned home and dug in front of the fireplace. There he found the treasure. All revelation will show that God is to be found nowhere else but within.
Traditional story

An American Indian of the Haida tribe, called Cowhoe, was kept on the warship HMS *Virago*, as a hostage when that vessel was sent in 1835 to rescue some Americans who had been taken prisoners by his tribe. He was well treated, and when set free the captain presented him with a New Testament, which of course he could not read, but which he kept carefully. The captain, on his return to England, being evidently highly impressed by the intelligence of the Haida, urged that missionaries should be sent to them.

When at length, in 1876, one arrived, he found Cowhoe was Chief, and still cherishing the English Testament. For forty years he had been waiting for the man whom he believed was sure to come to reveal to him the meaning of the words in 'God's Paper'.

In 1931 his son, Chief Henry Edenshaw, a lay delegate to the General Synod of the Canadian Church, stood up to show this same New Testament, still guarded as a sacred thing, and told how it had been given to his father.
Canadian Church News

When the Communists came to power in China not a few Christians were arrested and tried for their Faith. One was given the opportunity to reveal why he chose Christianity instead of the religion of his ancestors.

'I was in a deep pit,' he said, 'sinking in the mire, and helpless to deliver myself. Looking up I saw a shadow at the top, and soon a venerable face looked over the brink and said. "My son, I am Confucius, the father of your country. If you had obeyed my teachings you would never have been here." And then he passed on with a significant movement of his finger and a cheerless farewell, adding, "If you ever get out of this, remember to obey my teachings." But, alas! that did not save me.

'Then Buddha came along, and, looking over the edge of the pit he cried: "My son, just count it all as nothing. Enter into rest. Fold your arms and retire within yourself, and you will find Nirvana, the peace to which we all are tending." I cried: "Father Buddha, if you will only help me to get out, I will be glad to do so. I could follow your instructions easily if I were where you are, but how can I rest in this awful place?" Buddha passed on and left me to my despair. Then another face appeared. It was the face of a man beaming with kindness, and bearing marks of sorrow. He did not linger a moment, but leaped down to my side, threw his arms around me, lifted me out of the mire, brought me to the solid

ground above; then did not even bid me farewell, but took off my filthy garments, put new robes upon me, and bade me follow him, saying: "I will never leave thee nor forsake thee." That is why I became a Christian.
F. H. Drinkwater

USEFUL TEXTS

Revelation:
Through Jesus, *John 15:15*
By the Spirit, *1 Cor. 2:10; Eph. 3:1-6*
Through the prophets, *Deut. 18:18*

See also: A12 Holy Scripture
B2 The Good News
B24 Go tell everyone
C8 God's messengers
C38 Discerning God's will

B10
BAPTISM

'He will baptise you with the Holy Spirit.'
Mark 1:8

QUOTATIONS

Baptism points back to the work of God and forward to the life of faith.
J. A. Motyer

After their baptism in the Holy Spirit Christians walk in newness of life, the life of the new creation, the life of the age to come.
Alan Richardson

The day when a person is baptised is more important that the day when a person is ordained priest and bishop.
Raymond E. Brown

Baptism challenges all to be and to live as community of faith based on the Word and on the freedom and love that Christ has brought.
Leonard Durham

Concerning baptism, baptise in this way. Having first rehearsed all these things, baptise in the name of the Father and of the Son and of the Holy Ghost, in living water. But if you have not living water, baptise in other water; and, if thou canst not in cold, in warm. If you have neither, pour water thrice on the head in the name, etc . . . Before the baptism let the baptiser and the baptised fast, and others if they can. And order the baptised to fast one or two days before.
The Didache

HUMOUR

The baptism was well under way when the baby's six-year-old brother leaped up in the front pew and called out anxiously to the priest, 'Be careful, she bites!'

A Highland minister came to a lonely house on the margin of his parish to baptise the child of a shepherd who lived there. 'Are ye prepared?' he asked, 'Aye,' said the shepherd, 'I got a grand ham, ye ken, for dinner.' 'No, no,' said the minister. 'I mean spiritually prepared?' 'Aye, aye, minister. I got a quart jar from the inn!'

WORD PICTURES

In the world-famous Roman armies, the decisive act of becoming a soldier was called the *sacramentum*, that is, the military oath. The Christian Church adopted this word for the decisive act of becoming a solider of Christ; baptism, and especially the vows taken at baptism, were called the *sacramentum*. By becoming a Christian through the *sacramentum*, we cease to be civilians, and we become soldiers actively engaged in Christ's battle for the world.
Anon

When Clovis, King of the Franks, became a Christian, he was baptised in Rheims Cathedral by St Remigius. After his baptism Bishop Remigius took away his coat of arms, which had been three frogs, and replaced it by a coat of three lilies. The frogs were a symbol of ugliness, the lilies a symbol of beauty and purity. The Fleurs-de-lis have ever since been the coat of arms of the Kings of France.
Anon

In the sculptures and frescoes of the catacombs, as well as in the symbolic art of early Christianity, the dolphin occupies a prominent place. The dolphins, called 'the arrows of the sea' were in Greek mythology the great guides and deliverers of those 'in peril on the sea'. Hence they are constantly found as a device on ancient coins. One of the famous stories connected with the dolphin is that Arion, the sweet singer, had so enchanted the dolphins with his music that when forced to leap into the sea to escape his enemies, he was borne by them in safety to Taenarus. He is seen riding on a dolphin's back, while he –
  'With harmonious strains,
  requites his bearer for his friendly pains.'
  In Christian symbolism the dolphin is taken to represent Christ

as Guide and Deliverer. It points 'to him who through the waters of baptism opens up to mankind the paths of deliverance, causing them to so pass the waves of this troublesome world that finally they may come to the land of everlasting life.'
Anon

About 1877 a class of Zulu boys were being prepared for baptism. Among those who dropped in casually was a middle-aged man, Maqumusela, one of the King's soldiers, who, coming regularly, and staying long, at last asked for baptism with the rest.

But the King's word was that if any of his soldiers became Christians he would have him killed. This was put before Maqumusela, who, having gone away and thought and prayed, returned, and asked still to be baptised by the Anglican missionaries.

The King came to hear about it, and just before the baptism sent soldiers to put Maqumusela to death. He asked first for time to pray, and after prayers for himself, the missionaries, the King, the soldiers and Zululand, said to the soldiers who were sitting around, waiting, that he was ready. They were, however, so impressed that they could not perform their duty, but beckoned to another man near, who dispatched the first Zulu martyr.
Anon

Georgia's president, Edward Shevardnadze, has often been likened to 'a Stalin in reverse'. The Soviet dictator began his political life as a Georgian patriot, and then went on to rule the whole Soviet Union from the Kremlin, crushing the patriotic aspirations of his erstwhile Georgian compatriots. Shevardnadze, on the other hand, from being foreign minister of the Soviet Union went home to rule his native Georgia.

Now, it appears, he is the reverse of Stalin in another way. Stalin began life as an Orthodox believer – indeed, as a theological student – and then turned to Marxist atheism. Shevardnadze, after years as (at least officially) an atheist, announced on Sunday that he had been received into the Orthodox Church, taking the baptismal name of George, and hanging an icon of Our Lady on the wall, where once – he admits – Stalin's portrait hung.
Anon

There was for many centuries the custom in the Roman Church of celebrating the *pascha annotinum*, or the anniversary of baptism. It was a sort of 'class reunion' for the baptised, their sponsors, and the bishop, at which they celebrated the Eucharist together on what might be called their Christian birthday. The sense of the occasion is well caught in the opening collect of the Gelasian Sacramentary:

> O God, by your providence, the memory of the things that happened remains, while all that we could hope for in the future has been promised. Let the solemn occasion which we recall be permanently effective in our lives, so that we may remain faithful in practice to what we commemorate now.

If ever the celebration of Christian initiation begins to play the role in Christian community life that it used to play in the past, when it was the great community festival of the year, perhaps such annual reunions of the baptised will also revive. In the meantime, a growing awareness of our baptismal identity may make it more common for Christians to know at least the date of their baptism and to give thanks to God for his mercy on each successive anniversary.
Mark Searle

In Rio, a group of Christians was working with street children.
Every day boys from the street got together at one spot to chat, to discuss their problems and to share their fears and anger with one another. Many came regularly. The church people consisted of a Catholic priest, a Methodist, a priest of the Umbanda cult, a Presbyterian, and a young Lutheran pastor.

One day one of the boys said: 'I would like to be baptised.'
'In which church, then?' asked the Catholic.
'Which church? In ours here, of course.'
'But to which church building would you like to go?'
'Building? No, to our church, here on the street. I want to be baptised here among us.'

The Methodist said he couldn't issue such a certificate. The Catholic thought it wouldn't be possible to perform jointly with the man from the Umbanda religion. The boy stuck by his wish.

Finally, the pastor organised the necessary things: he laid a board over two crates and filled an old boot with water for flowers, which the children provided. The Catholic brought along a candle.

The baptism took place on the street, in the name of Jesus Christ.

Dorothee Soelle

USEFUL TEXTS

Baptism:
    Jesus' baptism, *Matt. 3:11, 13-17*
    By John the Baptist, *Matt. 3:5-12*
    Commanded by Christ, *Matt. 28:19-20*
    In the Early Church, *Acts 8:12, 36-38; 9:17-18*

See also: A38 Original Sin
           B36 The Family of God
           C26 The human condition
           C47 The indwelling spirit
           C49 Receive the Holy Spirit

B11
VOCATION

'Speak, Lord, your servant is listening.'
1 Samuel 3:10

QUOTATIONS

When I have learned to do the Father's will, I shall have fully realised my vocation on earth.
Carlo Carretto

Our vocation is to live in the Spirit, not to be more and more remarkable animals, but to be the sons and companions of God in eternity.
Anthony Bloom

Many are stubborn in pursuit of the path they have chosen, few in pursuit of the goal.
Frederich Nietzsche

God chooses those who are pleasing to him. He put a shepherd at the head of his people and of the goat-herd, Amos, he made a prophet.
St Basil

The vocation of each person merges, up to a certain point, with his very being: it can be said that *vocation and person become just one thing.* This means that in God's creative initiative there enters a particular act of love for those called not only to salvation, but also to the ministry of salvation.
Pope John Paul II

In God's house we must try to accept any job: cook or kitchen boy, waiter, stable boy, baker. If it pleases the king to call us into his private council, then we must go there, but without being too excited, for we know that our reward depends not on the job itself but on the faithfulness with which we serve him.
Pope John Paul I

WORD PICTURES

There was a rich man in a certain place. One day his son was sitting in his father's garden. At that time many birds came and ate up the fruits. Cattle trampled on the plants. The son saw but did not drive them away. 'Is it right for you to see your father's garden destroyed in this way and keep quiet? Can you not drive these things out?' said the people to him. 'My father has not asked me to do so,' said the son. 'So that is not my work.' Then the father, hearing of what happened, drove his son out of the house. For it is not a special voice, but the needs and imperfections of those around us which constitutes a call for God's service.
Sadhu Sindar Singh

Today we are living through an enormous revival of consciousness of the lay vocation. Is medicine, for example, a profession? Engineering a profession? Law a profession? But at the same time, they are vocations. What does it mean, a vocation? It means that everything you do in your life, for reasons of knowledge, education, practice and skill will become at the same time, a realisation of some part of the good ordained in the world by God himself, worked out in the world, paid for in the world by Christ himself.
Pope John Paul II

Each duty, office, vocation is God's gift, whether to man or to angels. Man indulges ardours and reluctances, choices, recoils, preferences; some gifts he styles trials, some burdens; angels seem to see and feel no difference between calling and calling, opportunity and opportunity. Angels doubtless estimate the gift by the Giver; men too often the Giver by the gift; not, that is, by the intrinsic value of the gift, but rather by their own taste or distaste for it.
Christina Rossetti

God has created me to do him some definite service. He has committed some work to me which he has not committed to another. I have my mission. I may never know it in this life, but I shall be told it in the next.

I am a link in a chain, a bond of connection between persons. He has not created me for naught. I shall do good. I shall do his work. I shall be an angel of peace, a preacher of truth in my own place while not intending it – if I do but keep his commandments.

Therefore, I will trust him. Whatever, wherever I am. I can never be thrown away. If I am in sickness, my sickness may serve him; in perplexity, my perplexity may serve him; if I am in sorrow, my sorrow may serve him. He does nothing in vain. He knows what he is about. He may take away my friends, he may throw me among strangers. He may make me feel desolate, make my spirits sink, hide my future from me – still he knows what he is about.
John Henry Newman

We read a story of St Anthony, who, being in the wilderness, led there a very hard and strait life, insomuch that none at that time did the like, to whom came a voice from heaven saying, 'Anthony, thou are not so perfect as a cobbler that dwelleth at Alexandria.' Anthony, hearing this, rose up forthwith, and took his staff and went till he came to Alexandria, where he found the cobbler. The cobbler was astonished to see so reverend a father come to his house. Then Anthony said to him 'Come and tell me thy whole conversation, and how thou spendest thy time.' 'Sir,' said the cobbler, 'as for me, good works have I none, for my life is but simple and slender. I am but a poor cobbler; in the morning when I rise, I pray for the city wherein I dwell, specially for all such neighbours and poor friends as I have; after, I set me at my labour, where I spend the whole day in getting my living, and I keep me from all falsehood, for I hate nothing so much as deceitfulness; wherefore, when I make to any man a promise, I keep it and perform it truly: and so I spend my time poorly with my wife and children, whom I teach and instruct, as far as my wit will serve me, to fear and dread God. And this is the sum of my simple life.'

In this story you see how God loveth those that follow their vocation and live uprightly, without any falsehood in their dealing. This Anthony was a great, holy man, yet the cobbler was as much esteemed before God as he.
Hugh Latimer

USEFUL TEXTS

Vocation:
    Worthy of, *Eph. 4:1*
    From God, *Rom. 8:30; 11:29*
    Obedience to one's, *1 Cor. 7:17-24*

See also: A10 Seeking perfection
           A22 Seeking God
           C16 Come follow me
           C38 Discerning God's will

B12
ON A MISSION

'The time has come,' Jesus said, 'and the kingdom of God is
close at hand. Repent, and believe the Good News.'
Mark 1:15

QUOTATIONS

The fact of the missions reveals the Church's faith in herself as the
Catholic unity of mankind.
J. C. Murray

Before Christ sent the Church into the world, he sent the Spirit
into the Church. The same order must be observed today.
John R. W. Stott

My son, if God has called you to be a missionary, your Father
would be grieved to see you shrivel down into a king.
Charles H. Spurgeon

Mission will not happen unless the Church goes beyond its own
life out into active care in the local neighbourhood.
David Sheppard

HUMOUR

It was the old missionary in Africa who gave the tribe of cannibals
their first taste of Christianity.

A young Canadian mission worker said that he was always looking
for guidance from the Lord and he had come to South America
because when he was considering his vocation he had suddenly
seen a chocolate bar with a Brazil nut. 'What would you have
done if it had been a Mars bar?' asked his sceptical friend.

WORD PICTURES

In his old age St Boniface longed once again to preach the Gospel to the Frisians, the people of his earliest mission, many of whom were still heathen. . . . He journeyed through its marshes and preached in its scattered villages. Many believed in his words, and he arranged to confirm a large number of newly baptised persons, at Dokkum, on June 5th, 755. Soon after sunrise on that day he was told that a heathen force was advancing against him. He called his clergy round . . . and went forth from his tent with them to meet his enemies. The younger men of his company wished to fight for their lives, but he forbade them, saying that they were taught in Scripture not to render evil for evil. He exhorted them to be of good courage; death would be short, they would soon reign with Christ for ever. He and nearly all his company were slain by the heathen, but his death was fruitful in providing many further conversions.

Anon

And the Lord said GO
And I said Who, me?
And he said Yes, you.
And I said
   But I'm not ready yet,
   And there is company coming
   And I can't leave my family.
   You know that there is no one to take my place.
And he said You're stalling.

And the Lord said GO
I said But I don't want to
And he said I didn't ask if you wanted to
And I said
   Listen I'm not the kind of person
   To get involved in arguments.
   Besides my family won't like it
   And what will the neighbours think?
And he said Baloney.

And yet a third time the Lord said GO
And I said Do I have to?
And he said Do you love me?
And I said
  Look, I'm scared.
  People are going to hate me
  And cut me into little pieces.
  And I can't take it all by myself.
And he said Where do you think I'll be?

And the Lord said GO
And I sighed
Here I am . . . send me.
Anon

I gave up my position of professor in the University of Strasbourg,
my literary work, and my organ playing in order to go as a Doctor
to Equatorial Africa. How did that come about? . . . I resolved,
when already thirty years old, to study medicine and to put my
ideas to the test . . . I had read about the physical miseries of the
natives in the virgin forests; I had heard about them from
missionaries, and the more I thought about it the stranger it
seemed to me that we Europeans trouble ourselves so little about
the great humanitarian task which offers itself to us in far-off
lands. The parables of Dives and Lazarus seemed to me to have
been spoken directly to us! And just as Dives sinned against the
poor man at his gate because for want of thought he never put
himself in his place, and let his heart and conscience tell him what
he ought to do, so we sin against the poor man at our gate.
Albert Schweitzer

In 1771, an English-speaking soldier-preacher who was being sent
to the colonies in response to young Francis Asbury's urgent
pleading for more preachers, received a stirring letter:
  Dear George, the time has arrived for you to embark for
  America. You must go down to Bristol where you will meet
  with T. Rankin, Captain Webb, and his wife. I let you loose,

George, on the great continent of America. Publish your message in the open face of the sun and do all the good you can.

I am, dear George, yours affectionately,

John Wesley.

When I was asked to write about a missionary I knew, a few people crossed my mind, such as Mother Teresa, then I stopped and thought, 'I can't write about one of these great people because I don't really know them. It's true I've heard their names and read and been told about them, but I don't know what they're like.'

The person I think is a missionary, and a good one, is my mother. This may sound peculiar but surely you don't have to be ordained to be a missionary. My mum's mission is to be a housewife and a mother to me and my family. My mum has never been selfish and put herself first before her family. I have never been starved or been without her endless love. Just like the famous missionaries my mother has needed a lot of courage. She could easily have gone off to bingo and left me, but she didn't. She made the supreme sacrifice of thinking about me before herself. I am very lucky to have a missionary mother.

An essay by a twelve-year-old girl

USEFUL TEXTS

Mission:

Of Christ;

    to do God's will, *John 6:38*

    to save the lost, *Luke 19:10*

    to reveal God, *Heb. 1:1-3*

    to fulfil the law, *Matt. 5:17*

Of all Christians;

    to make disciples, *Matt. 28; 16-20*

See also: B2   The Good News

              B24 Go tell everyone

              C12 The Church for all people

              C16 Come follow me.

B13
AUTHORITY

'Here is a teaching that is new,' they said,
'and with authority behind it.'
Mark 1:27

QUOTATIONS

Cast away authority, and authority shall forsake you.
Robert H. Benson

If you accept the authority of Jesus in your life, then you accept
the authority of his words.
Colin Urquhart

He who is firmly seated in authority soon learns to think security
and not progress.
J. R. Lovell

To despise legitimate authority, no matter in whom it is invested,
is unlawful; it is rebellion against God's will.
Pope Leo XIII

The vices of authority are chiefly from: delays, corruption, roughness
and facility (weakness).
Francis Bacon

I am convinced that people are open to the Christian message if it
is seasoned with authority and proclaimed as God's own word.
Billy Graham

The prevailing structures and practices of the institutional Church
are, with rare exceptions, not adapted to the exercise of lay
initiative, and need to be modified to allow for it.
Patrick Lally

Authority without wisdom is like a heavy axe without an edge, fitter to bruise than polish.
Anne Bradstreet

The lesson of history is clear: the Catholic Church preserved itself, its power and influence, at the cost of most of its dynamism and messianic drive. More than other institutions, the Church must fear not deviation but rigidity, not rebellious attempts to reach the reality behind itself, but its own natural tendency to identify itself with that reality.
David O'Brien

WORD PICTURES

I swear by God this sacred oath that I will render unconditional obedience to Adolf Hitler, the Führer of the German Reich and people, Supreme Commander of the Armed Forces, and will be ready as a brave soldier to risk my life at any time for this oath.
Oath of allegiance sworn by every member of the German Army between 1939 and 1945

'All authority in heaven and earth has been given to me' (Matthew 28:18) 'Authority in heaven and earth' is not an authority against man. It is not even an authority of man over man. It is the authority that enables man to be revealed to himself in his royalty in all the fullness of his dignity. It is the authority the specific power of which man must discover in his heart, through which he must be revealed to himself in the dimensions of his conscience and in the perspective of eternal life. Then the whole power of baptism will be revealed in him, he will know that he is 'plunged' in the Father, the Son and the Holy Spirit; he will find himself again completely in the eternal Word, in infinite love.
Pope John Paul II

Sometimes people are unjust and it is unpardonable when those people are ones responsible for justice. On 18th April 1689, there died in the Tower of London one of the unpleasantest characters in the history of England. He was Judge Jeffreys, whose brutal judgements caused his court to become known as the 'Bloody Assize'.

Out of the court he was a drunkard who revelled with brutal companions: in court he ranted at witnesses who were terrified by his blazing eyes and bellowing voice so that they sometimes answered wrongly and were given barbarous sentences.

After a rising against the King, Judge Jeffreys went to the West of England to try those concerned. At Winchester he sentenced an old lady to be burned; at Dorchester 292 people were sentenced to death or slavery; at Exeter 243 prisoners were sentenced in one batch; and at Taunton 255 were hanged. Eight hundred and forty-three were sent as slaves to the West Indies, including a party of schoolgirls.

When King James II fled from England, the judge thought it wise to follow his example, but he was recognised and nearly lynched before being imprisoned in the Tower. Judge Jeffreys, like some others in history, had great power but he used his power for evil rather than good.

Rowland Purton

USEFUL TEXTS

Authority:
> Jesus taught with, *Matt. 7:29*
> To forgive sin, *Matt 9:6*
> To cast out evil spirits, *Mark 3:15*
> None except from God, *Rom. 13:1*
> Submit to, *Titus 3:1*

See also: A14 The successors of the Apostles
           A24 Papacy
           A29 True obedience
           A32 Civic duty
           B14 Freedom to serve

B14
FREEDOM TO SERVE

'I made myself all things to all people in order to
save some at any cost.'
1 Corinthians 9:22

QUOTATIONS

The service that counts is the service that costs.
Howard Hendricks

Freedom is for people what air is for the birds.
Guillaume van der Graft

God forces no one, for love cannot compel and God's service,
therefore, is a thing of perfect freedom.
Hans Denk

All those who allow themselves a wrong liberty make themselves
their own aim and object.
Henry Suso

We find freedom when we find God; we lose it when we lose him.
Paul E. Scherer

Anything is free when it spontaneously expresses its own nature
to the full in activity.
John MacMurray

Make us masters of ourselves that we may be the servants of others.
Alexander Paterson

Freedom must be gained step by step, slowly. Freedom is a food
which must be carefully administered when people are too hungry
for it.
Lech Walesa

A Christian man is the most free lord of all, and subject to none; a Christian man is the most dutiful servant of all, and subject to everyone.
Martin Luther

Man must choose whether to be rich in things or in the freedom to use them.
Ivan Illich

'I say unrepentantly that I hope you find me difficult to pin down theologically. I want to be free to be the kind of person Christ wants me to be.'
George Carey

'We are prone to judge success by the index of our salaries or the size of our automobiles, rather than by the quality of our service and relationship to humanity.'
Martin Luther King

WORD PICTURES

Sign on the door of a Wiltshire village shop: 'Closed for lunch unless you want something.'
Peterborough

When Rabbi Baer's wife pressed her starving child to her bosom, the Rabbi heaved a rebellious sigh. Forthwith a voice from heaven thundered into his ear: 'Thou has lost thy share in the world to come.' 'It matters not,' said the Rabbi joyfully. 'The thraldom of reward has gone; henceforth I will serve God as a freeman.'
Hasidic story

Sir Winston Churchill had a pet budgerigar – Toby – which travelled with him everywhere and was allowed much freedom. One day, while Sir Winston was staying in Monte Carlo, Toby flew out of the window into the bright beckoning sunshine – and he never returned. His master reflected sadly, but philosophically, 'Freedom is the birthright of all God's creatures.'
Anon

A blind man and a lame man happened to come, at the same time, to a piece of very bad road. The former begged the latter to guide him through his difficulties. 'How can I do that,' said the lame man, 'as I am scarcely able to drag myself along? But if you were to carry me I can warn you about anything in the way, my eyes will be your eyes and your feet will be mine.' 'With all my heart,' replied the blind man, 'let us serve one another.' So taking his lame companion on his back they travelled in this way with safety and pleasure.
Aesop's Fables

During the early days of the nineteenth century a wealthy plantation owner was attracted by the heartbreaking sobs of a slave girl who was about to step up to the auction block to be sold. Moved by a momentary impulse of compassion, he bought her at a very high price and then disappeared into the crowd.

When the auction was over, the clerk came to the sobbing girl and handed her her bill of sale. To her astonishment, the unknown plantation owner had written 'Free' over the paper that should have delivered her to him as his possession. She stood speechless, as one by one the other slaves were claimed by their owners and dragged away. Suddenly, she threw herself at the feet of the clerk and exclaimed: 'Where is the man who bought me? I must find him! He has set me free! I must serve him as long as I live!'
Anon

In Budapest, a man went to the police station to ask for permission to emigrate to Western Europe.

'Aren't you happy here?' the police asked.

'I have no complaints,' said the Hungarian.

'Are you dissatisfied with your work?'

'I have no complaints.'

'Are you discontented with the living conditions?'

'I have no complaints.'

'Then why do you want to go to the West?'

'Because there I can have complaints,' explained the man.
Times, Hong Kong

Mother Teresa refused an offer of money from a rich Hindu gentleman to build a home for the dying. Why? Because he stipulated that it must be a vegetarian house.

Mother Teresa tries to give every dying perrson their last wish. Generally it is something like water from the Ganges (for a Hindu); sometimes a cigarette or a toffee apple; occasionally a chicken leg or chicken wing. In a vegetarian home she would not be able to give anyone chicken.

Anon

Slavery continues in Mauritania today. Tens of thousands of blacks are considered the property of their masters and are dependent entirely on their masters' will. Long hours are worked for no remuneration. They are denied education and do not have the right to marry or found a family. Children born to a slave woman are the property of her master; slave parents do not have any rights over their children. A slave couple in the cities may have a degree of family life, such as their own tent, but in the rural areas, there are no rules for such 'marriages'. Normally, when two slaves 'marry' the arrangements are made by their owners. Even though the woman is permitted to live in her husband's household, her original owner can call for her return to his house at any time; the will of the owners always taking precedence over those of the slaves.

The buying and selling of slaves still continues despite government denials. These transactions do not take place in open markets any more but discreetly among the Beydane tribes themselves.

Apart from the usual 'routine' punishments experienced by slaves in Mauritania – beatings with a wet cord while naked, denial of food and drink, prolonged exposure to the sun with hands and feet tied together – there are other more brutal methods of appalling cruelty far too terrible to be described in detail here since they involve physical mutilation. These dreadful punishments are meant not only to discipline the individual but to serve as a warning to others.

News from Africa

USEFUL TEXTS

Ministry:
   Example of Christ, *Mark 10:45*
   As servanthood, *Matt. 20:22-27*
   Of God's messengers, *1 Cor. 3:5*
   Of angels, *Ps. 103:20*

See also: B34   Human rights
            B45   Free will
            C1   Liberation from fear

B15
JESUS, FRIEND OF OUTCASTS

A leper came to Jesus and pleaded on his knees;
'If you want to' he said, 'you can cure me.'
Mark 1:40

QUOTATIONS

Life is filled with meaning as soon as Jesus Christ enters into it.
Stephen Neill

Jesus did not come to explain away suffering or remove it. He came to fill it with his presence.
Paul Claudel

What other people think of me is becoming less and less important; what they think of Jesus because of me is critical.
Cliff Richard

I believe there is no one lovelier, deeper, more sympathetic and more perfect person than Jesus. I say to myself that not only is there no one else like him, but there could never be anyone like him.
Feodor Dostoevski

HUMOUR

A young lad came home from his first Sunday school lesson. His mother asked, 'What did you learn today?' 'Oh,' he said, 'I learned about Jesus – and *sit down, sit down, sit down.*'

We all have heard the nursery rhyme: 'Humpty Dumpty'. A Christian mother had just repeated this rhyme to her four-year-old son. The boy thought for a moment, then, as if having suddenly come up with a solution, he said with bright-eyed confidence: 'Jesus could have done it!'

WORD PICTURES

A missionary who laboured on the east coast of Africa tells this story: One day a little black boy came to him and said, 'Was Jesus a white man or a black man?' The missionary was going to say right away that Jesus was a white man, but he happened to guess what was in the black boy's mind. He knew that if he said Jesus was a white man the boy would turn away with a sad look, thinking that everything that was good had been given to the white man. So the missionary thought a moment. He remembered that Jesus lived, when on earth, in a very warm country, that the people there were dark skinned, though not black. So he answered, 'No, Jesus was not a white man, nor a black man, but sort of between the two. He was kind of brown.' 'Oh, then he belongs to both of us, doesn't he?' exclaimed the little fellow with delight.
Anon

Sir Ernest Shackleton (who died in 1922), the leader of the famous Antarctic expedition, writes in *The Presence*: When I look back upon those days, with all their anxiety and peril, I cannot doubt that our party was divinely guided both over the snowfields and across the storm-swept sea. I know that during that long and racking march of thirty-six hours over the unnamed mountains and glaciers of South Georgia, it seemed to me often that we were not three, but four. I said nothing to my companions on the point, but afterwards Worsley said to me: 'Boss, I had a curious feeling on the march that there was another Person with us.'

Allow Christ to find you. Let him know all about you and guide you. It is true that following someone requires also making demands on ourselves. That is the law of friendship. If we wish to travel together, we must pay attention to the road we are to take.

If we go walking in the mountains we must follow the signs. If we go mountain climbing, we cannot let go of the rope. We must also preserve our unity with the Divine Friend whose name is Jesus Christ. We must co-operate with him.
Pope John Paul II

USEFUL TEXTS

Jesus and outcasts:
   Friend of, *Luke 7:34*
   Welcomes, *Luke 15:1-2*
   Came to invite, *Luke 5:32*
   Saviour, *Acts 2:36-38*

B16
CHRIST HEALS AND FORGIVES

Jesus said to the paralytic, 'my child, your sins are forgiven.'
Mark 2:5

QUOTATIONS

The healing acts of Jesus were themselves the message that he had come to set men free.
Francis MacNutt

It is easier to forgive an enemy than a friend.
Austin O'Malley

Health of body and mind is a great blessing if we can bear it.
John Henry Newman

Stronger than all the evils in the soul is the Word, and the healing power that dwells in him.
Origen of Alexandria

It is impossible to forgive whoever has done us harm if that harm has lowered us. We have to think that it has not lowered us but revealed our true level.
Simone Weil

There is not one moral virtue that Jesus inculcated but Plato and Cicero did inculcate before him. What then did Christ inculcate? Forgiveness of sins. This alone is the Gospel, and this is the life and immortality brought to life by Jesus.
William Blake

The end and lesson is the same – that Christ purges his friends of all that is not of him; that he leaves them nothing of themselves, in order that he may be wholly theirs; for no soul can learn the strength and the love of God until she has cast her weight upon him.
R. H. Benson

Be careful to preserve your health. It is a trick of the devil, which he employs to deceive good souls, to incite them to do more than they are able, in order that they may no longer be able to do anything.
St Vincent de Paul

The good Instructor, the Wisdom, the Word of the Father, who made man, cares for the whole nature of his creature. The all-sufficient physician of humanity, the saviour, heals both our body and soul, which are the proper man.
St Clement of Alexandria

PROVERBS

In every pardon there is love.
Welsh proverb

The offender never forgives.
Russian proverb

He who has health has hope; and he who has hope has everything.
Arab proverb

WORD PICTURES

He is a path, if any be misled;
he is a robe, if any naked be;
if any chance to hunger, he is bread;
if any be a bondman, he is free;
if any be but weak, how strong is he!
to dead men life he is, to sick men health,
to blind men sight, and to the needy wealth; –
a pleasure without loss, a treasure without stealth.
Giles Fletcher

In the pursuit of health this is even more obvious. For health means wholeness. It is concerned not simply with cure but with healing of the whole person in all his or her relationships; and this is what the Communion service is about.

Healing cannot be confined to any, or indeed every, level of human understanding or expectation. That is why too it shows up those twin deceivers, pessimism and optimism, as so shallow. The Christian takes his stand not on optimism but on hope. This is based not on rosy prognosis (from the human point of view mine is bleak, showing I'm dying of cancer), but, as St Paul says, on suffering. This, he says, trains us to endure, and endurance brings proof that we have stood the test, and this proof is the ground of hope in the God who can bring resurrection out and through the other side of death; though we carry death with us in our bodies (all of us) we never cease to be confident.

John Robinson

One of the most popular people at the court of King Henry I of England was Rahere, whose fun and humour raised many a laugh from all at court.

Then after King Henry's son was drowned in the *White Ship*, things were never the same. Rahere decided to go on a pilgrimage to Rome. There he caught a fever and was nursed back to health by the monks of the Hospital of the Three Fountains. Rahere was so impressed by the work of these monks that he decided to build a similar hospital in London. Then he had a dream, in which St Bartholomew, one of the original disciples of Jesus, blessed his plan, telling him where it should be built, on a piece of land belonging to the king.

His former friends were amazed when he returned to England dressed not in his finery but in the coarse clothing of a monk.

He told his story to the king, who readily gave him the land he required, known as the Smooth-field, or Smithfield, just outside the city of London. Rahere began clearing it with his own hands, but as the news spread, others offered to help him. Some gave their labour; others gave money to pay craftsmen.

Gradually the building rose – a simple hospital, a church and a priory, named after St Bartholomew. When Rahere died, on 20 September 1144, he was buried in his church. Today, St Bartholomew's is one of the most important of London's hospitals and known worldwide.

Rowland Purton

USEFUL TEXTS

Forgiveness of sin:

Forgiveness, *Exod. 34:7; Matt. 26:28*
Consequences of, *Exod. 20:5; Prov. 14:11; Rom 5:12*
Confession of sin, *Neh. 1:6; James 5:16; 1 John 1:9*

B17

THE CHURCH – BRIDE OF CHRIST

'I will betroth you to myself for ever, betroth you with
integrity and justice, with tenderness and love.'
Hosea 2:21

QUOTATIONS

Where three are gathered together, there is a Church, even though
they be laymen.
Tertullian

The Church owes to the Spirit its origin, existence and continued
life, and in this sense the Church is a creation of the Spirit.
Hans Kung

Spirituality really means 'Holy Spirit at work', a profound action
of the Holy Spirit in his Church, renewing that Church from the
inside.
Leon Joseph Suenans

As Gregory of Nyssa pictures it, Christ enters paradise bringing
with him his bride, humanity, whom he had just wedded on the
Cross.
Jean Danielou

The primary and full bride of Christ never is, nor can be, the
individual man at prayer, but only this complete organism of all
faithful people throughout time and space.
Friedrich Von Hugel

It is God who sanctified the Church; men in the Church are not,
any more than men in the world, holy of themselves . . . they are
themselves the *communio peccatorum* totally in need of justification and sanctification.
Hans Kung

The lance of the soldier opened the side of Christ, and behold . . .
from his wounded side Christ built the Church, as once the first
mother, Eve, was formed from Adam. Hence Paul says: Of his
flesh we are and of his bone. By that he means the wounded side
of Jesus. As God took the rib out of Adam's side and from it
formed the woman, so Christ gives us water and blood from his
wounded side and forms from it the Church . . . there the slumber
of Adam; here the death-sleep of Jesus.
St John Chrysostom

WORD PICTURES

The word *Church* used in most of the north European languages
comes from the Greek *kyriake oikia*, 'the family of the Lord'. It is
significant that when people sought a word to describe the reality
of what it means to be Church, the word they chose meant 'family
of the Lord'. . . . A brief look at some of the Vatican Council's
descriptions of the Church highlight how each of them relates to
the qualities of family . . . when the Church is described as the
bride of Christ, we are reminded of the resulting values of the
union and community he sets up.
Leonard Doohan

Under Pope Julius II the Church greatly increased its wealth and
political power. The story is told of how a poor monk travelled to
Rome and interviewed this pope, who showed him the vast riches
and priceless treasures of the Church. The amazed monk was shown
room after room filled with treasures of art, sculpture, jewels, gold
and silver. The proud pope said to the monk, 'You see, my friend, the
successor of Peter does not have to say, "Silver and gold have I
none".' 'Yes, Holy Father,' replied the monk, 'but by the same token
he can no longer say, "In the name of Jesus Christ, rise up and walk".'
John Sutherland Bonnell

On April 26, 1642, an immense crowd was gathered round the
triangular gallows at Tyburn, as an elderly Welshman, who had
come to be hanged, stood up in the cart to make his speech. He was
Edward Morgan, a Flintshire man who had been to school at Douai
and made priest at Salamanca. He had been imprisoned in the Fleet

for fourteen years, and suffered great hardships, being brought to trial under the Parliament. He waited till the crowd was quiet, and everybody was astonished at his cool and smiling demeanour. He began with the sign of the cross, and gave out a text . . . 'The Good Shepherd giveth his life for his sheep'. He explained that he was going to be hanged simply because he was a Roman Catholic priest, and was very glad to die for the Good Shepherd who died for his flock. 'I offer up my blood for the good of my country, and for a better understanding between the King and Parliament.'

Then he went on to preach a full sermon on the Unity of the Church, and persisted in finishing it in spite of several inter-ruptions. There is one God, one Faith, one Baptism, he said; so there must be one Church. He gave proof that the Catholic Church was the one true Church going back to the apostles, and showed that the recent sects are all too new to have any claim to be the Church of Christ. At the end he asked God to forgive all who had injured him, and also 'my own innumerable sins'.

Then, 'with a merry countenance', he told the hangman to do his duty and said: 'I pray thee, teach me what to do, for I never was at this sport before.' Whereupon the minister said: 'Mr Morgan, this is not a time to sport nor is it a jesting matter.' 'Sir,' he replied, 'I know it is no joking matter for me, but good sober earnest. But God loveth a cheerful giver, and I hope it is no offence to anyone that I go cheerfully and merrily to heaven.' He was allowed to hang until he was dead, before the rest of the sentence was carried out.

F. H. Drinkwater

USEFUL TEXTS

Church:
> Loved by Christ, *Eph. 1:22*
> Persecuted by Paul, *Gal 1:13*
> Gifts of, *1 Cor. 12:27-30*
> Bride, *2 Cor. 11:2; Eph. 5:31-32*

See also: A13 The Church is for sinners
> B36 The Family of God
> C12 The Church for all people

B18
SUNDAY

'The Sabbath was made for humankind, not humankind for the
Sabbath; so the Son of Man is master even of the Sabbath.'
Mark 2:27

QUOTATIONS

Day of all the week the best, emblem of eternal rest.
John Newton

If you want to kill Christianity, you must abolish Sunday.
François Voltaire

A world without a Sabbath would be like a man without a smile,
like a summer without flowers and like a homestead without a
garden. It is the joyous day of the whole week.
Henry Ward Beecher

PROVERBS

Rest and success are fellows.
French proverb

Come day, go day, God send Sunday.
English proverb

HUMOUR

During the Second World War, for basic training, the men were
divided according to their religious denominations and expected
to attend service at the Anglican, Roman Catholic or Jewish places
of worship, as the case might be. One of the men in an attempt to
evade attendance proclaimed himself an atheist.
   'Don't you believe in God?' asked his officer.
   'No,' said he.
   'Nor in keeping the Sabbath Day holy?'

'No, one day is as good as another to me.'

'Then,' said the officer, 'you are just the man we have been looking for. You will stay and clean out the latrines!'

A sporting vicar was making his way to church one Sunday evening when he saw two boys fishing. He stopped. 'My lads,' he said, 'do you not know that this is the Sabbath and you ought not to . . .' Just then one of the floats went under with a plomp. 'You've got a bite; you've got a bite, whip it up, you young slow coach,' yelled the vicar.

Those who are apt to keep their religion for use on Sundays, forgetting all their professions during the week, will do well to lay to heart the warning contained in the reply received by an applicant for a vacant post, who innocently observed, 'I have here a letter of recommendation from my minister.' 'That's very good as far as it goes,' replied the head of the firm as he read it, 'but we don't need your services on Sundays. Have you any references from anybody who knows you the other six days of the week?'

WORD PICTURES

A little girl trying to learn the Ten Commandments, was told by her mother to write them out. When she brought forth the result for inspection she had written, 'Remember the Sabbath day to keep it wholly.' The mother said, 'Why, don't you know how to spell better than that? The word should be "holy" not "wholly".' The Grandmother who was sitting by, said, 'Maybe the child has not made such a mistake. At least her idea of holy is nearer the truth. A day of rest should not be a shopping day or a decorating day.'
Anon

A family was on its way to a Sunday outing in the mountains. It was midmorning when they drove by a church. Worshippers, dressed in their Sunday best, were seen gathered at the front entrance. From the back of the car came the voice of five-year-old Karen: 'Daddy, aren't we going to go to church today?' In the front seat both father and mother exchanged embarrassed

glances. Since the question had been addressed to him, the father felt obliged to answer. 'We can worship God in the mountains,' was his short reply. There was a brief moment of silence, then from the back seat came the sage observation of which only a five-year-old is capable: 'But we won't, Daddy, will we?'
Anon

Children in the north of England, especially in Cumberland, used the following couplet to remember the Sundays from mid Lent to Easter:

Tid-Mid, Misera

Carlings, Palms, Pace Egg Day.

The name 'Carling Sunday' for Passion Sunday, as it used to be called, or the fifth Sunday in Lent, derives from the custom of people having carling nuts, a kind of pea, fried in butter. A pancake was made of these and it was eaten with salt and pepper. In the Midlands, Palm Sunday was known as 'Fig Sunday'. This custom may have had some connection with the cursing of the barren fig tree by Jesus. Even the poorest of people would contrive to get a handful of figs on Palm Sunday.
P.F.

Mr Girard, an atheist millionaire of Philadelphia, one Saturday ordered all his clerks to come the next day to his wharf and help to unload the newly arrived ship. One young man replied quietly:

'Mr Girard, I can't work on Sundays.'

'You know our rules?'

'Yes, I know, but I can't work on Sundays.'

'Well, step up to the desk, and the cashier will settle with you.'

For three weeks the young man could find no work, but one day a banker came to Girard to ask if he could recommend a man for cashier in a new bank. The discharged young man was at once named as a suitable person. Although Girard had dismissed the man, he recognised his sterling character. Anyone who would sacrifice his own interests for what he believed to be right would make a loyal, trustworthy cashier.
P.F.

Law is clear; law is manageable; we like law and law evades the wild demands of love; that's its attraction. Law limits. Love overflows. 'The pillars of Judaism were three: the law, the temple, the sabbath. Christ in a sense repealed them all. Christ made love the primary force and energy. He replaced the temple by his person, and transgressed the sabbath law, and defined its role as to serve not dominate the person. It's very hard to do this for people in power: 'The sabbath is made for man' is a revolutionary statement and not easily accepted. It cuts law down to size. It gives the primacy to the person; because law can be arrogant and often dominates and often oppresses.

Anon

USEFUL TEXTS

Sunday:
> First of week, *John 20:1*
> Breaking bread on, *Acts 20:7*

See also: A48 Worship
          B29 The Eucharist

B19
CONSCIENCE

'Whoever blasphemes against the Holy Spirit
can never have forgiveness.'
Mark 3:29

QUOTATIONS

A brave man risks his life but not his conscience.
Schiller

My conscience is captive to the Word of God.
Martin Luther

Let all thy converse be sincere, thy conscience as the noonday clear.
Thomas Ken

Conscience illuminated by the presence of Jesus Christ in the heart must be the guide of every man.
R. H. Benson

The worst thing in the world is not sin; it is the denial of sin by a false conscience – for that attitude makes forgiveness impossible.
Fulton Sheen

The testimony of a good conscience is the glory of a good man; have a good conscience and thou shalt ever have gladness.
Thomas à Kempis

Most of us follow our conscience as we follow a wheelbarrow. We push it in front of us in the direction we want to go.
Billy Graham

Men, as by a natural inspiration, have agreed to speak of conscience as the voice of God, as the Divinity within us.
William E. Channing

When a man is content with the testimony of his own conscience, he does not care to shine with the light of another's praise.
St Bernard of Clairvaux

Never stifle conscience, for when it speaks you are in the path of danger; only when you are safe is it silent, yet none the less watchful, unsleeping. Never try to displace that judge who never loses his seat, but sits moment by moment, weighing every thought and act in his balance.
Edward Clod

WORD PICTURES

A writer on Russia recorded that when it was discovered that the word for God had been printed with a capital letter in some school books, the initial was changed to lower case in each of a million copies before the edition was allowed to reach the pupils. But it is not only in Russia that it is a political crime to spell God with a capital G, but in every place where the state is elevated to supremacy over conscience.
Halford E. Luccock

An old Sioux Indian once asked a white man to give him some tobacco for his pipe. The man gave him a loose handful from his pocket. The next day the Indian came back and asked for the white man. 'For,' said he, 'I found a quarter of a dollar among the tobacco.' 'Why don't you keep it?' asked a person standing by. 'I've got a good man and a bad man here,' said the Indian pointing to his breast, 'and the good one say, "It is not yours; give it back to the owner." The bad man say, "Never mind, you got it, and it is your own now." The good man, "No, no! You must not keep it." So I didn't know what to do; and I thought to go to sleep; but the good man and the bad man kept talking all night, and troubled me; and now when I bring the money back, I feel good.'
Anon

I remembered one morning when I discovered a cocoon in the bark of a tree, just as the butterfly was making a hole in its case and preparing to come out. I waited a while, but it was too long appearing and I was impatient. I bent over it and breathed on it to warm it. I warmed it as quickly as I could and the miracle began to happen before my eyes, faster than life. The case opened, the butterfly started slowly crawling out and I shall never forget my horror when I saw how its wings were folded back and crumpled. The wretched butterfly tried with its whole trembling body to unfold them. Bending over it, I tried to help it with my breath. In vain. It needed to be hatched out patiently and the unfolding of the wings should be a gradual process in the sun. Now it was too late. My breath had forced the butterfly to appear, all crumpled before its time. It struggled desperately and, a few seconds later, died in the palm of my hand.

That little body is, I do believe, the greatest weight I have on my conscience.
Nikos Kazantzakis

The words of the Lord Jesus Christ guide man to God by means of his own conscience. Conscience in man is like an inner source of light and an organ of sight. The Lord Jesus compares it to the sense of sight, saying: 'If your eye is diseased, your whole body will be in darkness.' According to Christ's words we must be very attentive to the promptings of our conscience, for on this depends the inner truth of every man. Conscience first and foremost determines whether or not man lives in truth. Conscience like man's intellect is also fallible; it can sometimes make a mistake without knowing that it has done so. A man who is guided by such a conscience does not commit a sin.
Pope John Paul II

USEFUL TEXTS

Conscience:
    Maintaining a good, *Acts 24:16*
    Bears witness to God, *Rom. 2:15*
    Maintains truth, *1 Tim. 3:9*

See also: A2 Integrity
           A10 Seeking perfection
           A34 Hypocrisy and ambition
           B45 Free will
           C47 The indwelling Spirit

B20
GROWTH TO MATURITY

'Of its own accord the land produces first the shoot,
then the ear, then the full grain in the ear.'
Mark 4:28

QUOTATIONS

Growth begins when we start to accept our own weakness.
Jean Vanier

It takes a long time to bring excellence to maturity.
Publilius Syrus

Remember that bees make the sweetest honey from the flowers of
the thyme – a small and bitter herb.
St Francis of Sales

Mature people are made not out of good times but out of bad
times.
H. J. Schachtel

Mishaps are knives that either serve us or cut us as we grasp them
by the blade or by the handle.
James Russell Lowell

A price must be paid for extreme specialisation, even in holiness.
W. R. Inge

If you live among men the heart must either break or turn to
brass.
Nicolas Chamfort

The highest and most profitable reading is the true knowledge
and consideration of ourselves.
Thomas à Kempis

Many would be willing to have afflictions provided that they be not inconvenienced by them.
St Francis of Sales

Each soul is as great as the world, and in each soul there is room for all the tragedies of the world to be re-enacted, as every puddle is great enough to hold the sun.
R. H. Benson

A man has many skins in himself, covering the depths of his heart. Man knows so many things; he does not know himself. Why, thirty or forty skins or hides, just like an ox's or a bear's, so thick and hard, cover the soul. Go into your own ground and learn to know yourself there.
Meister Eckhart

As the light grows, we see ourselves to be worse than we thought. We are amazed at our former blindness as we see issuing from our heart a whole swarm of shameful feelings, like filthy reptiles crawling from a hidden cave. But we must be neither amazed nor disturbed. We are not worse than we were; on the contrary, we are better.
François Fenelon

Anyone who stops learning is old, whether at twenty or eighty. Anyone who keeps learning stays young. The greatest thing in life is to keep your mind young.
Henry Ford

WORD PICTURES

I walked a mile with Pleasure.
She chatted all the way,
but left me none the wiser
for all she had to say.
I walked a mile with Sorrow,
and ne'er a word said she;
but, oh, the things I learned from her
when Sorrow walked with me!
Robert Hamilton

'Excuse me,' said one ocean fish to another. 'You are older and more experienced than I, and will probably be able to help me. Tell me; where can I find this thing they call the Ocean? I've been searching for it everywhere to no avail!' 'The Ocean? But this is the Ocean,' said the older fish. 'Oh, this? But this is only water. What I'm searching for is the Ocean,' said the young fish, feeling quite disappointed as he swam away to search elsewhere.
Anon

The Managing Director of one of the largest commercial interests in the world was sitting in his New York office talking to a client. Suddenly a secretary came into the room obviously harassed, bearing in his hands a sheaf of impressive documents. He talked excitedly at great length seeking to impress upon his chief the desperate nature of his problem. 'Jones,' said the Managing Director, 'please don't forget rule three'. The secretary looked startled, then smiling, he folded his papers and left the room. Overcome by curiosity the client asked the Managing Director to tell him about rule three. 'Rule three,' said the Managing Director, 'is "Don't take yourself too seriously".' 'And what are rules one and two?' asked the client. 'There are no other rules in this business,' the Manager replied, 'only rule three.'
Cardinal John Heenan

Two little fir trees grew quite close together. One stood sheltered and guarded in a thick belt of trees, while the other had been planted in the open, with no protection of any sort.

On a winter's day, with the cold winds sweeping over it, or with the snow lying heavily on its branches, the lonely little fir tree looked as if it could not possibly grow strong. The sheltered tree grew much more quickly, for the trees and the underwood all around lent it warmth and kept it protected from the storms.

Years later, however, when a great storm blew over the forest, the little sheltered tree was blown completely down, and many more of the forest trees were destroyed in the gale. That tree had been so well taken care of, had so learned to depend on others, that it had never struck its roots deep down, and was not fit to stand alone. But

the lonely fir tree had spread its roots deeper and deeper in the
ground and stood firm and unmoved in the great storm.
Anon

In the apple bearing section of the State of Maine, my friend saw
an apple tree so loaded with fruit that, all around, the laden
branches were propped to keep them from the ground. When he
exclaimed about it, the owner of the orchard said, 'Go, look at
that tree's trunk near the bottom.' Then my friend saw that the
tree had been badly wounded with a deep gash. 'That is something we have learned about apple trees,' said the owner of the
orchard. 'When the tree tends to run to wood and leaves and not
to fruit, we wound it, gash it, and almost always, no one knows
why, this is the result: it turns its energies to fruit.' We must know
wounded apple trees in the human orchard of whom that is a
parable.
Henry Emerson Fosdick

No man has learned to live
until he can rise above the narrow confines
of his individualistic concerns
to the broader concerns of all humanity.
Length without breadth
is like a self-contained tributary
having no outward flow to the ocean.
Stagnant, still, and stale,
it lacks both life and freshness.
In order to live creatively
and meaningfully,
our self-concern must be wedded to other concern.
Martin Luther King

My life is but a weaving
between my Lord and me;
I cannot choose the colours,
he worketh steadily.

Oft-times he weaveth sorrow,
and I, in foolish pride
forget he sees the upper,
and I the underside.

Not till the loom is silent
and the shuttles cease to fly,
shall God unroll the canvas
and explain the reason why.

The dark threads are as needful,
in the Weaver's skilful hand,
as the threads of gold and silver
in the pattern he has planned.

He knows, he loves, he cares –
nothing this truth can dim;
he gives the very best to those,
who leave the choice with him.
Anon

USEFUL TEXTS

Growth:
    In grace and knowledge of God, *2 Pet. 3:18*
    In Christlikeness, *Eph. 4:13*
    In Christ, *Eph. 4:15*

See also: A2 Integrity
             A7 Poor in Spirit
             A10 Seeking perfection
             B26 The whole person

B21
TRUST IN GOD

'Why are you so frightened?
How is it that you have no faith?'
Mark 4:40

QUOTATIONS

Trust, like the soul, never returns once it is gone.
Publilius Syrus

God is faithful, and if we serve him faithfully, he will provide for our needs.
St Richard of Chichester

It is better to suffer wrong than to do it, and happier to be sometimes cheated than not to trust.
Samuel Johnson

To be trusted is a greater compliment than to be loved.
George Macdonald

An inflated balloon is vulnerable but how else can it fly?
Edward de Bono

When a train goes through a tunnel and it gets dark, you don't throw away your ticket and jump off. You sit still and trust the engineer.
Corrie ten Boom

He who trusts in himself is lost. He who trusts in God can do all things.
St Alphonsus Liguori

God is full of compassion and never fails those who are afflicted and despised if they trust in him alone.
St Teresa of Avila

In God alone is there faithfulness and faith in the trust that we may hold to him, to his promise, and to his guidance. To hold to God is to rely on the fact that God is there for me, and to live in this certainty.
Karl Barth

WORD PICTURES

As the marsh-hen secretly builds on the watery sod,
behold I will build me a nest on the greatness of God:
  I will fly in the greatness of God as the marsh-hen flies,
  in the freedom that fills all the space 'twixt the marsh and the skies:
by so many roots as the marsh-grass sends in the sod,
I will heartily lay me a-hold on the greatness of God.
Sydney Lanier

When Bulstrode Whitelock was about to embark as Cromwell's envoy to Sweden, in 1655, he was much disturbed in mind as he rested in Harwich on the preceding night, which was very stormy, while he reflected on the distracted state of the nation. It happened that a confidential servant slept in an adjacent bed, who, finding that his master could not sleep, said: Pray, sir, will you give me leave to ask you a question?' 'Certainly,' replied Whitelock. 'Pray, sir, don't you think God governed the world very well before you came into it?' 'Undoubtedly,' came the reply. 'And pray sir, don't you think he can take care of it while you are in it?' To this question Whitelock had nothing to reply, but turning about, soon fell asleep.
Anon

Father Lazarus, who had been a captain in the army, used to tell the story of how a certain peasant went to fetch wood for the furnace. Exhausted by his labours, he lay down to rest under a giant oak tree, and looking up at the branches of the oak and seeing the masses of fat acorns growing on them, thought to himself, 'It would have been better had pumpkins grown on the oak tree.' With this thought he shut his eyes, and suddenly an acorn fell and hit him hard on the lip. Whereupon the peasant said, 'I was wrong: God is cleverer than I am, and did well to make acorns and not pumpkins grow on oak trees. If that had been a pumpkin, it could have killed me with its weight.'

We all of us criticise God's work like this, instead of trusting him. The man who has committed himself to his holy will is at peace, whereas the one who strives to apprehend everything with his mind is unskilled in the spiritual life.
St Silouan

The story is told of a mother eagle that had built her nest on a ledge of rock jutting precariously over a steep and dangerous precipice. Soaring through the air one day, returning to her nest, she was startled by what she saw. Clinging desperately to the jagged edge of a rock at the top of the canyon was her baby eagle, struggling with all its might to prevent a fall that was sure to crush its body more than a thousand feet below.

Unable to get to the ledge before her little one would fall, the mother eagle, with the speed of lightning, swooped low beneath the jutting rock, spread her strong wings to break the fall of her darling, and with her precious cargo clinging to the feathers of her mighty wings glided safely to the canyon's floor.
Anon

Priests and nuns are becoming a prime target for confidence tricksters – or so it seems from the June *ad clerum* to clergy of the Westminster diocese. The bulletin contains several warnings against fraudsters who are targeting convents and presbyteries in a number of disguises. There is the 'pub worker' who rings the presbytery on a Sunday evening saying he needs £500 in change. He brings a cheque in exchange for the coins from the collection. The cheque bounces, and the name of the 'pub' is found to be false. Then there is 'Herman Otto Vahle', who uses false papers to con money out of convents and presbyteries on the grounds that he is a priest in need. Or 'Mr Stead' who rings up and claims he is from the Bourne Trust for the welfare of prisoners. Someone else will ring later that day, he says, asking for money for food or travel. If those at the presbytery will provide it, the Bourne Trust will reimburse them. It is all a hoax – that is not the way the Bourne Trust operates.

A trusting nature is a fine thing, but London clergy need to be streetwise too.

The Tablet

USEFUL TEXTS

Trust in God:
>   For peace, *Isa. 26:3*
>   For safety, *Prov. 29:25*
>   Forever, *Isa. 26:4*
>   Not in wealth, *Prov. 11:28; Luke 12:19-20*
>   Not in man, *Ps. 118:89; Jer. 17:5*

See also: A11 God's loving Providence
>   A19 Patience
>   B52 God is love
>   C39 Doing God's will

B22
DEATH

'Death was not God's doing, he takes no pleasure
in the extinction of the living.'
Wisdom 1:13

QUOTATIONS

It matters not how long you live, but how well.
Publilius Syrus

The ultimate evil is to leave the company of the living before you
die.
Seneca

Death is the golden key that opens the palace of eternity.
John Milton

This world's a city, full of straying streets;
and death's the market place, where each one meets.
William Shakespeare

Life levels all men: death reveals the eminent.
George Bernard Shaw

Death is the great adventure, beside which moon landings and
space trips pale into insignificance.
Joseph Bayly

For the Christian death interrupts nothing; it destroys nothing; it
liberates, not from the body, but from the empire of sin.
Robert Gleason

God makes the end of life a rest for broken things too broke to
mend.
John Masefield

The last act is always a tragedy, whatever fine comedy there may have been in the rest of life. We must all die alone.
Blaise Pascal

HUMOUR

Let us so live that when we die, even the undertaker will be sorry.
Anon

'Do you believe the dead can return, doctor?'
'If I did, I would change my job in a hurry.'
Eclats de Rire

Visitor to the churchyard: 'Are you the regular gravedigger?'
'No, sir,' replied Mick, 'I'm just filling in.'

The eminent surgeon was walking through his local churchyard one day when he saw the grave digger having a rest and drinking from a bottle of beer. 'Hey, you!' called the surgeon. 'How dare you laze about and drink alcohol in the churchyard! Get on with your job, or I shall complain to the vicar.' 'I should have thought you'd be the last person to complain,' said the grave digger, 'bearing in mind all your blunders I've had to cover up!'
Anon

The goldfish died after living in a bowl that was in the family lounge. The first time the baby sitter came over after the fish died she immediately noticed the empty bowl. 'Where's the fish?' she asked. Without hesitating, the family's three-year-old shot back, 'Oh, he's swimming with God.'
Anon

It is sobering to consider that when Mozart was my age he had already been dead for a year.
Ted Lehrer

Epitaph for Susan Blake, composed at her request
by St Thomas More:
Good Susan Blake in royal state
arrived at last at heaven's gate
(Some years later More added):
but Peter met her with a club
and knocked her back to Beelzebub.

Epitaph for an Irish priest:
Here I lie for the last time,
lying has been my pastime,
and now I've joined the heavenly choir
I hope I still may play the lyre.

Epitaph for a loving husband, by his widow:
Rest in peace – until we meet again.

Epitaph for an old soldier:
Though shot and shell around flew fast
on Balaclava's plain
unscathed he passed to fall at last,
run over by a train.

I was spending a few weeks with my daughter, as she was expecting her third baby. On the second day of my visit, I collected Matthew, aged five, from school.
Matthew: 'Granny, I didn't think you would still be here.'
Granny: 'Oh, yes, I am still here.'
Matthew: 'Well, I have been learning all about God. When people get old he takes them.'
    Then, looking up at me with a puzzled expression, he added:
    'He *must* have forgotten you.'
Mary Jones

He was surprised to read the announcement of his death in the morning paper, a confusion of similar names having taken place. Ringing up his friend Brown, he enquired, 'Did you see the announcement of my death in the paper this morning?' 'Yes,' was the unexpected answer, 'where are you speaking from?'

The ageing but still active French comedian, Maurice Chevalier, was asked how he felt about old age. 'I prefer it,' he said, 'to the alternative.'
K. Edwards

WORD PICTURES

For those who have put their trust in Christ now, death means that we shall be perfectly with him, more alive than ever, and free from pain, sickness, anxiety, depression and sin. On the memorial of Martin Luther King are these simple words:

Rev Martin Luther King Jr
1929-1968
'Free at last, free at last,
Thank God Almighty I'm free at last'

The Church is the only society on earth that never loses a member through death! As a Christian I believe, not just in life *after* death, but in life *through* death. In the words of a Russian Christian, 'The moment of death will be in the inrush of timelessness.'
David Watson

During the Second World War I had something to do with a canteen which was run for the troops in the town in which I was then working. Early in the war, we had billeted with us in our town a number of Polish troops who had escaped from Poland. Among them there was a Polish airman. When he could be persuaded to talk, he would tell the story of a series of hair-raising escapes. He would tell of how somehow he had escaped from Poland, how somehow he had tramped his way across Europe, how somehow he had crossed the Channel, how he had been shot down in his aeroplane once and crashed on another occasion.

He always concluded the story of his encounters with death with the same awe stricken sentence: 'I am God's man.'
William Barclay

The practice of using flowers at funerals has its origin in antiquity; not only did they smell sweet to disguise the odour of the corpse but they were also regarded as protectives against infection. When the plague was at its height, Dekker in *Wonderful Yeare*, 1603, records that rosemary, which could normally be bought at a price of twelve pence an armful, rose to six shillings a handful.

The traditional funeral emblematic flowers and trees are:

Oak – signifying virtue and majesty
Ivy – immortality
Passion flower – the crucifixion
White lily – futurity
Palm – martyrdom
Rosemary – remembrance
Cypress – symbol of life.

Rosemary was regarded by ancient and classical authorities as the most highly esteemed among flowers because it was believed to retard putrefaction.

Don Lewis

When Hare discovered death he ran back to the place where he lived. He shouted and cried: 'My people must not die!' He imagined the sloping rocks. They fell away. He imagined the big mountains. They fell apart. He imagined the place below the earth. Everything that lived in the soil stopped scurrying about; all froze and died. He imagined the skies high above him. The birds which had been flying stopped flying and fell to earth, dead.

He crawled into the place where he lived. He reached for his blanket, and rolled himself into it. He lay there and wept. There will not be enough earth for all that dies, he thought. There is not enough earth for all that dies. He buried himself in his blanket. He made no sound.

Alida Gersie

Peter Norman has died. May he rest in peace. In an adult Religious Studies class a few years ago we were discussing 'angels', and then went on to religious experiences and the research which has shown that 38 per cent of the population have at least one such experience in their lives. There were twelve people present and four confirmed that they had had such an experience. Peter told the group that his experience had lived with him all his life and had given a spiritual direction to it. This is his story:

When Peter was 12 he lived in the west of Ireland. Every Sunday morning he served the 11am Mass with his friend Sean. Sean would call for Peter at 10.30am and they would walk to the church together. Three months before Peter's experience Sean had been very upset when his grandmother died.

During the Saturday night of this particular weekend, Peter had a very vivid dream. He dreamt that Sean called for him, as usual, on the Sunday morning, but instead of walking to the church they walked out into the countryside to Sean's grandmother's cottage. At the garden gate Peter waited while Sean went up to the door and knocked. His grandmother opened the door, and said, 'Come in, Sean.' Peter came through the gate but the grandmother said, 'Not you Peter, another time.' And she went in with Sean.

Peter woke, had his breakfast and got ready for Mass. Sean, unusually, did not arrive; so Peter walked alone to Mass. When he got home he found his mother in the kitchen, very quiet. 'I have some very sad news, Peter,' she said. 'Sean died during the night. He was found dead in bed this morning.'

Knowing the sanctity of Peter's life I do not doubt his story for one moment.

A. P. Castle

Many years ago in a far off land in a quiet little village lived a young man called Bukin. He had one simple wish: to live forever. He went to a wise old woman in the village and told her what he sought. She said, 'That is very very difficult. I suggest that you go to see the old man of the forest.'

Bukin sought out the old man of the forest and told of his wish. 'That is very very difficult,' replied the old man of the forest. 'I shall live here until all the trees are felled.' 'That is not long enough for me,' replied Bukin. 'Then you had better visit the old man of the lake.' Bukin sought out the old man of the lake and repeated his wish. 'That is very very difficult,' replied the old man of the lake. 'I shall live here until all the water has dried up.' 'That is not long enough for me.' replied Bukin. 'Then you had better visit the old man of the mountain.' Bukin sought out the old man

of the mountain and shared his wish. 'That is very very difficult,'
answered the old man of the mountain. 'I shall live here until the
mountains fall.' 'That seems long enough for me,' replied Bukin,
and stayed with the old man of the mountain. Hundreds of years
passed and Bukin pined for his old village; he desperately wanted
to see again where he had been born, his parents had lived and so
on. The old man of the mountain pleaded with him not to go. 'It
has all changed,' he said, 'and it is dangerous for you.' Bukin
insisted. 'Then you must stay on the horse I give you. If you leave
the horse for any reason, you will die.'

Bukin rode to his old village and found everything had changed.
There were noisy vehicles and tall strange-looking buildings and
the people looked very odd. He was shocked by what he saw and
decided to return. As he left the city on his horse, he saw an old
cart, full of worn-out shoes, upturned at the side of the road. An
old horse stood lamely by the cart and an old man, his face
covered by a black hood stepped out into the road and pleaded
with Bukin for help. 'I can't get off my horse,' said Bukin. The old
man pleaded and pleaded. Bukin had not been asked to help
anyone for many many years; so he agreed. He dismounted and
helped to right the upturned cart.

'What are all these shoes?' asked Bukin. 'I am Death,' the old
man replied and they are the shoes that I have worn out chasing
after you.

P.F.

USEFUL TEXTS

Death:
   Consequence of sin, *Gen. 3:3; Rom. 5:12*
   End of earthly life, *Eccles. 9:10*
   Lot of all, *Heb. 9:27*
   Second death, *Rev. 20:14*

See also: A35 Preparing for death
            A42 Life after death
            B47 Dying to self
            C36 The Day of the Lord

B23
PASTORAL CARE OF THE SICK

'My grace is enough for you; my power is at its
best in weakness.'
2 Corinthians, 12:9

QUOTATIONS

Make sickness itself a prayer.
St Francis of Sales

I have always loved to think of devoted suffering as the highest,
purest, perhaps the only quite pure form of action.
Baron von Hugel

Jesus came to save persons not just souls. He came to help the
suffering in whatever way they were suffering. Sickness of the
body was part of the kingdom of Satan he had come to destroy.
Francis MacNutt

The sufferings of the sick are part of the messianic tribulations
which prepare us and the world for eternal life in glory.
Brian Newns

HUMOUR

'I want some grapes for my sick husband. Do you know if any
poison has been sprayed on these?' 'No, Madam, you'll have to
get that at the chemist's!'

A woman was telling her married daughter that the cold weather
was bad for her rheumatism. Her little granddaughter was present
and overheard the conversation. She didn't say anything then, but
that night when she went to bed she knew what she was going to
do. After she had said her usual prayers she concluded by saying:
'And please, God, make it hot for Gran!'

A priest was summoned in haste by a woman taken ill suddenly. He answered the call though somewhat puzzled, for he knew that she was not of his parish, and was, moreover, known to be a devoted worker in another parish. While he was waiting to be shown to the sickroom he fell to talking to the little girl of the house. 'It is very gratifying to know that your mother thought of me in her illness,' he said. 'Is your own priest away?' 'Oh, no,' answered the child in a matter-of-fact tone, 'he's home. Only we thought it might be something contagious – and we didn't want to take any risks!'

Anon

WORD PICTURES

The sick person, therefore, if a Christian, will desire the presence beside him of consecrated persons, who, together with all suitable technical services, are able to transcend this merely human dimension, so to speak, and, with thoughtful and patient delicacy, offer him the perspective of a vaster hope – that which was taught us by the cross, on which the Son of God was nailed for the redemption of the world.

In this perspective, 'every cross' put on man's shoulders acquires a dignity that is inconceivable on the human plane, and becomes a sign of salvation for him who carried it and also for others.

Pope John Paul II

So when the poor moaning creature comes, I lay my hand on his forehead and say to him, 'Don't be afraid! In an hour's time you shall be put to sleep, and when you wake you won't feel any more pain.' . . . The operation is finished and in the hardly lighted dormitory I watch for the sick man's awaking. Scarcely has he recovered consciousness when he stares about him and ejaculates again and again: 'I've no more pain! I've no more pain!' His hand feels for mine and will not let it go. Then I begin to tell him and others who are in the room that it is the Lord Jesus who has told the doctor and wife to come to Ogowe.

Albert Schweitzer

In the times of the opening up of the West, a prospector lay sick away out on the lonely mountainside, in Eastern Canada, thirty miles from doctor or medicine. Father Pat, a missionary priest, heard of it. He gathered together medicines and hit the trail. When nearing the cabin he came across three mounted miners, who saluted him with the question: 'Hello, parson! Where are you going?' He told them. 'Bill needs a doctor instead of a parson!' said they, and commenced to abuse the priest. They would not let him pass.

Quicker than lightning the priest jerked one of the miners off his horse, knocked another one off, and cleared the trail. He reached the sick man's side, and ministered to his wants. On returning the next day he met the three miners who had camped on the trail bent on revenge. While being abused he appeared meek as a lamb. The trio surrounded him in a threatening manner. Then the priest spoke. 'Will you see fair play if I fight one at a time?' said he. 'Yes, yes, yes,' exclaimed they, chuckling with delight at the prospect. A ring was formed, and soon one of the three measured his length on the ground. 'Come on,' said Father Pat, pleasantly, as the other two seemed somewhat dazed. One came on, and followed the first. 'Next,' said Father Pat. But the third miner took to his heels as though his Satanic Majesty was behind him instead of only a meek minister.

The priest bathed the bruises of the two prostrate miners, and after a few well-chosen words on the iniquity of fighting, went on his way.
Anon

USEFUL TEXTS

Sickness:
    Because of sin, *Lev. 26:14-16; 2 Chr. 21:12-15*
    Result of excesses, *Hos. 7:5; Prov. 25:16*
    Under God's control, *Deut. 32:39; 1 Cor. 11:30*
    Pray for those in, *Acts 28:8; Jas. 5:14-15*

See also: A35 Preparing for death
           B38 The suffering servant

B24
GO TELL EVERYONE

'Jesus summoned the Twelve and began to send them out
in pairs . . . to preach repentance.'
Mark 6:7, 13

QUOTATIONS

Whoever preaches with love preaches effectively.
St Francis of Sales

There is one thing stronger than all the armies in the world: an
idea whose hour is come.
Victor Hugo

The expertise of the pulpit can only be learned slowly and, it may
well be, with a strange mixture of pain and joy.
Donald Coggan

It is very important to live your faith by confessing it, and one of
the best ways to confess it is to preach it.
Thomas Merton

Avoid showing, if you can help it, any sign of displeasure when
you are preaching, or at least anger, as I did one day when they
rang the bell before I had finished.
St Francis of Sales

Whoever rights wrongs, feeds the hungry, cares for the dispossessed
not merely with enthusiasm but with dogged determination,
whoever is meek and poor of heart; whoever is sensitive towards
the numerous little heartaches people suffer is – knowingly or
unknowingly – an envoy of Christ. And whoever shares in Christ's
mission, shares in the fire of the Spirit.
Peter de Rosa

It is no use walking anywhere to preach unless we preach as we walk.
St Francis of Assisi

WORD PICTURES

The story is told of a famous preacher of the Jesuits, whose sermons converted men by scores – that it was revealed to him that not one of his conversions was owing to his talents or eloquence, but all to the prayers of an illiterate lay-brother who sat on the steps of the pulpit praying all the time for the success of the sermon.
Anon

An ancient historian points out this difference between Cicero, the polished speaker, and Demosthenes, the burning orator. After a great speech in Rome, every tongue was loud in the praise of Cicero. But the people who listened to Demosthenes forgot the orator. They went home with hurried stride, lowering brow, clenched fist, muttering in a voice like distant thunder, 'Let us go and fight Philip.'
Anon

The province of Shensi, in North China, contains one of the most ancient and interesting monuments in the world. It is the Nestorian Stone, a tablet that stands outside the walls of Sian-fu, the present capital of the province. It was set up in AD 781, and records the Christian mission to China under the Nestorian priest, Olopun, in 635. About 200 years later, on account of persecution, this tablet appears to have been buried, and the Christian community seems to have disappeared.

When, after 1,000 years' interval, in 1625, Jesuit missionaries came to this historic part of China, they discovered the famous tablet, and it was re-erected; and there, at Sian-fu, it probably still stands today.
Anon

If you go to Bedford you can visit the prison in which one of the most famous books in the world, *The Pilgrim's Progress*, was written. It tells the story of Christian, who sets off for the Celestial

city, helped by such people as Faithful and Hopeful and having his way barred by many such as Apollyon, a foul fiend, hobgoblins and evil spirits, and Giant Despair who lived in Doubting Castle. The book was first published on 18th February 1678. Its author, John Bunyan, was a man who knew what it was like to be thwarted in his work for God. He was a very powerful lay preacher and spent two spells in prison because he refused to leave off preaching in days when only clergymen were supposed to preach.
Anon

The alarm was given as the roof of the rectory at Epworth caught fire in the middle of the night. All but one walked out, leaving little John, aged six, trapped. A servant, standing on the shoulders of another, was just able to pull him through the window before the roof fell in.

Little did the Reverend Samuel Wesley realise that the boy who was dragged from the flames would one day set England on fire. At Oxford, John and some of his companions formed a club for prayer and Bible study, which became known as 'the Holy Club'. Because of their regular habits, they were also nicknamed 'Methodists'. Still John did not find the joy in his heart that he so anxiously wanted. His religion was very flat. On leaving Oxford, he spent two years as a missionary among the settlers in America, but it was back in London, on 24th May, 1738, that John Wesley's life was suddenly changed – converted into something much greater. It was as though he was filled with a new spirit. He knew then what he must do for God.

In no time, he was mounted on horseback and riding hither and thither – his aim to save England. He preached to thousands in the open air; he was frequently attacked; he was refused permission to preach in churches. His followers throughout the land became 'Methodists'.

John Wesley travelled 225,000 miles on foot or on horseback, declaring that he regarded the world as his parish, for the world must come to know the God whom Wesley came to know on 24th May, 1738.
Rowland Purton

USEFUL TEXTS

Mission:

Of Christ:
  to do God's will, *John 6:38*
  to save the lost, *Luke 19:10*
  to reveal God, *Heb. 1:1-3*
  to give his life, *Mark 10:45*
  to fulfil the Law, *Matt. 5:17*

Of Christians:
  to make disciples, *Matt. 28:15-20*

See also: B2 The Good News
           B12 On a mission
           C8 God's messengers

B25
QUIET – TIME FOR PRAYER

'You must come away to some lonely place all
by yourselves and rest for a while.'
Mark 6:31

QUOTATIONS

A man without prayer is like a tree without roots.
Pope Pius XII

The love which we bear to others remains the mark of the
authenticity of our contemplation.
Roger Sebury

Any trial whatever that comes to you can be conquered by silence.
Abbot Pastor

In the rush and noise of life, as you have intervals, step home
within yourselves and be still. Wait upon God and feel his good
presence; this will carry you evenly through your day's business.
William Penn

In troubled water you can scarce see your face; or see it very little,
till the water be quiet and stand still. So in troubled times you can
see little truth. When times are quiet and settled, then truth appears.
Selden

People who only know how to think about God during certain
fixed periods of the day will never get very far in the spiritual life.
In fact they will not even think of him in the moments they have
religiously marked off for 'mental prayer'.
Thomas Merton

Looking round on the noisy insanity of the world, words with
little meaning, actions with little worth, one loves to reflect on the

great empire of silence. The noble silent men, scattered here and there each in his department; silently thinking, silently working; whom no morning papers make mention of.
Thomas Carlyle

If the heart wanders, or is distracted, bring it back to the point quite gently and replace it tenderly in its Master's presence. And even if you did nothing in your hour (of meditation) but bring your heart back and place it again in our Lord's presence, though it went away every time you brought it back, your hour would be very well employed.
St Francis of Sales

The first step in contemplation is to consider steadily what God wants, what is pleasing to him, what is acceptable in his sight. And since we all make many mistakes and the boldness of our will revolts against the rightness of his, let us humble ourselves under the hand of the most high God.
St Bernard of Clairvaux

Contemplation is the awakening to the presence of God in the human heart and in the universe around us. Contemplation is knowledge by love.
Bede Griffiths OSB

We must reserve a little back shop, all our own, entirely free, wherein to establish our true liberty and principal retreat and solitude.
Montaigne

HUMOUR

Johnny liked church pretty well except for the bidding prayers, which he thought were far too long. So when his dad asked the priest to say grace one day at a meal, Johnny was worried. But, to his surprise, the prayer was brief and to the point. Pleased, Johnny said: 'You don't pray long when you're hungry, do you?'
Anon

Ten-year-old Robert had not done his homework the night before. And so he struggled through his written test in geography, doing a lot more guessing than he should have.

All evening, as his mind went back to the written test and some of the answers he had given, he was deeply troubled. What if too many of his answers had been wrong? What if he should not get a pass mark? That night, after he had said his prayers, he suddenly blurted the nervous postscript: 'And, please, God, make Paris the capital of Sweden!'
Anon

WORD PICTURES

An old man said: 'The man who hath learned by experience the sweetness of the quietness which is in his cell, doth not flee from meeting his neighbour because he is as one who despiseth him, but because of the fruits which he plucked from silence.'

One day last summer, after I'd been working on some songs, I left the harp before the open window. Suddenly I heard the sound of distant and very lovely music. It lasted only a few seconds and left me very puzzled. When it happened again I noticed that the sound came from the instrument and was caused by the gentle breeze from the open window playing on the harp strings.

At times of prayer we can be like that harp, by allowing sufficient calm to gather round us so that the Holy Spirit, the Breath of God, may play his music on us. But remember, it was a very gentle breeze and the music could be heard only because of the surrounding stillness.
Mary O'Hara

At the foot of a cliff, under the windows of the Castle Miramar, formerly the residence of the Mexican Emperor Maximilian, at a depth of eighty feet below the surface of the clear waters of the Adriatic, there was, years ago, a kind of cage fashioned by divers in the face of the rock. In that cage were some of the most magnificent pearls in existence. They belonged to the Archduchess Rainer.

Having been left unworn for a long time, the gems lost their colour and the experts were unanimous in declaring that the only means by which they could be restored to their original brilliancy was submitting them to a prolonged immersion in the depths of the sea. For some years they were kept lying in the crystal depths, and gradually regained their unrivalled beauty and splendour. The only secret of regaining the lost lustre of the inner life, the high desire, the fuller insight, is to get back again to those blessed depths from which the soul first received its bright touch of divine and holier things.

Anon

'No, I don't meditate,' he said. 'That's for the monks. Not my cup of tea at all.' So I asked him about his cup of tea. Where did it come from. I mean was the tea picked in Sri Lanka, India, China? And who picked it? Were they well paid? How were the leaves dried, packed and shipped? And where did the milk come from? Yes, I know the milkman brought it. But what about the cow – a black and white Friesian, brown-eyed Jersey, or what? Was the grass plentiful or had the sun dried it out? Then I asked him if he took sugar? It came from a plantation in the West Indies possibly. Think of the men and women who harvested it. Were they well paid? Then there's the cup. Did they use china clay from Cornwall, was it made in Staffordshire?

There are so many things to thank God for: all good gifts around us. And we've to thank God for the people who help us to use them. Plenty to meditate on there.

Brother Peter

USEFUL TEXTS

Prayer:
> Of faith, *Jas. 5:15*
> Of the righteous, *Prov. 15:29*
> Hindrance to, *1 Pet. 3:7*
> Of Christ, *John 17*
> For forgiveness, *Ps. 51:1-9*

See also: A1   The value of time
           A10 Seeking perfection
           C32 Prayer
           C47 The indwelling Spirit

B26
THE WHOLE PERSON

'Bear with one another charitably, in complete selflessness,
gentleness and patience.'
Ephesians 4:2

QUOTATIONS

True holiness consists in doing God's will with a smile.
Mother Teresa

May the outward and inward man be as one.
Socrates

If a man constantly aspires, is he not elevated?
Henry David Thoreau

'Tis not what man does which exalts him, but what man would do.
Robert Browning

Try not to become a man of success but rather try to become a
man of value.
Albert Einstein

The body is a vital source of gratification which we ignore or
dismiss only at the risk of violating our integrity.
Jack Dominian

We have become too spiritual in a 'holy, holy' sense, whereas we
should be biblically holy – that means facing up to the totality of
life, in the power of the Cross.
George MacLeod

Live for yourself – live for life, then you are most truly the friend
of man.
Kahlil Gibran

The more a person discovers himself the way he really *is*, the more he feels the need of God, and the more God manifests himself to such a soul.
Fulton Sheen

Even a cursory reading of the New Testament leaves a convincing impression that Jesus was typically Hebrew in his view of man; he did not divide man into body and soul, but he saw him as a whole person.
Francis MacNutt

We must not reject man in favour of God, nor reject God in favour of man: we must choose God and man, for the glory of God is man alive, supremely in Christ.
Leon Joseph Suenans

Every animal leaves traces of what it was; man alone leaves traces of what he created.
Jacob Bonowski

He who humbles himself shall be saved; he who bends shall be made straight; he who empties himself shall be filled.
Tao-Teh-King

Be lovingly attentive,
be lovingly intelligent,
be lovingly reasonable,
be lovingly responsible.
Bernard Longeran

PROVERB

The pleasures of the senses pass quickly; those of the heart become sorrows; but those of the mind are ever with us, even to the end of our journey.
Spanish proverb

WORD PICTURES

I wish I loved the Human Race;
I wish I loved its silly face;
I wish I liked the way it walks;
I wish I liked the way it talks;
And when I'm introduced to one
I wish I thought *What Jolly Fun!*
Sir Walter Raleigh

'I am a man and I count nothing that is human alien to me.' The sentence which, when first spoken in the Roman theatre, made it ring with applause. Trite as it is, we can scarce come upon it now without the whole heart rising to welcome it.

No character, we may affirm, was ever rightly understood till it had been first regarded with a certain feeling, not of toleration only, but of sympathy.
Thomas Carlyle

To be honest;
to be kind;
to earn a little
and to spend a little less;
to make, upon the whole,
a family happier for his presence;
to renounce, when that shall be necessary,
and not be embittered;
to keep a few friends,
but these without capitulation;
above all, in the same condition,
to keep friends with himself;
here is a task for all that a man has of
fortitude and delicacy.
Robert Louis Stevenson

There is an old legend which tells of a powerful genius who promised a beautiful maiden a gift of rare value if she would go through a field of corn and select the largest and ripest ear, and in doing so she was not to pause nor go backward nor wander hither and thither. The value of the gift was to be in proportion to the size and perfection of the ear. The maiden passed by many fine ears, but so anxious was she to get the largest and most perfect that she kept on without plucking any. Then the ears began to grow smaller and smaller, until finally they became so stunted that she was ashamed to pluck any, and not being allowed to go backward, she came out on the other side without any. For lack of decision she missed the very gift she coveted.

Tena F. Best

See also: A2   Integrity
           A10 Seeking perfection
           B20 Growth to maturity

B27
BREAD FROM HEAVEN

'It is my Father who gives you the bread from heaven,
the true bread; for the bread of God is that which
comes down from heaven and gives life to the world.'
John 6:32-33

QUOTATIONS

God is all to thee: if thou be hungry, he is bread; if thirsty, he is
water; if darkness, he is light; if naked, he is a robe of immortality.
St Augustine of Hippo

The heart preparing for communion should be as a crystal vial filled
with clear water in which the least mote of uncleanness will be seen.
St Elizabeth Seton

Here is bread, which strengthens men's heart, and therefore called
the staff of life.
Matthew Henry

The reality of our communion with Christ and in him with one
another is the increase of love in our hearts.
William Temple

WORD PICTURES

I like the story of little orphan Joe. Joe went to be examined by
the orphanage doctor. When he came back the nun asked, 'What
did he say to you, Joe?' And Joe answered, 'He said to me, "What
a miserable little specimen you are".' And then Joe added, 'But,
Sister, I don't think he knew I had made my first communion.'
    You see, that's what gives us value. You and I don't need to
fight and fume to win love and respect. For God who made us
likes us so much – even if really we are not very likeable – that he
comes to us in communion and comradeship.
Edwin White

Therefore in order that we may become of his Body; not in desire only, but also in very fact, let us become commingled with that Body. This, in truth, takes place by means of the food which he has given us as a gift, because he desired to prove the love which he has for us. It is for this reason that he has shared himself with us and has brought his body down to our level, namely, that we might be one with him as the body is joined with the head.

And to show the love he had for us he has made it possible for those who desire, not merely to look upon him, but even to touch him and to consume him and to fix their teeth in his flesh and to be commingled with him; in short, to fulfil all their love. Let us then, come back from that table like lions breathing out fire, thus becoming terrifying to the Devil and remaining mindful of our head and of the love which he has shown us.

St John Chrysostom

Napoleon was an artist in war, and his long succession of victories were the marvels of the world. One day some of his generals were discussing and comparing their master's great battles, and one of them ventured to ask him which was the happiest day of his life. They wondered if he would think of the Bridge of Lodi perhaps, the scene of his early triumph with the Army of Italy, a young general of twenty-six wresting Lombardy from the Austrians. Or more likely of the 'glorious sun' of Austerlitz, the shattering victory which made him master of Europe.

The Emperor looked thoughtful. 'Ah – the happiest day of my life? That was the day of my first Communion. I was near to God then.'

F. H. Drinkwater

It is told of Sadhu Sundar Singh that many years ago he was distributing gospels in the Central provinces of India and he came to some non-Christians on a train and offered a man a copy of John's Gospel. The man took it, tore it into pieces in anger and threw the pieces out of the window. That seemed the end, but it so happened in the Providence of God, there was a man idly walking along the line that very day, and he picked up, as he walked along, a little bit of paper and looked at it, and the words on it in his own language were 'the Bread of Life'. He did not know what it meant; but he enquired among his friends and one of them said: 'I can tell you, it is out of the Christian book. You

must not read it or you will be defiled.' The man thought for a moment and then said: 'I want to read the book that contains that beautiful phrase', and he bought a copy of the New Testament. He was shown where the sentence occurred – Our Lord's words 'I am the Bread of Life'; and as he studied the Gospel, the light flooded into his heart. Later he became a preacher of the Gospel in the Central Province of India. That little bit of paper, through God's Spirit, was indeed the Bread of Life to him.
Anon

O Christ, who holds the open gate,
O Christ, who drives the furrow straight,
O Christ, the plough, O Christ, the laughter
of holy white birds flying after,
lo, all my heart's field red and torn,
and Thou wilt bring the young green corn,
the young green corn divinely springing,
the young green corn for ever singing;
and when the field is fresh and fair
thy blessed feet shall glitter there,
and we will walk the weeded field,
and tell the golden harvest's yield,
the corn that makes the holy bread
by which the soul of man is fed,
the holy bread, the food unpriced,
thy everlasting mercy, Christ.
John Masefield

Useful texts

Bread:
    Unleaven for Passover, *Exod. 12:15, 17-20*
    In the tabernacle, *Lev. 24:5-9; Heb. 9:2*
    Miraculous provision of, *1 Kings 17:6; Matt. 14:19-21*
    'Bread of Life', *John 6:25-29*
    Eucharist, *Luke 22:7-19; 1 Cor. 11:23-29*

See also: A21 Feeding the hungry
            A44 Meeting Christ in the sacraments
            B29 The Eucharist

B28
THE FATHER
WHO DRAWS US TO HIMSELF

'No one can come to me unless he is drawn
by the Father who sent me.'
John 6:44

QUOTATIONS

The Father is our fount and origin, in whom our life and being is
begun.
John of Ruysbroeck

To know God and to live are one and the same thing.
Leo Tolstoy

I sought thee at a distance, and did not know that thou wast near.
I sought thee abroad, and behold thou wast within me.
St Augustine of Hippo

With God, we should feel like a child in its mother's arms, if he
carries us on the left arm or the right, it is all the same to us, we
let him do what he wants.
St Francis of Sales

There is need neither of art nor of science for going to God, but
only a heart resolutely determined to apply itself to nothing but
him, or for his sake, and to love him only.
Brother Lawrence

Father in Heaven, when the thought of thee wakes in our hearts,
let it not awaken like a frightened bird that flies about in dismay,
but like a child waking from its sleep with a heavenly smile.
Sören Kierkegaard

WORD PICTURES

It was well past midnight. Little four-year-old Tommy had been asleep for hours. Suddenly he awoke from a bad dream. Not knowing whether he was alone in the large, dark bedroom, he whispered into the darkness: 'Daddy, are you there?'

From the other side of the room came the comforting voice: 'Yes, Tommy, Daddy's here.' For a moment Tommy lay silent, still not quite sure his bad dream was imagined. Once more he whispered: 'Daddy, is your face toward me?' And once more the kind voice of his father assured him: 'Yes, Tommy, my face is toward your bed.' With that assurance the little fellow turned over, closed his eyes, and drifted back to peaceful slumber.
Anon

Some many years ago a certain Captain Dennis was in charge of a ship which sailed between Liverpool and New York. During one of his voyages he had all his family, besides a large crew, on board. One night while all were quietly sleeping a sudden squall of wind arose. It struck the ship with great force and threw her over on her beam ends. There was a great tumbling and crashing of things on board. The people awoke in a great fright. They were in great danger. Some jumped out of their berths and began to dress in a hurry, not knowing but that the vessel would soon sink.

The Captain had a little girl on board about eight years old. She woke with the rest of the people. 'What's the matter?' asked the frightened child. They told her a sudden squall had struck the ship and thrown her on her side. 'Is father on deck?' asked she. 'Yes, father's on deck.' 'Then it'll be alright,' she said, and quietly sank back on her pillow and went to sleep again.
Anon

In Bernard Shaw's play, *Saint Joan*, one of the officers asks, 'How do you mean? Voices?' The maid replies, 'I hear voices telling me what to do. They come from God.'

The weakling King Charles, whom she has helped to have crowned, impatiently exclaims, 'Oh your voices, your voices. Why don't the voices come to me? I am king, not you.'

Joan answers, 'They do come to you; but you do not hear them. You have not sat in the field in the evening listening for them. When the angelus rings you cross yourself and have done with it; but if you prayed with your heart, and listened to the thrilling of the bells in the air after they stop ringing, you would hear the voices as well as I do.'
Carl H. Elliot

USEFUL TEXTS

Fatherhood:
    Of God to all he created, *Deut. 32:6*
    Of God to all who believe in his Son, *Gal. 4:4-6*
    Of God to Jesus Christ, *Col. 1:3*

See also: B40 One God
             C20 Our Father in heaven
             C27 The Father who receives us back

B29
THE EUCHARIST

'For my flesh is real food and my blood is real drink.
Those who eat my flesh and drink my blood
live in me and I live in them.'
John 6:55-56

QUOTATIONS

The Eucharist is the silence of God, the weakness of God.
Carlo Carretto

The Eucharist is the Church at her best.
Gabriel Moran

The Eucharist is the means whereby those who once received the Spirit in baptism are constantly renewed in the Spirit until their life's end.
Alan Richardson

Our Lord did not say: 'Come unto me all ye faultless'; neither did he say, 'Be sure you tear yourselves to pieces first.' There are only three necessities of a good Communion – Faith, Hope and Charity. To rely utterly on God and be in charity with the world – this is the essential. What you happen to be feeling at the moment does not matter in the least.
Evelyn Underhill

LONGER QUOTATIONS

Concerning the Eucharist, give thanks in this way. First for the cup: 'We give thanks to thee, our Father, for the holy vine of David thy servant, which thou madest known to us through thy servant Jesus. To thee be the glory for ever.' And for the broken bread: 'We give thanks to thee, our Father, for the life and knowledge which thou madest known to us through thy servant Jesus. To thee be the glory for ever. As this broken bread was scattered upon the hills, and was gathered together and made one, so let thy Church be gathered together into thy kingdom from the ends of the earth; for thine is the glory and the power through Christ Jesus for ever.'

Let none eat or drink of your Eucharist, save such as are baptised into the name of the Lord. For concerning this the Lord hath said: 'Give not that which is holy to dogs.'
The Didache

We are that same body. What is the bread actually? The Body of Christ. What do communicants become? The body of Christ. In fact, just as bread is the result of many grains, and although remaining themselves are not distinguished from one another because they are united, so we too are mutually united with Christ. We are not nourished, some from one body, others from another, but all from the same Body.
St John Chrysostom

The gifts you ask of me for these brothers of mine – the only gift my heart can give – is not the overflowing tenderness of those special, preferential loves which you implant in our lives as the most powerful created agent of our inward growth, it is something less tender but just as real and of even greater strength. Your will is that, with the help of your Eucharist, between men and my brother men there should be revealed that basic attraction (already dimly felt in every love once it become strong) which mystically transforms the myriads of rational creatures into (as it were) a single monad in you, Christ Jesus.
Teilhard de Chardin

'Do this in remembrance of me.' There are two points to be noted here. First, we are commanded to use this sacrament, Jesus intended this by saying: 'Do this'. In the second place we do it in memory of his going to death for us.

So he said: 'Do this'. He could not have laid down a commandment more profitable or delightful, one more healthful or attractive,
one more like to life eternal. We shall study these point by point.
The sacrament profits us by forgiving our sins, and is of utmost use
to us by the outpouring of grace in our life. 'The father of spirits . . .
disciplines us for our good, that we may share in his holiness.'
Christ's holiness lies in his sacrificial action, that is, he offered
himself in the sacrament: to his Father to redeem us; to us for our
use. 'For their sake I consecrate myself,' he said. 'Christ, who
through the eternal Spirit offered himself without blemish to God,
will purify our conscience from dead works to serve the living God.'
St Albert the Great

. . . I receive in communion
the Body, divinised as being that of God.
I too become god
in this inexpressible union.
See what a mystery!
The soul then and the body
are one being in two essences.
Therefore these are one and two
in communion with Christ
and drinking his blood,
they are united in two essences,
united in this way to the essences of my God,
they become god by participation.
They are called by the same name as that of him
in whom they have participated on a level of essence.
They say that coal is fire
and the iron is black.
Yet when the iron is immersed in the fire
it appears as fire.
If it then appears as such,
we also can call it by that name.
We see it as fire,
we can call it fire.
St Simeon the New Theologian

WORD PICTURE

There is a strange legend that when Almighty God had finished the creation of his beautiful world, he called his angels together and asked them if they could think of anything further that was needed to complete it. 'There is nothing,' said the angels, 'but that a voice, strong and adoring, should praise God day and night, for his goodness.' Such a voice is heard in the Eternal Sacrifice which is offered continually from God's altar throughout the world.
Anon

See also: A44 Meeting Christ in the sacraments
          B18 Sunday
          B27 Bread from heaven

B30
MARRIED LOVE

'A man must leave his father and mother and be joined
to his wife, and the two will become one body.'
Genesis 2:24

QUOTATIONS

A happy marriage is the union of two good forgivers.
Robert Quillen

In the ideal marriage husband and wife are not loyal to each other
because it is their duty, but because it is their joy.
E. Merrill Root

None can be eternally united who have not died for each other.
Coventry Patmore

Together invite the Holy Spirit of love into your hearts and into
your homes.
Pope John Paul II

Sexual love in marriage is a relationship in which a couple affirm
each other's identity, by which they heal and sustain each other and
through which they make Christ sacramentally present to each other.
The English Catholic Bishops

Whenever Christ was confronted by people in sexual disarray he
took good care to safeguard sexuality by reminding them that they
had to avoid sin; that is to say to use their sexuality in a fully
human way.
Jack Dominian

I see no marriage that sooner fail than those contracted on account
of beauty and amorous desire.
Montaigne

Roman Catholic teaching maintains that human love is a precious gift, a sharing in the life and love of God himself. Unselfish love between persons is itself a way to God. It enriches the human personality. In married love a couple come together in a lifelong, life-giving union in which they give themselves totally and exclusively to each other. To be fully human and self-giving that love has to remain open to the possibility of new life. It provides the stability and affection necessary for the nurturing and development of the growing child. For all these reasons, the full sexual expression of love is reserved for husband and wife within marriage.
Basil Hume

A study conducted over a seven-year period at the University of Virginia found that one year after their divorce, 60 per cent of the men and 73 per cent of the women felt they made a mistake by splitting up. Even those who were miserable in their marriages said that if they had tried harder, they might have been able to work out their marital problems and stay together.
The Christophers

PROVERBS

More things belong to marriage than four bare legs in a bed.
French proverb

Do not choose your wife at a dance, but in the fields among the harvesters.
Czech proverb

HUMOUR

'My husband has only one fault. He can't seem to do anything right.'

Golden jubilarian husband's advice for happy marriage. 'When your wife isn't speaking to you, just don't interrupt.'

Wife to depressed husband: 'Look on the bright side, dear. When Mozart was your age, he'd been dead for 15 years.'
Punch

Wife: 'Why do you always lean out of the window when I sing?'
Husband: 'I want the neighbours to know it isn't me!'

A middle-aged woman clambered on to a bus with three sets of twins trailing behind her. When they were all seated in the bus, the conductor asked her: 'Do you always get twins?'

'Oh, no,' replied the woman, 'Hundreds of times we don't get anything.'
Anon

Father Vincent McNabb was speaking on Christianity at Hyde Park Corner when a woman heckler shouted, 'If I was your wife I'd put poison in your tea,' to which Father MacNabb replied, 'Madam, if I were your husband, I'd drink it.'
J. Vose

Wife, reading husband's fortune card from weighing machine: 'You are a leader with a magnetic personality and a strong character. You are intelligent, witty and attractive to the opposite sex.' She paused. 'It has your weight wrong too.'
Bernhardt

When I asked the class to explain the meaning of the word 'bachelor', one girl wrote, 'A very happy man'. 'Where did you get that idea?' I asked her. 'My father helped me with my homework,' she confessed.

On their 50th wedding anniversary, a couple summed up the reason for their long and happy marriage. The husband said, 'I have tried never to be selfish. After all there is no "I" in the word "marriage".' The wife said, 'For my part, I have never corrected my husband's spelling.'
Robert Brault

Wife (with newspaper): 'It says here that men grow bald because of the intense activity of their brains.'
Husband: 'Exactly. And women have no whiskers because of the intense activity of their chins!'

WORD PICTURE

By sexual union a man and woman say to each other, 'I love you. There is no one else in the world I love the way I love you. . . . I want to share my life and my world with you and I want you to share your life and your world with me. . . . I want us to build a future together that will be our future. . . . I will be faithful to you not just now but always. I will never let you down or walk out on you. . . . I will never put anyone in your place no matter what happens.'
Sexual Union Irish Bishops

USEFUL TEXTS

Marriage:
Permanent bond, *Matt. 19:5-6*
Instituted by God, *Gen. 2:18-24*
Honourable for all, *Heb. 13:4*
Means of preventing immorality, *1 Cor. 7:2-4*

See also: A46 Priesthood of the laity
B6   The Family
C5   The institution of marriage

B31
THE COMMANDMENTS OF LIFE

'Accept and submit to the word which has been planted
in you and can save your souls.'
James 1:21

QUOTATIONS

Man cannot break the laws of God, he can only break himself
against them.
G. K. Chesterton

The commands of God are all designed to make us more happy
than we can possibly be without them.
Thomas Wilson

The eleventh Commandment: Thou shalt not be found out.
George Whyte-Melville

I am not sure whether ethical absolutes exist. But I am sure that
we have to act as if they exist or civilisation perishes.
Arthur Koestler

Most people really believe that the Christian commandments (e.g.
to love one's neighbour as oneself) are intentionally a little too
severe, like putting the clock half an hour ahead to make sure of
not being late in the morning.
Sören Kierkegaard

The moral life of man is like the flight of a bird in the air. He is
sustained only by effort, and when he ceases to exert himself he falls.
James A. Froude

HUMOUR

An American bishop, invited to preach down South to a coloured
church, was asked by a venerable churchwarden: 'Have you ever
preached in the South before, sir?' 'No,' replied the bishop. 'I will

give you one piece of advice,' added the churchwarden. 'Don't lay out too much on them old Ten Commandments, for this is a most respectable congregation.'

An aged Scot told his minister that he was about to make a pilgrimage to the Holy Land. 'And when I'm there,' said the pilgrim, complacently, 'I'll read the Ten Commandments aloud frae the tap o' Mount Sinai.'

The minister looked at him with an eye of pity, and said, 'Sandy, tak' my advice: bide at hame and keep them.'
D. Williamson

A minister taking his morning walk came across a stonebreaker. After giving him a cheery 'Good morning', he remarked that he had a deal of work to get through. 'Aye,' said the man, 'them stones are like the Ten Commandments.' 'Why so?' replied the parson. 'You can go on breaking 'em,' came the reply, 'but you can never get rid of 'em.'

An Englishman and a Jew were talking about the ways of their respective races. 'You people,' said the Jew, 'have been taking things from us for thousands of years. The Ten Commandments for instance.' 'Well, yes,' said the other, 'we took them from you all right, but you can't say that we've kept them!'

At dinner a very pompous American woman was seated next to a rabbi. Wishing to impress him she said rather grandly: 'One of my ancestors signed the Declaration of Independence.' 'Indeed,' replied the rabbi, 'one of mine wrote the Ten Commandments!'

USEFUL TEXTS

The Commandments:
  Of God, *John 15:12*
  Of Christ, examples, *Matt. 5:16, 27-28, 31-32, 34*
  Of a father, *Prov. 6:20; 7:1*

See also: A29 True obedience
           C6   The Old Testament Law
           C39 Doing God's will

B32
THE WONDERS OF GOD

'He has done all things well,' they said, 'he makes
the deaf hear and the dumb speak.'
Mark 7:37

QUOTATIONS

Jesus was himself the one convincing and permanent miracle.
Ian MacLaren

God will do nothing without man. If God works a miracle, he
does it through man.
Paracelsus

The man who cannot wonder is but a pair of spectacles behind
which there are no eyes.
Thomas Carlyle

Let never day nor night unhallowed pass, but still remember what
the Lord hath done.
William Shakespeare

Miracles are not only not unlikely, they are positively likely; and
for this simple reason, because, for the most part, when God
begins he goes on. . . . If the divine Being does a thing once, he is,
judging by human reason, likely to do it again.
John Henry Newman

A miracle in the Biblical sense is an event which happens in a
manner contrary to the regularly observed processes of nature. . . .
It may happen according to higher laws as yet but dimly discerned
by scientists, and therefore must not be thought of as an irrational
irruption of divine power into the orderly realm of nature.
Alan Richardson

WORD PICTURES

A. J. Gossip used to love to tell a story about Mungo Park, the great explorer. He had been journeying for days and miles in the wilds of China, in the most desolate surroundings. Then quite suddenly he saw on the ground at his feet a little blue flower. And, as he saw it, he said gently, 'God has been here!'

There is the legend of a monk who had wandered into the fields when a lark began to sing. He had never heard a lark before, and he stood there entranced until the bird and its song had become part of the heavens. Then he went back to the monastery and found there a doorkeeper whom he did not know and who did not know him. Other monks came, and they were all strangers to him. He told them he was Father Anselm, but that was no help. Finally they looked through the books of the monastery, and these revealed that there had been a Father Anselm there a hundred or more years before. Time had been blotted out while he listened to the lark.
J. M. Barrie

Brother Tebaldo once told us something that he himself had seen. When St Francis was preaching one day to the people of Trevi, a noisy and ungovernable ass went careering about the square, frightening people out of their wits. And when it became clear that no one could catch it or restrain it, St Francis said to it, 'Brother ass, please be quiet and allow me to preach to the people.' When the donkey heard this it immediately bowed its head and, to everyone's astonishment, stood perfectly quiet. And the Blessed Francis, fearing that the people might take too much notice of this astonishing miracle, began saying funny things to make them laugh.
John Moorman

Owing to the excitement caused by several alleged miracles in the St Medard Cemetery in Paris in 1732, Louis XV had this sign placed upon the locked gates. 'By order of the King, God is hereby forbidden to work miracles in this place.' With similar arrogance the 'I' on the throne of our unsurrendered hearts forbids God to work his miracles within us.
John Schmidt

325

I am thinking now of those men who in 1917 held our country's freedom in that Retreat from Mons. And I remember how they came under our care, and told me the story of that miracle, 'The Angels from Mons'. Our line was held by only a few hundred men guarding the road to Paris, and the German cavalry charged at full strength, but, at a certain point, no horse would pass. They wheeled and stampeded, but they would not go on. Reinforcements were brought up, but always with the same result; and our men still held on.

I have no reason to doubt for one moment the story of that miracle. It did happen, and even if all those men did not see the vision, the horses did!
Anon

My grandfather was lame. Once he was asked to tell a story about his teacher and he told how the holy Baal Shem Tov used to jump and dance when he was praying. My grandfather stood up while he was telling the story and the story carried him away so much that he had to jump and dance to show how the master had done it. From that moment he was healed. This is how stories ought to be told.
Martin Buber

USEFUL TEXTS
Miracles:
   Attributed to:
   God's power, *Acts 15:12*
   Christ's power, *John 2:11*
   Spirit's power, *Matt. 12:28*
   To reveal God's glory, *John 11:40*

See also: A18 Balance in nature
           B39 Creation

B33
FAITH AND GOOD WORKS

'Faith is like that, if good works do not
go with it, it is quite dead.'
James 2:17

QUOTATIONS

Those prayers quickly ascend to God which the merits of our
works urge upon God.
St Cyprian

We must learn that to expect God to do everything while we do
nothing is not faith, but superstition.
Martin Luther King

You must live with people to know their problems, and live with
God in order to solve them.
Peter T. Forsyth

The hottest places in hell are reserved for those who, in a period
of moral crisis, maintain their neutrality.
Dante

A man must make his opportunity as oft as find it.
Francis Bacon

The Christian should resemble a fruit tree, not a Christmas tree.
For the gaudy decorations of a Christmas tree are only tied on,
whereas fruit grows on a fruit tree.
John R. W. Stott

It is faith's work to claim and challenge loving kindness out of all
the roughest strokes of God.
S. Rutherford

Faith is the power that you and I have to move mountains – if we are not too proud to push a barrow.
Peter Fletcher

Let a man first do good deeds, and then ask God for knowledge of Torah: let a man first act as righteous and upright men act, and then let him ask God for wisdom: let a man first grasp the way of humility, and then ask God for understanding.
Tanna Debe Eliyahu

WORD PICTURES

A teamster sought the Rabbi of Berditchev's advice as to whether he should give up his occupation because it interfered with regular attendance at the synagogue.

'Do you carry poor travellers free of charge?' asked the Rabbi.

'Yes,' answered the teamster.

'Then you serve the Lord in your occupation just as faithfully as you would be frequenting the synagogue.
Hasidic Story

Faith must be accompanied by works. Mohammed once overheard one of his followers say, 'I will loose my camel and commit it to God.' 'Friend,' said the prophet, 'tie thy camel and commit it to God.'

A little girl told a friend who was visiting her father that her brothers set traps to catch the birds. He asked her what she did. She replied, 'I prayed that the traps might not catch the birds.' 'Anything else?' 'Yes,' she said, 'I prayed that God would keep the birds out of the traps.' 'Anything else?' 'Yes, then I went and kicked the traps all to pieces.'
Christian Leader

In the history of the Scout Movement pride of place is given to the 'Good Turn' performed by a London newspaper boy. This scout, meeting Mr William Boyce, the American newspaper proprietor, in Fleet Street during a London fog, piloted him to his West End destination, refusing any reward. Mr Boyce was so impressed that,

on his return to America, he transplanted the Boy Scout movement there in 1910. Millions of American boys have since enjoyed Scout training as a result.
Anon

A person who is filled with the Holy Spirit speaks several languages. These several languages are the various ways of witnessing to Christ, such as humility, poverty, obedience and patience, with which we speak when we practise them towards our neighbour. Language comes alive when it speaks by deeds. Enough of talking; let actions speak. We are bloated with words and empty works. That is why we are accursed by the Lord, who cursed the fig tree on which he found no fruit but only leaves. It has been laid down as a law for the preacher, says St Gregory, that he should practise what he preaches. It is useless for a man to boast that he knows the law, if his behaviour contradicts his teaching.
St Anthony of Padua

There is a story to the effect that a poor man asked his rich brother: 'Why are you wealthy, and I am not?' The other answered: 'Because I have no scruples against doing wrong.' The poor brother began to misconduct himself, but he remained poor. He complained of this to his elder brother, who answered: 'The reason your transgressions have not made you wealthy is that you did them not from conviction that it matters not whether we do good or evil, but solely because you desired riches.' How much more applicable is this to doing good with the proper intention!
The Baalshem

USEFUL TEXTS

Faith:
   Gift of God, *Eph. 2:8*
   Condition of salvation, *Acts 16:31*

Works:
   Encouraged, *Matt. 5:16; Titus 2:7; 1 Pet. 2:12*

See also: C22 The Light of Faith
            C30 Increase our Faith

B34
HUMAN RIGHTS

'Wherever you find jealousy and ambition, you find disharmony and wicked things of every kind being done.'
James 3:16

QUOTATIONS

Rights are something other people grant you after you've fought tooth and nail for them.
Brendan Francis

When men say they have rights, they generally mean that they are suffering wrongs.
J. A. Spender

When people begin to ignore human dignity, it will not be long before they begin to ignore human rights.
G. K. Chesterton

Wherever there is a human being, I see God-given rights inherent in that being, whatever may be the sex or complexion.
William L. Garrison

Every man has by law of nature a right to such a waste portion of the earth as is necessary for his subsistence.
St Thomas More

Be as beneficent as the sun or the sea, but if your rights as a rational being are trenched on, die in the first inch of your territory.
Ralph Waldo Emerson

We hold these truths to be self-evident – that all men are created equal; that they are endowed by their Creator with certain unalienable rights; that among these are life, liberty, and the pursuit of happiness.
Thomas Jefferson – The Declaration of Independence

Justice impels us to desire and to insist that everyone receives what we all have a right to. The Christian is a witness and an apostle of justice in the world. He cannot bear any form of inequality, oppression or tyranny.
Max Thurian

What God had been and is doing in the world is what it takes to make and to keep human life human.
Paul Lehmann

God always takes his stand unconditionally and passionately on this side and on this side alone; against the lofty and on behalf of the lowly.
Karl Barth

God continues to be a 'scandal' to us. He challenges us through the situations of conflict, which are presented to us as claims to human dignity, and for acceptance with the differences inherent in being human. The challenge to Christians is to respond to the 'word of God' as presented to us through human beings who have specific needs as they strive to affirm their humanity.
Alan Falconer

WORD PICTURES
John Newton wrote a great hymn which the Church sings – 'Glorious things of thee are spoken'. When he wrote it he was sitting in the sunshine of a ship's deck while in the hatches slaves were groaning in anguish, shackled and being taken to be sold in some hellhole in London or America. We might call Newton a hypocrite. But he wasn't. He was morally asleep. Now is the time for good people everywhere to awake from their moral slumber, else some future generation will look upon us as insensitive to the evils around us as was John Newton who described the voyage as one of sweet communion with Jesus. The opportunity is here, let's not let it pass.

The tree of liberty
Without this tree, alake this life
is but a vale o' woe, man;
a scene o' sorrow mixed wi' strife,
nae real joys we know, man,
we labour soon, we labour late,
to feed the titled knave, man;
and a' the comfort we're to get
is that ayont the grave, man.

Wi' plenty o' sic trees, I trow,
the world would live in peace, man;
the sword would help to make a plough,
the din o' war wad cease, man.
Like brethren in a common cause,
we'd on each other smile, man;
and equal rights and equal laws
wad gladden every isle, man.
Robert Burns

The young man was explaining about his months in a South American prison. He gave a terrible account of interrogation and torture and then added: 'Of course there are many worse stories which I still cannot bring myself to repeat.' He was in his early twenties, not long married and only out of prison for one week.

He explained the Christian commitment which had led him to give up a comfortable career in the city to work with the peasants, a job which had led to conflicts with the authorities, imprisonment and torture. Now on his release from prison he planned to return to the rural area. 'But isn't that dangerous?' I ask. He shrugs. 'Possibly, yes, I suppose it is.'

I went to my home country and soon after heard the sequel. He had returned to work with the peasants, and just a few days after his arrival was standing beside the paddy field talking with some friends. Absorbed in their conversation, they didn't notice an unmarked car slowing to stop. From the car a man in civilian clothes pointed the automatic rifle and shot my friend dead. The car sped off before the stunned villagers could react.

In that brief instant the blood of yet another unnamed and little-known martyr had returned to the soil. His Christian obedience had meant death.
Ron O'Grady

See also: A21 Feeding the hungry
          A40 The equality of women
          B44 The dignity of the individual
          C1   Liberation from fear
          C33 Equality

B35
THE GRACE OF GOD

'The Lord spoke with Moses, but took some of the Spirit
that was on him and put it on the seventy elders.
When the Spirit came on them, they prophesied.'
Numbers 11:25

QUOTATIONS

Glory is perfected grace.
Meister Eckhart

We cannot seek grace through gadgets.
J. B. Priestly

Don't let go of me, God, hold on a bit longer.
Charles de Gaulle

He rideth at ease that is carried by the grace of God.
Thomas à Kempis

Yet in my walks it seems to me that the grace of God is in courtesy.
Hilaire Belloc

We are not drawn to God by iron chains, but by sweet attractions
and holy inspirations.
St Francis of Sales

God only asks from you what he gives you power to do.
Walsham How

Grace freely justifies me and sets me free from slavery to sin.
St Bernard of Clairvaux

Man is born broken; he lives by mending. The grace of God is the
glue.
Eugene O'Neil

Grace is nature's perfection, and therefore impairs nothing natural.
St Thomas Aquinas

A balanced soul, alight with tranquil grace within, is not afraid to look at the darkness without.
R. H. Benson

Grace is not sought nor bought nor wrought. It is a free gift of Almighty God to needy mankind.
Billy Graham

We cannot bridge the gap between God and ourselves through even the most intensive and frequent prayers; the gap betweeen God and ourselves can only be bridged by God.
Paul Tillich

WORD PICTURES

What an amazing, what a blessed disproportion between the evil we do, and the evil we are capable of doing, and seem sometimes on the very verge of doing! If my soul has grown tares, when it was full of the seeds of nightshade, how happy ought I to be! And that the tares have not wholly strangled the wheat, what a wonder it is! We ought to thank God daily for the sins we have not committed.
F. W. Faber

'There but for the grace of God, goes . . .'
Who used these famous words? They have been attributed to several saintly men, including John Bunyan, but the story is rightly told of John Bradford, the Protestant martyr, who was burnt at Smithfield on Sunday June 30th 1555. The story is that once, on seeing some criminals being taken to execution he exclaimed, 'There, but for the grace of God, goes John Bradford.'
Anon

In Nottingham is the Wesleyan chapel where William Booth, founder of the Salvation Army, was converted. A memorial tablet keeps fresh in recollection the fact that there this notable friend of the friendless received his baptism of spiritual power. Naturally, the chapel has become a shrine of pilgrimage for Salvation Army leaders from around the world.

One day an old man in the uniform of the Army was found by the minister of the chapel standing with uplifted eyes before the tablet. 'Can a man say his prayers here?' he asked. 'Of course,' was the minister's answer. And the old Salvation Army officer went down on his knees, and lifting his hands before the tablet prayed: 'O God, do it again! Do it again!'

That prayer is the touchstone of abiding reality in religion. Awareness that it is God, by his grace, who is the author of all good actions.
Anon

A distinguished visitor was spending a few days with the late Albert Schweitzer in Africa. Upon entering the dining room the first evening, he saw a piano which he described as old, broken down and warped.

After the meal was finished, Dr Schweitzer, as was his custom, sat at the keyboard of the decrepit instrument and began to play. Within a moment the room was filled with beautiful and majestic harmonies. Describing the incident later, the visitor wrote in his diary: 'The old piano seemed to *lose its poverty* in his hands.'
Anon

Clyde S. Kilby in *The Christian World of C. S. Lewis* tells of the first stage in the conversion of C. S. Lewis.

'It seemed to Lewis that God was as surely after him as a cat searching for a mouse.' He then quotes Lewis's own words:

'You must picture me alone in that room in Magdalen, night after night, feeling, whenever my mind lifted for even a second from my work, the steady, unrelenting approach of him whom I so earnestly desired not to meet. That which I greatly feared had at last come upon me.'

As he knelt down in prayer and admitted that God was God he felt himself, in his own words 'the most dejected and reluctant convert in all England'.

Lewis's experience did not end there, but that was certainly the beginning.

Sometimes conversion is unwilling submission by people fighting to the last ditch against it. In this case, it was a glorious liberation and emancipation, come all unexpectedly to one who was never thinking of it.

There is no 'standard' way of being converted. It is the fault of certain kinds of evangelism that it has in its mind a pattern which the conversion process ought to follow. There is no such pattern. It may come through the unwilling surrender of C. S. Lewis, or through the joyous splendour of revelation which came to Saul Kane. We must not force the grace of God into one mould. God works in many ways.
William Barclay

USEFUL TEXTS

Grace of God:
   Source of salvation, *Acts 15:11*
        forgiveness, *Eph. 1:7*
        faith, *Acts 18:27*
        justification, *Rom. 3:24*

See also: B51 One with Christ
           B52 God is Love
           C47 The indwelling Spirit

B36
THE FAMILY OF GOD

'The one who sanctifies, and the ones who are sanctified,
are of the same stock; that is why he openly calls
them brothers and sisters.'
Hebrews 2:11

QUOTATIONS

The Church is the family of God. It is seen in miniature in each
family.
John Ferguson

If thou hast seen thy brother, thou hast seen God.
St Clement of Alexandria

The word *Church* used in most of the northern European languages
comes from the Greek *kyriake oikia* 'the family of the Lord'.
Leonard Doohan

The Church is a family. To be Church, to live as church, means to
live as a part of this family, aware that we need others.
Leonard Doohan

God did not spare his only Son and he is not going to be soft on
his adopted ones either.
The Hermitage

'Create me' – this is the word that the Church, viewed as an idea,
addresses to mankind.
Josiah Royce

I must speed to my God before all things. My God, by this nature
my Father above, my brother in humanity, my Bridegroom in his
ardent love, and I his from eternity.
St Mechtild of Magdeburg

The family is clearly the foundational community of the Church which also means that once the foundation is established, it cannot be removed. The foundation status of the family is on-going, ordinary and essential.
David M. Thomas

Through his birth, that is, his incarnation, and baptism and passion and resurrection he delivered our nature from the sin of our first parents and death and corruption, and became the first fruits of the resurrection, and made himself the way and image and pattern, in order that we too following in his footsteps may become by adoption what he himself is by nature, sons and heirs of God and joint heirs with him.
St John of Damascus

The ministering angels wanted to sing a hymn at the destruction of the Egyptians, but God said: 'My children lie drowned in the sea, and you would sing?'
Rabbi Johanan

I am a part and parcel of the whole, and I cannot find God apart from the rest of humanity.
Mahatma Gandhi

Treat people as if they were what they ought to be, and you will help them to become what they are capable of being.
Johann von Goethe

HUMOUR

Every denomination has its share of fringe members who hang onto the Church by the membrane of an old childhood memory or a new social fashion. But the eggshell fragility of such allegiances is rarely acknowledged. Hence the point of this Canadian story about the man who was asked by an interviewer conducting a market research survey, 'What is your religious preference?' 'Well, I wouldn't call myself Christian,' came the reply, 'but you can put me down as Anglican!'

WORD PICTURES

Tolstoy tells the story of a man who stopped to give alms to a beggar. To his dismay he found that he had left his money at home. Stammering his explanation, he said, 'I am sorry, brother, but I have nothing.' 'Never mind, brother,' was the beggar's answer, 'that too was a gift.' The one word 'brother' meant more to him than money.
John Schmidt

To the unknown many
I raise no glass to the man whose fame
has spread from coast to coast,
whose talents have served to place his name
with those men honour most.

My toast is not for the lady fair,
whose grace and charming ways
have set men marvelling everywhere
and won her kindly praise.

I raise no glass to the hero who
has won deserved applause,
who has done as the brave alone may do
in a daring, righteous cause.

I drink no health to the one whose voice
mankind shall ne'er forget,
whose genius has made the world rejoice
and left it in her debt.

I raise my glass to the silent horde
spread o'er the world's expanse,
the unknown many who might have soared
but never had a chance.
Author unknown

If a man should be able to assent to this doctrine as he ought, that we are all sprung from God in an especial manner, and that God is the Father both of men and of gods, I suppose that he would

340

never have any ignoble or mean thought about himself. If Caesar should adopt you no one could endure your arrogance. What, then, and if you know you are the son of God, will you not be elated? Yet we do not so; but while these two things are mingled in the generation of man (body in common with the animals, and reason and intelligence in common with the gods), many incline to this kinship which is miserable and mortal, and some few to that which is divine and happy.
Epictetus

USEFUL TEXTS

Family of God – the Church:
    Loved by Christ, *Eph. 5:25*
    Head of, *Eph. 1:22*
    Persecuted by Paul, *Gal. 1:13*
    Pillar of truth, *1 Tim. 3:15*
    Gifts of, *1 Cor. 12:27-30*

See also: B34 Human rights
           C12 The Church for all people
           C17 International peace
           C24 Lord of all nations

B37
TRUE WISDOM

'I prayed, and understanding was given me; I entreated,
and the Spirit of Wisdom came to me.'
Wisdom 7:7

QUOTATIONS

No wise man wants a soft life.
King Alfred

Wisdom hath four virtues: prudence, temperance, courage, and
righteousness.
King Alfred

The writings of the wise are the only riches our posterity cannot
squander.
Walter Savage Landor

The days that make us happy make us wise.
John Masefield

There can be no wisdom disjoined from goodness.
Richard C. Trench

It is always wise to look ahead, but difficult to look further than
you can see.
Winston Churchill

The art of being wise is the art of knowing what to overlook.
William James

The height of wisdom is to take things as they are, and look upon
the rest with confidence.
Montaigne

The Delphic oracle said I was the wisest of all the Greeks. It is because that I alone, of all the Greeks, know that I know nothing.
Socrates

There is a very high rung which only one man in a whole generation can reach: that of having learned all secret wisdom and then praying like a little child.
Rabbi Mendel of Rymanov

What is that which shines through me, and strikes upon my heart without hurting it? And I shudder and kindle; shudder, inasmuch as I am unlike it; kindle, inasmuch as I am like it. It is Wisdom, Wisdom's self which thus shines into me.
St Augustine of Hippo

Knowing is a process of experiencing, understanding and judging.
Bernard Longeran

Science pursued with love of truth is a way to God.
William Johnson

PROVERBS

Everyone is wise until he speaks.
Irish proverb

Only a fool tests the depth of the water with both feet.
African proverb

The first step of wisdom is to know what is false.
Latin proverb

HUMOUR

And the Lord said unto Noah: 'Where is the ark which I have commanded thee to build?' And Noah said unto the Lord: 'Verily, I have had three carpenters off ill. The gopher wood supplier hath let me down – yea, even though the gopher wood hath been on order for nigh upon twelve months.'

And God said unto Noah: 'I want that ark finished even after seven days and nights.' And Noah said: 'It will be so.' And it was not so.

And the Lord said: 'What seemeth to be the trouble this time?' And Noah said unto the Lord: 'Mine subcontractor hath gone bankrupt. The pitch which thou commandest me to put on the outside and on the inside of the ark hath not arrived. The plumber hath gone on strike. Shem, my son who helpeth me on the ark side of the business, hath formed a pop group with his brothers Ham and Japheth. Lord, I am undone.'

And the Lord grew angry and said: 'And what about the unicorns, and the fowls of the air by seven?' And Noah wrung his hands and wept saying: 'Lord, unicorns are a discontinued line; thou canst not get them for love or money. And it hath just been told unto me that the fowls of the air are sold only in half dozens. Lord, Lord, thou knowest how it is.'

And the Lord in his Wisdom said: 'Noah, my son, I know; why else dost thou think I have caused a flood to descend upon the earth?'
E.R.A.

Seeing John Wesley coming along the street one day, a man straddled the pavement and said to him: 'I never get out of my way for a fool.' 'But I always do,' replied Wesley, as he stepped aside into the gutter.
Anon

WORD PICTURES

A great king once came to Solomon and asked him for a motto. 'It must be one', said he, 'that shall be as much use to me in times of trouble as in times of prosperity.' The wise king gave him his motto, and he had it engraved on a ring which he wore continually. It was this: 'Even this shall pass away.'
Anon

There were once two men who lived in a thirsty place where there was only about one shower of rain every three years, and nothing grew except cactus and lizards and sand fleas. Because they both grew so tired of being thirsty they went to Niagara. Stooping down, one filled a medicine bottle with the water and said: 'I think I shall come here every six months or so with a bottle or two.'

And the other built a house by the river.

Anon

An English lady travelling in Germany left a valuable fur coat in charge of a German woman in the carriage. When she returned, the German was wearing the coat, and said that it belonged to her. The guard tried in vain to discover to which of the two it belonged and finally sent them off to the consul. The consul asked to examine the coat, and brought it back a few moments later, saying: 'This is a very serious affair; whoever the coat belongs to has been smuggling cocaine. Here are the two packets I found in the coat.' The German woman excused herself and bowed herself out of the room, saying: 'Just my little joke.' The English woman said: 'I can't understand how they could have got there.' The consul replied: 'Don't worry, it is only salt, that I put there to find out whose coat it really was.'

John Arbuthnot

The playwright Dennis Potter, who died from cancer in 1994, said these words in his last interview with broadcaster Melvyn Bragg on TV's Channel 4.

'I'm almost serene. I can celebrate life. Below my window there's an apple tree in blossom. It's white. And looking at it – instead of saying, "Oh that's a nice blossom" – now, looking at it through the window, I see the whitest, frothiest, blossomest blossom that there ever could be. The nowness of everything is absolutely wondrous. If you see the present tense – boy, do you see it, and boy, do you celebrate it.'

Dennis Potter

There was a young prince of Persia who, on ascending the throne, summoned his wise men and asked them to prepare a history of the nations for his guidance. They came back in twenty years with twelve camels carrying six thousand volumes; but the king was busy with the cares of State, and sent them back to edit their works. Again in twenty years they came, and again they went back;

and so the process was repeated until there arrived at the palace an old wise man with a donkey, with a single volume on its back.

'Hasten! The king is dying,' the officer said. The wise man was taken to the king's bedside, and the king, his gaze falling on the book of history, said, with a sigh: 'Then I shall die without knowing the history of mankind.'

'Sire,' said the wise old man, 'I will sum it up for you in a few words: *they were born, they suffered, they died.*'
Old Legend

USEFUL TEXTS

Wisdom:
    Value of, *Job 28:12-28; Prov. 8:11; Eccles. 7:19*
    Given by God, *Eccles. 2:26; James 1:5*
    Prayers for, *2 Chron. 1:10; Ps. 90:12; Eph. 1:17*
    Personified, *Prov. 8:1*

See also: A2   Integrity
            B19 Conscience
            B20 Growth to maturity
            B26 The whole person

B38
THE SUFFERING SERVANT

'By his sufferings shall my servant justify many,
taking their faults on himself.'
Isaiah 53:11

QUOTATIONS

Pain is God's megaphone to arouse a deaf world.
C. S. Lewis

God whispers in our pleasures but shouts in our pains.
C. S. Lewis

Nothing great was ever done without much enduring.
St Catherine of Siena

I was able to use the machinery of it (pain) to explore a different
path into myself and into the world I was trying to respond to.
Dennis Potter

What is Calvary if just beyond it lies an Easter morning.
E. Stanley Jones

The more affliction for Christ in this world, so much the more
glory with Christ in the future.
St Philip Howard

There is a purity which only suffering can impart; the stream of
life becomes snow white when it dashes against the rocks.
Jean Paul Richter

PROVERBS

One does not get crucified, one crucifies oneself.
Bulgarian proverb

He who has come through the fire will not fade in the sun.
Hindu proverb

WORD PICTURES

There is a strange legend of a monk who was walking in the monastery garden alone, thinking of the Passion of our Lord, just before Holy Week. As he slowly paced along, he saw something lying in the path, and picked it up. It was the crown of thorns which our Lord had worn for our sakes, and he reverently carried it to the little chapel, and laid it upon the altar. Never had Holy Week been so well kept, for the sight of that crown of thorns made them realise the sufferings and the love of Jesus more than they had ever done before.

At last Easter Sunday dawned, and the monk rose early for his Easter preparations, and came to the chapel. As the sun shone through the window, it lighted up the altar, it touched the crown of thorns, and there in the Easter sunlight the thorns had blossomed into the most beautiful flowers.

It is a little parable. For it is suffering and sacrifice which bring forth the most splendid fruits.
M.C.C.

In Jocelyn Gibb's *Light on C. S. Lewis*, Nevill Coghill tells a story C. S. Lewis once told him.

Lewis married late in life. In his marriage he found the very perfection of love, but so soon the wife he loved so much died of cancer. Once when Lewis was with Coghill he looked across the quadrangle at his wife. 'I never expected', he said, 'to have in my sixties the happiness that passed me by in my twenties.'

'It was then', writes Nevill Coghill, 'that he told me of having been allowed to accept her pain.' 'You mean', said Coghill, 'that the pain left her, and that you felt it for her in your body?'
'Yes,' said C. S. Lewis, 'in my legs. It was crippling. But it relieved hers.'

O Lord, remember not only the men and women of good will, but also those of ill will. But do not remember all the suffering they have inflicted on us, remember the fruits we have borne, thanks to this suffering – our comradeship, our loyalty, our humility, our courage, our generosity, the greatness of heart which has grown

out of all this, and when they come to judgement, let all the fruits which we have borne be their forgiveness.
Found on a scrap of paper on the body of a dead child at Ravensbruck Concentration Camp

Sometimes all you can do is just cry. The Bible says that there is a time to weep.

I would say to someone who's hurting right now, just get angry with God. Better to get angry than walk away from him. Rant and rave if you must, scream and yell.

It's good to experience the depth of your pain, and, like that seed which falls into the ground and dies, experience that kind of Good.
Anon

In the musical *Sound of Music* Sister Maria, when confronted by a momentous decision which was to change the entire course of her life, spoke the well-known line of assurance: 'When God closes a door, somewhere he opens a window.' Millions of Christians who have faced many 'closed doors' (heartaches, trials, and disappointments) in their lives will rise up to say a hearty 'Amen' to her confident expression of faith.

In fact, many of the world's great have achieved their most heroic accomplishments in the face of 'closed doors'. John Milton wrote *Paradise Lost* and *Paradise Regained* after having been afflicted with total blindness. Beethoven wrote some of his greatest music, including his Ninth Symphony, after he was almost completely deaf.

From a hospital patient, dying of cancer, expressing her anger to God in poetry.
'God, you need to ask my forgiveness.
Your world is full of mistakes.
Some cells, like weeds in the garden,
are growing in the wrong place.
And we your children
have polluted our environment.
Why did you let it happen, God?

We prayed with faith, hope, love,
we perceived no change in our bodies or environment,
we are made sick by your world.
God you need to ask my forgiveness.
Was this why you sent your Son?'

Faced with the problem of evil let's attempt a mental exercise.
Let's imagine a world without evil. The challenge presented to
faith usually comes in the following form, 'How can there be a
loving God if he allows this to happen?'

Much suffering results from mechanical failure, for example
metal fatigue in an aircraft part; a fault that could lead to tragedy.
So does our all-loving God ensure that no metal parts fail? Or
engines fall off because a mechanic forgot to tighten a bolt? So
every time some unforeseen misfortune overtakes an aircraft in
flight, a miracle is automatically performed to put it right. So
aircraft maintenance is unnecessary and safety regulations pointless.

So too in all other realms of human activity; God stubs out our
cigarettes before they cause a fire, stops our ladders from slipping
when not erected correctly, etc. In our imaginary world God has
agreed to ensure that no drunken driver ever kills a child again.

In short, in our imaginary world the law of cause and effect has
been abolished, every human mistake will be corrected by a team
of invisible angels.

Without the principle of cause and effect the world becomes
irrational and the studies of Science impossible.
Based on an article by Clifford Longley

USEFUL TEXTS

Suffering Servant:
  Isa. 42:1; 49:3-6; 42:19

See also: B15 Jesus, friend of outcasts
            B49 Coping with doubt
            C13 Coping with grief

B39
CREATION

'What marvels the Lord worked for us. Indeed we were glad.'
Psalm 126:3

QUOTATIONS

Beauty is God's handwriting. Welcome it in every fair face, every fair sky, every fair flower.
Charles Kingsley

Creation: good broken up into pieces and scattered throughout evil.
Simone Weil

It is so impossible for the world to exist without God that if God should forget it, it would immediately cease to be.
Sören Kierkegaard

Creation is the language of God, time is his song, and things of space the consonants in the song. To sanctify time is to sing the vowels in unison with him.
Abraham Joshua Heschel

God created many worlds and destroyed many worlds before he created this one of heaven and earth.
The Midrash

Creation – happens to us, burns into us, changes us, we tremble and swoon, we submit. Creation – we participate in it, we encounter the creator, offer ourselves to him, helpers and companions.
Martin Buber

We believe that God had made all things out of nothing: because, even although the world hath been made of some material, that very same material hath been made out of nothing.
St Augustine of Hippo

Wherever ugliness is kept at bay, there the Spirit of God who is the God of beauty is doing his creative and re-creative labour.
Donald Coggan

A tree gives glory to God first of all by being a tree. For in being what God means it to be, it is obeying him. It 'consents' so to speak, to his creative love. It is expressing an idea which is in God and which is not distinct from the essence of God, and therefore a tree imitates God by being a tree.
Thomas Merton

Do not suppose that when God made heaven and earth and all things, he made one thing today and another tomorrow. Moses says so, of course, but he knew better; he only wrote for the sake of the populace, who could not have understood otherwise. God merely willed, and the world was.
Meister Eckhart

The more we learn about the wonders of our universe, the more clearly we are going to perceive the hand of God.
Frank Bormann

WORD PICTURES

This beautiful and oft-quoted poem was written by the saintly George Herbert (1593-1633) under the curious title of *The Pulley* – an allusion to man's need, at last, to be drawn up to God.

When God at first made man,
having a glass of blessings standing by,
'Let us,' said he, 'pour on him all we can;
let the world's riches, which dispersed lie,
contract into a span.'

So strength first made a way,
then beauty flowed, then wisdom, honour, pleasure;
when almost all was out, God made a stay,
perceiving that, alone of all his treasure,
rest in the bottom lay.

'For if I should,' said he,
'bestow this jewel also on my creature,
he would adore my gifts instead of me,
and rest in nature, not the God of nature:
so both should losers be.

'Yet let him keep the rest,
but keep them with repining restlessness;
let him be rich and weary, that at least,
if goodness lead him not, yet weariness
may toss him to my breast.'
George Herbert

The poet Caedmon is said to have been by occupation a cow-herd.
After receiving the gift of song, he entered the monastery of
Whitby, by the advice of St Hilda, its abbess. The following is a
translation from King Alfred's account of him:

> Caedmon was established in secular life until he had attained a
> considerable age, and had never learned any song. Moreover, at
> the banquets it was deemed the height of bliss that all those
> present should sing in turn to a harp which was passed round.
> When he saw the harp approaching him he would rise, filled
> with shame, from the assembly and return to his house. On one
> occasion he had thus left the feast and gone to the shed of the
> cattle which were committed to his care. At the usual time he
> lay down to rest and fell asleep. Then, in his sleep, a man stood
> before him greeting him and calling him by his name:
> 'Caedmon, sing me something.' Then he answered, 'I can sing
> nothing, and because of this I have left the feast.' But he that
> spoke with him said, 'Nevertheless you can sing to me.' He
> said, 'What shall I sing?' The vision answered, 'Sing to me of
> the Creation.' Then he soon began to sing in the praise of God
> the Creator verses and words which he had never heard.

From the Anglo Saxon

And I dream that these garden closes
with their glades and their sun-flecked sod
and their lilies and bowers of roses
were laid by the hand of God.

The kiss of the sun for pardon,
the song of the birds for mirth,
one is nearer God's heart in a garden
than anywhere else on earth.
Dorothy Frances Gurney

I left school as usual, accompanied by my pupil-daughter, and we set out to walk the mile to Southend to catch the 4.35pm bus to our village. We were approaching the centre of the town, chatting as we walked along, when I noticed, 50 yards ahead, an old pigeon walking across the road. It was just crossing the centre of the road when a BT van, driven by a young man, approached; the pigeon was directly in its path. The driver slowed and stopped, and waited for the road to be clear. The van proceeded and the pigeon had almost arrived at the gutter opposite my daughter and I, when a builder's small open-back truck approached. The young driver saw the pigeon, who was no longer an obstruction; he steered to the left and deliberately ran over the bird. He drove off laughing. My daughter was horrified as the pigeon twitched and then lay still. She demanded that we do something. I pointed out that there was nothing that we could do, and we went on to catch our bus.

I have used this story as a parable to illustrate the use of free will or the respect that can be given or refused to protect or destroy life.
A. P. Castle

Trees are the oldest living things in time, brooding witnesses of man and his queer ways – of the rise and fall of empires, the birth, progress and decay of what we call civilisation. There are two English oak trees in Norfolk, for example, which were 700 years old when William the Conqueror landed at Pevensey.

The oldest tree in the world – probably the oldest living thing – is the mighty Cypress tree in Chapultepec, Mexico, which has a trunk 118 ft in circumference and is believed to be more than 6,000 years old.
John Clement

USEFUL TEXTS

Creation:
Account of, *Gen. 1:1-2, 25*
Work of the Lord, *Ps. 104:1-35*
Work of the Word, *John 1:1-14*
Work of the Son, *Col. 1:13-17; Heb. 1:1-3*

See also: A18 Balance in Nature
B32 The Wonders of God

B40
ONE GOD

'Listen, Israel: The Lord our God is the one Lord.'
Deuteronomy 6:4

QUOTATIONS

We expect too much of God, but he always seems ready.
John F. Kennedy

God is not in need of anything, but all things are in need of him.
Marcianus Aristides

He who has gotten the whole world plus God has gotten no more than God by himself.
Meister Eckhart

God is an infinite circle whose centre is everywhere and whose circumference is nowhere.
St Augustine of Hippo

The hardness of God is kinder than the softness of men, and his compulsion is our liberation.
C. S. Lewis

God is not an idea, or a definition that we have committed to memory, he is a presence which we experience in our hearts.
Louis Evely

God is near, but God is different. God is here, but man is dependent.
Arthur Michael Ramsey

God wouldn't be the God that he is if we could prove that he was.
Gerald Priestland

What is impenetrable to us really exists, manifesting itself as the highest wisdom and the most radiant beauty.
Albert Einstein

The knower and the known are one. Simple people imagine that they should see God, as if he stood there and they here. This is not so. God and I, we are one in knowledge.
Meister Eckhart

What we make in our minds we call God, but in reality he dwells in our hearts.
Winston Churchill

The atheist staring from his attic window is often nearer to God than the believer caught up in his own false image of God.
Martin Buber

Children's Prayers

Dear God,
   I do not think anybody could be a better God. Well I just want you to know but I am not just saying that because you are God.
Charles

Dear God,
   I didn't think orange went with purple until I saw the sunset you made on Tue. That was cool.
Eugene

Dear God,
   It is great the way you always get the stars in the right places.
Jeff

Dear God,
   I don't ever feel alone since I found out about you.
Nora

PROVERBS

God has more than he has given away.
Czech proverb

God is a busy worker, but he loves help.
Basque proverb

HUMOUR

The teacher was talking to her junior class about God and how hard it was to know about God. 'Where is God?' the teacher asked. 'I know where God is,' called out one little boy, 'he's in my bathroom.'

'In your bathroom?' the teacher exclaimed.

'Yes, every morning my Dad goes to the bathroom door and he shouts, "My God, are you still in there!"'

Anon

WORD PICTURES

'I listen with reverence to the birdsong cascading at dawn from the oasis, for it seems to me there is no better evidence for the existence of God than in the bird that sings, though it knows not why, from a spring of untrammelled joy that wells up in its heart.' These lines are attributed to an Arab chieftain. He has all the simple proof he needed; proof which no theological disputation could ever present half so convincingly. That Arab chieftain had the sensitive ear, the receptive heart, and a mind able to interpret.

T.B.C.

When Robert Louis Stevenson was seeking for spiritual light and had found it, he wrote to his father, 'No man can achieve success in life until he writes in the journal of his life the words, *Enter God.*

Towards the end of his life Karl Rahner was questioned by an interviewer as to why he believed in God in spite of so many intellectual difficulties over faith today. The interviewer persisted in this line of inquiry to a degree that annoyed the famous theologian, who replied: 'Listen, I don't believe in God because I have worked everything out to the satisfaction of my mind. I continue to believe in God because I pray every day.'

When comedian George Burns was asked about his title role in the film, *Oh God*, the 82-year-old star explained that, 'It wasn't hard to play God. At my age, everything I do is a miracle.'

Neal Travis

The heart has its reasons, which reason knows not, as we feel in a thousand instances.

It is the heart which is conscious of God, not the reason. This then is faith: God sensible to the heart, not to the reason.

Blaise Pascal

Once upon a time the fishes of a certain river took counsel together and said: 'They tell us that our life and being is for the water, but we have never seen water, and know not what it is.'

Then some among them wiser than the rest said: 'We have heard that there dwelleth in the sea a very learned fish who knoweth all things; let us ask him to explain to us what is water.'

So several of their number set out, and came to where this sage fish resided. On hearing their request he answered them:

Oh ye who seek to solve the knot!

Ye live in God, yet know him not.

Ye sit upon the river's brink,

yet crave in vain a drop to drink.

Ye dwell beside a countless store,

yet perish hungry at the door.

This little parable has lived a thousand years in Persian literature.

Voltaire, as everyone knows, had little use for religion. He was one day walking with a friend when they passed a church. Voltaire raised his hat as they passed. 'I thought,' said the friend, 'that you did not believe in God.' 'Oh,' said Voltaire, 'we nod, but we do not speak.'

William Barclay

USEFUL TEXTS

Characteristics of God:
   Omnipotence, *Jer. 32:17, 27*
   Omnipresence, *Ps. 139: 7-12*
   Omniscience, *Amos 9:2-3*
   Foreknowledge, *Isa. 48:3-5*

See also: B28 The Father who draws us to himself
            B54 The Trinity
            C27 The Father who receives us back

B41
GENEROSITY

'I tell you solemnly, this poor widow has put more in than all
who have contributed to the treasury.'
Mark 12:43

QUOTATIONS
Nothing is impossible to a willing heart.
Thomas Heywood

Give what you have; to someone it may be better than you dare to
think.
Henry Wadsworth Longfellow

The return we reap from generous actions is not always evident.
Francesco Guiccrardini

When we are addressing God, who is infinitely rich, why ask for
sixpence?
Daniel Considine

PROVERBS
The quickest generosity is the best.
Arab proverb

When the hand ceases to scatter, the mouth ceases to praise.
Irish proverb

HUMOUR
A minister was once preaching at a little chapel on the subject of
'Giving'. During the sermon he was delighted when he saw a
member of the congregation go to the side of the chapel and place
a coin in a box, and a little later another did the same. Surely, the

minister thought, his sermon had never before met with such practical response. On leaving he was stopped by one of the men, who said: I hope we didn't disturb you, sir, but ours is a shilling-in-a-slot meter, and we should have been in darkness if we hadn't attended to it.'

London Evening Standard

A wealthy man attended a missionary service and gave a penny to the cause. On the way home he was caught in a storm. He crawled into a hollow tree for protection. The storm lasted longer than he thought, the tree began to swell from the moisture, and the man couldn't extricate himself. Thinking he was going to be squeezed to death he began thinking of all the mean sins he had committed. After a while he thought of the measly penny he had given to missions and he felt so small he crawled right out!

Anon

WORD PICTURES

There is a legend about the boy who gave up his five barley loaves and two small fishes so that Christ could feed the multitude. It tells how the boy hurried home, after all the fragments had been gathered, and told his mother about the exciting incident.

With eyes still big with wonder, he told her how his five little barley cakes and two dried fishes had multiplied in the Saviour's hand until there was enough to satisfy 5,000 hungry people. And then, with a wistful look, he added: 'I wonder, Mother, whether it would be that way with *everything* you gave him.'

Anon

Friar Juniper had so much compassion for the poor that he gave away his tunic and cowl to anyone in need. Therefore, the warden commanded him, by obedience, not to give away the whole of his tunic, nor any part of his habit. Now it fell out that Friar Juniper ere a few days had passed, happened on a poor creature, well-nigh naked, who asked alms of him for the love of God, to whom he said with great compassion: 'Naught have I, save my tunic, to give thee; and this my superior hath laid on me, by obedience, to give to no one; nay, nor even part of my habit; but if thou wilt take it off my back, I will not gainsay thee.' He spake not to deaf ears, for straightway this poor man stripped him of his tunic and went his way with it, leaving Friar Juniper naked.

When he returned to the friary he was asked where his tunic was, and he answered: 'An honest fellow took it from my back, and made off with it.' And the virtue of pity increasing within him, he was not content with giving away his tunic, but likewise gave books and church ornaments and cloaks, or anything he could lay his hands on, to the poor. And for this reason the friars never left things lying about the friary, because Friar Juniper gave all away for love of God and in praise of him.

Little Flowers of St Francis

I know a ranch in Colorado at the base of a mountain. From snow fields hundreds of feet above, two streams trickle down and divide. One grows until its waters are caught up by skilled engineers and made to irrigate a thousand ranches. The other runs into a blind valley and spreads into a lake with no outlet. There it poisons itself. In it are the carcasses of cattle who, thirsty and eager, have come to drink of the tainted flood. Some of them still stand upright in the miry bottom, their heads bent into the bitter tide, the flesh falling from their bones. The first lake has an outlet. It loses itself on a mesa and gives drink to the homes of men. The other turns in upon itself and kills everything that touches it. One loses life and finds it again in generosity – the other loses life in stagnation, never to find it again.

George Stewart

When Turner's picture of *Cologne* was exhibited in 1826, it was hung between two portraits by Sir Thomas Lawrence. The sky of Turner's picture was exceedingly bright, and it had a most injurious effect on the colour of the two portraits. Lawrence naturally felt mortified and he complained openly of the position of his pictures. On the morning of the opening of the exhibition, at the private view, a friend of Turner's, who had seen the *Cologne* in all its splendour, led a group of expectant critics up to the picture. He started back from it in consternation. The golden sky had changed to a dull colour. He ran up to Turner, who was in another part of the room, 'Turner, what have you been doing to your picture?' 'Oh,' muttered Turner, in a low voice, 'poor Lawrence was so unhappy. It's only lamp black. It'll wash off after the exhibition.'

Anon

When I think of all the people who have come through the Blue Door of our House of Hospitality in New York, my heart is filled with gratitude. This is especially true when I think of God's little ones, the *anawim* who often are known only to him.

I remember only the first name of the person whose story I am now going to relate. Maybe she never had a surname! Yet, I remember *her* very well. Every Saturday, rain or shine, cold or hot, she would come through the Blue Door. She would enter oh so softly and close the door gently behind her.

Slowly, with tired step, she would walk up to my desk, and, after a few words of greeting, lay on top of it in a tidy row four dirty pennies. Then she would explain, almost in a whisper, that this was all she had left of her pay to give to Christ in the poor. Then, with a little smile and a bow, she would ask for our prayers. Slowly, bidding everyone present a soft goodbye, she would walk out through the Blue Door, closing it very gently as she had closed it coming in.

She was a Negro, a widow. She earned her living by scrubbing a few office floors at night. Her name was Martha.

She brought her four pennies every week for four years. Then one Saturday, she did not come. I never saw her again. Months later someone along the street told me about a poor woman who was buried in an unmarked grave in a potter's field. I asked the woman's name. All they could remember was that her first name was Martha. Her surname? Nobody seemed to know.

Catherine de Hueck Doherty

USEFUL TEXTS

Generosity:
    Of God, *Ps. 103: 3-12*
    Example of, *Prov. 31:20*
    Command regarding, *Matt. 5:42*

See also: A5 One for another – unselfishness
          C18 Compassion
          C46 Loving kindness

B42
Signs of the Times

'Take the fig tree as a parable: as soon as its twigs grow supple
and its leaves come out, you know that summer is near.'
Mark 13:28

Quotations

There is nothing permanent except change.
Heraclitus

Modern man, more than in preceding generations, is a man 'on his
way'.
Pope John Paul II

When men are easy in their circumstances, they are naturally
enemies to innovations.
Joseph Addiston

Our fathers valued change for the sake of its results; we value it in
the act.
Alice Meynell

Christians are supposed not merely to endure change, not even to
profit by it, but to cause it.
Harry Emerson Fosdick

Every age has a blind eye and sees nothing wrong in practice and
institutions which its successors view with just horror.
Sir Richard Livingstone

When people shake their heads because we are living in a restless
age, ask them how they would like to live in a stationary one and
do without change.
George Bernard Shaw

The old order changeth, yielding place to new, and God fulfils himself in many ways, lest one good custom should corrupt the world.
Alfred, Lord Tennyson

'Should the Church move with the times?' The answer must be 'Yes'. Society has a lot to teach the Church about sex. But Christianity too embodies fundamental truths which – although in need of equally fundamental rethinking themselves – carry basic values which society ignores at its peril.
Jack Dominian

PROVERBS

There is no mortar that time will not loose.
French proverb

To change and to improve are two different things.
German proverb

HUMOUR

In Nelson's time, when His Majesty's ships were in harbour, ladies were allowed to sleep on board. The sailors were required to get up at the usual hour, but the ladies might please themselves. A nice problem of discipline thus arose. A solution was found in the fact that the ladies wore their stockings in bed, while the men slept bare footed. If (as usually happened) all the sailors did not appear punctually on deck, it was necessary for the boatswain to search for defaulters. He went along the bunks calling out 'Show a leg, show a leg!' The owner of a bare leg was promptly dealt with; but any leg wearing a stocking was allowed to return where it came from, and doubtless the boatswain would apologise to the lady in nautical terms. Evidently our sailors, being such innocent fellows, never thought of borrowing the ladies' stockings!
A.S.

WORD PICTURES

In Turkey, excavations in the Greco Roman ruins of Aphrodisias have uncovered some 300 fragments of inscribed stone panels. Fitted together like a giant jigsaw, they proved to be a table of fixed prices. In AD 301, Emperor Diocletian froze all prices to combat inflation. The items listed range from melons to marble.
Kenan Erim

'Let the great world spin forever down the ringing grooves of change.' Of this famous line, its author, Alfred, Lord Tennyson, wrote the following note:

> 'When I went by the first train from Liverpool to Manchester (1830) I thought that the wheels ran in a groove. It was black night and there was such a vast crowd round the train at the station that we could not see the wheels. Then I made this line . . .'

The words of Cyprian, Bishop of Carthage, written in the third century are as timely today as when he wrote them. He said:

> 'If I could ascend some high mountain and look out over this wide land, you know very well what I would see. Robbers on the high roads, pirates on the sea . . . selfishness and cruelty, misery and despair under all roofs. It is a bad world, an incredibly bad world, but in the midst of it I have found a quiet and holy people who have learned a great secret. They are despised and persecuted, but they care not. They are the masters of their souls. They have overcome the world. These people are the Christians and I am one of them.'

We are Survivors!
For those born before 1940!

We were born before television, before penicillin, polio, frozen food, Xerox, plastic, contact lenses, videos, frisbees and the Pill. We were born before radar, credit cards, split atoms, laser beams and ball-point pens; before dishwashers, tumble-dryers, electric blankets, air conditioners, drip-dry clothes . . . and before man walked on the moon.

We got married first and then lived together (how quaint can you be?). We thought 'fast food' was what you ate in Lent; a 'Big Mac' was an oversized raincoat and 'crumpet' we had for tea. We existed before house-husbands, computer dating, dual careers; when a 'meaningful relationship' meant getting along with cousins, and when 'sheltered accommodation' was where you waited for a bus.

We were born before day-care centres, group homes and disposable nappies. We never heard of FM radio, tape decks, electric typewriters, artificial hearts, word processors, yoghurt and young men wearing earrings. For us, 'time sharing' meant togetherness, a 'chip' was a piece of wood or a fried potato, hardware meant nuts and bolts and software wasn't a word.

Before 1940, 'Made in Japan' meant junk, the term 'making out' referred to how you did in exams, 'stud' was something that fastened a collar to a shirt and 'going all the way' meant staying on a double decker to the bus depot. Pizzas, McDonalds and instant coffee were unheard of. In our day, cigarette smoking was 'fashionable', 'grass' was mown, 'coke' was kept in a coalhouse, a 'joint' was a piece of meat you had on Sundays and 'pot' was something you cooked in. 'Rock Music' was Grandmother's lullaby, 'Eldorado' was an ice cream, a 'gay person' was the life and soul of the party and nothing more, while 'aids' just meant beauty treatment or help for someone in trouble.

We who were born before 1940 must be a hardy bunch when you think of the way in which the world has changed and the adjustments we have had to make. No wonder we are so confused and there is a generation gap today . . . *but* by the Grace of God . . . we have survived! Alleluia!

Anon

See also: A18 Balance in nature
          B34 Human rights
          C17 International Peace

B43
FORTY DAYS OF LENT

'The Spirit drove Jesus out into the wilderness and
he remained there for forty days.'
Mark 1:12

QUOTATIONS

Alms are but the vehicles of prayer.
John Dryden

If alms are lacking, our life does not yet converge fully towards God.
Pope John Paul II

Self-discipline never means *giving up* anything, for giving up is a
loss. Our Lord did not ask us to give up the things of the earth,
but to exchange them for better things.
Fulton Sheen

The cross that Jesus tells us to carry is the one that we willingly
take up ourselves – the cross of self-denial in order that we might
live for the glory of the Father.
Colin Urquhart

What other society has as its symbol a horrifying instrument of
torture and death – especially when the marks of that society are
meant to be love and peace.
David Watson

WORD PICTURES

Self-denial has a double objective: first, it drills and disciplines our
desires, so that we are masters of ourselves; and secondly, what we
deny to ourselves will be time, or money, free to give away.
   At Rouen there is a gloriously carved tower at the south angle of
the Cathedral, called the 'Butter Tower'. It is said it was built by
the offerings of the faithful who went without butter during Lent.
Anon

A certain American river used to do much damage in flood time, tearing down trees, swamping houses, and destroying the crops. At length the Government set to work to provide a remedy. Boats were sent with great dredges to deepen the river bed. An army of men came with spades to cut trenches and straighten the course of the river where it was crooked, and stone banks were built to keep the water from overflowing. So the river was shut in and kept in its course.

It was then that its good work began. The farms bore good crops, for they were safe from destruction. The villages were prosperous; and up and down the river came the great boats carried along by its deep and regular current. It was all the fruit of discipline.
Anon

There is a story of an Italian knight whose brother had been killed, and who pursued the assassin intending to be revenged. It was Good Friday morning, and as he rode up the hill his enemy approached, unarmed. The knight flung himself from his horse and raised his sword to strike, but the man fell on his knees and raised his arms in supplication. The knight hesitated, and as he did so, he became aware of a wayside crucifix, and looking at it, semed to see in the figure hanging there some strange likeness to his enemy. He could not kill him, and he put up his sword, and pardoned him under the shadow of that hanging cross. It was the beginning of a strange friendship; for the two men forsook the world, and together founded a great monastery.
Anon

An ancient Ash Wednesday custom was the making of a Jack o' Lent. This figure was made of straw and was dressed up in old clothes. It was supposed to represent Judas, the disciple who betrayed our Lord with a kiss. This figure was carried through the streets on Ash Wednesday and then set up in order that people might throw stones and sticks at it during the season of Lent. At the end of Lent, the Jack o' Lent was publicly burnt.
Charles Causley, a Christian poet, puts his own interpretation on Jack o' Lent:

Where are you running to, Jack o' Lent
your yellow coat so ruined and rent?
I'm going to the sea-shore as fast as I can
to try and find the Galilee man.

What will you have from him, Jack o' Lent,
before your thirty of silver is spent?
I'll have some fish and I'll have some bread
and some words to cure the pain in my head.

How long will it take you, Jack o' Lent,
your legs all crooked, your body all bent?
With the help of prayer and the help of praise
it'll take me forty nights and days.

Should you not find him, Jack o' Lent,
what will then be your intent?
I'll find the hungry and find the poor
and scatter my silver at their door.

What will you do then, Jack o'Lent,
if nobody takes a single cent?
I'll go to the rope-maker cunning and old
and buy me a collar against the cold.

Where will your lodging be, Jack o' Lent,
if house and home give no comment?
I'll climb as high as heaven's hem
and take my rest on a sycamore stem.

What can we do for you, Jack o' Lent,
if in the fire the tree is pent?
Take the fire and take the flame
and burn the curse from off my name.

What shall we do then, Jack o' Lent,
if all to ashes you are sent?
Take the cinders you can see.
Cross your brow, Remember me.
Charles Causley

USEFUL TEXTS

Forty Days:
  Gen. 7:4; Exod, 24:18; 1Kgs. 19:8; Matt. 4:2

See also: B47 Dying to self
            C37 Temptation
            C40 Reconciliation
            C41 Starting afresh

B44
THE DIGNITY OF THE INDIVIDUAL

'He not only died for us – he rose from the dead, and there at
God's right hand he stands and pleads for us.'
Romans 8:34

QUOTATIONS

Nothing surpasses the greatness or dignity of a human person.
Pope John Paul II

The true worth of a man is to be measured by the objects he pursues.
Marcus Aurelius

Reputation is what men and women think of us. Character is what
God and the angels know of us.
Thomas Paine

Live unto the dignity of thy nature, and leave it not disputable at
last, whether thou hast been a man.
Sir Thomas Browne

It is the final test of a gentleman – his respect for those who can
be of no possible service to him.
William Lyon Phelps

We must recognise that the motives and forces behind racism are
the anti-Christ, denying that man is made in the divine image.
Trevor Huddleston

Every man's life is a fairy tale written by God's fingers.
Hans Christian Andersen

If a man hasn't discovered something that he would die for, he
isn't fit to live.
Martin Luther King

The more faithfully you listen to the voice within you, the better you hear what is sounding outside of you.
Dag Hammarskjold

PROVERB

If people do not know much do not laugh at them, for every one of them knows something that you do not.
A gipsy proverb

WORD PICTURES

Can you walk on water? You have done no better than straw. Can you fly in the air? You have done no better than a bluebottle. Conquer your heart; then you may become somebody.
Ansari of Herat

Man is but a reed, the feeblest thing in Nature. But then he is a reed that thinks. It needs no gathering up of the powers of Nature to crush him: a vapour, a drop of water, will do it. But if the whole universe should fall upon him and crush him man would yet be more noble than that which slew him, because he knows he is dying, and the universe knows it not.

Therefore it is that our whole dignity lies but in this – the faculty of thinking. Let us think well.
Blaise Pascal

The Sunday school teacher had ended her Bible story and was asking questions of her primary tots. 'Why, do you think, does God love us all so very much?' she asked. There was a momentary silence as the children wrinkled their little brows and 'thought hard' for the proper answer. 'Why does God love us – so very much?'

Suddenly little Kristin's hand shot up. And without the slightest doubt about the correctness of her answer she blurted: 'Because he has only one of each of us.'
Only one of each of us!
Anon

My first visit to the Third World changed me. You cannot look into the eyes of a starving child and remain the same.

The first relief camp I was able to visit, with my colleague from CAFOD, was Quiha. The camp was enormous and hundreds of women and children were sitting in groups trying to keep warm with only simple ragged shawls. Many people were just lying on the ground and I sought as a simple priest to give comfort to many who were obviously close to death.

By the next morning in this one camp 300 people had died. I still have a vision of a small boy in another centre who took my fingers and rubbed them against his face, and put his fingers in his mouth to show he was hungry. He had only a loincloth around him. He would not let go of my hand. I thought this child is craving for food, craving for love.

There in a very simple, uncluttered way, I realised once again the fundamental needs of human beings. They need food just to live, and they need love, to be valued.
Cardinal Basil Hume

The morning came, but my servant appeared not. Doors were all open, the water was not drawn from the well, my servant had been out all night. My morning meal was not ready; my clothes were all lying unfolded.

As the hours passed by my anger grew, and I devised hard punishments for him. At last he came, late in the morning, and bowed low. I called out angrily: 'Go forth from my presence and never see my face again.'

He looked at me, and remained silent, and then said in a low, husky voice: 'My little daughter died last night.' And without another word he went to his daily task.
Rabindranath Tagore

From time to time, patients do ask us to end their suffering. If a patient asks me to kill him I would listen very closely: it would be very wrong to brush away such a courageous and awesome request. It is important to elucidate precisely why someone wishes to die: is he clinically (i.e. medically, chemically) depressed, for example, or

distressed at feeling a burden on relatives or carers? Many terminally ill patients do become depressed and respond well to anti-depressant therapy. Others feel better when they realise that their carers love and cherish them, however weak and broken. There does, however, remain a small core of people who find their debilitated and dependent state intolerable, and to these patients I would offer sedation, asking, 'Would you like to be more sleepy most of the time?' If they *would* like this we would prescribe regular sedative drugs, achieving a level of sedation that allows the patient to be woken for care and nourishment, and then drift off to sleep again. It sometimes happens that such people sleep their lives away over a few weeks or days – but I am clear that here the primary intention is the relief of emotional distress, not the ending of the person's life.
Sheila Cassidy

Apparently a wealthy society lady phoned Jung to request an urgent consultation the following day at 3pm in the afternoon. Jung said it wouldn't be possible because he was already committed to an important appointment at that time. Well, the next day, the lady in question happened to be sailing past Jung's garden which ran down to the shore of Lake Zurich. There was the famous doctor sitting on a small wall, his shoes and socks off, with his feet dangling idly in the water. As soon as she got home, the irate woman rang Jung to demand an explanation. 'You told me,' she exclaimed, 'that you couldn't see me because you had an important appointment. Nevertheless I saw you at that very hour, whiling away the time at the bottom of your garden.' 'I told you no lie,' Jung replied, 'I had an appointment, the most important appointment of the week, an appointment with myself.'
Anon

See also: B26 The whole person
            B34 Human rights
            B45 Free will
            C47 The indwelling Spirit

B45
Free Will

'Jesus never needed evidence about anyone;
he could tell what was in everyone.'
John 2:25

Quotations

Our wills are ours to make them thine.
Alfred Lord Tennyson

To deny the freedom of the will is to make morality impossible.
J. A. Froud

All theory is against freedom of the will; all experience for it.
Samuel Johnson

God is omnipotent – but powerless still
to stop my heart from wishing what it will.
Angelus Silesius

We glorify rugged wills; but the greatest things are done by timid
people who work with simple trust.
John La Farge

Those who deny freedom to others deserve it not for themselves,
and, under a just God, cannot long retain it.
Abraham Lincoln

God is not willing to do everything, and thus take away our free
will and that share of glory which belongs to us.
Niccolo Machiavelli

Our deeds are like the children born to us; they live and act apart
from our own will.
George Eliot

The difference between a 'weak' will and a 'strong' will lies not so much in the weakened will itself as in the lack of a strong deeply loved master purpose or ideal to direct the will.
Fulton Sheen

Proverbs

He who can follow his own will is a king.
Irish proverb

He who deliberates fully before taking a step will spend his entire life on one leg.
Chinese proverb

Humour

The old clergyman was without doubt the world's worst golfer. One day, on a fairly long straight hole he uncorked a towering drive straight towards the pin. The ball started to roll and as if drawn by a magnet continued to roll – over the apron – across the green – hit the pin and dropped into the hole.

The astounded clergyman turned his eyes towards heaven. 'Lord,' he begged, 'I'd rather do it myself.'
Cecil Bateman

Word pictures

Cherish no hate for thy brother who offends, because you have not offended like him. If your fellow man possessed your nature he might not have sinned. If you possessed his nature you might have offended as he has done. A man's transgressions depend not entirely upon his free choice, but often upon many other circumstances.
A Hasidic Rabbi

Pat Seed, a woman in her fifties, was told a few years ago that she had cancer and only six months to live. Instead of resigning herself to her situation (which would almost certainly have resulted in an early death), she immediately embarked on a fund-raising campaign in order to buy a sophisticated scanner for the early detection of cancer, for the Christie Hospital in Manchester. She worked so hard at this that she scarcely had time to think about anything else, including her own terminal illness. She not only outlived her six months; today, six years later, she has raised more than three million pounds for life-saving equipment. She has been presented with an MBE by the Queen at Buckingham Palace, and she has now been declared entirely free from cancer.

Moreover, over 5,000 patients have now been scanned by the equipment bought through her fund-raising, and probably many lives saved. Because she reacted positively to her situation she was able to change it radically. Pat Seed made this interesting comment in a newspaper interview: 'I heard about two cancer patients, both men, who like me were given six months to live. One went home, made arrangements for his funeral, and died a fortnight later. The other went home, looked at his seven children and thought: 'How on earth will this lot cope if I go?' Now, twenty years later, those children have grown up and he's still alive. Repeatedly it comes back to our attitudes which are often more important than the affliction itself.

P.F.

USEFUL TEXTS

Doubt:
   Mixed with faith, *James 1:6-8*
   In belief, *John 20:25-29*
   In trials, *Mark 4:40; 1 Pet. 1:6*

See also: C13 Coping with grief
           C22 The Light of faith
           C30 Increase our faith
           C41 Starting afresh

B46
CHRIST THE SACRAMENT OF GOD

'The Son of Man must be lifted up as Moses lifted up
the serpent in the desert, so that everyone who believes
may have eternal life in him.'
John 3:14-15

QUOTATIONS

Christ cannot live his life today in this world without our mouth,
our eyes, without our going and coming, without our heart. When
we love, it is Christ loving through us.
Leon Joseph Suenans

In Jesus we see the point in the evolution of the universe, when
the divine consciousness took possession of a human soul and
body and the plan of God in creation from the beginning was
revealed.
Bede Griffiths

The sign of Christ can only be deciphered if his human love and
surrender 'even unto death' is read as the manifestation of
absolute love.
Hans Urs von Balthasar

The man Jesus, as the personal visible realisation of the divine
grace of redemption is *the* sacrament, the primordial sacrament,
because this man, the Son of God himself, is intended by the
Father to be in his humanity the only way to the actuality of
redemption.
E. Schillebeeckx

Since the Holy Spirit proceeds from the love of the Father for the
Son, and through the Son is to be poured out over the whole
world, nothing is more appropriate than that the Son in his
humanity, as the head of all creatures, should represent and effect

this outpouring of the Holy Spirit in the outpouring of his blood, and that this latter outpouring should become the real sacrament of the other outpouring.
M. Scheeben

WORD PICTURES

In Malaya, during the Second World War, a sympathetic native was helping an escaping prisoner of war make his way to the coast – and from there to freedom. The two were stumbling through a virtually impenetrable jungle. There was no sign of human life and not even the slightest trace of a trail. Having grown weary and becoming somewhat wary, the soldier turned to his guide and asked, 'Are you sure this is the way?'
The reply came in faltering English. 'There *is* no way . . . I am the way.'

The story is told of a wayfarer who many years ago knocked on the door of a medieval English castle.
    'Please, sir, may I have lodging for the night?' he asked the stout man who answered the knock. 'This castle is not for pilgrims,' the grim-faced man replied as he made to close the door.
    'Are you the owner, sir?' the wayfarer inquired. 'I am'.
    'And who lived in this castle before you?' 'My father.'
    'And who will live in it when you are gone?' 'My son.'
    'And still you say, sir, this castle is not for *pilgrims*?'

In the earliest Christian art, that of the Catacombs, Christ is represented as the Greek Orpheus, with the lyre in his hand, drawing everything to him by his magic spell. These early Christians, standing near to the Greek civilisation, chose this, out of all the figures of Greek mythology, to express their ideas of the Lord whom they loved and worshipped. And this story of Orpheus is one of the noblest which has come down to us from the enchanted land of Hellas. Orpheus was the greatest of all musicians, for Apollo has bestowed upon him the lyre, which Hermes had invented. So wonderfully did he play that when his fingers touched the instrument the beast of the field drew near, and the birds were arrested in their flight, and even the things of Nature gathered spellbound around him. He could make the strings wail so pitiful a lament that tears trickled down the scarred cheeks of the rocks; while, when he sang of love, the world was filled with sudden sunlight, and even the wildest beast became tame and gentle.

It was thus the early Christians thought of Christ. They felt his drawing power, the strange spell which he had over everything. Possessed in their hearts, he transfigured nature, but most of all he transfigured them. He banished by his music the low and bestial instincts which raged within them, and made the most coarse and intractable gentle and docile and obedient.

B.D.

See also: A44 Meeting Christ in the sacraments
           B4   Mary – Handmaid of God
           B16 Christ heals and forgives
           B51 One with Christ

B47
DYING TO SELF

'I tell you, most solemnly, unless a wheat grain falls on
the ground and dies, it remains only a single grain,
but if it dies it yields a rich harvest.'
John 12:24

QUOTATIONS

All great virtues bear the imprint of self-denial.
William E. Channing

No man remains quite what he was when he recognises himself.
Thomas Mann

We are all serving a life sentence in the dungeon of self.
Cyril Connolly

In this world it is not what we *take* up, but what we *give* up, that
makes us rich.
Henry Ward Beecher

They that deny themselves for Christ shall enjoy themselves in Christ.
John Mason

WORD PICTURES

Henri Nouwen tells of a Lutheran bishop who was imprisoned in
a German concentration camp during World War II and beaten
by an SS officer in order to extract a confession from him about
his political action. The beatings continued to increase in
intensity, but the bishop maintained his silence. Finally, the
infuriated officer shrieked, 'Don't you know that I can kill you?'
The bishop looked in the eyes of his torturer and said, 'Yes, I
know – do what you want – but I have already died.'
    Instantly, as though paralysed, the officer could no longer raise
his arm. It was as if power over the bishop had been taken from

him. All his cruelties had been based on the assumption that the bishop's physical life was his most precious possession and therefore he would be willing to make any concession to save it. But with the grounds for violence gone, torture was futile.

Anon

Mothers will do almost anything to protect their children, self-love takes second place. When the thirty-year-old Margaret Clitherow, the butcher's wife of York was taken to court in 1586 accused of 'sheltering Catholic priests' in her house, she refused to plead guilty or not guilty. She declared that she had committed no crime and she would not plead 'not guilty' because the prosecution planned to put her children in the witness box to subject them to cross-questioning. As a mother she could not allow her children to feel later that they had caused their mother's death.

She knew the penalty, at that time, of refusing to plead. She would be taken to a public place and there, in a smock to cover her, be crushed to death under a door piled high with weights. And that is how she died; professing her Catholic Faith and witnessing to a mother's unselfish love. She was declared a saint in 1970.

Anon

A young friend has related to me how in her little sleepy English country town, a retired elderly sergeant, who had fought through the Boer War and who was now a quite average working man, told her the following experience of his own. He was riding in the Transvaal during that strenuous campaign, with a small troop of cavalry along a road between two British posts. A Boer patrol in ambush fired upon the troop – he himself was hit and slid off his horse; the rest effected their escape to the post nearby, whence they would bring help. All galloped off thus, except a quite young lieutenant of ancient lineage, luxurious nurture, and doubtless largely inarticulate intelligence and conviction, an Eton lad, come straight out to the war.

The lieutenant sprang from his horse, clasped the wounded man in his arms, and as the Boers renewed their fire shielded the sergeant with his body. The volley took its effect on the young man; a great gush of his blood streamed over the man he was

protecting. The sergeant saw that the officer was dying. 'How sad,' he said, 'that you, just starting on a long and brilliant life, should die thus for and instead of me – an elderly man of no special outlook or importance!' 'Sad? What could be better?' he exclaimed, and fell back, dead. That again, is supernatural.
Fredrich Von Hugel

In the *Arabian Knights* you will remember the story of the magnetic islands. These islands were so magnetic that when ships came near them they were wrecked. They were not drawn upon the rocks and dashed to pieces, nor was there any sudden explosion. These islands were simply so magnetic that they drew all the nails and bolts out of the ship and it fell to pieces.

This is the test which self-sacrifice applies to every life. When a life has been lived on a principle of selfishness, as the years go by, sacrifice applies this test and that life falls to pieces and comes to sorrow. As the sieve of life moves constantly, the little things slip through and there is nothing left of a selfish life. I challenge you to name any person who has attained any permanent degree of happiness who has not lived a life of self-denial.
Charles F Banning

USEFUL TEXTS
Unselfishness:
  In living, *Matt. 16:24-25; 1 Cor. 10:24*
  In true love, *1 Cor. 13:4-5*
Examples of:
  David, *1 Chron. 21:17*
  Paul, *1 Cor. 9:12-22; 10:33*
  Christ, *Mark 6:30-34*

See also: A5   One for another – unselfishness
           A7   Poor in spirit
           A10 Seeking perfection
           B26 The whole person

B48
CHRISTIAN UNITY

'The whole group of believers was united, heart and soul.'
Acts 4:32

QUOTATIONS

Our divisions prevent our neighbours from hearing the Gospel as
they should.
Pope John Paul II

Of what use is it to have many irons in the fire if the fire is going
out.
Eric Roberts

Church unity is like peace, we are all for it, but we are not willing
to pay the price.
Dr Visser't Hooft

It is not our differences that really matter. It is the meanness
behind that is ugly.
Mahatma Gandhi

The best creed we can have is charity towards the creeds of others.
Josh Billings

The responsibility of tolerance lies with those who have the wider
vision.
George Eliot

What wall or fort, strongly built with well-compacted and large
stones, is so impregnable against the assaults of the enemy, as the
united band of men joined by mutual love and sealed by oneness
of mind?
St John Chrysostom

The priest was describing to his bishop an inter-church gathering which was to finish up with a Catholic Mass. 'I told them all that only the Catholics would be able to come to Holy Communion. But at Communion time the non-Catholics came out as well.' 'What on earth did you do?' said the bishop. 'Well, I said to myself, what would Jesus do in a case like this?' 'Oh, my God,' said the bishop, 'you surely never did.'
Brian Green

Never resign yourself to the scandal of the separation of Christians – all so readily professing love for their neighbour, yet remaining divided. Make the unity of Christ's Body your passionate concern.
Taizé Community

HUMOUR

My daughter, aged about seven, came home from school and asked, 'What is a prostitute?'

As quick as a flash my youngest daughter, aged about five, replied, 'You know, it's what dad is.'

Shocked silence followed, then I asked her what she meant. 'You know,' she replied, 'not a Catholic.'
Bernadette Gray

There is a story going around among missionaries, of the cannibal who complains that since the ecumenical movement has been under way all missionaries taste alike!

An Irish Protestant who was dangerously ill and believed he was dying sent for a Catholic priest and was received into the Catholic Church. His Protestant friends were horrified and one of them asked him how he could thus forsake the creed for which he had stood all his life and go over to the enemy. 'Well,' said the sick man, 'it's this way. I said to myself, if anyone's got to die, better one of their lot than one of our lot.'
K. Edwards

A party of clergymen were attending a conference in Scotland. Several of them set off to explore the countryside. Presently they came to a river spanned by a temporary bridge. Not seeing the notice that said it was unsafe, they began to cross. A workman ran after them in protest. 'It's all right,' declared one of the ministers, not understanding the reason for the old man's haste. 'We're Presbyterians from the conference.' 'I'm no' caring aboot that,' came the reply, 'but if ye dinna get off the bridge you'll all be Baptists!' *Clyde Murdock*

Three clergymen – an Anglican priest, an Irish Catholic priest, and a Scots minister – were attending a conference in Scotland for Church unity. At the conclusion they decided to go for a day's fishing in the nearby loch and having hired a boat, set off and anchored a little way from the shore. They were having good luck with the fishing when suddenly the line of the Scots minister was fouled and, having no other of that particular tackle available, he decided to go ashore to get some more. Going down on his knees in the bow of the boat, he prayed very earnestly and then, stepping over the side, walked across the surface of the water to the shore, returning in like manner.

A little later the Anglican priest had need to go ashore and he also knelt down and prayed and then stepped over the side of the boat and walked over the water, returning in due course.

Presently, it was found that their supplies were running short so the first two priests looked at the Irish priest who said that he would go ashore to bring back replenishments. He also knelt and prayed and then stepped over the side of the boat as his companions had done previously. But he went right down in the water, and as the other two priests watched him sink, one said to the other: 'Perhaps for the sake of Christian unity, we should have pointed out where the stepping stones were!'
Anon

Just before visiting our new community hospital for the first time, I met with a Roman Catholic priest. We talked about supporting each other's ministry.

At the hospital I was pleased with the welcome accorded me as a minister. Especially impressive was a comfortable lounge marked 'Father's Room'. My Catholic colleague will be thrilled, I thought. But what about Protestant clergy? Do they have a special room, too? That's what I asked a passing nurse. She looked bewildered, then smiled and finally just plain laughed. Father's Room was in the maternity ward!
Jack Harris

WORD PICTURES

Bonhoeffer's last message as he was taken out to execution was to Bell (the Bishop of Chichester) through a British prisoner. . . . Tell him (he said) that for me this is the end but also the beginning – with him I believe in the principle of our universal Christian brotherhood which rises above all national interests, and that our victory is certain.
Wolf-Dieter Zimmermann and Ronald Gregor Smith

For thirty years the Abbé Paul Couturier taught mathematics. He was not a great orator but he was a man great in prayer, and from 1932 his prayers centered upon the unity of the Church.

In that year he spent some time in the diocese that had been ruled by Cardinal Mercier, that great Christian hero of the First World War and he caught something of his yearning to see the Churches brought together. After that the Abbé Couturier lived out the simple counsel of the Belgian Cardinal – 'In order to unite with one another, we must love one another. In order to love one another we must know one another. In order to know one another, we must meet one another.'

Most of all the Abbé Couturier showed that if we are to unite with one another we must pray for one another. He took the eight days from the Feast of St Peter at Rome on 18th January, to the Feast of St Paul on the 25th – a period that had earlier been used to pray for this purpose – and made it a week of prayer for unity in which all Christians could join.

When he died, a friend found the intentions for his last Mass on the altar. He said: 'The whole world was gathered on the Abbé's altar . . . along with the offering of his whole life.'
Kenneth Slack

Once a Jewess, intellectual and wealthy and thoroughly materialistic in outlook, she married the Jewish Richard and together they planned to have a pleasurable existence – until God erupted into their lives, challenged them, and conquered. Mrs Richard Wurmbrand had been imprisoned with 1,000 women, some of them society women who only possessed the evening dress they were wearing at the time of their sudden arrest. She had stories only to be equalled in the annals of the early Christians, and listening to her I was transported to the past, to the times of St Cyprian and my own Felicitas and I began to realise something of the intense veneration felt for heroic confessors of the faith, for my instinct was to kneel and kiss Mrs Wurmbrand's feet. She told of the nuns in her filthy overcrowded barrack room who, in the face of all threats, calmly went on singing psalms and praising God. Their captors finally decided to make an exhibition of them. Summoning the whole camp as witnesses, they ordered them on to the frozen lake in bare feet and scant clothing. They should have died of exposure and frostbite. Instead, their song grew louder and sweeter. So the dogs – great specially trained brutes of terrifying ferocity – were set on them to tear them to pieces. The camp set up a wail and begged for pity – in vain. The dogs hurtled themselves on to the ice, ran in circles round the nuns, and then sat down quietly without a growl or menace. In angry frustration, the warders ordered everyone back to their cells, sent for a doctor, and asked for examination of the prisoners after their exposure. Not a single sign of injury. The nuns sang on. The tale of their trial and victory very much resembles that of the Forty Martyrs of Sebaste which the higher critics would dismiss as myth – here it is a history in our own day. This, I felt, is where true ecumenism is to be found: no barriers whatever of confessional faiths. Only tribulations, anguish, persecutions, hunger, dangers, the sword, in fact the entire list given by St Paul in Romans – and over all, the joy of any man's inability to separate his own from Christ.
Felicitas Corrigan

On 3rd February 1943 a convoy of American ships was bringing reinforcements from St John's in Newfoundland to Greenland. In the darkness a German U-boat struck suddenly. The torpedo hit the SS *Dorchester* in a vulnerable spot at 3.55am and the 5,252-ton transport began to sink rapidly by the bow into the icy waters some 150 miles from Cape Farewell. There were fourteen lifeboats on board and all were quickly lowered. Only two, however, were used to good purpose – all the rest capsized. In such waters a man would have a life expectation of three to five minutes.

On the ship were four US Army chaplains: John P. Washington, a Catholic priest, Clark V. Poling and George L. Fox, Protestant ministers; and Alexander D. Goode, a Jewish rabbi. Unmindful of their own safety all four helped the officers to control the confusion which reigned and they encouraged the men and prayed with them. When the life-jackets ran short, each of the chaplains took off his own and gave it to a man who had none. As the doomed ship sank the men in the water could see the four chaplains on the deck, 'linked arm in arm, their voices raised in prayer'.

Of the 904 men on board only 299 were saved; the chaplains were not among them. One of the survivors, a coastguard officer, John J. Mahoney, owed his life to Chaplain Goode. The rabbi took off his gloves and gave them to him. The gloves kept his hands from freezing and miraculously enabled him to cling to a lifeboat for eight hours, awaiting rescue, while thirty-eight of the forty men in the boat froze to death or were swept overboard.
The Messenger

USEFUL TEXTS
Unity:
>   In Christ, *John 15:4-7; 1Cor. 3:23; Gal. 2:20*
>   In Church, *Gal. 3:28*
>   In mind and spirit, *1 Cor. 1:10; Phil. 1:27; 1 Pet. 3:8*

See also: A20 The Kingdom of God
>   B17 The Church – Bride of Christ
>   B36 The Family of God
>   B51 One with Christ

B49
COPING WITH DOUBT

'Why are you so agitated, and why are these doubts
rising in your hearts?'
Luke 24:38

QUOTATIONS

Doubt is the father of discovery.
Galileo

The end of doubt is the beginning of repose.
Petrarch

When unhappy, one doubts everything, when happy, one doubts
nothing.
Joseph Rowe

When in doubt, risk it.
Holbrook Jackson

Insecurity welcomes manacles to prevent its hands shaking.
Walter Lippmann

Doubt comes in at the window when enquiry is denied at the
door.
Benjamin Jowett

Give me the benefit of your convictions if you have any, but keep
your doubts to yourself, for I have enough of my own.
Goethe

For I kept my heart from assenting to anything, fearing to fall
headlong; but by hanging in suspense I was the worse killed.
St Augustine of Hippo

Underlying all life is the ground of doubt and self-questioning which sooner or later must bring us face to face with the ultimate meaning of our life.
Thomas Merton

PROVERBS

When in doubt do nowt.
English proverb

God will provide – ah, if only he would!
Yiddish proverb

HUMOUR

If only God would give me some clear sign! Like making a large deposit in my name at a Swiss bank.
Woody Allen

A husband, mulling over his bills, exclaimed: 'I'd give a thousand pounds to anyone who would do my worrying for me!' 'You're on,' answered his wife, 'where's the thousand?' Replied the husband, 'That's your first worry.'

WORD PICTURES

Several centuries ago a Chinese philosopher said: 'The legs of the stork are long, the legs of the duck are short. I cannot make the legs of the stork short; neither can I lengthen the legs of the duck. So why worry?'

Crossing the Atlantic, a vessel is often encircled by small ice floes like a flock of white sheep. When they started on their course southwards, the icebergs were ice-mountains. But the warm Gulf Stream plays on them beneath, and the sun on top, and they are always moving into a warmer atmosphere and growing smaller. So perhaps a man's doubts disappear in the glow of service for others kindling warmth.

At one time in his life Martin Luther was much depressed and found it very difficult to conceal his melancholy mood. Soon he noticed that his usually cheerful wife had put on her mourning garments and had adopted an unaccustomed attitude of sombre silence.

When he asked the reason for this sudden change, his pious Katie replied, 'Why, I thought that God had died, the way that you've been acting; and so I thought it proper that I should go in mourning.'

If there is a lesson
in the history of religious experience
in modern times,
it is that the quest for certainty
is self-defeating.

The more earnestly a man
seeks for certainty,
the more uncertain he becomes;
the more strenuously
he tries to remove all doubt
the more doubt he experiences.
John S. Dunne

USEFUL TEXTS

Will of Man:
   Free to choose, *Josh. 24:15; Deut. 30:19*
   Set free from Christ, *2 Tim. 2:26*
   In bondage to sin, *Prov. 5:22; Rom. 6:16*

See also: A2   Integrity
                B26 The whole person
                B44 The dignity of the individual

B50
THE GOOD SHEPHERD

'I am the good shepherd: the good shepherd is one
who lays down his life for his sheep.'
John 10:11

QUOTATIONS

The Resurrection became the confirmation of his victory; the victory
of the love of the Good Shepherd who says: 'They follow me.'
Pope John Paul II

Who can cancel the work of God himself, which the Son has
carried out in union with the Father? Who can change the fact
that we are redeemed? A fact as powerful and as fundamental as
creation itself? In spite of all the instability of human destiny and
the weakness of the human will and heart, the Church orders us
today to contemplate the might, the irreversible power of the
Redemption, which lives in the heart and hands and feet of the
Good Shepherd.
Pope John Paul II

WORD PICTURES

When a shepherd in Scotland was asked if his sheep would follow
the voice of a stranger, he replied: 'Yes, when they are sick; but
never when they are well. A sick sheep will follow anybody.'

A soldier lay dying on a Korean battlefield, and asked for a priest.
The Medic could not find one; but a wounded man, lying near,
heard the request, and said, 'I am a priest.' The Medic turned to
the speaker and saw his condition, which was as bad as that of the
other. 'It will kill you to move,' said he. But the priest replied,
'The life of a man's soul is worth more than a few hours of my life,'
and crawled to the dying soldier. He heard his confession, gave
him absolution, and the two died hand in hand.
Anon

Gladstone was on a holiday in Scotland, walking along a country lane, when a storm came up. The snow began to fall and the wind howled. As he walked along he noticed the sheep coming up out of the hollows and from underneath the trees, going out to stand on the bare hillsides facing the storm. A little later he met the old shepherd and said to him, 'Are not sheep the most foolish animals? Here is a storm pending and instead of remaining in shelter they are courting the fury of the blast. If I were a sheep, I should remain in the hollow.' The shepherd replied, 'Sair, if ye were a sheep, ye'd have mair sense.' Then he pointed out that down in the hollow drifts came, and death. Instinctively the sheep knew that their only safety was on the hills, facing the storm.
Anon

One evening General Garibaldi met a Sardinian shepherd who had lost a lamb out of his flock and was in great distress because he could not find it. Garibaldi became deeply interested in the man and proposed to his staff that they should scour the mountains and help to find the lost lamb. A search was organised, lanterns were brought, and these old soldiers started off full of eager earnestness to look for the fugitive. The quest was in vain however, and by and by all the soldiers returned to their quarters. Next morning Garibaldi's attendant found the General in bed fast asleep long after his usual hour for rising. The servant aroused him at length, and the General rubbed his eyes and then took from under his bed coverings the lost lamb, bidding the attendant carry it to the shepherd. Garibaldi had kept up the search through the night until he had found the lamb.
Anon

Archbishop Affre of Paris was murdered during the Revolution of 1848. Horror-stricken by the slaughter which for three days had been going on, he resolved to try whether it would be possible to reconcile the contending parties. Dressed in his pontifical robes, carrying the Cross and attended by two chaplains, he set out for the Place de la Bastille. The people, knowing his danger, fell on their knees and begged him to turn back. He answered quietly, 'It

is my duty. A good shepherd giveth his life for the sheep.' He was mortally wounded near the Bastille by a shot fired from a window. The insurgents, horror-stricken, carried him to a neighbouring hospital. When told he had only a few minutes to live, he said: 'God be praised! May he accept my life as an expiation for my omissions during my episcopate, and as an offering for this misguided people.' Then repeating once more, 'A good shepherd giveth his life for his flock,' he added, 'and may my blood be the last that is shed.' With these words on his lips he passed away.
Anon

USEFUL TEXTS

Shepherd, figurative of:
    God's provision, *Pss. 23; 78:52; 80:1*
    Prophets and priests, *Ezek. 34*
    Jesus, *John 10:11; 1. Pet. 2:25*

See also: B15 Jesus, friend of outcasts
            B38 The suffering servant
            C44 Feed my sheep

B51
ONE WITH CHRIST

'As a branch cannot bear fruit all by itself, but must remain part of the vine, neither can you unless you remain in me.'
John 15:4

QUOTATIONS

Everything leads to union with him, everything brings perfection excepting sin and what is not our duty.
Jean-Pierre de Caussade

I am in you and are me. We cannot be closer. We are two united, poured into a single form by an eternal fusion.
Mechthild of Magdelburg

We are the members of Christ, and Christ is our member. And my hand, the hand of me who is poorest of the poor, is Christ, and my foot is Christ.
Simeon the New Theologian

Christ has no body now on earth, but yours, no hands but yours, no feet but yours; yours are the eyes through which is to look out Christ's compassion to the world, yours are the feet with which he is to go about doing good, and yours are the hands with which he is to bless us now.
St Teresa of Avila

WORD PICTURES

In some parts of India there are provided along the road resting places for those who carry heavy loads on their heads. Such a resting place is called a *sumatanga*. These rests have a shelf where the traveller can easily drop his burden. Beneath is a shady recessed seat where he can quietly rest. Referring to one of these, a native Christian said, 'Christ is my *sumatanga*.'

A poor German schoolmaster, we are told, who lived in a humble house, in a small village, carved over his doorway this proud inscription: 'Dante, Molière, and Goethe live here.' That schoolmaster had learned the secret that the richness of life lies in one's spiritual companionships.

Turn now to a Christian like Paul and hear him say, 'I live; yet not I, but Christ liveth in me.' Unfortunately we have frozen words like that into theology. We have stiffened them into dogma until the life has gone out of them. If a schoolmaster can say that Dante and Molière and Goethe live with him, why cannot a man say that Christ lives in him.
Harry Emerson Fosdick

Coming together is a beginning, keeping together is progress: working together is success in the Christian assembly: for,
As One Flock, we are gathered together (John 10:16)
As One Family, we dwell together (Ps. 133:1)
As One Body, we are joined together (Eph. 4:16)
As One Temple, we are framed together (Eph. 2:21)
As One Household, we are built together (Eph. 2:19-20)
As One Kingdom, we are to strive together (Phil. 1:27)
As One Hierarchy, we are raised up together (Eph. 2:6)

There is in South India a story of a wealthy landowner who had some very quarrelsome sons, always jealous of one another and always arguing among themselves. On his deathbed he called them and divided his property among them. Then he called for some sticks to be brought, nicely tied into a bundle, and asked them one by one, beginning at the eldest to break the bundle. So long as they were thus closely bound together, they could not break any of the sticks. 'Now,' he said to the eldest, 'untie the bundle, and try to break the sticks singly.' This was not difficult, and soon each of the sticks, broken one by one, lay before them in two pieces.

The father thus taught them that – united they stood; divided they fell.
Anon

There is a legend of a saint whose wonderful deeds astonished the angels and they came to learn the secret of his piety. Everywhere the man went he diffused virtue as the flower gives out perfume, without being aware of it. The angels asked that the saint might be given the gift of miracles, and God consented. They asked the man if he would like by the touch of his hand to heal the sick. 'No,' he replied, 'I would rather God should do that.' 'Then would you like to convert guilty souls and bring them back to right paths?' 'No,' said the saint, 'it is the Spirit's mission to convert; I only pray.' 'Would you like to be a model of patience and draw men by your piety?' 'No, if men are attracted to me, they might be estranged from God.' 'What do you desire?' said the angels. 'That God would give me his grace; that I might do a great deal of good without knowing it.' The angels were perplexed. Finally they resolved that whenever the shadow of the man should fall where he could not see it, the shadow could cure disease and comfort sorrow. So it came to pass, as the saint passed along, the hearts of men were cheered wherever he walked.
Anon

See also: B25 Quiet – time for prayer
C47 The indwelling spirit
C48 One in us

B52
GOD IS LOVE

'Anyone who fails to love can never have known God,
because God is love.'
1 John 4:8

QUOTATIONS

Love is, above all, the gift of oneself.
Jean Anouilh

God wants the heart.
The Talmud

God loves all existing things.
St Thomas Aquinas

One loving heart sets another on fire.
St Augustine of Hippo

God has made thee to love him, and not understand him.
Voltaire

All virtue is loving right, all sin is loving wrong.
Hubert Van Zeller

All love, provided it is authentic, pure and disinterested, bears in
itself its own justification.
Pope John Paul II

What matters it to a truly loving soul whether God be served by
this means or by another.
St Francis of Sales

Love is the only force that can make things one without destroying
them.
Teilhard de Chardin

Human beings must be known to be loved, but divine things must
be loved to be known.
Blaise Pascal

Love is the greatest thing that God can give us; for himself is love:
and it is the greatest thing we can give to God.
Jeremy Taylor

And he alone is great who turns the voice of the wind into a song
made sweeter by his own loving.
Kahlil Gibran

The reality of our communion with Christ and in him with one
another is the increase of love in our hearts.
William Temple

Love is the result of love, it is intrinsically valuable. I love because
I love; I love in order to love. Love is a valuable thing only if it
returns to its beginning, consults its origin and flows back to its
source . . . when God loves, he wishes only to be loved in return,
assuredly he loves for no other purpose than to be loved. He
knows that those who love are happy in their love.
St Bernard of Clairvaux

It has the hands to help others.
It has the feet to hasten to the poor and needy.
It has the eyes to see misery and want.
It has the ears to hear the sighs and sorrows of men.
That is what love looks like.
St Augustine of Hippo

HUMOUR

An infatuated young man was sending his girlfriend a cable which
read: 'Ozzy loves his Woozy, Woozy, Woozy.'
  'You can have another "Woozy" without it costing any more,'
said the desk clerk.
  'No, thanks,' replied the young man, 'I think that would sound
rather silly.'
Anon

Making love is a mental illness that wastes time and energy.
Chinese Communist Manifesto

WORD PICTURES

Someday,
after mastering
the winds, the waves,
the tides and gravity,
we shall harness for God
the energies of love,

and then,
for the second time
in the history of the world,
man will discover fire.
Teilhard de Chardin

A little boy visiting in the home of an elderly woman was intrigued by a coloured wall motto bearing the biblical text: 'Thou God, seest me.' Noticing the child's interest, the kindly woman took the motto from the wall and began explaining it to the lad.

'Some people will tell you', she said, 'that God is always watching to see when you are doing wrong – so he can punish you. I don't want you to think of this motto in that way. Every time you read the words, "Thou God, seest me", I would rather have you remember that God loves you so much that he cannot take his eyes off you.'   •

Late have I loved you, O beauty so ancient and so new; late have I loved you! For behold you were within me, and I outside; and I sought you outside and in my ugliness fell upon those lovely things that you have made. You were with me and I was not with you. I was kept from you by those things, yet had they not been in you, they would not have been at all. You called and cried to me and broke upon my deafness; and you sent forth your beam and shone upon me, and chased away my blindness; you breathed fragrance upon me, and I drew in my breath and do not pant for

you; I tasted you and I now hunger and thirst for you; you touched me, and I now burned for your peace.
St Augustine of Hippo

The renowned theologian, Dr Karl Barth, was spending an evening within the intimate circle of friends. Curious to know more about the great theologian's thinking, one of these present asked him: 'What is the most profound thought that ever entered your mind?'

After a brief moment of reflection Dr Barth replied very simply: 'The most profound thought I have ever known is the simple truth: Jesus loves me, this I know, for the Bible tells me so.'

An ancient Chinese sage was once asked by his disciples what single thing would he do for humanity if it was in his power to do it.

Without hesitation he replied he would give back to words their original meaning. And if he could choose but one word above all others, what would that word be? It would be the word 'love' came the reply.
Anon

One of the great apostles of North America was the Franciscan Fra Junipero Serra. He was a young professor of philosophy at Majorca when in 1749 he was sent with one companion on the Mexican mission. On the way he wrote home to his parents, and told them of a slogan he had made for his future life: 'Always go forward, never turn back!' Arrived at Vera Cruz, he and his companion decided not to wait for the regular mule caravan, but started out to walk the 275 miles uphill to Mexico City. It was a dangerous journey through forests, with many perils especially poisonous snakes hanging from the trees. One night Fra Junipero found his leg painful and swelling from a small snake bite of which he had taken little notice. It was patched up somehow for the time, but the wound was never properly cured and the leg was a constant trouble for the rest of his life.

In Mexico he first spent nine years in the mountains of the Sierra Gorda among the Indians, learning their language, and learning also to love them. In 1767 he was appointed head of a Franciscan party in Lower California, where he started the mission of San Diego; and from there two years later he accompanied the troops who set out to colonise Upper California. Thus he began the great work of his life at the age of fifty-five.

Along the great coast road, alongside the military forts, he founded mission after mission, each of them with a housing estate and community centre for Indian converts. (Now they are great American cities such as the one he founded in honour of his own San Francisco of Assisi.) It is reckoned that he must have walked at least 13,000 miles in Mexico and Califormia, bad leg and all. He loved his California Indians (though they were not a very intelligent or attractive type) and fought hard and successfully for their rights as human beings. His customary greeting was 'Love God, my children!' and the Indians would reply 'Love God, our father!' He died at Monterey in 1784, and is buried there.
F. H. Drinkwater

USEFUL TEXTS

Love:
>Towards God, *Deut. 6:5*
>Towards Neighbour, *Matt. 22:39*
>Exemplified by Christ, *John 15:12*
>Obedience as proof of, *John 14:15*
>Importance of, *1 Cor. 13:1-3; 8-13*

See also: A9   Relationships
            A33 Love your neighbour
            B30 Married love
            C10 Love your enemies

B53
CONSECRATED IN TRUTH

'I have sent them into the world, and for their sake I consecrate
myself so that they too may be consecrated in truth.'
John 17:19

QUOTATIONS

The only way to speak the truth is to speak it lovingly.
Henry David Thoreau

Without a consciousness of truth itself doubt of truth would be
impossible.
Paul Tillich

If God were able to backslide from truth I would fain cling to
truth and let God go.
Meister Eckhart

Every man has a right to his opinion, but no man has a right to be
wrong in his facts.
Bernard M. Baruch

Truth is not only violated by falsehood; it may be equally outraged
by silence.
Henri Frederic Amiel

Only God is, only God knows, only God can do anything. This is
the truth, and with the help of my faith I discover this more
deeply every day.
Carlo Carretto

No one can bar the road to truth, and to advance its cause I'm
ready to accept even death.
Alexander Solzhenitsyn

Humour

I'll tell you one fact – it may be rather boring but it's interesting.
Barbara Cartland

Word pictures

If God held in his right hand all truth and in his left the ever-living
desire for truth – although with the condition that I should remain
in error for ever – and if he said to me, 'Choose', I should humbly
bow before his left hand, and say, 'Father, give; pure truth is for
Thee alone.'
Lessing

In 1922, when the Turks captured Smyrna, and drove out the
Greek Christians, they entered a boys' school where there were
about forty Christian boys between the ages of nine and fourteen.
The Turkish leader then assembled the boys and addressed them:

'Boys, if you put up your hands you will be allowed to remain in
this town, be clothed, cared for, and fed – but, you must become
Muslims; if you do not put up your hands, you will be shot.'

Not a boy put up his hand. They were at once shot. And so the
brave spirits of these young boys were carried up to join the noble
army of martyrs.
F. H. Drinkwater

In the first year of Hitler's power, out in a suburb of Berlin I sat
across the desk from Martin Niemoeller. Already he could see the
signs of the evils to come.

A few years passed and Martin Niemoeller was sent to the
concentration camp. Immediately his aged father came out of
retirement to take over his son's pastoral duties. Heinrich
Niemoeller preached as his son had, but in more guarded terms.
Before he died he told a friend of mine, 'Yes, it is terrible to have
a son in a concentration camp, but it would have been more
terrible if God had wanted a witness and Martin had been
unwilling to witness to the truth.'
Jack Finegan

When Aristotle, the Greek philosopher, who was tutor to Alexander the Great, was asked what a man could gain by uttering falsehoods, he replied, 'Not to be believed when he shall tell the truth.' On the other hand, it is related that when Petrarch, the Italian poet, a man of strict integrity, was summoned as a witness, and offered in the usual manner to take an oath before a court of justice, the judge closed the book, saying, 'As to you, Petrarch, your word is sufficient.'

USEFUL TEXTS

Truth:
  Attribute of God, *Isa. 65:16*
  Spirit of, *John 15:26*
  Christ is, *John 14:6*
  Word of God is, *John 17:17*

See also: A47 The Spirit of Truth
           C11 Talk
           C23 Zeal for what is right

B54
THE TRINITY

'Baptise them in the name of the Father and of the Son
and of the Holy Spirit, and teach them to observe all
the commands I gave you.'
Matthew 28:19-20

QUOTATIONS

God's purpose in creating us is that we may share in his very own
family life.
George A. Maloney

God, according to the Persons, is Everlasting Activity but according
to the Essence and its perpetual stillness, he is Eternal Repose.
John of Ruysbroeck

The Trinity becomes a reality in us as the guest of the soul. Why
go on searching for God beyond the stars when he is so close to
us, within us.
Carlo Carretto

So vast, so penetrating and all-embracing is this active and possessing
love of the Trinity that in its presence the silence of the creature is
absolute.
John of Ruysbroeck

We say that we know God by his energies. We do not affirm that
we can approach the essence itself. His energies come down to us,
but his essence remains unapproachable.
St Basil

In the earlier centuries of Christianity theology was a mysticism
about the indwelling Trinity, living within and transforming
Christians into divinised children of God.
George A. Maloney

HUMOUR

'Mother, today we learned all about the Blessed Trinity,' little Martha cried, rushing in from school. Everybody urged her to tell what she had learned. 'Well,' she said, 'there is the Father, and the Son, and the Holy Ghost' – she paused dramatically – 'and Amen isn't anybody.'
Contributed to Catholic Digest

WORD PICTURES

After much thinking and struggling, we have hit on a way, inadequate at best, of trying to explain in the family, three Persons in one God by comparing it to their own human father. At home, among the children, he is known as Daddy and his role is that of father. At work, among his fellow workers, he is known as Mr Newland and his role is that of wage earner. To Mother, he is known as Bill, and his role is husband, he is the same man, but he has three different roles to play. Very roughly, it draws a parallel to the three dispensations, as theologians call them, of the Persons of the Trinity. God the Father we think of as Creator. God the Son we think of as a Redeemer. God the Holy Ghost we think of as Divine Love.
Mary Newland

If we are made in the image of God, we are made in the image of the Trinity; and the life of the Trinity must in some sort be reflected in the pattern of our human life. Perhaps one such reflection is between the activities identified with each person of the Trinity and the no doubt only blurredly separable but nevertheless distinguishable categories of activity in which we engage. Thus to the Father is credited all that we understand by generation, creation, maintenance; and much of our human activity can be seen as co-operation in that work. Everything we do to awaken and cherish new life, to fashion, mould and develop our physical environment, shares in that work of the Father, fathering and mothering, designing and building, growing crops and breeding cattle, shaping and tending the landscape, manufacturing, organising, fashioning all kinds of things for our use and delight, all crafts, arts and technologies, in short every kind of making, fall under this head.

Likewise, all human works of compassion, healing, reconciliation, sacrifice, forgiveness, making amends, and making good again reflect the work of redemption and reconciliation identified most closely with the Son. All, that is, to use the current jargon, that falls under the heading of caring. And finally, the special role of the Holy Spirit is reflected in every positive idea and inspiration, however slight and humble, in every advance in knowledge and wisdom, in every flash of imagination, in every movement of the heart. The artist, lover, philosopher and inventor may embody and express this area of human experience most richly, but there is no one to whom it is foreign, for it covers the simplest ideas and feelings as well as the most elaborate.
John F. X. Harriott

. . . despite their orthodox confession of the Trinity, Christians are, in the practical life, almost mere 'monotheists'. We must be willing to admit that, should the doctrine of the Trinity have to be dropped as false, the major part of religious literature could well remain virtually unchanged. . . . Nowadays when we speak of God's incarnation, the theological and religious emphasis lies only on the fact that 'God' became man, that 'one' of the divine persons (of the Trinity) took on the flesh, and not on the fact that this person is precisely the person of the Logos.
Karl Rahner

One of the great classics in Byzantine iconography is the icon of the Trinity painted by the Russian monk, Andrei Rublev (*c.*1408-1425). He used an ancient, traditional image, known in the East from the earliest centuries, of the apparition of the three angels to Abraham by the oak of Mambre (Gen 18) to describe in iconic form the dogmatic teaching of the one Godhead and the three Persons in the Trinity. Using a circle as the basic form of composition, and intersecting circles and very vivid colours: blue, green, pink, brown, and purple, the iconographer depicts the three Persons: Father, Son and Holy Spirit as three angels brought into a oneness of deep peace and joyfulness.

Unlike so many attempts in Western art to depict the Trinity in images of a grey-bearded Father, with a more youthful son holding the globe of the world and the Spirit as a dove hovering over both of them, this Byzantine statement avoids the 'objectivisation' of making the Divine Persons look like human ones. It is a mystical vision, through harmony and relationship of colours and circular lines, of the inner trinitarian life of movement and rest, peace and joy, of a community of three in a oneness that constantly feeds to the Godhead for it is a nameless form.
George A. Maloney

USEFUL TEXTS

Trinity:
  Revealed at Jesus' baptism, *Matt. 3:16-17*
  Baptise in the name of, *Matt. 28:19*

See also: A37 Christ the King
           A47 The Spirit of Truth
           B28 The Father who draws us to himself
           B40 One God
           C47 The indwelling spirit

C1
LIBERATION FROM FEAR

'When these things begin to take place, stand erect, hold your
heads high, because your liberation is near at hand.'
Luke 21:28

QUOTATIONS

A vain shadow strikes the anxious with fear.
Ovid

We must not fear fear.
St Francis of Sales

We fear things in proportion to our ignorance of them.
Livy

Fear is an instructor of great sagacity.
Ralph W. Emerson

Fear nothing, blame nothing, flee nothing – so much as thy vices
and thy sins.
Thomas à Kempis

My sole fear was the fear of doing an unrighteous or unholy thing.
Socrates

Fears are educated into us, and can, if we wish, be educated out.
Karl Menninger

Fear is never a good counsellor and victory over fear is the first
spiritual duty of man.
Nikolai Berdyaev

Servile fear is no honour to God, for what father feels honoured
by his son's dread of the rod?
Walter Elliott

No man ever sank under the burden of the day. It is when tomorrow's burden is added to the burden of today, that the weight is more than a man can bear.
George Macdonald

Do not fear God, who wishes you no harm, but love him a great deal, who wishes you so much good.
St Francis of Sales

Fear imprisons, faith liberates; fear paralyses, faith empowers; fear disheartens, faith encourages; fear sickens, faith heals; fear makes useless, faith makes serviceable – and, most of all, fear puts hopelessness at the heart of life, while faith rejoices in its God.
Harry Emmerson Fosdick

We must fear God through love, not love him through fear.
Jean Pierre Camus

PROVERBS
All fear is bondage.
English proverb

Fear is a fine spur, so is rage.
Irish proverb

He who fears something gives it power over him.
Moorish proverb

Nothing ventured, nothing gained.
English proverb

He who rides on a tiger can never dismount.
Spanish proverb

Things never go so well that one should have no fear, and never so ill that one should have no hope.
Turkish proverb

HUMOUR

Tommy was very frightened of big dogs. One day, when he started to back away from a large alsatian, his mother scolded him for his timidity. 'You'd be afraid, too,' he replied, 'if you were as low down as I am.'

WORD PICTURES

Let then our first act
every morning be to
make the following
resolve for the day:
I shall not fear anyone on earth.
I shall fear only God.
I shall not bear ill will toward anyone.
I shall not submit to unjustice from anyone.
I shall conquer untruth by truth.
And in resisting untruth I shall put up with all suffering.
Mahatma Gandhi

The man with the bag of nails
And then came man, with his hammer and his bag of nails.
And he nailed the shining sun to the heavens, in case it should leave him cold.
And he nailed the bright moon fast to the silent sky, for fear of being left in darkness.
And he nailed the clouds to the shifting wind so they would not gather above him.
And he nailed down the salt sea and each fish fast within it.
And he nailed the bright birds to the empty air, and every creature that flew, or walked, or crawled, or slithered, he nailed hard in its allotted place.
And then came a carpenter's son. And man, afraid, took him and nailed him tight to a tree,
  for this man's tongue could loosen nails.
John Ballard

On the night of April 6th 1988 Father Dionisio Malalay, 33 years old, and known affectionately by his parishioners as Fr Diony, and

Rufino Rivera, a 69-year-old family man, were shot dead. The two of them had been leading a group of local Christians in their monthly prayer group at Rufino's house, in the parish of Tabina, on the Filipino island of Mindanao. They met to read the Scriptures, apply them to their daily lives and pray.

Arising from the discussions at these meetings the two leaders had heard of the extortion racket being run by the local constabulary against the local fisherfolk. The day before Fr Diony and Rufino had filed a complaint against the offending military men. During the prayer meeting there was a commotion outside and Fr Diony went with Rufino to the door of the house. They found an aggressive and agitated Constable Colipano with his cousin Nelson, a civilian. Diony tried to cool him down and reason with him; Rufino was frightened and identified Diony saying, 'Don't harm him, he's our priest.' A shot rang out and Fr Diony fell dead; Rufino struggled to restrain Colipano when Nelson fired and Rufino also died instantly. The assailants ran off shouting, 'Rebels, rebels', making out that they were defending themselves against members of the New People's Army who were to be found in the neighbouring hills.

The deaths of Fr Diony and Rufino spoke to the whole diocese as loudly as the death of Jesus. Their deaths shocked the bishop, clergy and lay leaders and they set out to use the Law to get justice. It took six long and painstaking years, after much obstruction and courage in the face of intimidation, but on 16th June 1995 the Colipano cousins were found guilty. Fr Diony and Rufino were courageous in standing up for the rights of the poor; but the poor were equally courageous in refusing to be intimidated by the Filipino military.
P.F.

USEFUL TEXTS

Fear:
  Commanded of all, *Ps 33:8*
  As beginning of wisdom, *Job 28:28*
  Reverential, in worship, *Heb, 12:28*

See also: B3   Joy in Christ
           B14 Freedom to serve
           C2   Joy of salvation

C2
THE JOY OF SALVATION

'God will guide Israel in joy by the light of his glory
with his mercy and integrity for escort.'
Baruch 5:9

QUOTATIONS

Joy is the infallible sign of the presence of God.
Leon Blay

We are all strings in the concert of his joy.
Jakob Boehme

To be able to find joy in another's joy, that is the secret of happiness.
George Bermans

Those who bring sunshine to the lives of others cannot keep it
from themselves.
J. M. Barrie

Following after God is the desire of happiness; to reach God is
happiness itself.
St Augustine of Hippo

Joy is prayer – Joy is strength – Joy is love – Joy is a net of love by
which you can catch souls.
Mother Teresa

Religion might be defined as the power which makes us joyful about
the things that matter. Fashionable frivolity might be defined as the
power which makes us sad about the things which do not matter.
G. K. Chesterton

God never ruffles the joy of his children, except to prepare them
for a certain, far greater joy.
Alessandro Manzoni

One of Satan's biggest lies is the claim that sin adds to human happiness. If this were true then the greatest sinners would be the happiest people. But the very reverse is the case.
W. T. Purkiser

This is the secret of joy. We shall no longer strive for our own way; but commit ourselves, easily and simply, to God's way, acquiesce in his will and in so doing find our peace.
Evelyn Underhill

The greatest honour you can give to God is to live gladly because of the knowledge of his love. If our joy gives honour to God, then it is our duty to be joyful.
Julian of Norwich

HUMOUR

Diogenes the Cynic was the founder of a school of philosophy which eschewed all worldly possessions. He lived in a barrel himself and it was there that he was visited one day by no less a personage than Alexander the Great. The Macedonian king stood in front of the opening to the barrel and asked the sage if there was anything he desired. 'Yes,' replied Diogenes, 'I should like you to stand out of my light.'

I have no weakness for shoes; I wear very simple shoes which are pump shoes. It is not one of my weaknesses.
(Imelda Marcos, after 3,400 pairs had been found in her wardrobes)

A man goes to a rabbi and complains: 'Life is unbearable. There are nine of us living in one room. What can I do?' The rabbi answers: 'Take the goat into the room with you.' The man is incredulous, but the rabbi insists: 'Do as you are told and come back in a week.' A week later the man comes back, half dead: 'We cannot stand it. The goat is filthy.' The rabbi tells him: 'Go home and let the goat out. And come back in a week's time.' A radiant man visits the rabbi a week later: 'Life is beautiful, rabbi. We enjoy every minute. No goat, only the nine of us.'
George Mikes

A Scotsman was once asked how many it took to convert him. 'Two,' he replied. 'Two! How was that? Didn't God do it all?' 'The Almighty and myself converted me,' he said. 'I did all I could against it, and the Almighty did all he could for it, and he won!'
Anon

WORD PICTURES

There is a legend along the Rhine that on a dark and cold night a thinly clad, half-starved man was toiling along one of its rugged paths. He looked with wistful eye at the bright light that streamed from the windows of the mansion, and listened to the sounds of feasting and strains of music. He had left the home of his youth in early life, and heard nothing from it for many years. He knew not that the magnificent property was his father's, and that he was the heir. Desperate, he asked for shelter there. At its gate he found an old servant who discovered who he was. Instantly he was ushered into the gaiety. His robes were changed to those of the heir. He had found his heritage. And so the Christian is often ignorant of all that belongs to him as a son of God.

TV shows seethe with myths and heroes. They guide decisions, inform perception, provide examples of conduct. Does that make our mass media culture 'religious'? I do not think we can explain its grip on people any other way.

The media's preachers tell us what our transgression is: our armpits are damp, our breath is foul, our wash is grey, our car is inadequate. They hold up models of saintly excellence before our eyes: happy, robust, sexually appreciated people who are free, adventurous, competitive and attractive. These blessed ones have been saved, or are on the way. And the sacramental means of grace that have lifted them from perdition are available to you and me – soaps, deodorants, clothes, pills, cars. Mass media culture is a religion, and we rarely get out of its Temple.
Harvey Cox

Every visitor when in Florence seeks out Michelangelo's statue of David, the shepherd lad. It is a masterpiece in marble. It stands nine cubits high, alert with all the wonderful expressiveness of artistic genius. The shepherd lad is equipped for mastery and stands with determined and expectant countenance ready for battle. The figure is erect, but the body is slightly curved as if in the act of hurling the fatal stone.

The statue has a history that is remarkable and splendidly suggestive. A hundred years or more before the time of Michelangelo, a magnificent block of Carrara marble was brought to Florence by a now unknown sculptor. He worked upon it, blocking out the figure which was in his mind, but suddenly bungled his work by cutting a great slice out of the side, which rendered it useless for him and so it was cast aside. There it lay for a century until the trained eye of Michelangelo rested upon it. Immediately he caught the possibility that lay in the stone, and soon it was taking on form under his hand. Outlining and fashioning, carving and chiselling, a majestic figure was soon stepping from the marble, and even the mutilation which had rendered it useless to the original workman became part of the majesty of the new design.

Out of the ruin another hand had wrought and other eyes despised, a world's masterpiece was fashioned.

Anon

See also: B3   Joy in Christ
           B16 Christ freely forgives

C3
SHARING POSSESSIONS

'Whoever has two tunics must share with anyone who has none.'
Luke 3:10

QUOTATIONS

When we can share – that is poetry in the prose of life.
Sigmund Freud

Those who have much are often greedy; those who have little always share.
Oscar Wilde

Let temporal things serve thy use, but the eternal be the object of thy desire.
Thomas à Kempis

It is easier to renounce worldly possessions than it is to renounce the love of them.
Walter Hilton

Give all thou canst; high heaven rejects the lore
of nicely calculated less or more.
William Wordsworth

If you have money, consider that perhaps the only reason God allowed it to fall into your hands was in order that you might find joy and perfection by throwing it away.
Thomas Merton

It is in the joyful simplicity of a life inspired by the Gospel and the Gospel's spirit of fraternal sharing that you will find the best remedy for sour criticism, paralysing doubt and the temptation to make money the principal means and indeed the very measure of human advancement.
Pope John Paul II

Poverty is the load of some, and wealth is the load of others, perhaps the greater load of the two. It may weigh them to perdition. Bear the load of thy neighbour's poverty, and let him bear with thee the load of thy wealth. Thou lightenest thy load by lightening his.
St Augustine of Hippo

The world's proverb is 'God help the poor, for the rich can help themselves', but to our mind, it is just the rich who have most need of heaven's help. Dives in scarlet is worse off than Lazarus in rags unless divine love shall uphold him.
Charles H. Spurgeon

A Christian's virtue is the only possession that cannot be conquered or destroyed.
Eusebius of Caesarea

PROVERB
To pretend to satisfy one's desires by possession is like using straw to put out a fire.
Chinese proverb

HUMOUR
'Er – about that umbrella I lent you last week.'
'Sorry, old chap, but I lent it to Brown. Were you wanting it?'
'Well, not for myself – but the chap I borrowed it from says that the owner's getting a bit anxious about it.'

WORD PICTURES
A merchant in quest of precious stones was one day riding through the bazaar of Damascus. A quivering beam of the sun upon a shelf caught his attention. There, shining with a light that never was on land or sea, was the jewel of his heart, the pearl of his dreams that henceforth would mean more than all the world for him. Dismounting from his camel he got permission to hold the pearl in the palm of his hand. Yes, it was worth the cost!

Excitedly he jumped on his camel and raced back to his palace. 'My wife,' he said exultantly as he entered the door, 'I have found at last what all my life I wanted most. But you and I will have to leave all this. To get the pearl it will take everything I have.'

'My husband,' answered the wife, 'I am not afraid to give up comfort or security. This palace is a trifling thing.'

Back to Damascus hurried the merchant. In return for the pearl he gave all his wealth. He and his wife spent the rest of their days in a shack. Their food was roots and bread. But the merchant was satisfied. Every day at noon he would hold up the pearl for the sun to shine upon; and there, in the palm of his hand, it would glow with the grace of unspeakable things.

In time the glory of it seemed to fade. The merchant and his wife were puzzled. At last they nodded their heads in understanding, and the merchant said to his wife, 'This pearl will be of worth to us only as we share it with the world.'
Allan A. Hunter

You and I are sitting down to breakfast in the twelfth richest country in the world. If at least a third of the world's inhabitants saw us eating now they would think we were rich beyond their wildest dreams. Most of us would find that a bit odd. We do not think of ourselves as being particularly rich. The rich are people like the Rothschilds and the Rockefellers. But the facts are undeniable. By comparison with the rest of the world we are a rich country, and you and I are among the rich people. Yet at least a third of the world's inhabitants are struggling for survival, and finding it harder all the time.
John Harriott

When Cortes and his followers were about to evacuate the capital city of Mexico in 1520, some of the men burdened themselves with treasure and gold. Cortes said, 'Be careful not to overload yourselves, he travels safest who travels lightest.' But those who paid no attention to his warning were weighed down and unable to escape in a terrible slaughter which followed, when they were crossing the causeway out of the city, and they were buried with their gold in the salt floods of the lake.
Anon

Let me tell you, Scholar, that Diogenes walked on a day, with his friend, to see a country fair; where he saw ribbons, and looking-glasses and nut-crackers, and fiddles, and hobby-horses and many other gimcracks; and having observed them, and all the other things that make a complete country fair, he said to his friend: 'Lord! How many things there are in this world, of which Diogenes hath no need!'
Isaak Walton

A Portugese romance tells the story of a young man who travelled to the Indies to seek his fortune, and in a few years returned to Lisbon with several ships laden with wealth.

'Now,' he thought, 'I will play a trick on my relations.' He put on some worn-out clothes and went to see his cousin Pedro.

'Here I am, your cousin, John: after some years in India, I have come back home. You see how I am fixed – can I stay in your house for a time?' 'Ah, my dear John, how I wish I could put you up! Alas there isn't a room free in my house.'

John went round to another friend, and another, and everywhere found the door closed against him. Then he returned to his ships, put on some expensive attire, sailed into the town with a fine retinue of servants, and purchased a large mansion in the main street. In a day or two his fabulous wealth was the talk of the city. 'Who could have imagined it!' said the relatives and friends who had received him so coldly. 'If only we had known! How differently we should have acted! But it's no good now – we have spoilt our chance with him for ever.'

Our Lord himself comes to us under the guise of all who need our help.
F. H. Drinkwater

See also: A7   Poor in spirit
          A21 Feeding the hungry
          A33 Love your neighbour
          B41 Generosity

C4
PERSONAL PEACE

'They will live secure, for from then on he will extend his
power to the ends of the land. He himself will be peace.'
Micah 5:4

QUOTATIONS

God takes life's pieces and gives us unbroken peace.
W. D. Gough

The blessed shall hear no vain words, but only the word – Peace.
Koran

Only the waters which in perfect stillness lie
give back an undistorted image of the sky!
Trench

He is the happiest, be he king or peasant, who finds peace in his
home.
Goethe

His face wore the utter peace of one whose life is hid in God's
own hand.
H. Hamilton King

When Christ came into the world, peace was sung; and when he
went out of the world, peace was bequested.
Francis Bacon

If the basis of peace is God, the secret of peace is trust.
J. B. Figgis

The world rests upon three things: upon truth, upon justice and
upon peace. All those three are really one, for when justice is done
the truth becomes an actuality, peace a reality.
The Talmud

Five great enemies to peace inhabit with us, namely, avarice, ambition, envy, anger, and pride. If these enemies were to be banished, we should infallibly enjoy perpetual peace.
Petrarch

Nice people must see themselves as nasty people before they can find peace. When they exchange their proud and diabolical belief that they never did anything wrong, for a hope for a Divine remedy for their mistakes, they will have attained to the condition of normality, peace and happiness.
Fulton Sheen

By all means use sometimes to be alone;
salute thyself; see what thy soul doth wear;
dare to look in thy chest, for 'tis thine own,
and tumble up and down what thou find'st there.
George Herbert

The definition of peace is that there should be harmony between two opposed factions. And so, when the civil war in our nature has been brought to an end and we are at peace within ourselves, we may become peace. Then we shall really be true to the name of Christ that we bear.
St Gregory of Nyssa

PROVERB

The wise man looks inside his heart and finds eternal peace.
Hindu proverb

WORD PICTURES

Guy de Maupassant's mother said to Eleonora Dusé, the great actress: 'What can I wish for you, madame? You are in the height of your glory: nothing more can come to you.'
'Peace,' Eleonora Dusé whispered humbly.

It is the will of God for us that in the world's most crowded street, in the din of life, when the rush and hurry are at their most intense

. . . in joy or sorrow, in love or in bereavement, in all that makes up our outer and inner life, we should have a place of retirement, a permanent retreat, ever at hand for renewal and peace. It is God's will for us that we should possess an Interior Castle, against which the storms of life may beat without being able to disturb the serene quiet within; a spiritual life so firm and so secure that nothing can overthrow it.
Evelyn Underhill

Father Paolo Turturro, parish priest in Palermo, launched a children's competition for a poem or painting dedicated to peace. There were 120,000 entries, including some from outside Sicily. The winner was a poem entitled 'Painting Peace':
I had a box of colours.
There was no red for the blood
of my wounds.
There was no black to paint
the mourning of my loved ones.
I didn't have yellow
for the world's jealousies.
I had blue:
I sat
and painted Peace.
Turturro used the title 'Painting Peace' for an organisation he founded to help the youths of Palermo and keep them out of the hands of the Mafia.
The Tablet

We 'inter-are', everyone is responsible for everything that happens in life. When you produce peace and happiness in yourself, you begin to realise peace for the whole world. With the smile that you produce in yourself, with the conscious breathing you establish within yourself, you begin to work for peace in the world. To smile is not to smile only for yourself; the world will change because of your smile. When you practise sitting meditation, if you enjoy even one moment of your sitting, if you establish serenity and happiness inside yourself, you provide the world with

a solid basis for peace. If you do not give yourself peace, how can you share it with others? If you do not begin your peace work with yourself, where will you go to begin it? To sit, to smile, to look at things and really see them, these are the basis of peace work.
Thich Nhat Hanh

USEFUL TEXTS
Peace:
    Fruit of the Spirit, *Gal. 5:22*
    Of God, *Phil. 4:7*
    Of Christ, *John 14:27*
    With one another, *Mark 9:50*

See also: A2 Integrity
          B19 Conscience
          C17 International peace

C5
THE INSTITUTION OF MARRIAGE

'There was a wedding at Cana in Galilee. The mother of Jesus was there and Jesus and his disciples had also been invited.'
John 2:1

QUOTATIONS

Every man who is happily married is a successful man, even if he has failed in everything else.
William Lyon Phelps

One of the great similarities between Christianity and marriage is that, for Christians, they both get better as we get older.
Jean Rees

Marriage resembles a pair of shears, so joined that they cannot be separated, often moving in opposite directions, yet always punishing anyone who comes between them.
P. Fontaine

The desire to be instantly understood and accurately responded to remains with us through life, and is one of the clearest expressions of closeness and love between people.
Jack Dominian

The happiest wife is not the one who marries the best man, but the one who makes the best of the man she marries.
Joseph Fort Newton

HUMOUR

Father: The man who marries my daughter will get a prize.
Young Man: May I see it, please?

'Your daughter has promised to marry me, sir.'
'Well, don't come to me for sympathy. I knew something like that would happen to you – hanging about the place every evening.'

The commercial traveller had proposed to Sarah, but she was a little dubious about accepting him. 'He's very irreligious,' she said, discussing the matter with her mother. 'He doesn't even believe in Hell.' 'Well, go ahead and marry him,' cut in her father. 'He'll soon find out how he's wrong!'

Priest: Do you take this man for better or worse?
Mandy: He can't be no worse, and dey is no hopes of his gettin' any better, so I takes him 'as is'.

The Archbishop had preached a fine sermon on the beauties of married life. Two old Irishwomen coming out from church were heard commenting upon his address.
''Tis a fine sermon his Reverence would be after givin' us,' said Bridget. 'It is indade,' replied Maggie, 'and I wish I knew as little about the matter as he does!'

Commenting on a certain cantankerous Scottish historian and his equally intolerable wife, the Victorian satirist Samuel Butler observed:
'It was very good of God to let Carlyle and Mrs Carlyle marry one another and so make only two people miserable instead of four.'

For eleven years Duncan had put up with the fat, interfering old woman. Now he could stand it no longer.
'She's got to go,' he said to his wife, 'I can't stand your mother another minute!'
'My mother!' exclaimed Duncan's wife, 'I thought she was *your* mother!'
Anon

Our four-year-old daughter, Marian, had been a bit mischievous and I had tried to correct her. I was sitting in the easy chair reading the paper. Her mother was sitting quietly on the sofa mending some clothes. Our daughter climbed on to the sofa very close to her mother and said, 'Do you think we married the right man, mother?'

A man had been in a public telephone booth for half an hour. He appeared to be very bored and, though he held the receiver to his ear, he made no attempt to speak. At last one of the crowd outside, exasperated with waiting, opened the door and asked abruptly. 'Are you speaking to anybody?' The silent one replied, 'Yes, I'm speaking to my wife.'

It was the young priest's first wedding, and he was desperately determined to conduct it without a hitch. Everyone could see he was nervous, but somehow he managed pretty well, for a while. Then came the words, 'If anyone, therefore, can show just cause why they may not be joyfully loined (instead of lawfully joined) together . . .' Hearing no protests, the young priest forged ahead to the ring ceremony, with growing confidence. But people in the pews pretty well lost theirs when he said, 'Now place the fing on her ringer.'

WORD PICTURES

Dietrich Bonhoeffer, sitting in a Nazi prison cell, once wrote a wedding sermon for a niece who was about to be married. In it he said, 'Marriage is more than your love for each other. It has a higher dignity and power, for it is God's holy ordinance, through which he wills to perpetuate the human race till the end of time. In your love you see only your two selves in the world, but in marriage you are a link in the chain of generations, which God causes to come and to pass away to his glory, and calls into his kingdom. In your love you see only the heaven of your happiness, but in marriage you are placed at a post of responsibility towards the world and mankind. Your love is your own private possession, but marriage is more than something personal – it is a status, an office.'

Ten Commandments for Marriage
1. Thou shalt not take thy partner for granted.
2. Thou shalt not expect perfection of each other.
3. Thou shalt be patient, loving, understanding, kind and true.
4. Thou shalt tend the garden of love daily.
5. Thou shalt take great care that thy partner's trust is never violated or diminished in any way.

THE INSTITUTION OF MARRIAGE C5

6. Thou shalt not forget thy wedding vows, remembering especially those important words, 'For better or worse'.
7. Thou shalt not hide thy true feelings. Mutual love provides a bright sunlit room where things of the heart can be discussed freely and without fear.
8. Thou shalt always respect each other as individuals. Degrading words and a sharp tongue cause grave distortions. Endearing terms ennoble, lift up, engender peace.
9. Thou shalt give thy marriage room to grow. Both partners should be willing to face the future together with confidence and trust. Today is a better day for them than yesterday, and tomorrow will find them closer still.
10. Thou shalt through all thy days reverence God, thy Creator, never forgetting that it is he who has made you.

'When you're a married man, Samivel, you'll understand a good many things as you don't understand now, but vether it's worth while goin' through so much to learn so little, as the charity boy said when he got to the end of the alphabet, is a matter o' taste. I rayther think it isn't.'
Charles Dickens: Pickwick Papers

Humanly speaking, Mary could not have been surprised that her son left home. It was something perfectly normal. Once they reach a certain age, children do leave their parents. They go out into the world to take up their calling as is commonly said. So Jesus too left the family circle, once when he was twelve and then, for good, when he was about thirty. At the time when Jesus leaves to take up his public ministry we find him with his mother – but already with disciples as well – attending the wedding feast at Cana in Galilee. St John has given us in his Gospel a detailed description of all that happened here. This was the occasion of Jesus' first miracle, in which Mary had a part to play. Let us recall it carefully. Let us remember the words heavy with meaning, exchanged by mother and son: the mother's request: 'They have no wine'; Jesus' reply: 'Woman, why turn to me? My hour has not come yet.' It is a highly significant reply. Mary must have heard in it an echo of what she had earlier heard from the lips of the twelve-year-old.

It again faces her with that hidden Father: 'I always do what pleases him' (John 8:29). But this time the Gospel writer does not add: 'But they did not understand what he meant.' Quite the reverse! Mary turns to the servants and says: 'Do whatever he tells you.'

From this it is possible to conclude that Mary knew what the Father willed. And that she also knew, without any doubt, that her son would not reject her request. Mary's request and the Father's will coincided.

Pope John Paul II

See also: B6   The Family
           B30 Married Love

C6
The Old Testament Law

'The precepts of the Lord are right, they gladden the heart. The
command of the Lord is clear, it gives light to the eyes.'
Psalm 19:8

Quotations

Wherever law ends, tyranny begins.
John Locke

Of law there can be no less acknowledged, than that her seat is the
bosom of God, her voice the harmony of the world.
Richard Hooker

There is but one law for all, namely, that law which governs all
law, the law of our Creator, the law of humanity, justice, equity –
the law of nature and of nations.
Edmund Burke

Moral law is more than a test, it is for man's own good. Every law
that God has given has been for man's benefit. If man breaks it,
he is not only rebelling against God, he is hurting himself.
Billy Graham

We need to free ourselves from the idea of God's law as a statute
imposed upon us from without and to substitute that of his spirit
as a principle governing life from within.
William Adams Brown

A noble law, it was, in truth, that God bestowed on us, and on the
tablets of each heart hath he inscribed it plain; that we should love
the Lord our God with all our heart and mind, and that no
creature share the love and reverence due to him.
Peter Valdes

There is nothing so dangerous as religion. It can congeal into legalism and ritualism.
Walter Kasper

PROVERBS

He that goes to law holds a wolf by the tail.
English proverb

God does not pay weekly, he pays at the end.
Dutch proverb

HUMOUR

After being found guilty of a criminal offence the defendant was asked whether he wished to say anything before sentence was passed.

'Yes,' he shouted, 'as God is my judge I am innocent.'

'You're mistaken,' the judge replied. 'He isn't; I am; you aren't; six months.'

'What is the greatest miracle recorded in the Old Testament?' enquired a teacher of her class.

'Joshua told his son to stand still, and he did,' promptly responded one of her pupils.

Most men will be familiar with the story of the boy, who, being asked, 'Who was the mother of Moses?' promptly replied, 'Pharaoh's daughter.' 'No,' expostulated the teacher, 'Pharaoh's daughter was not the mother of Moses. She found the little baby in an ark of bullrushes on the bank of the river.'

'Yes,' was the reply, 'I know that's what she said!'

WORD PICTURES

In the days before the Boer War the Jews in Pretoria came to President Kruger and asked if they, like the other 'denominations', could receive a grant of land on which to build their synagogue. This was promised without any difficulty. But when the grant was made the Jews discovered that their site was only half the size of the sites allotted to the other religions. They went to old Kruger again and asked the reasons. 'Well,' he said, 'you Jews only accept half the Bible, and not the best half of it either. If you agree to accept the whole Bible I will give you the whole block.'

Under the blue laws of the seventeenth and eighteenth centuries Puritans administered religion to unwilling subjects by means of the whipping post, the ducking stool, the stocks, fines, and prisons. Mrs Alice Morse Earle's history, *The Sabbath in Puritan New England*, lists such examples:

'Two lovers, John Lewis and Sarah Chapman, were accused and tried for sitting together on the Lord's day under an apple tree. A Dunstable soldier, for wetting a piece of old hat to put in his shoe to protect his foot, was fined forty shillings for doing this heavy work. Captain Kemble of Boston in 1656 was put in public stocks for two hours for his "lewd and unseemly behaviour" which consisted of kissing his wife in public on the Sabbath on the doorstep of his house after his return from a three-year voyage. A man who had fallen into the water absented himself from church to dry his only suit of clothes; he was found guilty and publicly whipped.'

USEFUL TEXTS

Law:
  Given through Moses, *Exod. 20*
  All to be obeyed, *Gal. 3:10*
  No one justified by it, *Rom. 3:20*
  Saved from, *Gal. 3:13*
  Christ is end of, *Rom. 10:4*

See also: A29 True obedience
            B4 Mary – Handmaid of God
            B31 The commandments of life

C7

THE HUMANITY OF CHRIST

They said, 'This is Joseph's son, surely?'
Luke 4:22

QUOTATIONS

God's only Son doth hug humanity into his very person.
Edward Taylor

God clothed himself in vile man's flesh so he might be weak enough to suffer woe.
John Donne

No man took his life; he laid it down himself.
R. H. Benson

We can hardly think of Jesus Christ without thinking of the sparrows, the grass, fig trees, sheep.
Vincent McHaff

Christ did not die a martyr. He died – infinitely more humbly – a common criminal.
Simone Weil

No one ever made more trouble than the 'gentle Jesus, meek and mild'.
James M. Gillis

Christ is a path – if any be misled;
he is a robe – if any naked be;
if any chance to hunger – he is bread;
if any be a bondman – strong is he!
Giles Fletcher

What was born of Mary, according to scripture, was by nature human; the Lord's body was a real one – real, because it was the same as ours. This was because Mary was our sister, since we are all descended from Adam. This is the meaning of John's words: 'The Word became flesh', as can be seen from a similar passage in Paul: 'Christ became a curse for us.' The human body has been greatly enhanced through the fellowship and union of the Word with it.
St Athanasius

WORD PICTURES

There is a story about a city that had erected a statue to a famous man. One day a stranger came to the city gate and asked of the boys that played in the shadow of the walls where he might find the statue. They told him and he passed on. Later on the stranger stopped a citizen and again asked the way. The citizen proudly answered, 'I am the man who first thought of the statue,' and he also told the stranger where to go. A third time the stranger sought direction, and the man of whom he asked replied, 'If anyone knows where the statue is, I should, for I had the contract of putting it up.'

The stranger found the statue, looked upon it thoughtfully for a time, and then retraced his steps. As he passed out of the city gate, one of the boys at play looked up into his face, and then gasped out to his companions, 'Boys, look! It is the man of the statue!' And in very truth the man in whose honour they had sacrificed and toiled, had walked in their streets, spoken with them face to face, and they knew him not.
D. Williamson

A certain artist, Sigismund Goetze, had a picture hung in the Royal Academy exhibition of 1904, entitled, 'Despised and Rejected of Men'. He showed Christ on the steps of St Paul's Cathedral. And the crowd are blind to his presence.

One man almost brushes against him as he passes, buried in his sporting newspaper. A scientist is too busy with his test-tube to see Christ. A dignitary of the Church, sleek, self-satisfied, with an air of piety, passes by oblivious of Christ. A nonconformist minister passes by so engaged in theological arguments and polemics that not even he sees Christ. A mob orator harangues the crowd of men on the rights of man, with never a look for the great Brother of all men. Only a nurse glimpses Christ and passes on.

That is the commonest situation of life. If Jesus Christ came again, there are many who would not bother to crucify him; he would not seem sufficiently important for that.
William Barclay

According to the old legend, the mother pelican wounds herself in order that she may give her blood to feed her little ones. There is a beautiful lectern in Durham Cathedral which represents a pelican with outstretched wings. Great red drops are on her breast, and in her bill was one great jewel to represent a drop of blood, as she bends to feed the little brood which gathers round her. The lovely jewel has since been stolen and has not been replaced.

Another bird legend is that of the robin red-breast. It is said that when our Lord hung suffering upon the Cross, a little brown bird, filled with love and sorrow, came fluttering down to his aid. There was so little it could do, but it plucked just one thorn from that awful crown. And ever since the robin's breast has borne the mark of the Precious Blood.
Anon

Here on the Mount of Olives looking down upon Gethsemane, you can more readily envisage what it took in those days to be a real man in the earthiest sense. I am sure you remember, dear friend, the day that we stood here and pondered together on the nitty-gritty details of those days after Palm Sunday when Jesus lived on this very patch of the hill where we were then standing. His feet must have been bruised, for you cannot walk through the Judean desert barefoot or in sandals without constantly striking your feet against rocks and stones and pebbles. Probably his skin was cracked; and likely enough he had fleas on him from riding the donkey. He and his disciples had sweated on the long pull up from Jericho; they must have all smelt of dried sweat since there were no showers in those days and no daily changes of clothes. And we asked ourselves how did they manage to clean themselves after emptying their bowels, since toilet paper and water closets were not yet invented? In the way still favoured by the Bedouin? People who live distant from the Mount of Olives may hold such considerations to be irrelevant. But they are far from irrelevant if you wish to stand in the sandals and enter into the mind of the man Jesus, this northern provincial of Galilean accent.

Donald Nicholl

Here is a man who was born in an obscure village, the child of a peasant woman. He grew up in an obscure village. He worked in a carpenter's shop until he was thirty, and then for three years he was an itinerant teacher. He never wrote a book. He never held an office. He never owned a home. He never had a family. He never went to college. He never travelled two hundred miles from the place where he was born. He never did one of the things that usually accompany greatness. He had no credentials but himself. He had nothing to do with this world except the power of his divine manhood. While still a young man, the tide of popular opinion turned against him. His friends ran away. One of them denied him. He was turned over to his enemies. He went through the mockery of a trial. He was nailed upon a cross between two thieves. His executioners gambled for the only piece of property he had on earth while he was dying – his coat. When he was dead he was taken down and laid in a borrowed grave through the pity of a friend.

Nineteen wide centuries have come and gone; today he is the centrepiece of the human race and the Leader of the column of progress.

I am far within the mark when I say that all the armies that ever marched, and all the navies that ever were built, and all the parliaments that ever sat, and all the kings that ever reigned, put together, have not affected the life of mankind upon this earth as powerfully as has that one solitary life.

James A. Francis

Useful texts

Humanity of Christ:
  Birth, *Matt. 1:18; Luke 2:2*
  Lost at 12, *Luke 4:21*
  Tempted, *Luke 4:1-13; Matt, 4:1-11*
  Angry, *Luke, 19:45; Matt, 21:12*
  Tired, *Luke 8:23*
  Grieved, *John 11:35*
  Like us, except for sin. *Heb. 4:15*

See also: A37 Christ the King
          B3   Joy in Christ
          B16 Christ heals and forgives
          C45 The Divinity of Christ

C8
GOD'S MESSENGERS

'Then I heard the voice of the Lord saying: "Whom shall I send?
Who will be our messenger?" I answered, "Here I am, send me."'
Isaiah 6:8

QUOTATIONS

The prophet lives with God rather than with his fellow men; and
he is confident that the word which he speaks is the word of God.
Benjamin Jowett

If you want to get across an *idea*, wrap it up in a *person*.
Ralph Bunche

The pontifical voice lingers less hauntingly and long than the
voice of one crying in the wilderness.
Catherine Carswell

The world is dark, and human agony is excruciating, but the
prophet casts a light by which the heart is led, into the thinking of
the Lord's mind.
Abraham Joshua Heschel

It is the prophetic interpretation of historical events which is the
vehicle of special revelation in the sense in which the Biblical and
Christian tradition understands that conception. Where there are
no prophets, there can be no special revelation.
Alan Richardson

HUMOUR

A patient from a nearby mental institution recently walked into
the local branch of Lloyd's Bank, Epsom, and said that he was a
prophet and God had sent him to pick up a million pounds. The
unflappable cashier's response was immediate, 'I'm sorry sir, God
banks with Barclays!'

WORD PICTURES

There are many old legends connected with the early days of Christianity. On the side of Weary All Hill at Glastonbury is a stone slab where St Joseph of Arimathea, the first apostle to Britain, is said to have stopped with his eleven comrades, having sailed from Bridgwater Bay, over what is now blue low-lying moorland. With a prayer, he drove his staff into the earth, and claimed this island for Christ. Legend has it that the wood of the staff sprouted, and took root, and on the next Christmas Day blossomed a thorn. Though the first shrub died, its offshoots are there still, and give their flower, be the weather what it may, every Christmas. It is said that the thorn will not live if transplanted from Glastonbury.

Anon

Who are the prophets?
They are a royal people
who penetrate mystery
and see with the spirit's eyes.
In illuminating darkness they speak out.
They are living, penetrating clarity.
They are a blossom blooming only
on the shoot that is rooted in the flood of light.

Hildegard of Bingen

There is no doubt that people can foresee the future. Four hundred years before Christ was crucified, the Greek thinker, Socrates, foretold his crucifixion. 'The perfect righteous man,' he said (his disciple, Plato, recorded the words in his *Republic*), 'will be scourged and bound, and at last, after suffering every kind of torture, he will be crucified.'

An Amos walks the beaten paths of Tekoa, but he hears a divine voice which no other vine-dresser in Tekoa ever caught; a Bunyan tramps about England mending pots and pans, but above the din of his lowly task he catches voices that presently are to reverberate immortally through *Pilgrim's Progress*; a Lincoln steers his

awkward raft down the Mississippi and ties up near a slave auction block. But out of his rough routine labour a voice sounds which no other raftsman ever heard; a Riis tramps the round of a New York reporter in search of news, and out of the ugly tenements through which his duties carry him catches a challenge from the God of social justice which makes him a veritable prophet; and a lad of Galilee at a common carpenter's bench, shaping the same yokes of wood for the necks of cattle which countless other carpenters have shaped, dreams his way into a vision of the coming kingdom of God when man shall wear the spiritual yoke which he shall shape for them as easily and as gratefully as these toiling bearers of burdens shall wear the wooden yokes which he is now making. In every case the majesty of the commonplace lies not so much in the task itself as in the spirit which the great soul brings to the task.
Frank S. Hickman

See also: B2 The Good News
          B9 Revelation
          B24 Go tell everyone

C9
THE BEATITUDES

'Blessed are those who trust in the Lord,
whose hope is the Lord.'
Jeremiah 17:7

QUOTATIONS

Beatitude means having everything you want and wanting nothing wrongly.
St Augustine of Hippo

Jesus clothes the beatitudes with his own life.
Carl F. Henry

The beatitudes are a call to us to see ourselves, to live with ourselves, in a way that probably does not come easily to most of us.
Simon Tugwell

If the Sermon on the Mount is the précis of all Christian doctrine, the eight beatitudes are the précis of the whole of the Sermon on the Mount.
Jacques B. Bossuet

The more we live and try to practise the Sermon on the Mount, the more shall we experience blessing.
Martin Lloyd-Jones

Happiness-seeking is the common human drive; this Jesus recognised, but inverted the maxims of the world for his disciples, saying: Happy are they who seek poverty of spirit, mercy and justice.
Paul Frost

LONGER QUOTES

Jesus starts off by telling them it's a damn sight better to be poor and humble than rich and haughty; better to be hard up and happy than rich and miserable, any day of the week. Then he says that people who act mean and spiteful, always on the make, money-grubbers and misers, they're no good to themselves nor to anybody else. The ones who don't ask too much, they'll get a proper share, because whatever they get will be enough; but those who always want more and more, the ones who're never satisfied and always on the make, they'll never know happiness, either in this life or the next
Bernard Miles

Our Lord tells us that the poor in spirit are the lucky ones. To be so, we have to stop thinking simply in terms of money and begin to look at the world through the eyes of the poor, and to feel as they feel. It is not just occasionally missing a meal or not being able to afford a packet of cigarettes which will help us to do so, but every snub, every deprivation, every time we suffer rejection, every occasion on which we are ignored or contradicted. It is that experience of poverty which will give us some share in the condition of the poor, and spark the emotion which is needed for their defence. And it is through that experience that we slowly come to learn what is truly precious in ourselves and in the world that lies about us.
John Harriott

Poverty is not a question of having or not having money. Poverty is not material. It is a beatitude. 'Blessed are the poor in spirit.' It is a way of being, thinking and loving. It is a gift of the Spirit. Poverty is detachment and freedom and, above all, truth. Go into almost any middle-class home, even a Christian one, and you will see the lack of this beatitude of poverty. The furniture, the drapes, the whole atmosphere are stereotyped, determined by fashion and luxury, not by necessity and truth.

This lack of liberty, or rather this slavery to fashion, is one of the idols which attracts a great number of Christians. How much

money is sacrificed upon its altar! – without taking into account that so much good could otherwise be done with it. Being poor in spirit means, above all, being unrestrained by what is called fashion; it means freedom.
Carlo Carretto

WORD PICTURE

'Blessed are the meek . . . for they shall inherit the earth.' Some of the greatest Christians are those who have been meek or humble, and one who will be remembered as such is St Swithun.

St Swithun's Day is 15th July, a day on which people give an eye to the weather, for tradition says that whatever the weather is like on St Swithun's Day, it will continue so for the next forty days. There is an old rhyme which reads:

St Swithun's Day, if thou dost rain,
for forty days it will remain;
St Swithun's Day, if thou be fair,
for forty days 'twill rain na mair.

But St Swithun had little to do with the weather and records show that the rhyme is not always correct. He was a Bishop of Winchester in Saxon times, who became the chief adviser to the king on religious matters. Though born of a noble family and a friend of kings and princes, he was a very humble man, who is said always to have walked wherever he went instead of riding. When he was dying, he asked to be buried outside the church instead of in a place of honour and this wish was granted. About a hundred years later, the cathedral was rebuilt and the remains of St Swithun were carried into the cathedral. It was 15th July, 971 and it is on this day that he is still remembered – a good man and a kindly bishop, who gave himself in the service of both kings and ordinary folk.
Rowland Purton

See also: B2   The Good News
         B3   Joy in Christ
         C2   Joy of salvation

C10
LOVE YOUR ENEMIES

'Love your enemies, do good to those who hate you,
bless those who curse you.'
Luke 6:27

QUOTATIONS

Every man is his own chief enemy.
Anacharsis

A man cannot be too careful in the choice of his enemies.
Oscar Wilde

Often we attach and make ourselves enemies, to conceal that we
are vulnerable.
Friedrick Hietgsche

Love makes everything lovely; hate concentrates itself on the one
thing hated.
George McDonald

Perhaps with charity one shouldn't think. Charity like love should
be blind.
Graham Greene

Give the enemy not only a road for flight, but also the means of
defending it.
Scipio Africanus

None but myself ever did me any harm.
Napoleon Bonaparte

There is more to be feared from unspoken and concealed, than
from open and declared hostility.
Cicero

An open foe may prove a curse, but a pretended friend is worse.
Benjamin Franklin

Doing an injury puts you below your enemy;
revenging one makes you but even with him;
forgiving it sets you above him.
Benjamin Franklin

I owe much to my friends, but all things considered, it strikes me
that I owe even more to my enemies. The real person springs to
life under a sling, even better than under a caress.
André Gide

There is so much good in the worst of us,
and so much bad in the best of us,
that it ill behoves any of us,
to find fault with the rest of us.
Author unknown

PROVERBS

Love makes all hard hearts gentle.
English proverb

An enemy may chance to give good counsel.
English proverb

Take heed of enemies reconciled, and of meat twice boiled.
Spanish proverb

WORD PICTURES

A certain king, after conquering his enemies, took them into his
favour and had them about his court. His courtiers remonstrated
with him, saying that he should have destroyed them. 'But I
destroy my enemies in the most effective way of all,' he answered,
'when I make them my friends.'

Once upon a time in an Eastern city there was a riot. The people were hungry and blamed the Caliph. When he rode through the streets of the city some of the citizens mobbed him; and one man more desperate than the rest, caught him by the beard and but for the intervention of the guard would have dragged him from the saddle.

Order was restored, food distributed, and the discontent subsided; but a shopkeeper named Hassan sought to curry favour with the Caliph by telling him of the name of the man who had pulled him by the beard. The man's name was Khasim.

The ruler sent for him. Khasim arrived at the palace trembling with fear. He threw himself at the Caliph's feet, begging for mercy. 'Get up, Khasim. I did not send for you to punish you, but to warn you that Hassan is a bad neighbour; for he it was that told me that you were my chief assailant in the riot. Go in peace, and never trust a tale-bearer,' said the Caliph.

F. H. Drinkwater

There was a cholera epidemic in Paris during 1832. A Sister of Charity who was going to the hospital one day was rudely insulted by a workman; he followed her, shouting bad language, and would have struck her if not prevented by the bystanders, but she went quietly on to her duty.

A few days later a new patient was brought to the hospital, already crowded with hundreds, with deaths every few minutes. 'No room – not even for one more!' said the officials at the door. The new patient was being turned away when Sister Marie happened to pass and recognise him; it was the man who had so insulted her. 'Oh, don't send him away! I will find a corner for him somewhere – I will look after him myself.' He was taken in, and the Sister tended him unceasingly, in addition to all her other patients. He did not recognise the Sister as one of those he had insulted, for he had insulted so many.

On the eighth day he was out of danger, but found a new nurse looking after him. 'Where is Sister Marie?' he asked. 'She took the cholera herself and died during the night.'

F. H. Drinkwater

449

A soldier wrote to a German mother: 'As a member of a Commando unit raiding a village in France, it became my duty to kill your son. . . . I earnestly ask your forgiveness, for I am a Christian. . . . I hope I may, some day after the war is over, talk with you face to face.'

This German mother received the note several months later, and she wrote to the English soldier in turn: 'I find it in my heart to forgive you, even you who killed my son, for I too am a Christian. . . . If we are living after the war is over I hope you will come to Germany to visit me, that you may take the place in my home, if only for a time, of my son whom you killed.

Edwin A. Goldsworthy

USEFUL TEXTS

Enemy:
   Help when in trouble, *Exod. 23:4-5*
   Do good to and love, *Luke 6:35*
   Pray for, *Matt. 5:44*
   Last to be destroyed, *1 Cor. 15:26*
   Of the Cross, *Phil. 3:18-19*

See also: A9 Relationships
             A33 Love your neighbour
             B15 Jesus, friend of outcasts
             B52 God is Love

C11

TALK

'It is out of the abundance of the heart
that the mouth speaks.'
Luke 6:45

QUOTATIONS

Words are nails for fixing ideas.
H. Giornale

From a slip of the foot you may soon recover, but a slip of the
tongue you may never get over.
Benjamin Franklin

I have often regretted my speech, but never my silence.
Publilius Syrus

Would you have men think well of you? Hold your tongue.
Blaise Pascal

The slanderous tongue kills three; the slandered, the slanderer,
and him who listens to the slander.
The Talmud

Conversation is the art of telling people a little less than they want
to know.
Franklin Jones

If people would only stop talking where they stop knowing, half
the evils of life would come to an end.
Edward Everett Hale

The best conversation is that in which the heart has a greater share
than the head.
La Brunjère

The genius of communication is the ability to be both totally honest and totally kind at the same time.
John Powell

We seldom repent talking too little, but very often talking too much; a common trivial maxim which everybody knows and nobody practises.
La Brunjère

Refrain from listening to worldly tales, that you may not in any way stain your soul with the spattering of mud.
St Basil

Be at peace regarding what is said or done in conversation: for if good, you have something to praise God for, and if bad, something in which to serve God by turning your heart away from it.
St Francis of Sales

PROVERBS
Whoever gossips to you will gossip of you.
Spanish proverb

What is said when drunk has been thought out beforehand.
Flemish proverb

The tongue has no bones, but it can break your back.
Italian proverb

God gave a man two ears and only one mouth. Why don't we listen twice as much as we talk?
Chinese proverb

HUMOUR
A real Christian is a person who can give his pet parrot to the town gossip.
Billy Graham

Gossip specialist: 'I won't go into all the details; in fact, I've already told you more about it than I heard myself.'

Husband to wife at sale: 'If you're sure it'll make you too happy for words, I'll buy it!'

'I hear Mrs Jones has completely lost her voice.'
'Poor dear! I must call on her. I've been wanting to have a good talk with her for a long time.'

Two Englishmen were crossing the Atlantic in the *Queen Elizabeth II*. Though they shared the same stateroom and sat side by side in deck chairs, they did not address each other, as they had not been introduced. Finally, just as New York was in sight, one decided to break the ice.
'Going over?' he drawled.
'I rather thought I would,' came the reply. 'And you?'

The late Margaret Mead was once interviewed by a young and hesitant journalist, a little awed by his famous guest. 'Why do you always carry that forked staff around with you?' he ventured nervously. 'I find it helps to start conversations,' was her deadpan reply.
Anon

Mrs Brown (very annoyed): 'Look here, Mrs Green, Mrs Gray told me that you told her the secret I told you not to tell her.'
Mrs Green: 'Oh the mean creature, and I told her not to tell you that I told her.'
Mrs Brown: 'Well, look here. Don't you tell her that I told you she told me.'

For three years Amy Clegg's parrot had not said a single word, and eventually she became convinced it was simply a stupid parrot unable to learn to speak English. Then one day as she was feeding it a piece of lettuce as a special treat, the parrot suddenly squeaked: 'There's a maggot on it; there's a maggot on it!' Amy

Clegg was astonished. 'You can talk!' she exclaimed. 'But why haven't you spoken all the three years that I've been keeping you?' 'Oh,' replied the parrot, the food has been excellent up to now.'

Have you heard about the Trappist monk, whose superior decided to permit a periodic lifting of the silence rule? Well, one morning at breakfast he said, 'Brother Michael, you may make an observation,' and Michael, after considerable thought, commented, 'The marmalade in this place is too chunky.' Five years later the dispensation was repeated. 'Brother Ignatius, would you care to make a remark?' 'I find it too runny,' was his contribution; then silence was resumed. After a further five-year interval the superior invited Brother Peter to say something. 'I think there's far too much controversy in this place,' he summed up.

WORD PICTURES

'Then you should say what you mean,' the March Hare went on.
    'I do,' Alice hastily replied; 'at least – at least I mean what I say – that's the same thing, you know.'
    'Not the same thing a bit!' said the Hatter. 'Why, you might as well say, 'I see what I eat' is the same thing as 'I eat what I see!'
Alice in Wonderland

'When this pen flows too freely,' run the instructions given with a fountain pen, 'it is a sign that it is nearly empty, and should be filled.' The caution would seem to apply to human beings. Gossip, slander, idle chatter, all testify to the emptiness of the mind and are a damaging sign.
Forward

Socrates in an anonymous anecdote about gossip:
    'Have you heard, O Socrates –'
    'Just a moment, friend,' said the sage. 'Have you made sure that all you are going to tell me is true?'
    'Well, no. I just heard others say it.'
    'I see. Then we can scarcely bother with it unless it is something good. Will it stand the test of goodness?'

'Oh no, indeed. On the contrary.'

'Hmm. Perhaps it is necessary that I know this in order to prevent harm to others.'

'Well, no –'

'Very well, then,' said Socrates. 'Let us forget about it. There are so many worthwhile things in life; we can't afford to bother with what is so worthless as to be neither true nor good nor needful.'
The Liguorian

'I have gossiped about my neighbour,' the woman confessed to her priest. 'One day I saw her stagger about in the yard, so I told a few friends that she had been drunk. Now I find her staggering was caused by a leg injury. How can I undo this gossip I started?'

The priest excused himself for a moment, returned with a pillow and asked the woman to follow him to the side porch. He took out a knife, cut a hole in the pillow and emptied the feathers all about the yard, among shrubs, flowers, even up in the trees. A few feathers floated across the street, heading for unknown destinations.

The priest turned to the woman. 'Will you go out now and gather up every one of the feathers?'

The woman looked stunned. 'Why that would be impossible!'

'Exactly,' replied the priest sorrowfully. 'So it is with your gossip.'

The cloud of suspicion that hung over Robert Edwards for 27 years has lifted at last.

Those who accused him now know that he did not murder his wife, Lena, all those years ago.

The gossips were silenced after Mrs Edwards was found living in a hostel in the city where she vanished.

The story began on August 26, 1968, when she popped out to the shops and was never seen again.

Gossip ran riot in City Road, Walton, Liverpool.

Neighbours could not believe that a mother would walk out on her children, Tom, then aged 11, Carole, six, and Elaine, five.

Within days, police were at Mr Edwards' door with a search

warrant. When they found nothing, they dug up his back yard then the floor of his cellar.

Mr Edwards vehemently denied harming his wife. The police found no evidence against him, and eventually logged Mrs Edwards as a missing person.

But neighbours remained suspicious of her husband. He said: 'People would point at me in the street. I was the man who had murdered his wife and buried her in the back yard.

'When police didn't find a body there, people kept asking where I had put her. Lena's family haven't spoken to me since.'
Andrew Loudon

USEFUL TEXTS

Gossip:
    Consequences of, *Prov. 16:28*
    Forbidden under the law, *Lev. 19:16*
    Result of idleness, *1 Tim. 5:13*

See also: A2   Integrity
          A9   Relationships
          A47 The Spirit of Truth
          B53 Consecrated in Truth

C12
THE CHURCH FOR ALL PEOPLE

'Grant all the foreigner asks so that all the peoples
of the earth may come to know your name.'
1 Kings 8:43

QUOTATIONS

For where the Church is, there is the Spirit of God; and where the
Spirit of God is, there is the Church and every form of grace, for
the Spirit is truth.
St Irenaeus

Locality, nationality, particularity are essential marks of the
universal Church; the local congregation is the embodiment at a
given place and time of the Church of all the world.
Alan Richardson

All the denominations have fallen prey to the capitalist machine.
With what remnant of moral authority can we demand structural
change if our own institutions are linked to the old structures.
Helder Camara

The Church is not a finished, solidly built and furnished house, in
which all that changes is the successive generations who live in it.
The Church is a living reality which has had a history of its own
and still has one.
Karl Rahner

I am of the Church, come dance with me in the church.
Mary Robinson

I'd like to see my Church more relevant to the millions of people
who read popular papers like the *Sun*. I passionately believe God
is relevant to everyday life . . . but I know it is often a giant yawn
to real people.
George Carey

The Church is a house with a hundred gates: and no two men
enter at exactly the same angle.
G. K. Chesterton

What the Catholic Church needs in Western culture is
  a renewed spirituality
    based on the liturgy with a particular emphasis on Scripture,
    so as to recapture the basic concept of Christian community,
  a renewed sense of service to those who are in need,
  and the courage to share with fellow Christians
    providing society with radical witness to Gospel values.
Cormac Murphy-O'Connor

WORD PICTURES

No other institution is left standing which carries the mind back
to the times when the smoke of sacrifice rose from the Pantheon,
and when camelopards and tigers bounded in the Flavian
amphitheatre. The proudest royal houses are but of yesterday
when compared with the line of the Supreme Pontiffs. That line
we trace back in an unbroken series from the Pope who crowned
Napoleon in the nineteenth century to the Pope who crowned
Pepin in the eighth; and far beyond the time of Pepin the august
dynasty extends, till it is lost in the twilight of fable.

    The republic of Venice came next in antiquity. But the Republic
of Venice is gone, and the Papacy remains. The Papacy remains, not
in decay, not a mere antique, but full of life and youthful vigour. The
number of her children is greater than in any former age. Her
acquisitions in the New World have more than compensated her for
what she has lost in the Old. Her spiritual ascendancy extends over
the vast countries which lie between the plains of the Missouri and
Cape Horn, countries which a century hence may not improbably
contain a population as large as that which now inhabits Europe.

    Nor do we see any sign which indicates that the term of her long
dominion is approaching. She saw the commencement of all the
governments and of all the ecclesiastical establishments that now
exist in the world; and we feel no assurance that she is not destined
to see the end of them all. She was great and respected before the

Saxon had set foot on Britain, before the Frank had passed the Rhine, when Grecian eloquence still flourished in Antioch, when idols were still worshipped in the temple of Mecca. And she may still exist in undiminished vigour when some traveller from New Zealand shall, in the midst of a vast solitude, take his stand on a broken arch of London Bridge to sketch the ruins of St Paul's.
Macaulay's Essays

The Church must preserve her identity as a family, united in the diversity of her members. She must be the leaven which helps society to react as it did to the early Christians: 'See how they love one another.' With this picture of the Church before our eyes – a picture that is certainly not idealised unrealistically but matured by trial and suffering – we call on everybody to overcome unlawful and dangerous differences. We must recognise each other as brothers in the love of Christ that unites us.
Pope John Paul II

Some churches are like lighthouses, built of stone, so strong that the thunder of the sea cannot move them – with no light at the top. That which is the light of the world in the Church is not its largeness, nor its services celebrant with pomp and beauty, not its music, not the influences in it that touch the taste or instruct the understanding: it is the Christlikeness of its individual members.
Henry Ward Beecher

Saint Paul says that precepts kill. The Church should follow Saint Paul. No one is saved by precepts. They are saved by grace and by being given a high ideal to follow. The Church shouldn't worry whether its rules are obeyed or not, it should ask whether men are fired with the ideal of the Gospel. A Church which refers to the Gospel is a Church which isn't obsessed by imposing laws and observances, but which offers an ideal to all.
Cardinal Martini

See also: A6   Light of the world
          A13 The Church is for sinners
          A43 Believing community
          B17 The Church – Bride of Christ

C13
COPING WITH GRIEF

'When the Lord saw her, he felt sorry for her.
"Do not cry," he said.'
Luke 7:13

QUOTATIONS

Afflictions are but the shadow of God's wings.
George MacDonald

Sorrow is a fruit: God does not make it grow on limbs too weak
to bear it.
Victor Hugo

Light griefs can speak; but deeper ones are dumb.
Seneca

Those who have known grief seldom seem sad.
Benjamin Disraeli

There are times when sorrow seems to be the only truth.
Oscar Wilde

The half of music, I have heard men say, is to have grieved.
Ralph Waldo Emerson

Often it is required to leave God for God, renouncing his
sweetness to serve him in his sorrows and travails.
St Francis of Sales

The flood of grief decreaseth when it can swell no longer.
Francis Bacon

Facing and accepting a loss is the first step of managing bereavement.
Only life which deliberately picks up and starts again is victorious.
James Gordon Gilkey

Sorrow you can hold, however isolating, if nobody speaks to you. If they speak, you break down.

Bede Jarratt

Sorrow makes us all children again – destroys all differences of intellect. The wisest know nothing.

Ralph Waldo Emerson

HUMOUR

An Irishman lying on his deathbed was questioned by his sorrowing wife if there was anything she could do to make him more comfortable. 'Anything ye ask,' she said, 'I will get for ye.'

'Please, Bridget,' he replied, 'I think I'd like a wee taste of the ham I smell boiling in the kitchen.'

'Arrah, go on,' said she, 'Divil a bit of that ham ye'll get. It's for the wake.'

Anon

WORD PICTURES

A few years ago explorers opened an Egyptian tomb which had been closed for three thousand years. There stood the exquisitely carved coffin of a little child with this inscription: 'Oh, my life, my love, my little one. Would God I had died for thee.' Instinctively the men uncovered their heads, then resealed the tomb, and left. Love and sorrow are as old as the human heart and God.

D. B. Knox

There are shadows in all good pictures, but there are lights, too, if we choose to contemplate them. If anything could soothe the first sharp pain of a heavy loss it would be – with me – the reflection that those I mourned, by being innocently happy here and loving all about them, had prepared themselves for a purer and happier world. The sun does not shine upon this fair earth to meet frowning eyes, depend upon it.

Charles Dickens

The Arabs have a saying that all sunshine makes the desert. It is even so. Just as sun and shower are alike needful for the development of the flower, so are joy and grief for the culture of the soul.

From vintages of sorrow are deepest joys distilled;
and the cup outstretched for healing is oft at March filled.
God leads to joy, through weeping; to quietness, through strife;
through yielding, unto conquest; through death, to endless life.
Henry Durbanville

Now consider first the myrrh. It is bitter; and this is a type of the bitterness which must be tasted before a man can find God, when he first turns from the world to God, and all his likings and desires have to be utterly changed . . .

But there is yet another myrrh which far surpasses the first. This is the myrrh which God gives us in the cup of trouble and sorrow, of whatever kind it may be, outward or inward. Ah, if thou couldst but receive this myrrh as from its true source, and drink it with the same love with which God puts it to thy lips, what blessedness would it work in thee! And what joy and peace and an excellent thing were that! Yes, the very least and the very greatest sorrows that God ever suffers to befall thee, proceed from the depths of his unspeakable love; and such great love were better for thee than the highest and best gifts beside that he has given thee or ever could give thee, if thou couldst but see it in this light.
John Tauler

USEFUL TEXTS

Grief:
Results from:
    Hardness of heart, *Mark 3:5*
    Disease, *Job 2:11-13*
    Death, *2 Sam. 19:1-2*
    Rebelliousness, *Isa. 63:10*

See also: A25 Courage
             B38 The Suffering Servant
             B49 Coping with doubt
             C18 Compassion

C14
FORGIVENESS

'I tell you that her sins, her many sins, must have been forgiven
her, or she would not have shown such great love.'
Luke 7:47

QUOTATIONS

A noble mind disdains not to repent.
Alexander Pope

He who repents having sinned is almost innocent.
Seneca

Forgiveness to the injured doth belong.
But they ne'er pardon who have done wrong.
John Dryden

When a man injures me I strive to lift up my soul so high that his
offence cannot reach me.
Descartes

The man who is truly forgiven and knows it, is a man who forgives.
Martyn Lloyd-Jones

Above all, no reproaches about what is passed and cannot be
altered! How could a man live at all if he did not grant absolution
every night to himself and his fellows.
Goethe

Chronic remorse is a most undesirable sentiment. If you have
behaved badly, repent, make what amends you can, and address
yourself to the task of behaving better the next time. On no
account brood over your wrongdoing. Rolling in the muck is not
the best way of getting clean.
Aldous Huxley

We may, if we choose, make the worst of one another. Everyone has his weak points; everyone has his faults; we may make the worst of these; we may fix our attention constantly upon these. But we may also make the best of one another. We may forgive, even as we hope to be forgiven.

A. P. Stanley

HUMOUR

During one rare hot summer, a German gentleman had to spend three weeks in hospital. On a real scorcher of a day the chaplain made his call and asked the sick man if he could do anything for him. The German and his room-mate asked for ice cream. Less than an hour later a young boy appeared with two succulent cornets. He told them he had been to confession and the priest had told him to bring them the ice cream as a penance and not to lick them.

J. Vose

A good Presbyterian minister in old Scotland, of the staid and orthodox type, had in his congregation a poor old woman who was in the habit of saying, 'Praise the Lord!' when anything particularly helpful was said.

This practice greatly disturbed the minister, and one New Year's Day he went to see her. 'Betty,' he said, 'I'll make a bargain with you. You call out "Praise the Lord" just when I get to the best part of my sermon, and it upsets my thoughts. Now if you will stop doing it all this year, I'll give you a pair of wool blankets.' Betty was poor, and the offer of the blankets looked very good. So she did her best to earn them.

Sunday after Sunday she kept quiet. But one day a minister of another type came to preach – a man bubbling over with joy. As he preached on the forgiveness of sins and of all the blessings that follow, the vision of the blankets began to fade and fade, and the joys of salvation grew brighter and brighter. At last Betty could stand it no longer and jumping up she cried, 'Blankets or no blankets, Hallelujah!'

C. Johnson

Leaflet announcement by a Glasgow church: 'There will be a "Parish Sin-a-long" on Monday at 7.30.'
William McCaffrey

WORD PICTURES

Robert Bear still remembers every detail of the day three years ago when he was forced to say goodbye to his wife and six children, after being shunned by his Church for criticising an elder. 'We went into the vestry and I kissed her,' he says softly. 'I remember saying, "Well I suppose this is the last time I will ever get to kiss you." She didn't say a word. Nor did the children. They wouldn't even touch me. They never spoke to me again.'

When he came out of the small room, church officials escorted him right to the graveyard gate. 'Don't come back,' they said. Both his parents died that week, refusing to acknowledge they still had a son. Emotionally broken, he let the farm deteriorate. Pretty soon it was bought by a neighbour and he had to move into a caravan. He still doesn't understand what he has done to deserve this.

In the eyes of the Reformed Mennonite Church, whose 500 members live in isolated rural communities in Canada, the Devil is within Bear and has seized his heart and voice. They will forgive him and reunite him with his family if he will admit that the Devil was inside him and that he has cast it out and begs forgiveness.

Robert Bear, aged 48, says he won't beg forgiveness. He is fighting for his family to be returned to him in an appeal before the State Supreme Court.

O man, forgive thy mortal foe,
nor ever strike him blow for blow;
for all the souls on earth that live,
to be forgiven must forgive;
forgive him seventy times and seven,
for all the blessed souls in heaven
are both forgivers and forgiven.
Author unknown

Almost hidden in a secluded corner of a New York cemetery is a small gravestone polished smooth by the wind and weather of many years. The stone bears no name, nor is there any date inscribed on it. Still legible on the face of the stone, however, in letters that neither wind nor weather has been able to erase, is one solitary word, 'forgiven'. No monument, no obelisk, no vaulted mausoleum marks the final resting place of the anonymous person who lies buried there – only a simple stone – and the single word 'forgiven'.

There was a crash from the lounge; something had been broken. My 13-year-old daughter was larking around with two boy-friends and I had suspected that they were throwing cushions around. I stormed into the lounge to find all three sitting silently and innocently watching TV. At the foot of one wall, on which had hung a set of four plates, lay the debris of one; it was a set that I had bought my wife for Christmas two years before. The set was now destroyed. I was livid. I shouted at the three teenagers and demanded to know who the culprit was. No one knew. The plate, they said, had 'just fallen off the wall'. I exploded and lay the blame on my daughter. 'You will pay for it,' I said.

Later when the boys had gone and I had calmed down, I asked again for the name of the culprit. My daughter admitted that it was her fault; they had been throwing cushions and hers had hit the plate. I said that she was forgiven, but she would have to pay for the replacement. It took several years until someone put me in touch with the Bradford Exchange. At 18 my daughter parted with £35 to cover the cost of a replacement.

God will always forgive us but we must put right any injustice or damage that we have done others. Restitution has to be made. A.P.C.

Magdalen at Michael's gate
tirled at the pin;
on Joseph's thorn sang the blackbird,
'Let her in! Let her in!'

'Hast thou seen the wounds?' said Michael:
'Know'st thou thy sin?'
'It is evening, evening,' sang the blackbird,
'Let her in! Let her in!'

'Yes, I have seen the wounds,
and I know my sin.'
'She knows it well, well, well,' sang the blackbird,
'Let her in! Let her in!'

'Thou bringest no offerings?' said Michael.
'Nought save sin.'
And the blackbird sang, 'She is sorry, sorry, sorry!
Let her in! Let her in!'

When he had sung himself to sleep,
and night did begin,
one came and open'd Michael's gate,
and Magdalen went in.
Henry Kingsley

On her 25th birthday, on 1st December 1964, Sister Anwarite was murdered for refusing to give in to the sexual demands of rebel soldiers under the command of Colonel Pierre Olombe.

Born in 1939, fourth of five daughters of a pagan family, Anwarite was baptised at 5 years of age. She joined a congregation of African Sisters of the Holy Family when she was 16; she took the name Clementine and she qualified as a teacher.

There was a rebel resistance movement in northern Zaire at that time and a bloody civil war was raging. Sister Anwarite's community of thirty-four nuns was taken from their convent by lorry to Isiro. Two drunken soldiers demanded that Anwarite and another sister be their 'wives'. Their superior refused to leave their side and when all three were threatened with death, Sister Anwarite said, 'Why kill them, kill me.' The colonel, Pierre Olombe, beat her with a gun; she replied, 'I'm ready to die.' The soldiers crowded round her, and witnesses heard her say, 'I forgive you because you don't know what you are doing.' She was stabbed by bayonets and then the colonel shot her in the chest; she died an hour later in the arms of her Sisters.

Her body was reclaimed from a communal pit and buried at Isiro Cathedral. Three hundred thousand people attended the ceremony at Kinshasa when the Pope in 1985 declared her 'Blessed' (a step towards canonisation).

Colonel Pierre Olombe served five years imprisonment, during which he became a Christian. He was present, and received a special word of forgiveness, when Pope John Paul II beatified Sister Anwarite.

P. F.

USEFUL TEXTS

Forgiveness:
  Of human sin:
  By God, *Ps. 130:4*
  By Christ, *Acts 10.43*
  Among believers, *Eph. 4:32*
  Of enemies, *Luke 6:27*

See also: A26 The Sacrament of Penance
          A27 As we forgive those
          B16 Christ heals and forgives
          C27 The Father who receives us back
          C40 Reconciliation

C15
PREJUDICE

'There are no more distinctions between Jew and Greek, slave and free, male and female, but all of you are one in Christ Jesus.'
Galatians 3:28

QUOTATIONS

Prejudice is the reasoning of the stupid.
Voltaire

Passion and prejudice govern the world; only under the name of reason.
John Wesley

A great many people think they are thinking when they are merely rearranging their prejudices.
William James

Men are usually down on what they are not up to.
Hoyt M. Dobbs

I am convinced there is no more evil thing in the present world than race prejudice – none at all.
H. G. Wells

Prejudices subsist in people's imagination long after they have been destroyed by their experience.
Ernest Dimnet

Familiarity causes us to see things according to our prejudices, and the result is that we do not see things as they are.
James Mahoney

WORD PICTURES

There is a legend in the Talmud of a traveller coming at twilight to a camping place. As he looked off yonder he saw a strange

object. Through the gathering dusk it seemed to take the shape of a terrible monster, and he resolved to go closer to see, if possible, what it was. Drawing nearer, he saw that it was a man. Much of his fear then vanished. Thereupon he ventured still nearer and found that not only was the object a man like himself but that it was his own brother.
George Willets

She spoke of heaven
and an angelic host;
she spoke of God
and the Holy Ghost;
she spoke of Christ's teachings
of man's brotherhood;
yet when she had to sit beside a Negro once –
she stood.
Elizabeth Hart

I dislike abuse of the mind. I was in Northern Ireland on one of my frequent trips to that place and there was a nice lady, and I said to her, 'How do you get on with the violence?' She says, 'It's awful, Jimmy, but the danger is that we're learning to live with it now. We've come to expect it and we just hear about it and learn to live with it. It is a great sadness to us.' Then, she carried on in the same tone of voice, 'I will never be happy until every Catholic in Northern Ireland is dead.'

That saddened me beyond measure because this was a dear lady unfortunately abusing her mind. It is an abuse of the mind to want to kill Protestants or Catholics, or anybody or anything.
Jimmy Saville

I felt drained of strength and thought; yet somehow I managed to leave that office, navigate the passage, lift and corridor, and walk out of the building into the busy sunlit street. I had just been brought face to face with something I had either forgotten or completely ignored for more than six exciting years – my black skin. It had not mattered when I volunteered for aircrew service in 1940, it had not mattered during the period of flying training or when I received my wings and was posted to a squadron; it had not mattered in the hectic uncertainties of operational flying, of living and loving from day to day, brothered to men who like myself had no tomorrow and could not afford to fritter away today on the absurdities of prejudice; it had not mattered when, uniformed and winged, I visited theatres and dance halls, pubs and private houses.

I had forgotten about my black face during those years. I saw it daily yet never noticed its colour. I was an airman in flying kit while on His Majesty's business, smiled at, encouraged, welcomed by grateful civilians in bars or on the street, who saw not me, but the uniform and its relationship to the glorious, undying Few. Yes, I had fogotten about my skin when I had so eagerly discussed my post-war prospects with the Careers Officer and the Appointments people; I had quite forgotten about it as I jauntily entered that grand, imposing building . . .

Now as I walked sadly away, I consciously averted my eyes from the sight of my face reflected fleetingly in the large plate glass windows. Disappointment and resentment were a solid bitter rising lump inside me; I hurried into the nearest public lavatory and was violently sick.

E. R. Braithwaite

See also: A40 The equality of women
          A41 Spiritual blindness
          B15 Jesus, friend of outcasts
          C1 Liberation from fear

C16
COME FOLLOW ME

'Another to whom he said "Follow me", replied,
"Let me go and bury my father first." But he answered,
'Leave the dead to bury their dead.'
Luke 9:59-60

QUOTATIONS

Christianity is asceticism without rigorism and love without sentimentality.
Baron F. Von Hugel

Nothing is more depressing and more illogical than aggressive Christianity.
Gerald Vann

The main business of a Christian soul is to go through the world turning its water into wine.
Andrew Long

The world around us will recognise us as disciples of Jesus when they see our prayers being answered.
Colin Urquhart

If we were willing to learn the meaning of real discipleship and actually to become disciples, the Church in the West would be transformed, and the resultant impact on society would be staggering.
David Watson

WORD PICTURES

A Christian . . .
    is a mind through which Christ thinks.
    is a heart through which Christ lives.
    is a voice through which Christ speaks.
    is a hand through which Christ helps.

'Are you a Christian, Uncle Lawrence?' 'No, my dear; if anything a Confucian, who, as you know, was simply an ethical philosopher. Most of our caste in this country, if they only knew it, are Confucian rather than Christian. Belief in ancestors, and tradition, respect for parents, honesty, moderation of conduct, kind treatment of animals and dependants, absence of self-obtrusion, and stoicism in face of pain and death.'
John Galsworthy

Love has still another meaning. Namely, it is closely connected with the direction of a person's vocation. A person goes in the direction which his love chooses. How else, for example, can we understand the vocation of a nun? There's a young girl, just like all her classmates she goes to the school-leaving party, on excursions and I don't know what else, then suddenly, one day, she knocks at the novitiate door.

After that, what will she do in life? She'll do what I often see just looking round Cracow: run up and down stairs from six in the morning till ten at night, nursing the sick, the ones who have no one to take them in, whom the hospitals have discharged and left to their families. But the families very often don't get on with them. And in all this she will be so serene, a bride, a very bride.

She has chosen a very great love. And it is always a cause for astonishment when the voice of the Bridegroom is heard, overwhelming all else and bidding one follow him.
Pope John Paul II

It was Pliny who left the world the only account by an eye-witness of the destruction of Pompeii, who left us also the first mention of Christianity in secular history. The Roman scholar and ruler is troubled by the strange new sect calling themselves Christians, and writes concerning them to the Emperor Trajan. These letters were written about AD 103.
Pliny to Trajan
It is my invariable rule to refer to you in all matters about which I feel doubtful. Who can better remove my doubts or inform my ignorance? I have never been present at any legal examination of

Christians, so that I do not know what is the nature of the charge against them, or what is the usual punishment. Whether any difference or distinction is made between the young and persons of mature years, whether repentance for their fault entitles them to pardon, whether the very profession of Christianity unaccompanied by any criminal act is a subject of punishment – on all these points I am in great doubt. Meanwhile, as to those who have been charged before me with being Christians, I have observed the following method.

I asked them whether they were Christians; if they admitted it I repeated the question twice; if they persisted I ordered them at once to be punished. I could not doubt that, whatever might be the nature of their opinions, such inflexible obstinacy deserved punishment. Some were brought before me, with the same infatuation, who were Roman citizens; these I took care should be sent to Rome.

An anonymous information was laid before me containing a great number of names. Some said they neither were and never had been Christians; they repeated after me an invocation of the gods, and offered wine and incense before your statue (which I had ordered to be brought for that purpose, together with those of the gods), and even reviled the name of Christ; whereas there is no forcing (it is said) of those who are really Christians into any of these acts. These I thought ought to be discharged.

Some among them, who were accused by a witness in person at first confessed themselves Christians, but immediately after denied it. They declared that their offence was summed up in this, that they met on a stated day before daybreak, and addressed a form of prayer to Christ, as to a divinity, binding themselves by a solemn oath; not for any wicked purpose, but never to commit fraud, robbery, theft; never to break their word, or to deny a trust when called upon to deliver it up; after which it was their custom to separate, and then reassemble to eat together a harmless meal. From this custom, however, they desisted after the proclamation of my edict, by which, according to your command, I forbade the meetings of any assemblies.

USEFUL TEXTS

Discipleship:
  The cost of, *Luke 14:25-33*
  Responsibility, *2 Tim. 2:2-8*
  Characterised by love, *John 21:15-18*

See also: A22 Seeking God
           B11 Vocation
           B24 Go tell everyone
           C41 Starting afresh

C17
INTERNATIONAL PEACE

'Now towards her I send flowing peace, like a river,
and like a stream in spate the glory of the nations.'
Isaiah 66:12

QUOTATIONS

It takes two to make a peace.
John F. Kennedy

Peace is not made at the council tables or by treaties, but in the
hearts of men.
Herbert Hoover

Yes, we love peace, but we are not willing to take wounds for it,
as we are for war.
John Andrew Holmes

Nothing except a battle lost can be half so melancholy as a battle
won.
Duke of Wellington

The atomic bomb is here to stay; the one question is whether we
human beings are here to stay too.
Harry Emerson Fosdick

My religion is based on truth and non-violence. Truth is my God
and non-violence is the means to reach him.
Mohandes Gandhi

If we let people see that kind of thing, there would never again be
any war.
*Senior Pentagon official on reasons why the US military censored
footage showing Iraqi soldiers sliced in two by US helicopter fire*

PROVERBS

A bad peace is better than a good war.
Russian proverb

Who is narrow of vision cannot be big of heart.
Chinese proverb

WORD PICTURES

I dip't into the future, far as human eye could see,
saw the vision of the world, and all the wonders that would be;
till the war drum throbbed no longer, and the battle flags were furl'd
in the Parliament of Man, the Federation of the world.
Alfred, Lord Tennyson

It is said that during World War I an English pacifist printed the Sermon on the Mount and had it circulated widely; no notes or comments, just the words of Jesus. He was put in jail for conduct prejudicial to the national safety!

Give me the money that has been spent in war, and I will clothe every man, woman, and child in an attire of which kings and queens would be proud. I will build a schoolhouse in every valley over the whole Earth. I will crown every hillside with a place of worship consecrated to the gospel of peace.
Charles Sumner

The following lines were found inscribed on the wall of a shelled house in a devastated French village during the First World War:
War provokes pillage,
pillage brings ruin,
ruin brings patience,
patience implies peace;
thus does war produce peace.

Peace provokes abundance,
abundance brings arrogance,
arrogance brings war;
thus does peace produce war.
Author unknown

One day a little boy asked his parents. 'How do wars break out? How are they declared?' So the father, who was very learned in economic matters, started talking about wheat, oil and all the things that divide the world. But the mother thought the little boy was far too small to understand such things, and she said, 'Let me explain it.' The mother began to explain, and the father grew angry, and a great argument developed. The little boy was very frightened indeed, and held up his hands and cried, 'Stop, stop! Now I know how wars begin.'
Irene Laure

Building up peace by works of peace is difficult. It demands that truth be restored, in order to keep individuals, groups and nations from losing confidence in peace and from consenting to new forms of violence. Restoring peace means in the first place calling by their proper names, acts of violence in all their forms. Murder must be called by its proper name: murder is murder; political or ideological motives do not change its nature, but are in the contrary degraded by it.

The massacre of men and women, whatever their race, age or position, must be called by its proper name. Torture must be called by its proper name: and, with the appropriate qualifications, so must all forms of oppression and exploitation of man by man, of man by the State, of one people to another people. The purpose of doing so is not to give oneself a clear conscience by means of loud all-embracing denunciations – this would no longer be calling things by their proper names – nor to brand and condemn individuals and peoples, but to help to change people's behaviour and attitudes, and in order to give peace a chance again.
Pope John Paul II

The late Albert Einstein, during his declining years, granted a press conference to a number of newspaper reporters.

After they had plied him with questions on many subjects, one reporter asked: 'Mr Einstein, would you care to make a prediction as to the kind of weapons that will be used in the third world war?' Modestly he shook his head and said: 'No, I would not venture a prediction.' After the briefest hesitation he added, 'But I'll tell you what will be the chief weapon in the fourth world war.'

The reporters were all ears and every pencil was poised in anticipation of the old man's prediction. What would be the chief weapon in the fourth world war?

With an air of finality, the old man gave a one-word reply – clubs? It took a moment or two for the aged scientist's reply to register, but as it did, a grim silence settled over the assembled group.

Anon

Not long ago I visited a small well-kept church in a country town and happened to notice a specification for a new altar cross with the cost attached. £2,700. Pax Christi, the only Catholic organisation in this country devoted to ending the arms trade, promoting peace education, defending the rights of conscientious objectors and working for peace in Northern Ireland, gets a grant from the national Catholic purse of £2,000 a year – less than the amount that one small parish can spend on a new cross.

Bruce Kent

'Tell me the weight of a snowflake,' a coal-mouse asked a wild dove. 'Nothing more than nothing,' was the answer.

'Listen then,' said the coal-mouse to the wild dove. 'I sat on a branch of a fir tree, close to its trunk, when it began to snow, not heavily, but gentle without any violence. Since I didn't have anything better to do, I counted the snowflakes settling on the twigs and needles of the branch. Their number was exactly 3,741,952. When the next snowflake dropped onto the branch – nothing more than nothing, as you say – the branch broke off.'

The dove flew off back to Noah's Ark. She thought about the story for a while and said to herself: 'Perhaps there is only one person's voice lacking for peace to come about in the world.'

Kurt Kauter

See also: A33 Love your neighbour
          B34 Human rights
          C4   Personal peace
          C10 Love your enemies

C18
COMPASSION

'A Samaritan traveller who came upon him was moved
with compassion when he saw him.'
Luke 10:33

QUOTATIONS

Compassion is the root of religion; pride the root of sin.
Tulsi Das

Man may dismiss compassion from his heart, but God will never.
William Cowper

God does not wish us to remember what he is willing to forget.
George A. Buttrick

Perchance that I might learn what pity is, that I might laugh at
erring men no more.
Michelangelo

Unless you are deliberately kind to every creature, you will often
be cruel to many.
John Ruskin

Compassion will cure more sins than condemnation.
Henry Ward Beecher

Justice seeks out the merits of the case, but pity only regards the
need.
St Bernard of Clairvaux

'I am that I am,' said God to Moses, by which he intimated that
he created the world in mercy, and will always rule the world in
mercy.
The Midrash

Nobody can judge men but God, and we can hardly obtain a higher or more reverent view of God than that which represents him to us as judging men with perfect knowledge, unperplexed certainty and undisturbed compassion.
Frederick W. Faber

God created a reminder, an image.
Humanity is a reminder of God.
As God is compassionate,
let humanity be compassionate.
Abraham J. Heschel

There is no wilderness so terrible, so beautiful, so arid and so fruitful as the wilderness of compassion. It is the only desert that shall truly flourish like the lily.
Thomas Merton

WORD PICTURES

Once a poor villager came to a town to earn money for the Passover. After nightfall on his return to the village, laden with purchases, his horse and wagon fell into a pit made swampy by the spring rains. A rich man passing by, heard his cries, and helped his own driver to extricate the villager. He roped the latter's wagon to his carriage, and accompanied the poor man to his hut. On beholding the abject poverty in which the villager and his family lived, the magnate gave him a large sum of money.

When the wealthy man died and was brought before the heavenly tribunal, it seemed as if his demerits because of certain business dealings would result in his sentence to eternal punishment. Suddenly an Angel of Mercy appeared, and asked that the heavenly scales be used to determine whether the worth of his good deeds outweighed his sins. When consent was given, the Angel placed in the scale of good deeds the poor villager and his family whom the rich man had saved from misery. But this did not suffice. The horse and the wagon were added, but they did not help enough. Then the Angel placed on the scale the mud and mire out of which the rich man had helped rescue the villager,

and, lo, the scale of good deeds dipped with its weight, and the magnate was saved from eternal punishment.
Rabbi Israel of Rizbyn

Some of the followers of St Bernard, who had caught his spirit of helping people, decided to leave the comforts, and beautiful churches of Italy, where they loved to worship, to settle upon the top of a great mountain pass which is now known by the Saint's name. They went there because they felt compassion for the travellers who lost themselves on those snow-covered mountains, and were sometimes buried in the snow and died of cold. They determined therefore to live near at hand in order to rescue these poor wanderers.

They trained dogs to help them in their work. These dogs were sent out in pairs: one had a flask of brandy round his neck, the other a warm cloak strapped to him. These wonderful dogs knew what their work was. If they found a stranger, they led him to the monastery; if, by their sense of smell they traced one buried in the snow, they would scratch away the snow and uncover him, and then bark till the sound reached the listening monks, who would then follow the sound, and come to the rescue of the traveller.

One St Bernard dog saved twenty-two lives, and it would be impossible to say how many storm-pressed travellers have thanked God for putting it into the hearts of the monks of St Bernard to build their mountain hospice and to train their faithful dogs.
Anon

USEFUL TEXTS

Compassion:
  Of Jesus, *Matt. 9:36*
  Of God, *Deut. 13:17; Ps. 78:38*
  Of Good Samaritan, *Luke 10:33-34*
  As a mark of believers, *1 Pet. 3:8*

See also: A17 Gentleness
           A23 Mercy
           A33 Love your neighbour
           C46 Loving kindness

C19
FRIENDSHIP

'Jesus came to a village, and a woman named Martha
welcomed him into her house.'
Luke 10:38

QUOTATIONS

Friendship – one soul in two bodies.
Pythagoras

Judge not thy friend until thou standest in his place.
Rabbi Hillel

God is everybody's friend . . . or he should be.
Humphrey Bogart

Go oft to the house of thy friend, for weeds choke the unused path.
Ralph Waldo Emerson

Promises may get friends, but it is performance that keeps them.
Owen Feltham

Blessed is he who hungers for friends – for though he may not
realise it, his soul is crying out for God.
Habib Sahabib

It is a true saying that a man must eat a peck of salt with his friend
before he knows him.
Cervantes

Everything that is mine to give, even to my life, I may give to one
I love, but the secret of my friend is not mine to give.
Philip Sidney

You make more friends by becoming interested in other people
than by trying to interest other people in yourself.
Dale Carnegie

Friendship is to be purchased only by friendship. A man may have authority over others; but he can never have their heart but by giving his own.
Thomas Wilson

The impulse of love that leads us to the doorway of a friend is the voice of God within and we need not be afraid to follow it.
Agnes Sanford

So long as we love, we serve; so long as we are loved by others I would almost say that we are indispensable; and no man is useless while he has a friend.
Robert Louis Stevenson

It is a poor or false friendship that will allow a friend to perish without help, that dare not lance an abscess to save his life.
St Francis of Sales

Life is to be fortified by many friendships.
Sydney Smith

WORD PICTURES

Today I have added to my wealth a priceless treasure. To find it I did not have to dive to the bottom of the sea, nor blast the granite mountain side, nor dig a field, quarry a mine, nor play a sharper's trick. I looked straight into a man's clear eye, spoke a true word, received a signal of understanding, and now, for life, I have a friend.
Anon

A true friend is one who will recognise me when necessity compels me to wear shabby clothes; who will take my hand when I am sliding downhill, instead of giving me a push to hasten my descent; who will lend me a dollar when I really need it, without demanding two dollars security; who will come to me when I am sick; who will pull off his coat and fight for me when the odds are two to one against me; who will talk of me behind my back as he talks to my face.
Anon

Every man will be thy friend
whilst thou hast wherewith to spend;
but if store of crowns be scant,
no man will supply thy want.

He that is thy friend indeed,
he will help thee in thy need;
if thou sorrow, he will weep;
if thou wake, he cannot sleep.

Thus of every grief in heart
he with thee doth bear a part.
These are certain signs to know
faithful friend from flattering foe.
Richard Barnfield

Love will teach us all things: but we must learn how to win love;
it is got with difficulty: it is a possession dearly bought with much
labour and in a long time, for one must love not sometimes only,
for a passing moment, but always. There is no man who doth not
sometimes love: even the wicked can do that.

And let not men's sin dishearten thee: love a man even in his sin,
for that love is a likeness of the divine love, and is the summit of
love on earth. Love all God's creation, both the whole and every
grain of sand. Love every leaf, every ray of light. Love the animals,
love the plants, love each separate thing. If thou love each thing
thou wilt perceive the mystery of God in all; and when once thou
perceive this, thou wilt thenceforward grow every day to a fuller
understanding of it; until thou come at last to love the whole world
with a love that will then be all-embracing and universal.
Feodor Dostoevski

When the Anglican Bishop, Bishop King, was a young man, he
was a curate in a village. One wet cold night he had come home
very tired and had just got his boots off, when his landlady came
in and said that a farmer, living three miles off across the fields,
had met with a serious accident and wanted King to come at once.
She did not know the messenger, and he refused to come in

because he was so wet. King put on his boots again and started off; but it was very dark and he missed the man who had brought the message. When he reached the house to which he had been summoned, the door was opened to his knock by the farmer himself, hale, hearty and much surprised to see his visitor. No message had been sent, and, greatly mystified, King went home. The man who had summoned him had gone, and the matter remained unexplained.

Some years afterwards, in another part of the country, King was ministering to a dying man in hospital, and the man said: 'Don't you remember me, Sir?' The Bishop could not recall him until he gave his name, which was that of a very bad character who had lived years ago in that village where King had been a curate. The man went on: 'It was lucky for you that you brought a friend with you that night when you thought you had a call to the farm. I meant to murder you, only I couldn't as there were two of you.' The Bishop had seen and heard nothing that night, but the man was certain that he had been accompanied by a second great-coated figure walking beside him.

Charles Lindley Wood

USEFUL TEXTS

Friendship:
> With God, *Ps. 25:14*
> With the angry, *Prov. 22:24*
> With the world, *James 4:4*
> A continuing relationship, *Prov. 17:17*
> Betrayal in, *Ps. 41:9*
> With Jesus, *John 15:14*

See also: A9   Relationships
>   A33 Love your neighbour
>   B15 Jesus, friend of outcasts

C20
OUR FATHER IN HEAVEN

'Father, may your name be held holy, your kingdom come.'
Luke 11:2

QUOTATIONS

Sheer joy is his and this demands companionship.
St Thomas Aquinas

If the earth is our mother, God is our Father, and we need faith in
God as our Father, to save us from a mother-fixation to earth.
H. G. Wood

I have a creed, none better and none shorter. It is told in two
words – the first of the Paternoster. And when I say these words I
mean them.
Oliver Wendell Holmes

The belief that God is the Father and man is the child of God is
not an insight which can be gained directly – it is not an insight at
all. On the contrary, it must be believed, ever and again, as the
miraculous act of God.
Rudolf Bultmann

If we address him as children, it is because he tells us he is our
Father. If we unbosom ourselves to him as a friend, it is because
he calls us friends.
William Cowper

What deep mysteries, my dearest brothers, are contained in the
Lord's Prayer! How many and great they are! They are expressed
in a few words but they are rich in spiritual power so that nothing
is left out; every petition and prayer we have to make is included.
It is a compendium of heavenly doctrine.
St Cyprian

The nature of the Trinity is one in three; it is God; but that which makes the unity is the Father, from whom and to whom the order of persons runs its course, not in such a way that the nature is confused, but that it is possessed without distinction of time or of will or of power.
St Gregory of Nazianzus

PROVERBS

God has more than he has given away.
Czech proverb

When the Devil says his Paternoster, he means to cheat you.
Spanish proverb

WORD PICTURES

Bishop Brooks taught me no special creed or dogma; but he impressed upon my mind two great ideas – the fatherhood of God and the brotherhood of man – and made me feel that these truths underlie all creeds and forms of worship. God is love, God is our Father, we are his children; therefore the darkest clouds will break, and though right be worsted, wrong shall not triumph.
Helen Keller

These lines of Charles Thompson may help in a tendency to be self-centred while praying:
    You cannot pray the Lord's Prayer,
    and even once say 'I'.
    You cannot pray the Lord's Prayer,
    and even once say 'My'.
    Nor can you pray the Lord's Prayer,
    and not pray for another;
    for when you ask for daily bread,
    you must include your brother.
    For others are included
    in each and every plea:
    from the beginning to the end of it,
    it does not once say 'Me'.

St Cyril was a boy who became a Christian at Caesarea in Cappadocia, third century. His rich pagan father reviled him, beat him, and at last turned him out of the house; but nothing could quench the joy in his heart, and he won many other boys to a Christian life also.

Soon he was brought before the tribunal as a Christian. Threats failed to move him. Then the magistrate offered to release him if he would return to his home and inheritance. 'Leaving home did not trouble me,' he answered. 'There is a real home waiting for me, much grander and more beautiful, where my Father in heaven lives.'

They took him to the fire as if for execution, then back to the tribunal. 'Why don't you get on with it?' he asked. As nothing could shake his firmness, he was led forth again to die. Some Christians around were weeping, but Cyril said: 'You ought to be a joyful escort for me. Evidently you do not know the City where I am going to live!' He watched the fire being kindled, and died in it brave to the last, with his mind fixed on his heavenly home.
F. H. Drinkwater

Until last September I had never once prayed in all my life, at least not in the literal sense of the word. I had never said any words to God, either out loud or mentally. I had never pronounced a liturgical prayer. I had occasionally recited the *Salve Regina*, but only as a beautiful poem.

Last summer, doing Greek with T . . ., I went through the 'Our Father' word for word in Greek. We promised each other to learn it by heart. I do not think he ever did so, but some weeks later, as I was turning over the pages of the Gospel, I said to myself that since I had promised to do this thing and it was good, I ought to do it. I did it. The infinite sweetness of this Greek text so took hold of me that for several days I could not stop myself from saying it over all the time. A week afterwards I began the vine-harvest. I recited the 'Our Father' in Greek every day before work, and I repeated it very often in the vineyard.

Since that time I have made a practice of saying it through once each morning with absolute attention. If during the recitation my attention wanders or goes to sleep, in the minutest degree, I begin

again until I have once succeeded in going through it with absolutely pure attention. Sometimes it comes about that I say it again out of sheer pleasure but I only do it if I really feel the impulse.
Simone Weil

USEFUL TEXTS

Fatherhood:
    Of God to all he created, *Deut. 32:6*
    Of God to all who believe, *Gal. 4:4-6*
    Of God to Jesus Christ, *Col. 1:3*

See also: A22 Seeking God
              B28 The Father who draws us to himself
              C27 The Father who receives us back

C21
RISE ABOVE MATERIALISM

'Be on your guard against all kinds of greed; for one's life
does not consist in the abundance of possessions.'
Luke 12:15

QUOTATIONS

You can see what God thinks of money, when you see the people
he gives it to.
Abraham Lincoln

The rich man is not one who is in possession of much, but one
who gives much.
St John Chrysostom

It is not a sin to have riches, but it is a sin to fix our hearts upon
them.
St John Baptist de la Salle

The world may be divided into those who take it or leave it and
those who split the difference.
Ronald A. Knox

The rich in this world cannot be made useful for the Lord, unless
their riches have been cut out of them.
Shepherd of Hermas

If you want to destroy a nation, give it too much – make it greedy,
miserable and sick.
John Steinbeck

Man today attempts to escape his guilt through the electrifying effects
of consumer society, through seeking different ways of being amused,
through the merchandising of peace by commercial means.
Roger Schutz

Jesus, on whom be peace, has said: The world is merely a bridge; you are to pass over it, and not to build your dwellings on it.
Old inscription on a mosque at Agra

Money can buy the husk of many things, but not the kernel. It brings you food, but not appetite, medicine, but not health; acquaintances, but not friends; servants, but not faithfulness; days of joy, but not peace and happiness.
Henrik Ibsen

Money can't buy friends, but you can get a better class of enemy.
Spike Milligan

PROVERBS

Riches are like salt water – the more you drink the more you thirst.
Roman proverb

When money speaks, the truth is silent.
Russian proverb

HUMOUR

My little granddaughter eagerly searched under her pillow one morning after having a tooth extracted. She burst into tears after discovering that the tooth had not been replaced by a coin during the night. Trying to comfort her, I said: 'Darling, you don't still believe in those old fairy stories, do you?' 'Maybe not,' she replied, 'but I still believe in money.'

A housewife was having difficulty with her gas bills. Every month after she sent her cheque she was notified that she had sent either too much money or not enough. After a few months of this, it appeared that she and the gas company would never agree on how much she owed. The problem was finally solved when one kindly soul in the company's office checked the payments and sent the customer a little handwritten note that read: 'Please pay the amount I have circled for you in red. Up to now you have been paying the date.'

The Sunday School teacher was talking to her class of ten-year-olds when she suddenly asked: 'Now, why do you think the Children of Israel made a Golden Calf?'

The children were silent until one little boy put up his hand and said: 'Please, Miss, perhaps it was because they didn't have enough gold to make a cow.'

'Madam, is that your little boy burying my jacket in the sand?'

'No, that's my neighbour's little boy. Mine is the one sailing your hat in the sea.'

Every morning a train commuter dropped 5p on the tray of a blind man selling shoe laces at the station, but he never took any laces. One day, when he put down his usual 5p, the beggar touched him on the shoulder.

'It's all right,' said the traveller, 'I don't want any laces.'

'It's not that sir,' said the beggar. 'Since the Budget, the price of shoelaces has gone up to 10p.'

WORD PICTURES

If of thy mortal goods thou art bereft,
and from thy slender store two loaves alone are left,
sell one, and with thy dole
buy hyacinths to feed thy soul.
Sadi, Persian poet of the 12th century

There is an old legend in India that Buddha once lived on the earth as a man, and that one night he was overtaken by a storm, and sought shelter in the humble hut of a fisherman, who took care of him, gave him supper and a bed, with no knowledge of who his guest really was. Before the stranger departed the next morning, the Great Buddha revealed himself. 'I am Buddha,' he said. 'You have been very kind to me; you have been unselfish, and I will grant you any wish you make.' The man, being very poor, asked for gold. The great Buddha said, 'Gold acquired without effort is a curse, and not a blessing. I will give you the gold, but I will also give you the method of earning it. In the little horseshoe curved beach in front of your house,' continued the great man, 'is a certain pebble. If you touch it with iron, it will make the iron gold. Find the pebble, and you will have all the gold you want.'

The man wore an iron bracelet on his wrist. He began that very hour to search for the pebble, beginning at one end of the beach and working very carefully and with great interest, picking up every pebble he could find, touching it to his bracelet and then casting it into the sea so that he would not have to pick it up again. For half a day he worked diligently, picking up the pebbles and touching the bracelet. The sun was hot. The perspiration poured down his face. He became fatigued, discouraged, and after a while the motions of picking up the pebble, touching it to the bracelet and throwing the pebble into the sea became mechanical. Finally, he looked down at his wrist. The bracelet had turned to gold. The pebble which had wrought the miracle had been tossed into the sea.

P. Fontaine

For Las Vegas is a city entirely devoted to the idea of entertainment, and as such it proclaims the spirit of a culture in which all public discourse takes the form of entertainment. Our politics, religion, news, athletics, education and commerce have been translated into congenial adjuncts of show business. . . . The result is that we are a people on the verge of amusing ourselves to death.

Neil Postman

In the last century, a tourist from America paid a visit to a renowned Polish rabbi, Hofetz Chaim. He was astonished to see that the rabbi's home was only a simple room filled with books, plus a table and a bench.

'Rabbi,' asked the tourist, 'where is your furniture?'

'Where is yours?' replied Hofetz Chaim.

'Mine?' asked the puzzled American. 'But I'm only passing through.'

'So am I,' said the rabbi.

Tales of the Hasidim

Let us not be distressed over the loss of worldly goods; such losses are a small matter. My own father taught me this early in life. When some misfortune happened at home, he would remain serene. When our house caught fire and the neighbours said, 'Ivan Petrovich, your house is burnt down,' he replied, 'With God's help I'll build it up again.' Once we were walking along the side of our field, and I said, 'Look, they're stealing our sheaves.' 'Aye, son,' he answered me, 'the Lord has given the corn and to spare, so if anyone steals it, it means he is in want.' Another day I said to him, 'You give a lot away in charity, while some who are better off than we are give far less.' To which he replied, 'Aye, son, the Lord will provide.' And the Lord did not confound his hope.
Archimandrite Sophrony

USEFUL TEXTS
Money:
    Love of, a root of evil, *1 Tim. 6:10*
    Associated with greed, *2 Kgs. 5:19-27*
    Not to be loaned for interest, *Lev. 25:37; Deut. 23:19*

See also: A7 Poor in spirit
           A21 Feeding the hungry
           C29 Not through luxury

C22
THE LIGHT OF FAITH

'It was for faith that our ancestors were commended.'
Hebrews 11:2

QUOTATIONS

Faith is the sight of the inward eye.
Alexander Maclaren

To believe is difficult. Not to believe is impossible.
Victor Hugo

The opposite of sin is not virtue but faith.
Sören Kierkegaard

Faith is not jumping to conclusions. It is concluding to jump.
W. T. Purkiser

Historial facts never create faith, only faith creates faith.
John Macquarrie

I believe in Christianity as I believe in the sun – not only because I see it, but because by it I see everything else.
C. S. Lewis

Faith is to believe what we do not see, and the reward of this faith is to see what we believe.
St Augustine of Hippo

Faith is the bird that sings while dawn is still dark.
Rabindranath Tagore

I do not want merely to possess a faith; I want a faith that possesses me.
Charles Kingsley

Faith makes the uplook good, the outlook bright, the inlook favourable, and the future glorious.
Raymond Edman

There's nothing that can help you understand your beliefs more than trying to explain them to an inquisitive child.
Frank Clark

The life of faith is a continually renewed victory over doubt, and continually renewed grasp of meaning in the midst of meaningless.
Leslie Newbign

God wants us to approach life, full of expectancy that God is going to be at work in every situation as we release our faith in him.
Colin Urquhart

PROVERBS

Fear knocked at the door. Faith answered. No one was there.
English proverb

It is by believing in roses that one brings them to bloom.
French proverb

A person consists of his faith. Whatever is his faith, even so he is.
Hindu proverb

HUMOUR

A vicar ran out of petrol, but the filling station was only 100 yards away. He hadn't an empty can, so he used the baby's potty that was in his car, to put the petrol in. As he was pouring it into the tank, one of his parishioners passed by. 'Heavens, Vicar,' he said, 'you've more faith than I have!'

A climber fell off a cliff. As he tumbled down into the deep gorge he grabbed hold of a branch of a small tree. 'Help,' he shouted. 'Is there anyone up there?' A deep majestic voice from the sky echoed through the gorge. 'I will help you, my son. But first you must have faith in me.' 'All right, all right. I trust you,' answered the man. The voice replied, 'Let go of the branch.' There was a long pause and the man shouted again, 'Is there anyone else up there?'

WORD PICTURES

One of the few famous and enduring slogans from World War II was coined by an Army Chaplain in the Philippines, namely: 'There are no atheists in foxholes.'

Artists, in a way, are religious anyhow. They have to be: if by religion one means believing that life has some significance, and some meaning, which is what I think it has. An artist couldn't work without believing that.
Henry Moore

When Moses threw the wand into the Red Sea, the sea, quite contrary to the expected miracle, did not divide itself to leave a dry passage for the Jews. Not until the first man had jumped into the sea did the promised miracle happen and the waves recede.
Jewish legend

Two friends were once going swimming, when they began discussing religion. Just as they were going into the sea, one said to the other, 'What wouldn't I give to find a faith?'
'How much do you want it?' asked his friend.
'Oh, very much indeed,' replied the seeker.
To his amazement, his friend suddenly seized him and pressed his head under water, and, in spite of his struggles, held him there till he was nearly suffocated. When at last he released his grip, and his victim could stand up and breathe again, he demanded to know what he meant by his behaviour.
'What did you want most in the world just now?' asked his friend.
'Why, air, of course,' said the seeker.
'Well,' was the response, 'when you want a faith as much as you wanted air just then, you'll find it.'
Anon

You do not have to sit outside in the dark. If, however, you want to look at the stars, you will find that the darkness is most certainly required. The stars neither require it nor demand it.
Annie Dillard

The rabbi asks his students: 'How can we determine the hour of dawn, when the night ends and the day begins?'

One of his students suggested: 'When from a distance you can distinguish between a dog and a sheep.'

'No,' was the answer of the rabbi.

'Is it when one can distinguish between a fig tree and a grapevine?' asked a second student.

'No,' said the rabbi.

'Please tell us the answer then,' said the students.

'It is, then,' said the wise teacher, 'when you can look into the face of human beings and you have enough light (in you) to recognise them as your brothers and sisters. Up until then it is night, and darkness is still with us.'
Old Hasidic tale

Five years ago I came to believe in Christ's teaching and my life suddenly changed. . . . It happened to me as it happened to a man who goes out on some business and on the way suddenly decides that the business is unnecessary and returns home. All that was on his right is now on his left and all that was on his left is now on his right; his former wish to get as far as possible from home has changed into a wish to be as near as possible to it. The direction of my life and my desires became different and good and evil changed places. . . .

I, like the thief on the cross, having believed Christ's teaching, had been saved . . . I, like the thief, knew that I was unhappy and suffering . . . I, like the thief on the cross, was nailed by some force to that life of suffering and evil. And, as, after the meaningless suffering and evils of life, the thief awaited the terrible darkness of death, so did I await the same thing.

In all this I was exactly like the thief, but the difference was that the thief was already dying while I was still living. The thief might believe that his salvation lay there beyond the grave but I could not be satisfied with that because besides a life beyond the grave life still awaited me here. But I did not understand that life. It seemed to me terrible. And suddenly I heard the words of Christ and understood them, and life and death ceased to seem to me evil, and instead of despair I experienced happiness and the joy of life undisturbed by death.

Leo Tolstoy

USEFUL TEXTS

Faith:
> Condition of salvation, *Acts 16:31*
> Way of life, *Eph. 6:16*
> Object of, *John 14:1*
> Gift of God, *Eph. 2:8*

See also: B33 Faith and good works
C30 Increase our faith

C23
ZEAL FOR WHAT IS RIGHT

'Jesus said to his disciples, "I have come to bring fire to the
earth, and how I wish it were blazing already."'
Luke 12:49

QUOTATIONS

Zeal without tolerance is fanaticism.
John Kelman

Zeal without knowledge is the sister of folly.
John Davies

Violent zeal for truth hath an hundred to one odds to be either
petulancy, ambition or pride.
Jonathan Swift

Nothing spoils human nature more than false zeal. The good
nature of a heathen is more God-like than the furious zeal of a
Christian.
Benjamin Whichcote

PROVERBS

Zeal, when it is a virtue, is a dangerous one.
English proverb

Zeal without knowledge is a runaway horse.
English proverb

WORD PICTURES

A Hindu boy came to England for his education: he was already
married! At Oxford he became interested in the Christian religion,
was converted and baptised. He was a young prince, and his first
duty on his return to his native land was to tell his father of his
new faith. The rage and grief of the parents were great. He was
turned out of the house into a cowshed, and there left, hungry and

sad. His mother brought him a dish of the favourite curry he had often longed for amid the strange meals of foreign lands but before he might eat she had a condition: 'Say, "I am not a Christian".' He refused, and the plate was taken away.

Hungrier and thirstier he grew, and at length, hearing a scratching outside, he found a low-caste man, a sweeper (whom in the old days, to touch was defilement) offering him water. Now, in spite of his ingrained repugnance, he was thankful to receive it.

The next morning he heard sounds of mourning – it had been given out that he was dead, drowned in the courtyard well – therefore his girl-wife was widowed. From the cowshed he could see her being led across the courtyard in her bright clothes and jewels, then she was thrown down, and they were torn from her, and the rest of the cruel treatment that a Hindu widow receives was dealt out to her; while the boy-husband watched, powerless to help.

That night, with the help of the friendly sweeper, he escaped to a mission station near by; later the poor little 'widow' was also discovered, and brought to Christianity, and the husband and wife were reunited in Christian marriage.

Nicholas Garlick was a yeoman's son in Derbyshire, went to Worcester College, Oxford, and became a schoolmaster at Tideswell. He had loved from his boyhood the daughter of the lord of the manor there, but she was too far above him in station, and at last he renounced his hopes and turned instead to the service of God. He became a priest at Rheims, and worked in his own county with great drive and enthusiasm. In the Armada year, 1588, he was captured in a hiding-place at Padley Hall by Topciffe (through information by a traitor) and executed with two other priests at Derby. As he stood on the ladder he suddenly threw among the crowd a number of loose papers, written in prison, in defence of the Catholic Faith. Everyone into whose hands those papers fell was subsequently received (it is said) into the Catholic Church.
F. H. Drinkwater

'If a job is worth doing, it is worth doing well.' This sums up the attitude of an engineer with an unusual name, Isambard Kingdom

Brunel. Born on 9th April, 1806, he was to become one of the greatest engineers of railways, docks, bridges, tunnels, canals, and ships.

He was the son of an engineer, Sir Marc Brunel, and followed in his father's footsteps, assisting him in building a tunnel under the Thames. But his big opportunity came when designs were invited for a bridge over the River Avon below Bristol. This bridge would have to span a deep gorge, which was no easy task, but Isambard got busy and his plans were accepted. Work began but had to stop because there was not enough money but it was finally completed after Brunel's death as a memorial to him.

Meanwhile, his enthusiasm drove him on. He had become interested in railways and became an engineer for the Great Western Railway, the present Western Region of British Rail. He was responsible for laying about 1,200 miles of railway track, for which he also designed bridges and tunnels. His railway ran from London to Bristol and beyond. But why stop there? Beyond lay the Atlantic Ocean and America. So Brunel turned his attention to the ships and designed several that were capable of crossing the Atlantic.

His greatest, *The Great Eastern*, was larger than any ship of her day and caused Brunel so much worry that he died in 1859 in bad health.

Isambard Kingdom Brunel was a man of great talent. He was never one to tackle a job half-heartedly, but took pride in his work and entered every job with great enthusiasm.
Rowland Purton

USEFUL TEXTS
Zeal:
  Of God, *2 Kings 19:31; Isa. 26:31*
  Encouraged, *1 Thess. 2:11-12*
  For Law, *Acts 21:20*
  Misguided, *Rom. 10:2*

See also: A2 Integrity
           C8 God's messengers
           C39 Doing God's will

C24
LORD OF ALL NATIONS

'I am coming to gather the nations of every language.
They shall come to witness my glory.'
Isaiah 66:18

QUOTATIONS

What will God say to us if some of us go to him without the others.
Charles Péguy

For all in common she prays,
for all in common she works,
in the temptations of all she is tried.
St Ambrose

It seems to me that catholicity is not only one of the notes of the Church, but according to the divine purposes, one of its securities.
John Henry Newman

Loyalty, nationality, particularity are essential marks of the universal Church; the local congregation is the embodiment at a given place and time of the Church of all the world.
Alan Richardson

As long as Catholicism lasts, it will feel the need for reform, for a more perfect assimilation of its actuality to the ideal which illumines its path.
Karl Adam

WORD PICTURES

In 1869, after great labour, Dr J. G. Paton printed his first book, a translation into Aniwan of various passages of Scripture. He had to work with a broken press and scanty type, but after long and patient toil the volume was ready for his people.

One old chief had a great desire to 'hear it speak'. While the book was being printed Namakei came, morning after morning, saying: 'Missi, it is done? Can it speak?' 'At last,' says Dr Paton, 'I could say yes.' 'Does it speak my words?' asked the chief. 'It does.' 'Let me hear it speak.'

I read to him a few sentences, and he fairly shouted for joy. 'It speaks my own language! Oh give it to me.' He grasped it, turned it round every way, and closing it with a look of great disappointment, handed it back, saying, 'I cannot make it speak. It will never speak to me!'

'You do not know how to make it speak yet,' I answered, 'I will teach you.' As I showed him the book again I noticed the old chief strained his eyes, and I suspected he could not see the letters through the dimness of age. I hunted up a pair of spectacles and managed to fit him. At first he was afraid to put them on, thinking of sorcery. At last he yielded, and was overjoyed to see the letters clearly. He cried: 'I see it all now! This is what you told us about Jesus. He opened the eyes of blind men. The word of Jesus has come to Aniwan. He has sent me these glass eyes. I have got back the sight I had when I was a boy.'

I drew ABC on the sand in large letters, and showed him the same on the book. Fixing these in his mind, he exclaimed: 'I have lifted up ABC! They are here in my head, and I will hold them fast. Give me other three.'

He learnt very fast. He used to say to the young people: 'You say it is hard to read. But be strong and try. If an old man like me can do it, how much easier it ought to be for you.'
Anon

The word 'catholic' – the adverb is *kath' 'olou*, or the later adjective *katholikos*, rendered in Latin by the loan word 'catholicus' or 'universalis' means: referring to or directed towards the whole, general. In classical Greek the word is used above all for general statements (universals as distinct from individuals) . . . In the New Testament the word is used once (Acts 4:18) as an adverb meaning 'thoroughly', 'completely', 'totally'.
Hans Kung

At Lindisfarne Aidan trained a number of Northumbrian boys who became prominent in the Church, among them Chad, later bishop of Lichfield, and Wilfrid who became bishop of York. Wilfrid travelled south to Canterbury, went on to Rome and decided that the customs of his own church were wrong and that Rome was right. He was a quarrelsome man and an enthusiastic convert to the Roman view. Back in Northumbria he led a party against his own bishop, Colman, who, like Aidan, had come back from Iona. The king supported Colman; the queen, a Kentish princess, backed Wilfrid. The king decided that this must stop. The controversy was not only unseemly but awkward. The king, for instance, found himself keeping Easter while the queen had got no further than Palm Sunday. He called a synod at Whitby which Bede described. As a result Colman returned to his native Ireland. The Northumbrian church became fully integrated in the Western Church, but it long retained, especially in the field of art, the marks of its Celtic origin.

Anon

USEFUL TEXTS

Nation:
  Gospel preached to every, *Matt. 24:14; Rev. 14:6*
  Believers from every, *Rev. 15:9*
  All organically connected, *Acts 17:26*
  Abraham father of many, *Gen. 17:4-5*

See also: A6 Light of the world
  B8 The Word
  B28 The Father who draws us to himself
  C12 The Church for all people

C25
HUMILITY

'For all who exalt themselves will be humbled and
those who humble themselves will be exalted.'
Luke 14:11

QUOTATIONS

Humility is the truth about ourselves loved.
C. Carey-Elwes

It is always the secure who are humble.
G. K. Chesterton

I believe the first test of a truly great man is his humility.
John Ruskin

Who is free from defects? He lacks everything who thinks he lacks
nothing.
St Bernard of Clairvaux

The only wisdom we can hope to acquire is the wisdom of
humility – humility is endless.
T. S. Eliot

The greatest among men is always ready to serve and yet is
unconscious of the service.
Helena P. Blavatsky

Pride changed angels into devils; humility makes men into angels.
St Augustine of Hippo

Whosoever therefore grounds his virtue in humility, he shall never
err.
John of Ruysbroeck

We do not have to acquire humility. There is humility in us – only we humiliate ourselves before false gods.
Simone Weil

Humility is the luxurious art of reducing ourselves to a point, not to a small thing or a large one, but to a thing with no size at all, so that to it all the cosmic things are what they really are – of immeasurable stature.
G. K. Chesterton

Holiness is not in one exercise or another, it consists in a disposition of the heart, which renders us humble and little in the hands of God, conscious of our weakness but confident, even daringly confident, in his fatherly goodness.
St Thérèse of Lisieux

It is certain that the poor more easily achieve the blessing of humility than the rich. Gentleness goes with poverty, pride more commonly with riches. And yet, very many rich people do use their wealth for works of charity rather than as a means to puff their pride. This spirit counts as among its greatest profits what it spends in relieving distress and hardship in others.
St Leo the Great

PROVERBS

Too much humility is pride.
German proverb

The boughs that bear most hang lowest.
English proverb

HUMOUR

'I used to be terribly conceited.'
   'Really?'
   'Yes, but my psychiatrist straightened me out, and now I'm one of the nicest guys in town!'

A rather pompous landowner met a local farmer one morning and said to him: 'Why, Brown, you're getting quite bent. Why don't you stand up straight, like me?'

In reply, Farmer Brown said: 'Do you see yon field of corn?' And when the other nodded, went on, 'Well, you'll notice that the full heads hang down, and the empty ones stand up.'

If I think I'm in danger of getting carried away with the notion of my own importance, I remember what the girl from Madam Tussaud's said when she came to see me. I asked her what happened if people they have made images of cease to be personalities. 'Well,' she said, 'we did melt down Alan Ladd last week.'

As far as I am concerned, that's just about the size of it.
André Previn

WORD PICTURES

If you want to realise your own importance, put your finger into a bowl of water, take it out and look at the hole.
Robert Burdette

There is a story told of Mr Gladstone who invited his tenants and workers to dinner. It was a very good dinner, served in the very best style, complete with napkins and finger bowls.

One man who had never been at such a dinner before started drinking from his finger bowl. Some guests who knew the real purpose of the bowls started sniggering, whereupon Mr Gladstone immediately lifted his finger bowl and drank from it.
Anon

There is no true and constant gentleness without humility; while we are so fond of ourselves, we are easily offended with others. Let us be persuaded that nothing is due to us, and then nothing will disturb us. Let us often think of our own infirmities, and we shall become indulgent towards those of others.
Francis Fenelon

If ever I'm disappointed with my lot in life, I stop and think about little Jamie Scott. Jamie was trying for a part in his school play. His mother told me that he'd set his heart on being in it, though she feared he would not be chosen.

On the day the parts were awarded, I went with her to collect him after school. Jamie rushed up, eyes shining with pride and excitement. Then he said those words that remain a lesson to me: 'I've been chosen to clap and cheer.'
Marie Curling

A reporter who once asked the great Italian composer, Giuseppe Verdi for his full postal address, was told:
   'I think that *Italy* will be sufficient.'

Years ago a young American girl visited the home of Beethoven. She sat down at the piano of the great artist and played through with pride his *Moonlight Sonata*. When she had finished she turned to the stern old caretaker of the house and said to him, 'I suppose many great people come here?' 'Yes,' said the man, 'Paderewski was here last week.' 'And did he play on Beethoven's piano?' she asked. 'No,' said the old man; 'he said he wasn't worthy.'
Southern Churchman

In order to depict our Christian path more clearly, let us adopt the method of the Fathers and make an analogy. When we look at an ancient tree reaching high up to the clouds, we know that its roots, deep in the ground, must be correspondingly powerful. If the roots did not stretch down into the dark depths of the earth, as deep, perhaps, as the tree is high; if the mass and strength of the roots did not parallel the size and weight of the visible part of the tree, they could not nourish the tree or keep it upright – the lightest breeze would blow it down. So it is in man's spiritual life. If we recognise the greatness of our calling in Christ – that we have been chosen before the foundation of the world (Ephesians 1:4) by the eternal Divine Providence to receive the adoption of sons (Galatians 4:5) – we shall be, not puffed up but genuinely

humble. A downward movement, into the blackness of hell, is indispensable for all of us if we are to continue steadfast in the Christian spirit. So we must be ever conscious of our primeval nothingness, continually condemning ourselves harshly in all things. And the more man abases himself in self-condemnation, the higher will God exalt him. 'I tell you . . . every one that exalteth himself shall be abased; and he that humbleth himself shall be exalted' (Luke 18:14).
Archimandrite Sophrony

USEFUL TEXTS

Humility:
  Of Christ, *Matt. 11:29*
  God teaches, *Deut. 8:3*
  God is with those who have, *Isa. 57:15*
  Of a child, *Matt. 18:4*

See also: A2 Integrity
           A7 Poor in spirit
           A10 Seeking perfection
           B20 Growth to maturity

C26

THE HUMAN CONDITION

'A perishable body presses down the soul, and this tent
of clay weighs down the teeming mind.'
Wisdom 9:15

QUOTATIONS

We are never so happy or so unhappy as we think.
La Rochefoucald

What history does is to uncover man's universal sin.
Herbert Butterfield

Human nature will find itself only when it fully realises that to be
human it has to cease to be beastly or brutal.
Mahatma Gandhi

All one's life is music, if one touched the notes rightly and in tune.
John Ruskin

We grumble because God puts thorns with roses; wouldn't it be
better to thank God that he puts roses with thorns.
O. S. Marden

Humanity does not pass through phases as a train passes through
a station: being alive, it has the privilege of always moving yet
never leaving anything behind. Whatever we have been, in some
sort we are still.
C. S. Lewis

The children of Israel did not find in the manna all the sweetness
and strength they might have found in it; not because the manna
did not contain them, but because they longed for other meat.
St John of the Cross

The Cross looks grim, but one thing is sure. That dream of perfect bliss which lures us to evade it will not come true. The primrose path of dalliance is early overrun with briers; and if we must be pierced with thorns, it is more kingly to wear them as a crown.
B. H. Streeter

If humanity is shaped by its surroundings, its surroundings must be made human.
Karl Marx

To be really alive, to be really human, one needs . . . discipline, wisdom, artistry, and a little foolishness.
Anon

I haven't asked you to make me young again. All I want is to go on getting older.
Konrad Adenauer's reply to his doctor

PROVERBS
He does not cleanse himself of his sins who denies them.
Latin proverb

HUMOUR
When you're down in the mouth, think of the Prophet Jonah. He came out all right!
American business motto

Eve was so jealous of Adam that when he came home each night she used to count his ribs!

Two youngsters in different pre-Easter Baptismal classes were overheard exchanging notes on their progress. One announced proudly, 'We're up to original sin.' 'That's nothing,' scoffed the other. 'We're past redemption.'
Morton Sands

Can you imagine what the life of Adam and Eve must have been in the Garden of Eden before the apple episode? The inescapable monotony of their existence! Eve put up the job about the apple. What was the result? They were fired from the Garden of Eden. Adam got a job and went to work. Eve got some clothes to wear, and when they met at night, they had something to talk about.
Daniel Frohman

WORD PICTURES

There's something that pulls us upwards
and there's something that pulls us down;
and the consequence is we wobbles
twixt muck and a golden crown.
Anon

Over every aspect of human life there hangs the prospect of a possible better, inviting us to achieve it, but without proof that we shall succeed, or even that it is worth our while to make the attempt. The coward within asks for the proof; crying out that the venture is not safe, and summoning the will to disbelieve has no difficulty in finding reasons for rejecting the invitation. The hero, on the contrary, finds in the terms offered the exact conditions to which his nature is fitted to respond. He finds his own nature as hero exquisitely adapted to the nature of the universe as dangerous – on that side the ringing challenge, on this the joyous response; man and the universe engaged together as loyal confederates in the task of creating a better-than-what-is.
L. P. Jacks

There is an old tale about Satan walking in the Street of Life, sulking in the shadows with his hunting dogs, the little imps of human weakness. A man, Albert, came walking down the street; Satan said to a little imp, scowling with a bitter face: 'Go, get him for me!' Quickly the imp crossed the street, silently and lightly hopped to the man's shoulder. In his ear he whispered, 'You are discouraged.' 'No,' said the man, 'I am not discouraged.' 'You are discouraged!' insisted the imp. This time the man replied, 'I don't think I am.' Louder and more decidedly, the little imp repeated, 'I tell you, you are discouraged.' Albert dropped his head and murmured: 'Well, I suppose I am.' The little imp darted back to Satan and said proudly, 'I've got him; he's discouraged.'

Another man, Carlson, passed. Again, old Satan said: 'Get him for me!' The proud little demon of discouragement repeated his tactics. The first time he said, 'You are discouraged,' the man replied, emphatically, 'No.' The second time Carlson replied, 'I tell you I am not discouraged.' The third time he said, 'You lie! I am not discouraged,' and he walked down the street, his head erect, going straight towards the light. The imp of discouragement returned to his master, crestfallen. 'I couldn't get him,' he reported. 'Three times I told him he was discouraged. The third time, he called me a liar, and that discouraged me!'
P. Fontaine

The point was emphasised when Gill Pickup quoted an American headteacher, who had once told her staff: 'I am a survivor of a concentration camp. My eyes saw what no person should witness. Gas chambers built by learned engineers. Children poisoned by educated physicians. Infants killed by trained nurses. Women and babies shot and burned by high school and college graduates. So I am suspicious of education. My request is: help your students become human. Your efforts must never produce learned monsters, skilled psychopaths, educated Eichmanns. Reading, writing and arithmetic are important only if they serve to make our children more human.'
ATL Report

See also: A15 Sin
            A38 Original Sin
            B22 Death
            B49 Coping with doubt
            C37 Temptation

C27
THE FATHER WHO RECEIVES US BACK

'His father saw him and was moved with pity. He ran to the boy,
clasped him in his arms and kissed him tenderly.'
Luke 15:20

QUOTATIONS

Going away from the Father always brings with it a great destruction.
Pope John Paul II

That which you confess today, you will perceive tomorrow.
Coventry Patmore

The only true forgiveness is that which is offered and extended
even before the offender has apologised and sought it.
Sören Kierkegaard

God likes forgiving big sins more than small ones. The bigger they
are the gladder he is and the quicker to forgive them.
Meister Eckhart

WORD PICTURES

In the timber mountains of the Northwest of USA a five-year-old
boy was lost. Night came. The citizens and rangers searched
frantically every cave and mountainside. Snow began to fall.
Blanket upon blanket covered the forest floor, but no Bobby
could be found. The next morning the father, fatigued from an all-
night search, kicked against what seemed to be a log in the path,
but when the snow fell loose, a small boy sat up, stretched,
yawned, and exclaimed: 'Oh, Daddy! I've found you at last!'

The singing nun who topped the charts world-wide with her song,
Dominique, was found dead yesterday after taking a drug over-
dose. Sister Smile – Jeannine Deckes – committed suicide with

companion Annie Berchet. A note from both of them said: 'We are going together to meet God our Father. He alone can save us from financial disaster.' Their bodies were found in the 52-year-old ex-nun's flat in Ware, Brussels.

Sister Smile's record in 1963 made her a star – a film starring Debbie Reynolds was even made of her life – but she died penniless. Three years ago she was ordered to pay tax on royalties. But her ex-convent had taken the income from the record.
Daily Mail

For the Father only one thing is important: that his son has been found again; that he has not completely lost his humanity; that, in spite of everything, he has the firm resolve to live again as a son, precisely because of his awareness of his unworthiness and sin. 'Father I have sinned, I no longer deserve to be called your Son.' Our reconciliation with God, the return to the Father's house, is carried out by means of Christ. His passion and death on the Cross are set between every human conscience, every human sin, and the infinite love of the Father. This love – ready to raise and forgive – is nothing but mercy.

Each of us, in personal conversion, in the firm resolution to change our ways, agrees to carry out a personal spiritual labour, which is the prolongation and reflection on the saving work of our Redeemer. Here is what Paul, the Apostle of reconciliation, says: 'For our sake God made the sinless one into sin, so that in him we might become the goodness of God' (2 Corinthians 5:21).
Pope John Paul II

See also: A26 The Sacrament of Penance
          B28 The Father who draws us to himself
          C20 Our Father in heaven
          C41 Starting afresh

C28
LORD OF THE OPPRESSED

'From the dust he lifts up the lowly, from the dungheap he raises the poor to set them in the company of princes.'
Psalm 112

QUOTATIONS

While hunger rules, peace cannot prevail.
Patrick O'Mahony

Everyone who accepts God in Christ accepts him through the cross.
Pope John Paul II

Theirs is an endless road, a hopeless maze, who seek for goods before they seek for God.
St Bernard of Clairvaux

HUMOUR

A millionaire entered a Post Office and saw an elderly couple standing at the counter drawing their old age pensions. Going up to them he said: 'How would you like to spend a week at my residence? I will give you both a wonderful time.'

Well, the old couple agreed and so the millionaire took them off to his house in his Rolls and as he had promised, saw that they had a really good holiday, with excellent food, colour television and many luxuries which they never dreamed they would ever have. At the end of the week he walked into the library where the old boy was enjoying a quiet glass of wine and smoking a cigar. 'Well,' he said, 'have you enjoyed yourself?' 'Indeed, I have,' the old boy replied. 'But, can I ask you a question?' 'Certainly,' replied the millionaire. 'Then,' said the other, 'who's the old woman I've been sleeping with all the week?'

WORD PICTURES

It is infinitely easier to suffer in obedience to a human command than to accept suffering as free, responsible men. It is infinitely

easier to suffer with others than to suffer alone. It is infinitely easier to suffer as public heroes than to suffer apart and in ignominy. It is infinitely easier to suffer physical death than to endure spiritual suffering. Christ suffered as a free man alone, apart and in ignominy, in body and in spirit, and since that day many Christians have suffered with him.
Dietrich Bonhoeffer

John Wesley was walking one day with a worried man who expressed his doubt of God's goodness. 'I don't know what I shall do with all this worry and trouble,' he said. At that moment Wesley noticed a cow looking over a stone wall. 'Do you know,' asked Wesley, 'why that cow is looking over that wall?' 'No,' replied his troubled companion. 'I will tell you,' said Wesley – 'because she cannot see through it. That is what you must do with your wall of trouble – look over it and above it.'
Anon

For not only did Christ die and rise again many years ago but with his death and resurrection he has struck the chords of human history with a note that goes on ringing across the centuries until the end of time. . . . He dies in every prisoner of conscience, in every woman who cannot feed her children, in all those who suffer in Northern Ireland and in those whose racial origins place them at the margin of our society. He rises today in every peasant who wins the right to land on which to grow food for those he loves; in every person unjustly imprisoned who is set free . . . and in every country whose people win the struggle for self-determination.
Liverpool Pastoral Congress Official Report

A man I know was badly injured by a drunken motorist at the age of 15. His leg was amputated, but he happily married, until, after six years, his wife left him for another man. Yet he was determined to make the best of life and work for others, which he did. Then he got the idea of starting up a pen-friendship with a cripple worse off than himself.

He was put in touch with a fellow who had been struck on the

head by a cricket ball at the age of nine and who had lost all use of his arms and legs; an incurable who had been in hospital for over 40 years. This man answered my friend with a three-page letter from which cheerfulness, optimism and good spirits shone through every sentence. And how do you think he ended his letter? 'I thank God,' he said, 'I thank God that I'm able to write my own letters by holding the pen in my mouth.'
Gordon Albion

What Christ did was to use the suffering he encountered as a gate through which to enter a new dimension of love, faith and courage. Humanly speaking he became a richer personality and the effects of his response – 'Father forgive them'; 'Into thy hands I commend my spirit' – have spilled over and proved psychologically as well as ontologically redemptive for many from his own time until ours. He does not explain the why of suffering, he does not glorify it, but he identified it as a vital material in the making of ourselves.
John Harriott

USEFUL TEXTS

Oppression:
    Deliverance from, *Ps. 72:4*
    Commanded to relieve, *Isa. 1:17*
    Of poor and needy, *Amos. 4:1; 5:11*
    Not to be guilty of, *Lev. 25:14*

See also: A21 Feeding the hungry
             B15 Jesus, friend of outcasts
             B38 The suffering servant
             B50 The Good Shepherd

C29
NOT THROUGH LUXURY

'Woe to those ensconced so smugly in Zion and to those
who feel so safe on the mountain of Samaria.'
Amos 6:1

QUOTATIONS

Superfluities do not hurt.
St Augustine of Hippo

Too much plenty makes the mouth dainty.
Benjamin Franklin

Luxury is an enticing pleasure, a bastard mirth, which hath honey
in her mouth, gall in her heart, and a sting in her tail.
Francis Quarles

Luxury is the first, second and third cause of ruin of reputation.
It is the vampire which soothes us into a fatal slumber while it
sucks the lifeblood of our veins.
Hamilton Malue

Most of the luxuries and many of the so-called comforts of life are
not only not indispensable, but positive hindrances to the elevation
of mankind.
H. D. Thoreau

PROVERBS

If you have no money, be polite.
Danish proverb

When your fortune increases, the columns of your house appear
to be crooked.
Armenian proverb

WORD PICTURES

An ancient seal of the Moravian Church shows an ox standing loose, between a plough and an altar, with the motto, 'Prepare for labour or sacrifice.'

A poor mother when asked why she was spending precious money to exchange her black and white television set for a colour receiver, replied, 'I don't want my children growing up not knowing what colour is!'

Pervading materialism imposes its dominion on man today in many different forms and with an aggressiveness that spares no one. The most sacred principles, which were the sure guides for the behaviour of individuals, and society, are being hollowed out by false pretences concerning freedom, the sacredness of life, the indissolubility of marriage, the true sense of human sexuality, the right attitude towards the material goods that progress has to offer.

Many people now are tempted to self-indulgence and consumerism, and human identity is often defined by what one owns. Prosperity and affluence, even when they are only beginning to be available to larger strata of society, tend to make people assume that they have a right to all that prosperity can bring, and thus they can become more selfish in their demands.

Everybody wants a full freedom in all the areas of human behaviour and new models of morality are being proposed in the name of would-be freedom. When the moral fibre of a nation is weakened, when the sense of personal responsibility is diminished, then the door is open for the justification of injustice, for violence in all its forms, and for the manipulation of the many by the few. The challenge that is already with us is the temptation to accept as true freedom what in reality is only a new form of slavery.
Pope John Paul II

See also: A7   Poor in spirit
              A21 Feeding the hungry
              C21 Rise above materialism

C30
INCREASE OUR FAITH

The apostles said to the Lord, 'Increase our faith.'
Luke 17:5

QUOTATIONS

The religion of the atheist has a God-shaped blank at its heart.
H. G. Wells

When faith becomes blind, it dies.
Mahatma Ghandi

A simple, childlike faith in a Divine Friend solves all the problems that come to us by land or sea.
Helen Keller

If a man believes and knows God, he can no longer ask, 'What is the meaning of my life?' But by believing he actually lives the meaning of his life.
Karl Barth

Faith always implies the disbelief of a lesser fact in favour of a greater. A little mind often sees the unbelief without seeing the belief of a large one.
Oliver Wendell Holmes

Faith is a crusade – no weaklings need apply. No, I take that back. For we have here a regimen that makes weak men strong and cowards brave.
Henry M. Edmonds

If we desire to enter into our supernatural inheritance, the deep tranquillity of faith, coming unto God, must be completely absorbed by the thought that he is; and rewards, in such ways as we can endure, them – and them only – that diligently seek him for his own sake alone.
Evelyn Underhill

I can't understand how all this can happen. It's enough to make one lose one's faith in God!
Eva Braun writing to a friend from Hitler's bunker during the siege and bombing of Berlin in April 1945

All I have seen teaches me to trust the Creator for all I have not seen.
Ralph Waldo Emerson

I cannot hear what you say for listening to what you are.
Robert Louis Stevenson

HUMOUR

The vicar was explaining the difference between knowledge and faith to his congregation.

'In the front row,' he said, 'we have Mr Heather with his wife and three children. Now, she *knows* they are her children – that's knowledge. He *believes* they are his children – that's faith.'

WORD PICTURES

Was it Archimedes who said, 'Give me a lever long enough and a place to put it on, and I will move the world'? There is such a lever, and it is called 'Faith'; there is a place to put it on, and it is called 'God'; and there is a power that can swing that lever, and it is called 'Man'.
Richard M. Steiner

It is the custom in Edinburgh for four buglers to blow out the 'last post' each evening from the castle. There is a legend, which lingered late among some of the citizens, that long ago one of the buglers was murdered at the place of duty; and it was believed that on the last day in March, the anniversary of the crime, after the buglers had sounded their call, those who listened might hear another peal – the summons of the ghostly bugler.

Amid the many challenging cries of today there are still heard the voices of some who stand upon their towers calling men to faith and loyalty. The most authoritative voices of the day challenge the hearts of men to believe.
Anon

A vessel was stranded on a sand bar in Dublin harbour. Tugboats tugged and foamed trying to pull her off, but without avail. A giant stationary engine was brought, cables laid, but the vessel did not budge. A college lad, standing by, said, 'If you'll bring me two barges, I'll take her off.' The barges were brought. 'Place them one on either side of the vessel. Then run the cables under the vessel and fasten them firmly to the two barges.' This done he said, 'Now wait for the tide.' And when God's great ocean began to come in with the tide the barges began to creak, the cables strained, and up rose the stranded vessel, free.
H. S. Putnam

There comes a time in your life, when you play as it were a game of cards against Faith. It is the oldest of all games: you and she, across the green table of Earth, are confronted; and the rule is, that you play first. You sit and stare, across the table, at the backs of her cards. You have a strong hand: you hold the cruelty of Nature, and the iniquities of Man; the facts of drink, insanity, inherited disease; the misery of the unemployed. What a hand you have got, what a hand! Come, you begin. Those eighteen, on whom the town of Siloam fell, and slew them – try that card. The game sways now to you, now to her, till the fan of your hand is thinned. You will find that she, no less than you, has a strong hand, stronger than you thought: and, if you live long enough, she is likely to win. For she holds, with much else that is worth having, certain cards you will never beat: and she is an old and skilful player. Be careful to keep your temper over the game: and, of course, you play not for money but for Love.
Stephen Paget

Freda was a neighbour and a devoted member of our Church community. Her husband retired from the RAF, then worked for Southend Airport, but retired early because of ill health. We all admired Freda because she was so loyal to her non-Christian, unbelieving husband who was only interested in aircraft and socialising in the local club; he was renowned for his consumption of alcohol and his womanising. Through many infidelities Freda would say, 'He may be unfaithful to me, but one day he will need me.'

Eventually his health deteriorated and he was housebound and dependent upon his wife who cared faithfully for him. He was at home for four years. He learnt that he had cancer.

One day, as Pastoral Lay Assistant, I thought a visit was long overdue, although we saw Freda on a Sunday, and on calling learnt that Phil had just been admitted to hospital. I promised to visit him in hospital, but a few days later, before I could do so, I received a call from Freda at the hospital. She told me that Phil had just died; she had been with him all night and the family had arrived that morning. She asked if I would go to the hospital and say a prayer with them. With the parish priest's approval I arrived at the quiet room just off the hospital ward.

Phil lay just as he had died; a daughter was holding his hand and sobbing; the elder daughter and his two sons stood stoically by. Freda seemed relaxed and welcoming. I said appropriate prayers from the Ritual and then stepped back to put a comforting arm around Freda. She told me that while they were alone during the night Phil had regained consciousness and asked her to pray with him. This was an answer to her prayers because he was not only not baptised, he had never shown any interest in religion. After a while he lapsed into unconsciousness. Freda then asked, 'Did I do the right thing?' 'What was that?' I asked. 'Well I got some water and baptised him. Do you think that I did the right thing?' 'Yes,' I replied confidently, 'I'm sure you did.' Freda had had more than enough faith for the both of them.

A. P. Castle

See also: B33 Faith and good works
C22 The Light of faith

526

C31
THANKSGIVING

'Finding himself cured, one of them turned back praising God
at the top of his voice and threw himself at the feet of
Jesus and thanked him.'
Luke 17:15-16

QUOTATIONS

Be thankful for the least gift, so shalt thou be meet to receive greater.
Thomas à Kempis

There is as much greatness of mind in acknowledging a good turn
as in doing it.
Seneca

The worship most acceptable to God comes from a thankful and
cheerful heart.
Plutarch

God has two dwellings – one in heaven and the other in a thankful
heart.
Isaak Walton

Pride slays thanksgiving, but a humble mind is the soil out of
which thanks naturally grow.
Henry Ward Beecher

A thankful heart is not only the greatest virtue, but the parent of
all the other virtues.
Cicero

Gratitude is the fairest blossom which springs from the soul.
Ballou

There is not a more pleasing exercise of the mind than gratitude.
Joseph Addison

Let never day nor night unhallowed pass but still remember what the Lord hath done.
William Shakespeare

O Lord, that lends me life, lend me a heart replete with thankfulness!
William Shakespeare

Thanksgiving for a farmer, doth invite God to bestow a second benefit.
Robert Henrick

PROVERB

Who does not thank for little will not thank for much.
Estonian proverb

HUMOUR

A little girl was going to a party and her mother told her to be a good girl and to remember, when she was leaving, to thank her hostess. When she arrived home the mother asked if she had thanked her hostess and the little girl replied: 'No, the girl in front of me did and the lady said, 'Don't mention it' – so I didn't.'

WORD PICTURES

My little daughter said, 'Daddy, I am going to count the stars.' 'Very well,' I said, 'go on.' By-and-by I heard her counting, 'Two hundred and twenty-three, two hundred and twenty-four. Oh dear!' she said, 'I had no idea there were so many!'

I sometimes say in my soul, 'Now, Master, I am going to count your blessings.' Soon my heart sighs, not with sorrow, but burdened with such goodness, and I say to myself, 'I had no idea that there were so many.'
Mark Pearse

If one should give me a dish of sand and tell me there were particles of iron in it, I might look for them with my eyes, and search for

them with my clumsy fingers, and be unable to detect them; but let me take a magnet and sweep through it, and how would it draw itself the almost invisible particles by the mere power of attraction! The unthankful heart, like my finger in the sand, discovers no mercies; but let the thankful heart sweep through the day, and as the magnet finds the iron, so it will find in every hour some heavenly blessings; only the iron in God's sand is gold.
Henry Ward Beecher

The legend goes that two angels were once sent down from heaven, each with a basket. They went from place to place, to poor houses and rich houses, visiting the children saying their prayers, the people in the churches, old and young. Then at length they came flying back with their loads. The basket borne by one angel was laden, but that of the other was very light, hardly worthwhile, one would have thought, to go so far and collect so little. 'What have you in your basket?' asked one angel of the other. 'I was sent to collect the prayers of all the people who said, 'I want', and 'Please give me', answered the angel who carried the heavy load. 'And what have you in yours?' 'Oh,' replied the other angel, sadly, 'I have been sent to collect the "Thank yous" of all the people to whom the great God had sent a blessing; but see how few have remembered to give!'

Would you know who is the greatest saint in the world? It is not he who prays most or fasts most; it is not he who gives most alms, but it is he who is always thankful to God, who receives everything as an instance of God's goodness and has a heart always ready to praise God for it.

If anyone would tell you the shortest, surest way to all happiness and perfection, he must tell you to make a rule to thank and praise God for everything that happens to you. Whatever seeming calamity happens to you, if you thank and praise God for it, you turn it into a blessing. Could you therefore work miracles you could not do more for yourself than by this thankful spirit; it turns all that it touches into happiness.
William Law

529

USEFUL TEXTS

Thanksgiving:
   Response of believer, *Col. 2:7*
   To accompany prayer, *Phil. 4:6*
   Offered to God, *Pss. 69:30, 100:4, 147:7*

See also: A17 Gentleness
            A39 The Glory of God
            A48 Worship
            B41 Generosity

C32
PRAYER

'Now will not God see justice done to his chosen who cry to him day and night even when he delays to help them?'
Luke 18:7

QUOTATIONS

Prayer is the key of the morning and the bolt of the evening.
Mahatma Ghandi

A generous prayer is never presented in vain.
Robert Louis Stevenson

Prayer enlarges the heart until it is capable of containing God's gift of himself.
Mother Teresa

Real power in prayer flows only when man's spirit touches God's spirit.
Catherine Marshall

The biggest problem in prayer is how to 'let go and let God'.
Glenn Clark

The degree of our faith is the degree of our prayer. The strength of our hope is the strength of our prayer. The warmth of our charity is the warmth of our prayer.
Carlo Carretto

Man discovers that mortification of the senses and the mastery of the body, confer on prayer a greater efficacy.
Pope John Paul II

Really to pray is to stand to attention in the presence of the King and to be prepared to take orders from him.
Donald Coggan

When one is in very great pain and fear it is extremely difficult to pray coherently, and I could only raise my mind in anguish to God and ask for strength to hold on.
Sheila Cassidy

We know that it is God's will that we should ask. We are not absolutely sure that it is his Will that he should grant. If we were quite sure what God intended to do, we should not pray.
John H. Newman

When you long to pray as much as you long to breathe when your head is being held under water – only then can I teach you to pray.
Anon

Those who know the path to God can find it in the dark.
Ian Maclaren

We can do nothing unless divine aid supports us. This divine aid is at hand for all who seek it with truly humble and devout heart. To seek thus is to sigh for divine aid in fervent prayer. Prayer then is the mother and origin of every upward striving of the soul.
St Bonaventure

PROVERB

Pray to God in the storm – but keep on rowing.
Danish proverb

WORD PICTURES

They asked the abbot Macarius, saying, 'How ought we to pray?' and the old man said, 'There is no need of much speaking in prayer, but often stretch out thy hands and say, "Lord, as Thou wilt and as Thou knowest, have mercy upon me." But if there is war in thy soul, add, "Help me." And because he knoweth what we have need of, he showeth us his mercy.'

Spin carefully,
spin prayerfully,
leaving the thread with God.
Anon

Two went to pray! Or rather say
one went to brag, th' other to pray:

one stands up close and treads on high,
where th' other dares not send his eye;

one nearer to God's altar trod,
the other to the altar's God.
R. Crashaw

A Hindu fable illustrates a better kind of prayer, in which we can see a great truth:
Once the birds could not fly, but grovelled and crept and hopped about, seeing nothing above the hedges, bearing on their backs a heavy and – to them apparently – useless weight of feathers. One day they decided to bear it no longer, and stretched and wriggled to get rid of the burden: and behold! their very efforts unfolded their wings which bore them aloft, soaring up to God's blue vault of heaven.

We are told that at the top of every music manuscript of the great Johann Sebastian Bach appear the two Latin words: 'Iesu, iuval!' – 'Jesus, help!' The world's mightiest master of music did not dare place his fingers on the organ or compose a single melody without first calling on his Lord for help.
Anon

A small boy was seen kneeling reverently as if in prayer, but the words he was heard to be saying were the letters of the alphabet! The sympathetic grown-up who had watched this, on questioning the little chap, found out that he knew God liked his children to pray to him but he didn't know any prayers, so he was telling him the alphabet, which he had just learnt.
Anon

A thought-provoking story comes from Christine Benson, a project worker for Central Bradford Baptist Fellowship – not the kind of background one usually associates with inter-faith

worship. She tells of a visit she paid to a Muslim friend just after she had had 'rather an upsetting meeting'. It was coming up to prayer time so she asked her Muslim friend to pray for her. Christine Benson tells how 'I sat on the settee and I prayed my prayer, and she knelt in the corner and she prayed her prayer. And we were virtually praying together. And then, when she finished praying, she sat by me and she said, 'What is it that has upset you?' And I shared it with her, and she put her arms round me and we were so close we were just like sisters.
The Tablet

The fool's prayer
The royal feast was done; the king
sought some new sport to banish care,
and to his jester cried: 'Sir Fool,
kneel now, and make for us a prayer!'

The jester doffed his cap and bells,
and stood the mocking court before;
they could not see the bitter smile
behind the painted grin he wore.

He bowed his head, and bent his knee
upon the monarch's silken stool;
his pleading voice arose: *O Lord,
be merciful to me, a fool!*

No pity, Lord, could change the heart
from red with wrong to white as wool;
the rod must heal the sin; but, Lord,
be merciful to me, a fool!

'Tis not by guilt the onward sweep
of truth and right, O Lord, we stay;
'tis by our follies that so long
we hold the earth from heaven away.

These clumsy feet, still in the mire,
go crushing blossoms without end;
these hard, well-meaning hands we thrust
among the heart-strings of a friend.

The ill-timed truth we might have kept –
who knows how sharp it pierced and stung!
The word we had not sense to say –
who knows how gladly it had rung!

Our faults no tenderness should ask,
the chastening stripes must cleanse them all;
but for our blunders – O, in shame
before the eyes of heaven we fall.

Earth bears no balsam for mistakes;
men crown the knave and scourge the tool
that did his will; but thou, O Lord,
be merciful to me, a fool!

The room was hushed; in silence rose
the king, and sought his gardens cool,
and walked apart, and murmured low,
Be merciful to me, a fool!
Rowland Hill

USEFUL TEXTS

Prayer:
    Of Christ, *John 17*
    Hindrance to, *1 Pet. 3:7*
    Continuing in, *Col. 4:2*
    Of faith, *James 5:15*
    Of the righteous, *Prov. 15:29*

See also: A22 Seeking God
                A48 Worship
                B25 Quiet – time for prayer
                B29 The Eucharist

C33
EQUALITY

'The Lord is a judge who is no respecter of personages.'
Ecclesiasticus 35:12

QUOTATIONS

It is not true that some human beings are by nature superior and others inferior. All men are equal in their natural dignity.
Pope John XXIII

He who treats as equal those who are far below him in strength really makes them a gift of the quality of human beings, of which fate has deprived them.
Simone Weil

I want to be the white man's brother, not his brother-in-law.
Martin Luther King

One man is as good as another – and a great dale bether, as the Irish Philosopher said.
William M. Thackeray

PROVERBS

Before God and the bus driver we are all equal.
German proverb

We are all born equal, and are distinguished alone by virtue.
Latin proverb

HUMOUR

The two farm hands were having an argument and Garge, who had 'discovered' the amazing new principle that all men were equals, was having great difficulty in making Willum understand the principles of his new-found creed. 'It's share and share alike,' he said, 'If you've got something someone else hasn't, then you give them half.' Willum seemed to be getting the general drift of it. 'I see,' he said, 'You mean that if you had a thousand pounds and I hadn't you'd give I half?' Garge nodded. 'That's the ticket,' he said. Said Willum, 'And if you had two moty cars, then you'd give I one?' Again Garge nodded. Said Willum, 'And if you had a pig and I hadn't, then you'd give I half?' Garge thought that one out quickly. Then he said, 'No ruddy fear – I've *got* a pig.'

WORD PICTURES

'Can you find no other way?' asks Sir Arthur Wardour of the beggar when the two men are cut off by the tide. 'I'll give you a farm . . . I'll make you rich.' 'Our riches will soon be equal,' says the beggar, and looks out across the advancing sea.
Sir Walter Scott

In my own country (South Africa) where there are many races, and where race difference is established and maintained by law, it is difficult for many members of the so-called superior groups to serve those of the so-called inferior groups. For every white man who would help an old black woman across a busy street, there would be some who would not; though perhaps some of those would wish that they could do so. But once the barrier is crossed, the whole personality becomes richer and gentler. There is only one way in which man's inhumanity to man can be made endurable to us, and that is when we in our own lives try to exemplify man's humanity to man.
Alan Paton

Suppose a person, even an entire group is ignored by the media? Until fairly recently, America was full of 'invisibles'. Blacks were ignored in literature. On radio, they became Amos 'n Andy played by two white men. On film they became comic servants. They were never shown as cowboys, though in real life about a third of the post-Civil War cowhands were black. Deadwood Dick was black as coal, but on film he turned pink-cheeked and blue-eyed.

Blacks made their first public appearance on TV when they turned to violence. Suddenly they were no longer invisible. For one brief moment, they could be seen on TV. At which point they were also seen on the streets. But that moment passed quickly. The media

image soon shifted from the real blacks – unemployed, uneducated, hungry – to 'media blacks' – well dressed, professionally employed, college educated. Real blacks once more became invisible.
Edmund Carpenter

One night a Negro was walking along Forty-second Street in New York, from the railway to the hotel, carrying a heavy suitcase and a heavier valise. Suddenly a hand took hold of the valise and a pleasant voice said: 'Pretty heavy, brother! Suppose you let me take one. I'm going your way.' The Negro resisted but finally allowed the young white man to assist him in carrying his burden, and for several blocks they walked along, chatting together like cronies. 'And that,' said Booker T. Washington, years afterwards, 'was the first time I ever saw Theodore Roosevelt.'
Onward

We hold these truths to be self-evident:
that all men are created equal;
that they are endowed by their Creator
    with inherent and inalienable rights;
that among these are life, liberty, and the pursuit of happiness;
that to secure these rights, governments are instituted among men,
    deriving their just powers from the consent of the governed;
that whenever any form of government becomes destructive of these ends it is the right of the people to alter or to abolish it, and to institute new government, laying its foundation on such principles, and organising its powers in such form, as to them shall seem most likely to effect their safety and happiness.
From the American Declaration of Independence

USEFUL TEXTS
Equality:
    2 Cor. 8:13; Phil. 2:6; John 5:18

See also: A9   Relationships
           A40 The equality of women
           B34 Human rights
           B44 The dignity of the individual

C34
THE VALUE OF LITTLE THINGS

'In your sight, Lord, the whole world is like a grain
of dust that tips the scales, like a drop of morning
dew falling on the ground.'
Wisdom 11:22

QUOTATIONS

Little strokes
fell great oaks.
Benjamin Franklin

The trivial round, the common task,
will furnish all we need to ask.
John Keble

The smallest thing by the influence of eternity is made infinite and
eternal.
Thomas Traherne

A little thing is a little thing, but faithfulness in a little thing
becomes a great thing.
Plato

Faithfulness in little things is a big thing.
St John Chrysostom

There is nothing small in the service of God.
St Francis of Sales

Accomplish the great task by a series of small acts.
Tao Te Ching

HUMOUR

Among the records preserved in the College of Pestology (52
Bedford Square, London) is a receipt for two guineas paid in July

1827 to the Bug Destroyer to His Majesty King George IV for destroying bugs in four bedsteads!

WORD PICTURES

In the American Civil War one of the Federal ships had what seemed to be a small superficial leakage. It was not thought necessary to countermand the order that she should take part in a coming conflict. At the crisis of the engagement it was found that sea water had got into the gunpowder magazine and rendered nearly the whole of it useless. On that powder hung victory or defeat. The little leak was neglected, and inferior force won.

In one of his essays Tolstoy says of Brulof, a celebrated Russian painter, how one day he corrected his pupil's study. The pupil, having glanced at the altered drawing, explained, 'Why, you only touched it a tiny bit!' But Brulof replied, 'Art begins where the tiny bit begins.' 'That saying,' Tolstoy goes on, 'is strikingly true, not of art alone, but of all life.'

I come in the little things,
saith the Lord;
yea! on the glancing wings
of eager birds, the softly pattering feet
of furred and gentle beasts, I come to meet
your hard and wayward heart. In brown bright eyes
that peep from out of the brake, I stand confest.
On every nest
where feathery Patience is content to brood,
and leaves her pleasure for this high emprise
of motherhood –
there doth my Godhead rest.
Evelyn Underhill

An old legend tells us that Jesus and his disciples were going one summer day from Jerusalem to Jericho. Peter was at his side. On the road lay a horseshoe, which the Master desired Peter to pick up. But the disciple let it lie. Jesus, however, stooped and picked

it up. In the village he exchanged it for a measure of cherries. When they came to a hill and the way lay between heated rocks, Peter was tormented with thirst and fell behind. Then the Master dropped a ripe cherry every few steps, teaching him that things despised often come to unexpected uses.
Edgar W. Work

A man who had hitch-hiked from coast to coast of the USA, and who had walked many miles in the process, was asked what he found the hardest to endure. To the surprise of his questioner, it was not the steep mountains or the dazzling sun or the scorching desert heat that had troubled him most, but – in the words of the traveller – 'it was the sand in my shoe'.

Hearts good and true
have wishes few,
in narrow circles bounded;
and hope that lives
on what God gives
is Christian hope well founded.
Small things are best,
grief and unrest
to rank and wealth are given;
but 'little things'
on 'little wings'
bear little souls to heaven.
Frederick W. Faber

Many years ago two men were on board a sailing ship, going back to their home in a far-off island, when one of them noticed a little grain of corn at his feet. He picked it up and examined it. 'It's a grain of corn,' said he. 'If it were a sackful it might be of some use!' And he threw it away again carelessly. But the other man picked it up, put it in his pocket, and treasured it till they reached their island home. Then he sowed it. It grew into a plant, and yielded a tiny crop, so small as to be laughable. But he sowed that again, and the next time the result was enough to fill a cup. This again he sowed, and there was enough to give a few grains to each of his many friends. So the crop grew, and in the end yielded an abundant harvest. The little grain of corn was the means of introducing corn to the islands.

USEFUL TEXTS

Little things:
Luke 9:17; Luke 19:17

See also: A5   One for another – unselfishness
A18 Balance in Nature
B20 Growth to maturity
B33 Faith and good works

C35
HOPE

'Ours is the better choice, to meet death at men's hands, yet relying on God's promise that we shall be raised up by him.'
2 Maccabees 7:14

QUOTATIONS

Hope is the first thing to take some sort of action.
Vincent McHaff

Hope ever urges us on and tells us tomorrow will be better.
Albius Tibullus

Everything that is done in the world is done by hope.
Martin Luther

To be a sinner is our distress but to know it is our hope.
Fulton Sheen

Every child comes into the world with the message that God does not yet despair of man.
Rabindranath Tagore

Hope is a lover's staff; walk hence with that, and manage it against despairing thoughts.
Shakespeare

Hope is the best possession. None are completely wretched but those who are without hope, and few are reduced so low as that.
Hazlitt

I am a man of hope, not for human reasons nor from any natural optimism, but because I believe the Holy Spirit is at work in the Church and in the World, even where his name remains unheard.
Joseph Suenans

Optimism is the faith that leads to achievement, but nothing can be done without hope.
Helen Keller

All human wisdom is summoned up in two words – wait and hope.
Alexander Dumas

Love means to love that which is unlovable, or it is no virtue at all, forgiving means to pardon the unpardonable, or it is no virtue at all, faith means believing the unbelievable, or it is no virtue at all. And to hope means hoping when things are hopeless, or it is no virtue at all.
G. K. Chesterton

PROVERB

If it were not for hope the heart would break.
English proverb

WORD PICTURES

Human wisdom says, Don't put off until tomorrow
what can be done the same day.
But I tell you that he who knows how to put off until tomorrow
is the most agreeable to God.
He who sleeps like a child
is also he who sleeps like my darling Hope.
And I tell you, Put off until tomorrow
those worries and those troubles which are gnawing at you today,
and might very well devour you today.
Put off until tomorrow those sobs that choke you
when you see today's unhappiness,
those sobs that rise up and strangle you.
Put off until tomorrow those tears which fill your eyes
and your head

flooding you, rolling down your cheeks.
Because between now and tomorrow, maybe I, God,
will have passed your way . . .
Blessed is he who puts off, that is to say,
Blessed is he who hopes. And who sleeps.
Charles Péguy

There is a story of a smith of the Middles Ages who was taken
prisoner and confined in a dungeon. Because of the knowledge
his craft had taught him he carefully examined the heavy links that
bound him, expecting somewhere to find a flaw that would show
him a weak place which could soon be made to yield. But
presently he dropped his hands hopelessly. Certain marks told
him that the chain was of his own making, and it had always been
his boast that one of his workmanship could not be broken. There
are truly no chains so hard to break as those of our own forging,
but they are not hopeless. The worst possible habits will yield to
human resolution and strength from above.
D. Williamson

Sometimes we are lamps without light, extinguished, but with
possibilities not realised. Well, I have come to light a flame in your
hearts, should the disappointments you have suffered, the
expectations that have not come true, have put it out. I want to
say to each of you that you have capacities of goodness, honesty
and industry; real, deep capacities, often unsuspected, sometimes
made even greater and more vigorous by hard experience.

Rest assured that I have come in your midst because I love you,
and have confidence in you; to show you personally this affection,
this trust I have in you, and to tell you that I do not fail to raise
my prayer to God so that he may always sustain you with that love
which he manifested by sending us his only begotten Son, Jesus
Christ, our Brother. He, too, experienced suffering and need, but
he indicated to us the way and offers us his help to overcome
them.
Pope John Paul II

USEFUL TEXTS

Hope:
Characteristics of:
   blessed, *Titus 2:13*
   sure, *Heb. 6:19*
   good, *2 Thess. 2:16*

Inspires:
   purity, *1 John 3:3*
   courage, *Rom. 5:4-5*
   joy, *Rom. 12:12*

Of Christian:
   Salvation, *Rom. 5:1-5*
   Christ, *1 Cor. 15:19*

See also: A6   Light of the world
           A19 Patience
           B21 Trust in God
           C1   Liberation from fear

C36
THE DAY OF THE LORD

'The day is coming now, burning like a furnace; and all the
arrogant and evildoers will be like stubble.'
Malachi 3:19

QUOTATIONS

Thoughts and feeling do not matter. We shall be judged only by
our will.
Daniel Considine

Don't wait for the last judgement. It takes place every day.
Albert Camus

The coming of Christ will be an indication of the moral order of
the universe and a revelation of God's sovereign purpose in
history.
William Fitch

Human beings judge one another by their external actions. God
judges them by their moral choice.
C. S. Lewis

Thou art the Judge. We are bruised thus.
But, the Judgement, join sides with us.
Robert Browning

HUMOUR

A German missionary in Africa went home on leave and came
back with a fine set of large coloured pictures to illustrate his
sermons. They were a great success. Every Sunday after the
sermon the natives rushed to the picture and discussed it with
excitement.

One day, the sermon was on Hell. The natives seemed very
impressed, and the priest went off to breakfast hoping that the

picture of the lost souls would fix the impression. Before he got inside his house he heard screams of delight and laughter, and turned round to see his congregation dancing with glee in front of the picture of hell. Very indignant, he strode back to the crowd. 'Silence! What do you mean by all this noise? Hell is not a laughing matter!' One of the natives took him by the arm up to the picture. 'Don't you see, Father! Look – all the people in hell are white!'

After Mass one morning, I offered to take home three ladies, all pillars of the church and all in their 80s. As we drove along they started discussing the Sunday reading. 'The last Days will mean an increase in earthquakes.' 'But we won't need to worry about that,' said one of the women. 'The earthquakes will all be at the bottom of the sea.' 'They will?' I said, barely disguising my scepticism. 'Oh, yes!' she answered confidently. 'The Bible says the earthquakes will be in "diver's places".'

Driving my four children to school/nursery/playgroup, Rebecca, aged about six at the time, suddenly said:
    'Mummy, when's Jesus coming? I want to meet him.'
    Me (flippantly): 'He's been and gone, dear.'
    Rebecca: 'I don't understand – I want to meet him.'
    Me: 'Well you can't.'
    Rebecca: 'Why can't I meet him?'
    Me (wearily): 'Rebecca, Jesus was here one thousand nine hundred and eighty-one years ago.'
    Rebecca: 'Oh . . . Did you meet him?'
Melanie Riches

'My wife is an Eighth Day Adventist.'
'Don't you mean a Seventh Day Adventist?'
'No – she's always late for everything.'

WORD PICTURES
Though the mills of God grind slowly, yet they grind exceeding small.
Though with patience he stands waiting, with exactness grinds he all.
H. W. Longfellow

An elder said: Do not judge a fornicator if you are chaste, for if you do, you too are violating the law as much as he is. For he who said thou shalt not fornicate also said thou shalt not judge.

It is the face of the Incarnate God
shall smite thee with that keen and subtle pain.
The sight of him will kindle in thy heart
all tender, gracious, reverential thought.
Thou wilt be sick with love, and yearn for him,
and feel as though thou couldst but pity him,
that one so sweet should e'er have placed himself
at disadvantage such, as to be used
so vilely by a being so vile as thee.
There is a pleading in his pensive eyes
will pierce thee to the quick, and trouble thee,
and thou wilt hate and loathe thyself; for, though
now sinless, thou wilt feel that thou has sinned,
as never thou didst feel; and wilt desire
to slink away, and hide thee from his sight,
and yet wilt have a longing aye to dwell
within the beauty of his countenance.
And these two pains, so counter and so keen –
the longing for him, when thou seest him not;
the shame of self at thought of seeing him –
will be thy veriest sharpest purgatory.
John Henry Newman

USEFUL TEXTS
Day of the Lord:
  Jer. 45:10; 1 Thess. 5:2

See also: A31 Heaven
          A42 Life after death
          B22 Death

C37
TEMPTATION

'Jesus was led by the Spirit through the wilderness,
being tempted there by the devil for forty days.'
Luke 4:1

QUOTATIONS

Every moment of resistance to temptation is a victory.
Frederick W. Faber

The absence of temptation is the absence of virtue.
Goethe

No man is matriculated to the art of life till he has been well
tempted.
George Eliot

Beware no man more than of yourself; we carry our worst enemies
with us.
Charles H. Spurgeon

The devil tempts us not. It is we who tempt him, beckoning his
skill with opportunity.
George Eliot

You cannot run away from a weakness; you must some time fight
it out or perish. And if that be so, why not now and where you stand.
Robert L. Stevenson

Here, too, amidst all the dangers and the trials we and others must
sing Alleluia, 'for God is faithful and he will not let you be tempted
beyond your strength' as St Paul says. So then we must sing here
also Alleluia. Man is still a sinner, but God is faithful. Scripture
does not say, 'He will not let you be tempted,' but, 'He will not let
you be tempted beyond your strength, but with the temptation will
also provide the way of escape, that you may be able to endure it.'
St Augustine of Hippo

The happiness of a man in this life does not consist in the absence but in the mastery of his passions.
Alfred, Lord Tennyson

Every temptation is great or small according as the man is.
Jeremy Taylor

WORD PICTURES

Go to dark Gethsemane,
ye that feel the tempter's power.
Your Redeemer's conflict see,
watch with him one bitter hour.
James Montgomery

Christian life means a walking; it goes by steps. There is a straight fence run for us between right and wrong. There is no sitting on that fence. No; only walking, one side or other. You can hardly look across without stepping through.
R. W. Barber

There is hardly any power in the mechanical world greater than that of the wedge. Once get the thin edge in, it is only a question of time and force how far the remainder shall be driven. The hardest stone, the toughest wood, are not able to resist its power for separation. Beware the thin edge of sin.

In the old legend the sirens sang so sweetly that all who sailed near their home in the sea were fascinated and drawn to their shore only to be destroyed. Some tried to get safely past the enchanted spot by putting wax in their ears, so that they should not hear the luring, bewitching strains. But Orpheus, when he came, found a better way. He made music on his own ship which surpassed in sweetness that of the sirens and thus their strains had no power over his men.

The best way to break the charm of this world's alluring voices is not to try to shut out the music by stopping our ears, but to have our hearts filled with the sweeter music of the joy of Christ. Then temptation will not have power over us.
R.H.

551

An Arab fable tells of a miller who was startled by seeing a camel's nose thrust in at the window of a room where he was sleeping. 'It is very cold outside,' said the camel, 'I only want to get my nose in.' The nose was allowed in, then the neck, finally the whole body. Soon the miller began to be inconvenienced by such an ungainly companion in a room not large enough for both.

'If you are inconvenienced,' said the camel, 'you may leave; as for myself I shall stay where I am.' 'Give but an inch,' says Lancelot Andrewes, 'and the devil will take an ell; if he can get in but an arm, he will make shift to shove in his whole body. As we see, if the point of a nail have once made entry, the rest will soon be in.
A.M.C

The story goes of a young certified accountant, who was given an opportunity to make £10,000 in a few months' time by a course of action which in other days would have been regarded as dishonest. He asked his mother for her opinion. After a few moments' silence she replied, 'Jim, you know when I come to wake you in the morning I shake you hard and you don't stir. And I shake you even harder and you give a little moan. And finally I shake you as hard as I can and you open one sleepy eye. I'd hate to come in morning after morning and find you awake.' He turned the job down and has been sleeping soundly since.
Anon

USEFUL TEXTS

Temptation:
    In the garden, *Gen. 3:1-5*
    Prayer to avoid, *Matt. 6:13*
    Of Christ, *Luke 4:1-13*
    Common to all, *1 Cor. 10:13*
    Not from God, *James 1:13-14*

See also: A15 Sin
            A38 Original Sin
            B19 Conscience
            C26 The human condition

C38
DISCERNING GOD'S WILL

'My Lord, the Lord,' Abram replied, 'how am I to know
that I shall inherit it?'
Genesis 15:8

QUOTATIONS

A possibility is a hint from God.
Sören Kierkegaard

God's will is not an itinerary but an attitude.
Andrew Dhuse

Prayer is no other but the revelation of the will or mind of God.
John Saltmarsh

That which is often asked of God, is not so much his will and way,
as his approval of our way.
S. F. Smiley

Let your will be one with his will, and be glad to be disposed of
by him. He will order all things for you. What can cross your will,
when it is one with his will, on which all creation hangs, round
which all things revolve?
H. E. Manning

If we stand in the openings of the present moment, with all the
length and breadth of our faculties unselfishly adjusted to what it
reveals, we are in the best condition to receive what God is always
ready to communicate.
T. C. Upham

Every hour comes with some little fagot of God's will fastened
upon its back.
F. W. Faber

Neither go back in fear and misgiving to the past, nor in anxiety and forecasting to the future; but lie quiet under his hand, having no will but his.
H. E. Manning

Proverb

If you want to disobey God, seek a place where he cannot see you.
Arab proverb

Word pictures

The present moment is the only moment in which any kind of action is possible. If I want to do the will of God, I must recognise that the divine will is always something I must do now – I cannot receive now what God will offer me tomorrow. But I can receive now what he is offering me now. And each moment God is offering me some grace (gift) for my acceptance or some command for my obedience.
Nevill Ward

How to find out God's will
1) Pray. 2) Think. 3) Talk to wise people but do not regard their decision as final. 4) Beware of the bias of your own will but do not be too much afraid of it. God never necessarily thwarts a man's nature and likings, and it is a mistake to think that his will is in the line of the disagreeable. 5) Meanwhile do the next thing, for doing God's will in small things is the best preparation for doing it in great things. 6) When decision and action are necessary, go ahead. 7) Never reconsider the decision when it is finally acted upon. And 8) You will probably not find out till afterward, perhaps long afterward, that you have been led at all.
Henry Drummond

Nothing is small or great in God's sight; whatever he wills becomes great to us, however seemingly trifling, and if once the voice of conscience tells us that he requires anything of us, we have no right to measure its importance. On the other hand, whatever he would not have us do, however important we may think it, is as nought to us. How do you know what you may lose by neglecting this duty, which you think so trifling, of the blessing which its faithful performance may bring? Be sure that if you do your very best in that which is laid upon you daily, you will not be left without sufficient help when some weightier occasion arises. Give yourself to him, trust him, fix your eye upon him, listen to his voice, and then go on bravely and cheerfully.

Jean Nicolas Grou

Towards the end of the thirteenth century, in Florence, a young girl of noble family, Piccarda Donati, entered a convent of Franciscan nuns against the will of her family. She made her vows, but one day her brother forced his way in and dragged her home, where she was compelled to marry a turbulent noble named Rossellino da Tosa. In a short time, still only a young girl, she fell ill and died.

She was a relative of Dante, who some years later was writing the *Paradiso*. In this poem, he tells us that in the first or lowest of the heavens, that of the moon, he saw one of the spirits, a young and beautiful girl, who seemed to wish to speak with him, and he asks her name. 'If you look at me carefully, you will soon know. I am Piccarda.'

Then he recognises her, though she is so transfigured by celestial joy that he had not known her at first. She explains that she is in the lowest heaven because she had failed to keep her vow, though submitting only to force. 'I see you are happy,' said Dante. 'But tell me – do you not long for a higher place in heaven, where you would know more and love more?' The idea amuses Piccarda. She smiles at the question, and so do the other spirits that cluster round listening. 'Our will is at rest, brother,' she says, 'we could not wish for the higher heavens for that would be out of harmony with the Will of God, who placed us here. Love makes our will one with God's Will. In his will is our peace.'

F. H. Drinkwater

Useful texts

Will of God:
Christ's resignation to, *Matt. 26:39; John 6:38-39*
Asking for, *Matt. 6:10*
Directing early missions, *Acts 18:21; Rom. 15:30-32*

See also: A41 Spiritual blindness
B11 Vocation
B47 Dying to self
C39 Doing God's will

C39
DOING GOD'S WILL

'This,' God added, 'is what you must say to the children of Israel:
'I AM has sent me to you.'
Exodus 3:14

QUOTATIONS

Our wills are ours, to make them Thine.
Alfred, Lord Tennyson

The centre of God's will is our only safety.
Betsie Ten Boom

If God sends us on stony paths, he provides strong shoes.
Corrie Ten Boom

All heaven is waiting to help those who will discover the will of
God and do it.
J. Robert Ashcroft

There are no disappointments to those whose wills are buried in
the will of God.
Frederick Faber

God's will on earth is always joy, always tranquillity.
Frederick Faber

This is how men get to know God – by doing his will.
Henry Drummond

I hope that when I have done what I can, he will do with me what
he pleases.
Brother Lawrence

I find the doing of the will of God leaves me no time for disputing
about his plans.
George Macdonald

Self-will should be so completely poured out of the vessel of the soul into the ocean of the will of God, that whatever God may will, that at once the soul should will; and that whatever God may allow, that the soul should at once willingly embrace, whether it may be in itself sweet or bitter.
Louis de Blois

Seek not to have things happen as you choose them, but rather choose them to happen as they do, and so shall you live prosperously.
Epictetus

Holiness is the joy of doing God's will.
Pope John Paul II

HUMOUR

During the American Civil War a lady exclaimed effusively to President Lincoln: 'Oh, Mr President, I feel so sure that God is on our side, don't you?' 'Ma'am,' replied the President, 'I am more concerned that we should be on God's side.'
K. Edwards

WORD PICTURES

The eminent John Newton once said: 'If two angels came down from heaven to execute a divine command, and one was appointed to sweep the streets, they would feel no inclination to change employments.' And why not? Because each would have the sure conviction that he was doing what his Lord had asked him to do and that by his service, great or humble, he was glorifying God.
Anon

St Ignatius Loyola one day said to Fr Lainez: 'Suppose God let you choose, either to go to heaven now, or to stay on earth with the chance of doing something for his glory; which would you choose?' 'I would make certain of heaven now,' replied Fr Lainez. 'Well,' said the saint. 'For my part, I would remain on earth, to do the will of God. As for saving of my soul, I am sure God would take care of it. I don't believe he would let anyone perish who, for love of him, had delayed entering heaven.'

Another name for doing God's will is 'duty'. Duty simply means concentrating on what is God's will for us now; and that means turning away from all else for the time being. Many never learn to turn away from pleasant distractions but the reliable 'man of duty' takes it for granted.

In Nelson's signal before Trafalgar, the operative word was 'duty'. The signal as Nelson wrote it was 'England confides that every man this day will do his duty.' The signals officer, Lieutenant Pascoe, suggested that some time would be saved if the word 'expects' could be substituted for 'confides', so Nelson agreed to the change. But no other word would have done instead of 'duty'.

When Collingwood (Captain of the ship leading the attack) received the message he said: 'Why doesn't Nelson stop sending signals? We all know what we are doing.' But there are always some of us that can do with a reminder.

F. H. Drinkwater

See also: A41 Spiritual blindness
            B11 Vocation
            B47 Dying to self
            C38 Discerning God's will

C40
RECONCILIATION

'It was God who reconciled us to himself through Christ and gave us the work of handing on this reconciliation.'
2 Corinthians 5:18

QUOTATIONS

The tragedy is not that things are broken.
The tragedy is that they are not mended again.
Alan Paton

Vengeance is too little. Pardon is very much bigger and greater.
Irène Lare, French resistance leader

Nothing is so deadening to the divine as an habitual dealing with the outside of holy things.
George Macdonald

PROVERBS

Repentance is the May of the virtues.
Chinese proverb

WORD PICTURES

When Dostoyevsky, the Russian novelist, knew that he had but a little time to live he made his children come into his room, and begged their mother to read the parable of the Prodigal Son. He listened with his eyes closed, absorbed in his thoughts. 'My children,' he said in his feeble voice, 'never forget what you have just heard. Have absolute faith in God, and never despair of his pardon. I love you dearly, but my love is nothing compared with the love of God for all those he has created. Even if you should be so unhappy as to commit a crime in the course of your life, never despair of God. You are his children; humble yourselves before him as before your father, implore his pardon, and he will rejoice over your repentance, as the father rejoiced over that of the Prodigal Son.
D. Williamson

Poor Gainsborough lay dying. He thought of the small rivalries and misunderstandings which had kept him and Reynolds apart, and he sent begging Reynolds to visit him. Reynolds went, and many a tear has been shed over the reconciliation of these two splendid men. Gainsborough bravely talked of getting better, and had some of his pictures brought to his bedside to show his friend. But his words began to fail, and his last utterance to Reynolds was: 'We are all going to Heaven, and Van Dyck is of the company.'
My Magazine

There is another word that must be part of the vocabulary of every Christian, especially when barriers of hate and mistrust have been constructed. This word is reconciliation. 'Leave your offering and be reconciled with your brother.' This command of Jesus is stronger than any barrier that human inadequacy or malice can build. Even when our belief in the fundamental goodness of every human being has been shaken or undermined, even if long-held convictions and attitudes have hardened our hearts, there is one source of power that is stronger than every disappointment, bitterness or ingrained mistrust, and that power is Jesus Christ, who brought forgiveness and reconciliation to the world.
Pope John Paul II

A madman came into a shop carrying a hammer; he swung it at the china and smashed it all to pieces. People stopped, rushed across from elsewhere, and gazed in astonishment. Some hours later a little old man came into the shop with a box under his arm: he took off his coat, put on his glasses and very, very patiently, among all those broken pieces, began mending the pots. No one, you can be perfectly sure, stopped to watch him!
Aristide Briand

At the period of history when Britain maintained a presence in the north-west frontier of India, two English officers, Colonel Stoddart and Captain Conolly, were sent to Bukhara on Government business. They never returned, but news at length came that both had been murdered, after terrible treatment, by the Amir.

Nineteen years passed and then one day in St Petersburg in Russia, an old English prayer book was found by a visitor in the house of a Russian officer. Its fly-leaf and the margins were covered with pencilled notes. It had been picked up on a stall in Bukhara, but the Russian officer to whom it belonged could not read it. His visitor, however, could. It had belonged to Captain Conolly, and the pencilled notes told how from December till June he and Colonel Stoddart had spent months of suffering, half-clad in the bitter cold of an Afghan winter, wounded, ill-treated, and with no change of clothes. At last they were led to an open square outside the prison, where, before a crowd of natives, Stoddart was executed. Then Captain Conolly was offered his life if he would become a Muslim, but he replied, 'I will not be a Muslim. I am ready to die.' And he too was beheaded.

Now, the Russian officer's visitor knew Conolly's family, and sent the prayer book to England to the Captain's sister, and his sister endowed a bed in the frontier hospital for Afghan tribesmen.

When the hospital patients heard this story they would say, with amazement, 'The sister of that man pays that men of the nation who killed him may be cured? Has she forgotten about his death?' 'No,' is the reply. 'It is that he may not be forgotten that she does it. That is the way of Christian Reconciliation.'
Anon

USEFUL TEXTS
Reconciliation:
>   To God, *Rom. 5:10-11*
>   To brother, *Matt. 5:23-24; 18:15-17*
>   Of whole creation, *Col. 1:19-20*

See also: A26 Sacrament of penance
            A27 As we forgive those
            B16 Christ heals and forgives
            C14 Forgiveness

C41
STARTING AFRESH

'All I can say is that I forget the past and I strain ahead
for what is still to come.'
Philippians 3:14

QUOTATIONS

All things change, nothing perishes.
Ovid

They must often change who would be constant in happiness and
wisdom.
Confucius

O God, always one and the same, if I know myself I shall know thee.
St Augustine of Hippo

Here below to live is to change, and to be perfect is to have
changed often.
John Henry Newman

Any change, even a change for the better, is always accompanied
by drawbacks and discomfort.
Arnold Bennett

It is a secret both in nature and state, that it is safer to change
many things than one.
Francis Bacon

Very often a change of self is needed more than a change of scene.
A. C. Benson

PROVERB

To change and to improve are two different things.
German proverb

WORD PICTURES

The fact that we may have had a stormy past should not frighten us. Storms that were bad in the past become good in the present if they encourage us to reform and to change; they become jewels if they are given to God.
Pope John Paul I

The other day while trying my luck at ice skating I fell – many times. Each time it seemed more difficult to get up until someone yelled, 'Get up on your knees first.' I tried it and it worked. Later I thought – there are so many ways in which we fall and fail; what better advice than to 'Get on your knees first', then pull yourself up. This works too.
Roberta Lash

We do not read lessons to tree seeds, instructing them how to develop. We know that they will come to all that there is in them by the simple operation of opening up. But men come to it by very different processes – by rebirth in every faculty, again and again and again. Scores of men have to be born again and again before they come to their fullness. As every tree on the death of winter, awakes, as it were, with a new resurrection in the spring, so men should be coming constantly to higher ideals of manhood and the uses of occupation, the uses of society, and the uses of the physical world, and of the bodies in which they are.
Phillips Brooks

The ship on which he had booked his passage was lying in the blue harbour ready to sail. On board were the missionary's books and possessions. Only Raimon Lull himself was not there. He was facing the hardest moment of his life. Though he knew the ship was waiting for him he could not leave his room in the town. For suddenly he had felt terribly afraid. He sat there alone, thinking of the unknown country to which he was going, of the fierce Saracens who had just triumphed over the Crusaders in Palestine and were bitterly angry because their brother Moors had been slain in Spain by Crusaders like Raimon's father. For the moment he forgot the real reason why he was sailing to meet these fierce and cruel men; he thought only of what they might do to him. Perhaps they would torture him or keep him imprisoned for life in a dark dungeon. No, he simply could not go. So his belongings were brought ashore again. The boat sailed without him.

Feeling that he had failed his Master, Raimon Lull's shame and sorrow were so great that he became very ill with a high fever. But his courage was beginning to come back. When his friends brought him news that another ship was ready in the harbour and loaded to sail for the port of Tunis, he begged them to put his books on board and to carry him down to the ship. They did as he asked, but seeing how ill he was they carried him ashore again, in spite of all his pleading, just before the hour of sailing.

Soon came the news of a third ship that was making ready to sail, and Raimon Lull made up his mind that at all costs he would be put on board and would sail this time. As the ship sailed out of the harbour into the open sea, Lull felt the courage of Christ take hold of him in place of the old fears. 'From this moment,' he wrote, 'I was a new man. All fever left me almost before we were out of sight of land.' So the ship sailed southward to the great Moslem city of Tunis.
Phyllis Garlick

See also: A25 Courage
          B14 Freedom to serve
          C1   Liberation from fear

C42
THE RISEN LORD

'Three days afterwards, God raised him to life and allowed
him to be seen, not by the whole people but
only by certain witnesses.'
Acts 10:40

QUOTATIONS

Christ has turned all our sunsets into dawns.
St Clement of Alexandria

To renounce all is to gain all; to descend is to rise; to die is to live.
Karl Rahner

Christianity is in its very essence a resurrection religion. The concept
of resurrection lies at its heart. If you remove it, Christianity is
destroyed.
John R. W. Stott

The resurrection that awaits us beyond physical death will be but
the glorious consummation of the risen life which already we have
in Christ.
D. T. Hiles

Let no one rob us of our birthright that the Resurrection of Jesus
Christ was a real event. He was raised physically to life and we
shall be raised physically to that new life in God.
George Carey

HUMOUR

The kindergarten-age child came home from Sunday school Easter
Sunday and told his mother he could understand about Christ but
not about the roses and asked his mother, 'Why was Christ a rose?'

WORD PICTURES

The little white or violet-veined wood sorrel is sometimes called *Hallelujah* because it blooms about Easter, the time of the singing of Alleluias.

Before Christ's coming the Tuscans made their tombs face the west, for death meant for them the close of life's day and the passing into eternal night. After Christ's coming the tombs face the east, for the Easter day had come with its radiant promise, bringing life and immortality to light. In this changed attitude is the secret of that overwhelming joy which Christianity brought into the world. It threw a 'light upon the mountain-tops of death, which made them lovely'.

The same vivid contrast is to be found in the Catacombs. In one chamber, which dates back to the time of Julius Caesar, the tombs are marked with the signs of pagan gloom and hopelessness. The inscriptions are either cynical at the expense of the gods, or embittered in their complaints. Hard by is a chamber where are buried those who suffered the extremities of persecution at the hands of men – martyrs who were burned, or crucified, or sawn asunder, or thrown to the beasts. But here there is no gloom: lilies adorn the tombs expressive of immortality, the inscriptions express a serene joy: the whole chamber is decked as if for marriage rather than death, and the spirit pervading it is a gladness that excludes all sorrow. And that which created this was the conscious presence of the living Christ, and the present participation of his followers in the joy set before them.
James Burns

One ancient symbol of Christian belief in the resurrection is the phoenix. This bird symbolised hope and the continuity of life after death.

According to legend, only one phoenix could live at a time. The Greek poet Hesiod, writing in the eighth century BC, said it lived nine times the lifespan of the long-living raven. When the bird felt death approaching, it built itself a pyre of wild cinnamon and died in the flames. But from the ashes there then arose a new phoenix, which tenderly encased its parent's remains in an egg of myrrh and flew with them to the Egyptian city of Heliopolis, where it laid them on the Altar of the Sun. These ashes were said to have the power of bringing a dead man back to life.

Scholars now think that the germ of the legend came from the Orient, and was adopted by the sun-worshipping priests of Heliopolis as an allegory of the sun's daily setting and rebirth. In Christian art the resurrected phoenix became a popular symbol of Christ risen from the grave.

P.F.

There is an old story that, when the Battle of Waterloo was being fought, the people in England were dependent upon a system of semaphore signals to learn of the tide of battle which was being waged fiercely on the opposite side of the Channel – against Napoleon Bonaparte. One of these signals was on the tower of Winchester Cathedral.

Late in the day it flashed the disheartening signal: 'Wellington defeated.' Just at that moment one of those sudden English clouds of fog obscured the signal, and the whole countryside was plunged into deep despair. Suddenly the fog lifted and the remainder of the message became clearly visible: 'Wellington defeated . . . the enemy!' Within the space of a moment sorrow was turned into joy, and defeat was swallowed up in victory.

P.F.

John and Michael were well aware that over seventy people had been killed trying to escape over the Berlin wall but they were determined to try. With the help of a friend who lived in West Berlin they worked out a plan. First they searched for a tall block of flats on their side of the wall. It had to face a house that wasn't quite so tall on the west side of the wall. When they had found No. 5 Schmoller Strasse, they needed a fibreglass bow, steel arrows, 100 metres of fishing line and some quarter-inch-diameter steel wire.

They hid in the top of the house for fifteen hours until conditions were just right. At a signal flashed by torch from the house on the other side at 5am as it was just getting light, they opened a window and fired the arrow with the line attached over the house opposite. The arrow sailed over the house to where their friend was waiting. He pulled in the line with the cable attached to it, and secured it to the back of his car. Each of the escapers had to wait for the moment when the Communist guards in their observation towers were looking the other way. Then, hitched to a pulley made to run down the wire, Michael, followed by John, sailed over the death wall to the house on the other side, passing over the wall from the closed-in unhappiness of East Berlin to joy and freedom.

T.C.

USEFUL TEXTS

Resurrection:
    Of Jesus, *John 20:1-20*
    Disciples witness to, *Acts 1:22*
    Hope of Believers, *Rom. 6:5; 1 Cor. 15:13*

See also: A44 Meeting Christ in the sacraments
             C43 The Living One
             C45 The Divinity of Christ
             C47 The indwelling spirit

C43
THE LIVING ONE

'You believe because you can see me.
Happy are they who have not seen and yet believe.'
John 20:29

QUOTATIONS

Life is Act, and not to Do is death.
Lewis Morris

Life alone can impart Life.
Ralph W. Emerson

Life loves no lookers-on at his great game.
A. H. Clough

Commit thyself to God to whom nothing perishes or dies.
Thomas à Kempis

Time wasted on existence – used in Life.
E. Young

Higher Life gives deeper death.
George MacDonald

Mohammed's truth lay in a holy Book – Christ's in a sacred Life.
William Houghton

Without sacrifice there is no resurrection. Nothing grows and blooms
save by giving. All you try to save in yourself wastes and perishes.
André Gide

WORD PICTURES

A man was once conversing with a Brahmin priest, and he asked him:
'Could you say "I am the Resurrection and the Life"?' 'Yes,' replied
the priest, 'I could say that.' 'But could you make anyone believe it?'
   Christ proved his superiority right there. His character and his
actions were back of his words.

The editor of one of our leading religious newspapers was walking along some cliffs near Eastbourne, England, one Easter morning. On his walk he met an old fisherman, and during their conversation together, the editor was struck by the simple faith of the old fisherman in his risen Saviour. 'How do you know that Christ is risen?' he asked. 'Sir,' came the reply, 'do you see those cottages near the cliffs? Well, Sir, sometimes when I'm far out at sea I know that the sun is risen by the light that is reflected by yon cottage windows. How do I know that Christ is risen? Why, Sir, do I not see his light reflected from the faces of some of my fellows every day, and do I not feel the light of his glory in my own life? As soon tell me that the sun is not risen when I see his reflected glory, as tell me that my Lord is not risen.'

Years ago an old municipal lamplighter, engaged in putting out his lights one by one, was met by a reporter who asked him if he never grew tired of his work in the cold dark night of labour. 'Never am I cheerless,' said the old man, 'for there is always a light ahead of me to lead me on.' 'But what do you have to cheer you when you have put out the last light?' asked the news writer. 'Then comes the dawn,' said the lamplighter.

A man of the world might have asked Jesus the same question. One light after another did he put out: the lamp of popular acclaim, the lamp of patriotic approval, the lamp of ecclesiastical conformity – all for the sake of God's love which burned in his heart and showed him a better way. At last even the light of his life was to flicker out on the hill called Calvary. What then? We hear his voice, 'Into thy hands I commend my spirit', and then dawn came.
Carl Knudsen

You have heard how wonderfully silk is made – in a way such as God alone could plan – how it all comes from an egg resembling a tiny peppercorn. . . . When in the warm weather the mulberry trees come into leaf, the little egg, which was lifeless before its food was ready, begins to live. The caterpillar nourishes itself upon the mulberry leaves until, when it has grown large, people place near it small twigs, upon which, of its own accord, it spins

silk from its tiny mouth until it has made a narrow little cocoon in which it buries itself. Then this large and ugly worm leaves the cocoon as a lovely little white butterfly.
St Teresa of Avila

There is an ancient legend which tells of a monk who is said to have found the crown of thorns that had mockingly encircled the brow of the Master. It goes on to tell how the saintly man carried it into the chapel of the cathedral on Good Friday morning and set it upon the altar. What a ghastly looking thing it was, rugged, cruel, and stained with blood. It was no wonder his flock merely glanced at it for a moment of their devotions and turned away sick at its ugliness. But it was a true symbol of Good Friday. All the ugliness of men's hearts which crucified the Lord, all the physical horrors, the mental nausea and spiritual torture through which our Lord passed, were indicated in the crown of mockery that he wore.

Very early Easter morning the monk hurried to the chapel to remove the symbol of sin, suffering and death. He knew it would be strangely out of place in the glory of the resurrection morning. Imagine his surprise when, upon opening the door, he found the place full of a beautiful fragrance. At first all he saw was the sun shining through a stained-glass window directly upon the altar upon which the thorns lay. Fixing his gaze upon the spot on which the sun had concentrated its glory upon the altar, he saw the crown of thorns. But the thorns and barrenness of the twisted twigs had undergone a marvellous transformation; the whole thing had blossomed into roses of the rarest beauty and the most delicate fragrance. The symbol of crucifixion and death had become the emblem of loveliness and life.
Samuel Parsons

See also: A44 Meeting Christ in the sacraments
C42 The Risen Lord
C45 The Divinity of Christ
C47 The indwelling spirit

C44
FEED MY SHEEP

'Lord, you know I love you.' Jesus said to him, 'Feed my sheep.'
John 21:17

QUOTATIONS

Do not offer advice which has not been seasoned by your own performance.
Henry S. Haskins

Whatever advice you give, be short.
Horace

We may give advice, but we can never prompt behaviour.
François de la Rochefoucauld

No gift is more precious than good advice.
Desiderius Erasmus

He that won't be counselled can't be helped.
Benjamin Franklin

Many receive advice, only the wise profit by it.
Publilius Syrus

'Tis not enough to help the feeble up, but to support him after.
Shakespeare

To help all created things, that is the measure of our responsibility; to be helped by all, that is the measure of our hope.
Gerald Vann

There are people in life, and there are many of them, whom you will have to help as long as they live. They will never be able to stand alone.
William Osler

Advice, as it always gives a temporary appearance of superiority, can never be grateful, even when it is most necessary or most judicious.
Samuel Johnson

I am sad at the number of young women and girls who come to me for help. They have been pressured into sexual activity without any accompanying love and tenderness. They feel used and betrayed. My role is never to condemn, only to pick up the hurt women, to reassure them that God loves and treasures them; that they are still beautiful in his sight. They need their dignity restored. I am glad that as a priest, I seem able to do this.
Fr John, RC parish priest

PROVERBS

He that will not be counselled cannot be helped.
French proverb

Help your brother's boat across and your own will reach the shore.
Hindu proverb

Teeth placed before the tongue give good advice.
Bulgarian proverb

HUMOUR

The ward sister had noticed that the new curate was taking an unusually long time doing his 'visits' – as he passed her desk she remarked this fact. 'Well, sister,' the priest replied, 'the list on your desk does say 24 RC and 4P.' Whereupon the sister, hardly able to contain her mirth, gasped – 'But, Father, that's my breakfast list for tomorrow – 24 Rice Crispies and 4 Porridge!'

A nervous young curate was visiting one of his parishioners, a sharp-tongued old lady, in the late autumn. 'Well,' he said, 'winter draws on, eh?' 'As a matter of fact I have,' replied the old lady tartly. 'I'd welcome you kept your advice to yourself.'
K. Edwards

Perhaps one of the only positive pieces of advice that I was ever given was that supplied by an old courtier who observed: 'Only two rules really count. Never miss an opportunity to relieve yourself; never miss a chance to sit down and rest your feet.'
Edward, Duke of Windsor

Recently, it is reported that archaeologists discovered, in the sands of the Near East, the evidence of the first recorded suicide. The skeleton clutched in one hand a Hebrew dagger and in the other a piece of parchment that read, 'I advise 100-1 on Goliath'!

WORD PICTURES

Man is a person; the need for secrecy and the need to reveal belong to a person's nature. These needs are closely united. Together they indicate the need for Someone before man can reveal himself.

Even more, man needs Someone who can help him to understand his own mystery. That Someone must, moreover, win absolute trust; he must, in revealing himself, show that he is worthy of this trust. He must confirm and reveal that he is the Lord and, at the same time, the Servant of man's spiritual mystery.

This is precisely how Christ revealed himself. His words, 'I know my own and my own know me', are clearly confirmed by the words that follow, 'I lay down my life for the sheep'. That is the spiritual character of the Good Shepherd.
Pope John Paul II

USEFUL TEXTS

Shepherd:
  Duties of, *Ps. 23:2; Matt. 18:12; 1 Sam. 17:34-35*
  Figurative of, *Pss. 23, 78:52, 80:1; Ezek. 34*
  Jesus, *John 10:11; 1 Pet. 2:25*

See also: A21 Feeding the hungry
           B50 The Good Shepherd

C45
THE DIVINITY OF CHRIST

'The Father who gave them to me is greater than anyone and no
one can steal from the Father. The Father and I are one.'
John 10:29-30

QUOTATIONS

Christ is not valued at all unless he be valued above all.
St Augustine of Hippo

Jesus never claims to be God, personally; yet he always claims to
bring God completely.
John A. T. Robinson

They should have known that he (Christ) was God. His patronage
should have proved that to them.
Quintus Tertullian

Christ stimulates us, as other great men stimulate us, but we find
a power coming from him into our lives that enables us to respond.
That is the experience that proves him to be the universal Spirit.
It does not happen with others.
William Temple

Of the human body of Christ you can say that first it suffered, and
then it was glorified and made glad; but throughout that temporal
sequence the Godhead remains unchanged, and unchanged
precisely in its knowledge and willing of, and its will to share in,
that which Christ on the Cross took to himself and made his own
and in his glorification turned into glory.
Gerald Vann

WORD PICTURES

Here in this human life we meet the living God. It is God himself,
personally present and redeemingly active, who comes to meet
men in this Man of Nazareth. Jesus is more than a religious genius,

576

such as George Fox, and more than a holy man, such as the lovable Lama in Kipling's *Kim*. He himself knows that he is more. The Gospel story is a tree rooted in the familiar soil of time and sense; but its roots go down into the Abyss and its branches fill the Heavens; given to us in terms of a country in the Eastern Mediterranean no bigger than Wales, during the Roman Principate of Tiberius Caesar in the first century of our era, its range is universal; it is on the scale of eternity. God's presence and his very Self were made manifest in the words and works of this Man.

In short, the Man Christ Jesus has the decisive place in man's ageless relationship with God. He is what God means by 'Man'. He is what man means by 'God'.
J. S. Whale

Then I see the Saviour over me,
Spreading his beams of love, and dictating the words of this mild
    song . . .
I am not a God afar off, I am a brother and friend;
Within your bosom I reside, and you reside in me;
Lo! we are One; forgiving all Evil; Not seeking recompense . . .
William Blake – from Jerusalem

A famous Russian writer describes a dream which was full of meaning to him.
I saw myself, in dream, a youth, almost a boy, in a low-pitched wooden church. The slim wax candles gleamed, spots of red, before the old pictures of the saints. A ring of coloured light encircled each tiny flame. Dark and dim it was in the church. . . . But there stood before me many people, all fair-haired, peasant heads. From time to time they began swaying, falling, rising again, like the ripe ears of wheat, when the wind of summer passes in slow undulation over them.

All at once some man came up from behind and stood beside me. I did not turn towards him; but at once I felt that this man was Christ. Emotion, curiosity, awe mastered me suddenly. I made an effort . . . and looked at my neighbour. A face like everyone's, a face like all men's faces. The eyes looked a little upwards, quietly and intently. The lips closed, but not compressed, the upper lip, as it were, resting on the lower; a small beard parted in two. The hands folded and still. And the clothes on him like everyone's.

'What sort of Christ is this?' I thought. 'Such an ordinary, ordinary man! It can't be!' I turned away. But I had hardly turned my eyes away from the ordinary man when I felt again that it really was none other than Christ standing beside me.

Again I made an effort over myself. . . . And again the same face, like all men's faces, the same everyday though unknown features. And suddenly my heart sank, and I came to myself. Only then I realised that just such a face – a face like all men's faces – is the face of Christ.
Ivan Turgnev

See also: A37 Christ the King
            A44 Meeting Christ in the sacraments
            B4   Mary – Handmaid of God
            B8   The Word
            B46 Christ the Sacrament of God

C46
LOVING KINDNESS

'By this love you have for one another, everyone
will know that you are my disciples.'
John 13:35

QUOTATIONS

No one is kind only to one person at once, but to many persons
in one.
Frederick W. Faber

Be like a tree. The tree gives shade even to him who cuts off its
boughs.
Sri Chaitanya

It is a kindness to refuse gently what you intend to deny.
Publilius Syrus

Wise sayings often fall on barren ground; but a kind word is never
thrown away.
Arthur Helps

There is nothing so kingly as kindness, and nothing so royal as truth.
Alice Cary

Men are rich not in proportion to their avarice, but to their
benevolence.
L. Larcom

Getting money is not all a man's business: to cultivate kindness is
a valuable part of the business of life.
Samuel Johnson

PROVERBS

A kind word is like a Spring day.
Russian proverb

One kind word can warm three winter months.
Japanese proverb

By a sweet tongue and kindness, you can drag an elephant with a hair.
Persian proverb

HUMOUR

A man went to see his bank manager to ask for a loan. After he had taken particulars, the bank manager said: 'By rights I should refuse your request, but I will give you a sporting chance. Now, one of my eyes is made of glass. If you can tell me which one it is, I will grant you the loan.'

The customer looked at the other intently for a few moments and then said: 'It's your right eye.' 'That's correct,' said the bank manager. 'How did you guess?' 'Well,' replied the customer. 'It's the kind and sympathetic one.'

WORD PICTURES

I think of every single person who has been kind to me in my prison life . . . down to the poor thief who, recognising me as we tramped round the yard at Wandsworth, whispered to me in the hoarse prison voice men get from long and compulsory silence: 'I am sorry for you; it is harder for the like of you than it is for the likes of us.'
Oscar Wilde

A smile costs nothing but creates much. It enriches those who receive without impoverishing those who give. It happens in a flash, and the memory of it sometimes lasts for ever. None are so rich that they can get along without it, and none so poor but are richer for its benefits. It is rest to the weary, daylight to the

discouraged, sunshine to the sad, and Nature's best antidote for trouble. Yet it cannot be bought, begged, borrowed or stolen, for it is something that is no earthly good to anybody till it is given away.
Dale Carnegie

Life is mostly froth and bubble,
two things stand like stone:
kindness in another's trouble;
courage in your own.
Adam L. Gordon

What a comfort it was to see Florence Nightingale pass by! She would speak to one and nod to another; she could not do it to all, you know, for we were lying there by hundreds, but we could kiss her shadow as it fell, and lay our heads on the pillow again content.
A soldier's letter from the Crimea

I've read a great deal over the years about the unhappy Franz Kafka but have never read anything by him. His story and his stories seem to be surrounded and impregnated by so much gloom that I had no desire to risk being sucked in. Nevertheless, there must have been something special about a man who could do what he did in the final months of his life when he was dying of tuberculosis.

Kafka met a child in the street, crying because she had lost her doll. He explained to her that, while the doll had, indeed, gone away, he, by a happy coincidence, had just met it and that the doll had promised to write. In the weeks that followed, Kafka did, indeed, write letters to the little girl in which the doll told about its travels and presumably brought sweet magic into that child's life. I'd like to be able to think of something like that.
A.M.

One day, so says an old legend, God gave a banquet for all his servants, and a really grand feast it was. All the virtues came and had a fine time. Humility was there, sitting in the lowest place at the table. Patience was there and didn't mind at all being served last. Faith and Hope sat together. Everyone was having a wonderful time.

At the height of the banquet, Charity noticed that two of the virtues were strangers to each other. He was surprised because he thought they were always together and he had purposely placed them side by side for just that reason. He came down to them and asked each one whether she had met her partner before. When they said that they had not, Charity introduced them: 'Kindness, I want you to meet Gratitude.' Both the virtues were so surprised to find out who the other was. Kindness said to Gratitude: 'We are supposed to be always together. Where one of us is, the other should be. Isn't it a pity that we have never really met before?'
P. Fontaine

USEFUL TEXTS
Kindness:
    Of the Lord, *1 Pet. 2:3*
    In speech, *Prov. 31:26*
    In Ministry, *2 Cor. 6:6*
    To those in need, *1 John 3:17*
    To all, *Gal. 6:10*

See also: A17 Gentleness
             A33 Love your neighbour
             B41 Generosity
             C18 Compassion

C47
THE INDWELLING SPIRIT

'Those who love me will keep my word,
and my Father will love them, and we shall come
to them and make our home with them.'
John 14:23

QUOTATIONS

Interior growth is only possible when we commit ourselves with
and to others.
Jean Vanier

Take care that the divinity within you has a creditable charge to
preside over.
Marcus Aurelius

As the flint the fire, as in the seed the tree,
so is God's likeness hid in everything I see.
Angelus Silesius

As the Spirit is the loving presence between the Father and the
Son, he can be present to us only by his work of love.
George A. Maloney

The seed of God is in us.
Now the seed of a pear tree grows into a pear tree
and a hazel seed into a hazel tree;
a seed of God grows into God.
Meister Eckhart

Just as the work of Christ would be devoid of power without the
'power from on high' in a Pasch without Pentecost, so would the
Way remain unwalkable, the Truth unknowable and the Life
unliveable. The Spirit comes to make possible in men all that
Christ is by nature by the gracious gift of his presence.
Thomas Hopko

O stupendous prodigy, of an incomprehensible God, who works and yet is mysteriously incomprehensible! A man bears consciously in himself God as light, him who has produced and created all things, holding even the man who carried him. Man carries him interiorly as a treasure which transcends words, written or spoken, any quality, quantity, image matter and figure, shaped in an inexplicable beauty, all entirely simple as light, he who transcends all light.
St Symeon the New Theologian

The difference between a good and a bad man does not lie in this, that the one wills that which is good and the other does not, but solely in this, that the one concurs with the living inspiring spirit of God within him, and the other resists it, and can be chargeable with evil only because he resists it.
William Law

I am learning now, as a prisoner, to have no desires. I am seeking him who died for me. I desire him, who rose for our sake. Birth stands before me. Let me receive pure light. When I am come to it, I shall at last be a man. Let me become an imitator of the suffering of my God. If a man bears God within himself, he will understand what I desire, and will pray for me, that I may pass over to it.
St Ignatius of Antioch

WORD PICTURES

It isn't the Devil in humanity that makes man a lonely creature, it's his Godlikeness. It's the fullness of the Good that can't get out or can't find its proper 'other place' that makes for loneliness.
Fynn

Once upon a time or rather at the birth of Time, when the gods were so new that they had no names, and man was still damp from the clay of the pit whence he had been digged, man claimed that he, too, was in some sort a god.
The gods weighed his evidence, and decided that man's claim was good. Having conceded man's claim, the legend goes that

they came by stealth and stole away this godhead, with intent to hide it where man should never find it again. But this was not so easy. If they hid it anywhere on earth the gods foresaw that man would leave no stone unturned till he had recovered it. If they concealed it among themselves they feared man might batter his way up even to the skies.

And while they were all thus at a stand, the wisest of the gods said, 'I know. Give it to me!' He closed his hand upon the tiny, unstable light of man's stolen godhead, and when that great hand opened again the light was gone. 'All is well,' said Brahm, 'I have hidden it where man will never dream of looking for it. I have hidden it inside man himself.'
Rudyard Kipling

In my heart I place the feet,
the golden feet of God.
If he be mine, what can I need?
My God is everywhere:
within, beyond man's highest word,
my God existeth still:
in sacred books, in darkest night,
in deepest bluest sky,
in those who know the truth, and in
the faithful few on Earth.
An Indian fragment from the tenth century

One day is much like another in the spiritual life, in the search for God. But from time to time there is a sudden, unexpected revelation or shining forth of God. You suddenly realise that God is everywhere, in everything and everyone. Call it insight, epiphany, baptism in the Spirit, or any other name, it is the same experience: the God within me reveals his presence, fleetingly, and all the rest of my days are changed permanently. Something happens that I did not merit and that I cannot explain or communicate. But it is more real than any communicable experience, and I cannot formulate it or capture it in words. For to do so would be to have some hold on God, who cannot be captured in a phrase or formula. Nor can I, by remembering it, recapture the experience. It is a gift; it is grace. The spirit blows where it will.

Murray Bodo

I have read somewhere about an old sculptor who had, among many other pieces of work in his workshop, the model of a beautiful cathedral. It was covered with the dust of years, and nobody admired it, although it was an exact model, inside and out, of a fine cathedral. One day the old attendant placed a light inside the model, and its gleams shone through the beautiful stained-glass windows. Then all stopped to admire its beauty. The change that was wrought by the light within was marvellous. It is so with us all. We must have the light within.

This is the incomparably 'Good News': Jesus Christ lives within us. We are, in the words of St Ignatius of Antioch (d. 115), *Christ bearers* (*Christophoroi*). The kingdom of God is truly within us. What amazing love God has for us in that he gave us his only-begotten Son (John 3:16) who in the flesh was able to die for love of us and to image the infinite love that the Father has for us, each one of us, but through that death the Father glorified him. (Ph 2:9).

In his risen existence the full Jesus Christ, God-Man, can now be in us and we, by his Holy Spirit, can be in *him*. This is God's greatest gift, the Spirit unseparated from the risen Christ. The two personalised relations within the Trinity are communicated to the Christian. This gift contains both Jesus Christ and the Holy Spirit who have their full being in relationship to the Father.

George A. Maloney

USEFUL TEXTS

Holy Spirit:
  Ps. 51:11; Isa. 63:10; Matt. 12:32

See also: B44 The dignity of the individual
              B51 One with Christ
              C47 The indwelling spirit
              C49 Receive the Holy Spirit

C48
ONE IN US

'Father, may they be one in us, as you are in me
and I am in you.
John 17:21

QUOTATIONS

The Holy Spirit is the skilled craftsman who unites us with God.
It is he who incorporates us in Christ Jesus, who teaches us what
we must say to the Father.
Carlo Carretto

Become as God; then ah! What joy is thine!
Thou drinkest God with every sip of wine.
Angelus Silesius

We are the wire, God is the current. Our only power is to let the
current pass through us.
Carlo Carretto

Unless we are personally committed, the wind of the Spirit cannot
blow through us.
George MacLeod

When we are united to Jesus we are *in sinu Patris*. This is the life
of *pure love* which presupposes the effort to do always what is
most agreeable to the Father.
Columba Marmion

We possess God, not in the sense that we become exactly as he,
but in that we approach him as closely as possible in a miraculous,
spiritual manner, and that our innermost being is illumined and
seized by his truth and his holiness.
St Augustine of Hippo

This indwelling Holy Spirit teaches us how to pray deeply in the heart. He leads us beyond our idols constructed about God to live in the mystery of the circular movement of the Father, Son and Spirit, inter-love relationships.
George A. Maloney

We are the members of Christ, and Christ is our member. And my hand, the hand of one who is the poorest of the poor, is Christ, and my foot is Christ. And I, the poorest of the poor, am the hand of Christ and the foot of Christ. I move my hand, and Christ moves, who is my hand. For you must know that divinity is undivided. I move my foot and my foot shines as he shines. Do not say that this is blasphemy, but confirm this, and adore Christ who has made you in this way. For you also, if such is your desire, will become one of his members. And so all the members of each one of us will become the members of Christ, and Christ our member, and he will make all that is ugly and ill-shapen, beautiful and well-shapen, in that he adores it with the splendour and majesty of his Godhead. And we shall all become gods and intimately united with God, and our bodies will seem to us immaculate, and since we have partaken of the semblance of the whole body of Christ, each one of us shall possess all of Christ. For the one who has become many remains the one undivided, but each part is all of Christ.
Symeon the Younger

Useful texts

Trinity:
    Revealed at Jesus' baptism, *Matt. 3:16-17*
    Baptise in name of, *Matt. 28:19*
    Creation, *Gen. 1:1; Ps. 104:30*
    Salvation, *2 Thess. 2:13-14; Titus 3:4-6*

See also: B44 The dignity of the individual
              B51 One with Christ
              C49 Receive the Holy Spirit

C49
RECEIVE THE HOLY SPIRIT

'As the Father sent me, so am I sending you.' After saying this
he breathed on them and said, 'Receive the Holy Spirit.'
John 20:21-22

QUOTATIONS

The personality of the Holy Spirit is hidden in a personalised
Humility that characterises Love itself.
George A. Maloney

Remember that you have received the spiritual seal, the spirit of
wisdom and understanding, the spirit of counsel and strength, the
spirit of knowledge and godliness, the spirit of holy fear. Preserve
what you have received. God the Father has sealed you. Christ the
Lord has confirmed you and has given you the guarantee of the
Spirit in your heart, as you have learned from the apostolic teaching.
St Ambrose

You are not only free, but also holy; not only holy, but also just;
not only just, but also sons; not only sons, but also heirs; not only
heirs, but also brothers of Christ; not only brothers of Christ, but
also joint heirs; not only joint heirs, but also members; not only
members but also the temple; not only the temple, but also the
instruments of the Spirit.
St John Chrysostom

WORD PICTURES

I have a glove here in my hand. The glove cannot do anything by
itself, but when my hand is in it, it can do many things. True, it is
not the glove, but my hand in the glove that acts. We are gloves.
It is the Holy Spirit in us which is the hand, who does the job. We
have to make room for the hand so that every finger is filled.
    The question on Pentecost is not whether God is blessing our

own plans and programmes but whether we are open to the great opportunities to which his Spirit calls us.

Once the Lord said to a faithful evangelist, 'You have been working for me with the utmost sincerity, for seven years. All that time I have been waiting for the moment that I could start to work through you.'
Corrie ten Boom

One of the 'labours' imposed upon Heracles was to cleanse the stables of Augeas. The stables had a herd of three thousand oxen, and the stalls had not been cleansed for thirty years. According to the bond the stables were to be cleansed in a single day. Heracles accomplished the task not by his own labour, but by directing the river Alpheus and making it run through the stables. It is only thus that the heart of man can be cleansed, not by fighting individual impurities by unaided effort, but by letting in the river of cleansing. Here is the joy and the method of overcoming sin.
G. B. F. Hallock

The origin of Confirmation can first be seen in the third-century *Apostolic Tradition of Hippolytus* of Rome. Here, it was a rite of presenting the newly baptised and anointed Christians to the assembly of the Faithful. A presentation rite was necessary at that time since baptism was done privately and in some other place due to the rule that one was baptised and anointed in the nude. Once clothed, the new Christians were then taken to the assembly and presented formally to it by the bishop laying his hand on their heads, praying for an outpouring of the Holy Spirit upon them, and then by anointing their heads a second time with fragrant oil, chrism.
Aidan Kavanagh

We may possibly think that the vegetables and fruits of the earth have always existed in their present state for the use of man.
But that is not the case. The wild plant is generally of little use as food, and only becomes valuable through our care.

The wild cabbage as it grows on some ocean cliff has a long

stalk and a few raw green leaves with a sharp and unpleasant taste. It has by the long cultivation of man been brought to its present state. The wild pear tree is an ugly bush, bristling with fierce thorns, and bearing a rough, hard and bitter fruit, in no way comparable with the delicious mellow pear of some cared-for country orchard today. It is not without care and cultivation that the fruit of the Spirit can be gained.

The most common word for worship in the New Testament comes sixty-six times. It could be translated 'I come towards to kiss'. God is love, and he wants us to respond to him in love. He wants us to enjoy a love-relationship with him, expressed partly through praise. People today need to know that God loves them as individuals, just as they are, with all their faults and failings. Often the common feeling is that God, if he exists at all, is a million miles away, aloof, distant, far removed from our personal needs, seemingly silent to all our cries for help. Those who believe in him are usually afraid of him, unsure of him and only too ready to believe that sickness is some sort of punishment for past sins. Comparatively few know, deep within their hearts, that God really loves them more than they could ever begin to imagine. However, when we 'come to kiss', by opening our hearts to him in worship, we are able to receive his love poured into our hearts by the Holy Spirit (Romans 5:5). Whatever our feelings may be (and feelings are fickle) we become aware of God's personal love for us. Interestingly the Christian mystics of the past have often referred to God's Spirit as his kiss, so that being filled with his Spirit is simply allowing ourselves to be kissed by God.
David Watson

See also: A46 Priesthood of the laity
A47 The Spirit of Truth
C47 The indwelling spirit

APPENDIX ONE

SUNDAY THEMES
ASB Lectionary of the Church of England

	Theme	Sections
Before Christmas		
9th Sunday	The Creation	A18/A39/B28/B32/B39/C20
8th Sunday	The Fall	A13/A15/A28/A30/A38/B45/C26/C37
7th Sunday	The Election of God's People: Abraham	A43/B4/B36/B40
6th Sunday	The Promise of Redemption: Moses	A29/B4/B9/B40/C6/C20/C35
5th Sunday	The Remnant of Israel	A3/A7/A22/A30/B1/B38/C1
Advent		
1st Sunday	The Advent Hope	A1/A2/A4/B1/C1/C2/C35
2nd Sunday	The Word of God in the Old Testament	A12/B4/B8/C6/C8
3rd Sunday	The Forerunner	A2/A5/A7/A22/C25/C29
4th Sunday	The Annunciation	A4/A40/B7/B41/B44/C7
After Christmas		
1st Sunday	The Incarnation	A4/B4/B7/B46/C7
2nd Sunday	The Holy Family	A4/B6/B7/B30/C5/C7
After Epiphany		
1st Sunday	Revelation: The Baptism of Jesus	B9/B10/B11/C7
2nd Sunday	Revelation: The First Disciples	A14/B2/B9/C16
3rd Sunday	Revelation: Signs of Glory	A39/B9/B32
4th Sunday	Revelation: The New Temple	A20/B4/B9/C45
5th Sunday	Revelation: The Wisdom of God	A12/B2/B9/B37/C9
6th Sunday	Revelation: Parables	A12/B9/B24
Before Easter		
9th Sunday	Christ the Teacher	A6/B2/B24/B50/C9
8th Sunday	Christ the Healer	B3/B16/B23/B32/B46/C13
7th Sunday	Christ the Friend of Sinners	A13/A44/B15/B16/B50
Lent		
1st Sunday	The King and the Kingdom: Temptation	A15/A38/C26/C37
2nd Sunday	The King and the Kingdom: Conflict	A15/A38/C15/C28/C37
3rd Sunday	The King and the Kingdom: Suffering	A35/B15/B38/C13/C38
4th Sunday	The King and the Kingdom: Transfiguration	A39/B8/C23/C45
5th Sunday	The King and the Kingdom: The Victory of the Cross	A29/A37/B38/C10
Palm Sunday	The Way of the Cross	A29/B15/B38/B39
Easter Sunday		A42/C42/C43/C45

After Easter

1st Sunday	The Upper Room/The Bread of Life	A44/B27/B29
2nd Sunday	The Emmaus Road/The Good Shepherd	B50/C44
3rd Sunday	The Lakeside/The Resurrection and the Life	C42/C43
4th Sunday	The Charge to Peter/The Way, the Truth and the Life	A47/C44
5th Sunday	Going to the Father	B28/C20/C27
Sunday after Ascension	The Ascension of Christ	A39/B51/C48
Pentecost		A47/B53/C47/C48
Trinity Sunday		B40/B54/C20/C45/C48

After Trinity

1st Sunday	The People of God/The Church's Unity and Fellowship	A43/B48/C48
2nd Sunday	The Life of the Baptised/The Church's Confidence in Christ	B17/B21/C12
3rd Sunday	The Freedom of the Children of God/ The Church's Mission to the Individual	B14/B44/C1/C12
4th Sunday	The New Law/The Church's Mission to All People	A13/A33/B12/B52/C10
5th Sunday	The New Person	A5/A10/B26/B47/C47
6th Sunday	The More Excellent Way	A10/B11/C38/C39/C47
7th Sunday	The Fruit of the Spirit	A2/A5/A17/A19/B3/B41/C46
8th Sunday	The Whole Armour of God	A3/B21/B35/C32/C35
9th Sunday	The Mind of Christ	A6/A23/A27/A33/C18/C39
10th Sunday	The Serving Community	A1/A7/A21/B14/C3/C17
11th Sunday	The Witnessing Community	A8/A32/A43/B24/B33/C21
12th Sunday	The Suffering Community	A7/A21/B15/B38/C13/C18
13th Sunday	The Family	A46/B6/B32/C5
14th Sunday	Those in Authority	A14/A32/B13
15th Sunday	The Neighbour	A9/A33/C10/C46
16th Sunday	The Proof of Faith	A29/B21/B33/C1/C22
17th Sunday	The Offering of Life	A2/A5/A39/A46/A48/B47
18th Sunday	The Life of Faith	A1/A10/C22/C30
19th Sunday	Endurance	A3/A19/A25/B21/B49/C13
20th Sunday	The Christian Hope	A20/A31/B51/C35
21st Sunday	The Two Ways	A19/A23/C18/C46
22nd Sunday	Citizens of Heaven	A16/A20/A31/B51

APPENDIX TWO

SUNDAY THEMES
For use with the Roman Catholic three-year cycle of Readings

The material is arranged in three parts, A, B, and C to correspond with the three year cycle.
The themes are those which are suggested by one or more of the Sunday readings.

YEAR A	Theme	Text	Section	Related Sections
Advent				
1st Sunday	The value of time	Rom. 13:11	A1	A19/B25/C34
2nd Sunday	Integrity	Isa. 11:5	A2	B19/B20/B26/C23
3rd Sunday	Perseverance	Matt. 11:6	A3	A19/B49/C30/C35
4th Sunday	Emmanuel Mary's Child	Isa. 7:14	A4	A37/B4/B8/B46/C45
Of the Year	*(for Christmas see Year B)*			
2nd Sunday	One for another – unselfishness	Isa. 49:3	A5	A33/B41/B47/C34
3rd Sunday	Light of the world	Ps. 27:1	A6	A37/B4/B8/B46
4th Sunday	Poor in spirit	Matt. 5:3	A7	A11/C21/C25/C29
5th Sunday	The light of example	Matt. 5:16	A8	A9/A33/B24
6th Sunday	Relationships	Matt. 5:37	A9	A33/B6/B30/B52/C10/C19
7th Sunday	Seeking perfection	Matt. 5:48	A10	A20/A22/B26/C47
8th Sunday	God's loving providence	Matt. 6:26	A11	A7/A19/B21/C39
9th Sunday	Holy Scripture	Matt. 7:24	A12	B2/B9/B24/C6
10th Sunday	The Church is for sinners	Matt. 9:13	A13	B17/C12/C27
11th Sunday	The successors of the Apostles	Matt. 10:1	A14	A24/A45/B13
12th Sunday	Sin	Rom. 5:12	A15	A13/A38/C37
13th Sunday	The Saints	Matt. 10:41	A16	A10/B26/B51/C8
14th Sunday	Gentleness	Matt. 11:30	A17	A19/B41/C18/C46
15th Sunday	Balance in Nature	Rom. 8:20	A18	B32/B39/B42/C34
16th Sunday	Patience	Matt. 13:28	A19	A11/B21/C39
17th Sunday	The Kingdom of God	Matt. 13:52	A20	A31/B17/B51/C39
18th Sunday	Feeding the hungry	Matt. 14:16	A21	A33/B15/C21/C29
19th Sunday	Seeking God	1 Kgs. 19:12	A22	A10/B28/C16/C38
20th Sunday	Mercy	Isa. 56:1	A23	A17/C14/C18/C46
21st Sunday	Papacy	Matt. 16:18	A24	A14/B13/B17/C44
22nd Sunday	Courage	Matt. 16:21	A25	B35/C13/C41
23rd Sunday	The Sacrament of penance	Matt. 18:18	A26	A27/B16/C14/C40
24th Sunday	As we forgive those	Matt. 18:22	A27	A26/B16/C14/C40
25th Sunday	Work	Matt. 20:8	A28	A1/A18/A36/A39
26th Sunday	True obedience	Phil. 2:7	A29	A14/A32/B13/B31/C25
27th Sunday	God's sinful people	Isa. 5:7	A30	A15/A34/A38
28th Sunday	Heaven	Isa. 25:7	A31	A20/B3/B51/C48
29th Sunday	Civic duty	Matt. 22:21	A32	A29/B14/B33/B34
30th Sunday	Love your neighbour	Matt. 22:39	A33	A9/B52/C10/C19
31st Sunday	Hypocrisy and ambition	Matt. 23:3	A34	A2/A15/B26/B44
32nd Sunday	Preparing for death	Matt. 25:13	A35	A42/B21/B22/B23/B41
33rd Sunday	Using talents	Matt. 25:15	A36	A1/A28/A39
34th Sunday	Christ the King	1 Cor. 15:25	A37	A4/A44/B4/B8

Lent

1st Sunday	Original Sin	Rom. 5:12	A38	A15/B10/C26/C37
2nd Sunday	The Glory of God	Matt. 17:2	A39	A20/B40/C31/C39
3rd Sunday	The equality of women	John 4:27	A40	B34/B44/C33
4th Sunday	Spiritual blindness	John 9:26	A41	A22/B49/C26
5th Sunday	Life after death	John 11:25	A42	A31/B22/C35

Eastertide	*(for Easter Day see Year C)*			
2nd Sunday	Believing community	Acts 2:42	A43	B17/B36/C12
3rd Sunday	Meeting Christ in the sacraments	Luke 24:30-31	A44	A37/B4/B46/B51/C45
4th Sunday	The Priesthood	Ps. 23:1	A45	A14/A46/B13
5th Sunday	Priesthood of the laity	1 Pet. 2:9	A46	B10/B44/C49
6th Sunday	The Spirit of Truth	John 14:16-17	A47	B53/C47/C48
7th Sunday	Worship	Acts 1:14	A48	B25/B29/C32

YEAR B	*Theme*	*Text*	*Section*	*Related Sections*
Advent				
1st Sunday	Waiting on the Lord	Mark 13:35	B1	A1/A22/A35/B21/C36
2nd Sunday	The Good News	Isa. 40:9	B2	B9/B12/B24/C2
3rd Sunday	Joy in Christ	1 Thess. 5:16	B3	B51/C2/C47
4th Sunday	Mary – Handmaid of God	Luke 1:38	B4	A4/A40/B7
Christmas				
Christmas Day	A Saviour is born for us	Luke 2:11	B5	A4/B3/C2/C7
Sunday in Octave	The family	Ecclus. 3:2	B6	A9/B30/C5
1st January	Mary, Mother of God	Luke 2:16	B7	A4/A40/C7/C45
2nd January	The Word	John 1:1	B8	A4/A37/B4/C45
Epiphany	Revelation	Eph. 3:3	B9	A12/B2/B24/C8/C38
Sunday after Epiphany	Baptism	Mark 1:8	B10	A38/B36/C26/C47/C49

Of the Year				
2nd Sunday	Vocation	1 Sam. 3:10	B11	A10/A22/C16/C38
3rd Sunday	On a mission	Mark 1:15	B12	B2/B24/C12/C16
4th Sunday	Authority	Mark 1:27	B13	A14/A24/A29/A32/B14
5th Sunday	Freedom to serve	1 Cor. 9:22	B14	B34/B45/C1
6th Sunday	Jesus, friend of outcasts	Mark 1:40	B15	A21/A33/B38/C3
7th Sunday	Christ heals and forgives	Mark 2:5	B16	A15/A26/A27/C22/C27/C40
8th Sunday	The Church – Bride of Christ	Hos. 2:21	B17	A13/B36/C12
9th Sunday	Sunday	Mark 2:27	B18	A48/B29
10th Sunday	Conscience	Mark 3:29	B19	A2/A10/A34/B45/C47
11th Sunday	Growth to maturity	Mark 4:28	B20	A2/A7/A10/B28
12th Sunday	Trust in God	Mark 4:40	B21	A11/A19/B52/C39
13th Sunday	Death	Wisd. 1:13	B22	A35/A42/B47/C36
14th Sunday	Pastoral care of the sick	2 Cor. 12:9	B23	A35/A52/B38
15th Sunday	Go tell everyone	Mark 6:7-13	B24	B2/B12/C8
16th Sunday	Quiet – time for prayer	Mark 6:31	B25	A1/A10/C32/C47
17th Sunday	The whole person	Eph. 4:2	B26	A2/A10/B20
18th Sunday	Bread from heaven	John 6:32-33	B27	A21/A44/B29

19th Sunday	The Father who draws			
	us to himself	John 6:44	B28	B40/C20/C27
20th Sunday	The Eucharist	John 6:55-56	B29	A44/B18/B27
21st Sunday	Married love	Gen. 2:24	B30	B8/C13
22nd Sunday	The commandments of life	Jas. 1:21	B31	A29/C6/C39
23rd Sunday	The Wonders of God	Mark 7:37	B32	A18/B39
24th Sunday	Faith and good works	Jas. 2:17	B33	C22/C30
25th Sunday	Human rights	Jas. 3:16	B34	A21/A40/B44/C1/C33
26th Sunday	The Grace of God	Num. 11:25	B35	B51/B52/C55
27th Sunday	The Family of God	Heb. 2:11	B36	B10/B34/C12/C17/C24
28th Sunday	True Wisdom	Wisd. 7:7	B37	A2/B20/B26
29th Sunday	The Suffering Servant	Isa. 53:11	B38	B15/B19/B49/C13
30th Sunday	Creation	Ps. 126:3	B39	A18/B32
31st Sunday	One God	Deut. 6:4	B40	B30/B54/C27
32nd Sunday	Generosity	Mark 12:43	B41	A5/C18/C46
33rd Sunday	Signs of the times	Mark 13:28	B42	A18/B34/C17
34th Sunday	Christ the King	(see A37)		

Lent

1st Sunday	Forty days of Lent	Mark 1:12	B43	B47/C37/C40/C41
2nd Sunday	The dignity of the individual	Rom. 8:34	B44	B26/B34/B45/C47
3rd Sunday	Free will	John 2:25	B45	A2/B26/B44
4th Sunday	Christ the Sacrament of God	John 3:14	B46	A44/B16/B51
5th Sunday	Dying to self	John 12:24	B47	A5/A7/A10/B26

Eastertide *(for Easter Day see Year C)*

2nd Sunday	Christian unity	Acts 4:32	B48	A20/B17/B36/B51
3rd Sunday	Coping with doubt	Luke 24:38	B49	C13/C22/C30/C41
4th Sunday	The Good Shepherd	John 10:11	B50	B15/B38/C44
5th Sunday	One with Christ	John 15:4	B51	B25/C47/C48
6th Sunday	God is Love	1 John 4:8	B52	A9/A33/B30/C10
7th Sunday	Consecrated in Truth	John 17:19	B53	A47/C11/C23
Trinity Sunday	The Trinity	Matt. 28:19-20	B54	A37/A47/B28/B40/C47

YEAR C	*Theme*	*Text*	*Section*	*Related Sections*
Advent				
1st Sunday	Liberation from fear	Luke 21:28	C1	B3/B14/C2
2nd Sunday	Joy of salvation	Ba. 5:9	C2	B3/B14/C1
3rd Sunday	Sharing possessions	Luke 3:10	C3	A7/A21/A33/B41
4th Sunday	Personal peace	Mic. 5:4	C4	A2/B19/C17

Of the Year *(for Christmas see Year B)*

2nd Sunday	The institution of marriage	John 2:1	C5	B6/B30
3rd Sunday	The Old Testament Law	Ps. 19:8	C6	A29/B4/B31
4th Sunday	The humanity of Christ	Luke 4:22	C7	A37/B3/B16/C45
5th Sunday	God's messengers	Isa. 6:8	C8	B2/B9/B24
6th Sunday	The Beatitudes	Jer. 17:7	C9	B2/B3/C2
7th Sunday	Love your enemies	Luke 6:27	C10	A9/A33/B15/B52
8th Sunday	Talk	Luke 6:45	C11	A2/A9/A47/B53
9th Sunday	The Church for all people	1 Kgs. 8:43	C12	A6/A13/A43/B17
10th Sunday	Coping with grief	Luke 7:13	C13	A25/B38/B49/C18

11th Sunday	Forgiveness	Luke 7:47	C14	A26/A27/B16/C27/C40
12th Sunday	Prejudice	Gal. 3:28	C15	A40/A41/B15/C1
13th Sunday	Come follow me	Luke 9:59-60	C16	A22/B11/B24/C41
14th Sunday	International peace	Isa. 66:12	C17	A33/B34/C4/C10
15th Sunday	Compassion	Luke 10:33	C18	A17/A23/A33/C46
16th Sunday	Friendship	Luke 10:38	C19	A9/A33/B15
17th Sunday	Our Father in heaven	Luke 11:12	C20	A22/B28/C27
18th Sunday	Rise above materialism	Luke 12:15	C21	A7/A21/C29
19th Sunday	The Light of faith	Heb. 11:2	C22	B33/C30
20th Sunday	Zeal for what is right	Luke 12:49	C23	A2/C8/C39
21st Sunday	Lord of all nations	Isa. 66:18	C24	A6/B8/B28/C12
22nd Sunday	Humility	Luke 14:11	C25	A2/A7/A10/B20
23rd Sunday	The human condition	Wisd. 9:15	C26	A15/A38/B22/B49/C37
24th Sunday	The Father who receives us back	Luke 15:20	C27	A26/B28/C20/C41
25th Sunday	Lord of the oppressed	Ps. 112	C28	A21/B15/B38/B50
26th Sunday	Not through luxury	Amos 6:1	C29	A7/A21/C21
27th Sunday	Increase our faith	Luke 17:5	C30	B33/C22
28th Sunday	Thanksgiving	Luke 17:15-16	C31	A17/A39/A48/B41
29th Sunday	Prayer	Luke 18:7	C32	A22/A48/B25/B29
30th Sunday	Equality	Ecclus. 35:12	C33	A9/A40/B34/B44
31st Sunday	The value of little things	Wisd. 11:22	C34	A5/A18/B20/B33
32nd Sunday	Hope	2 Macc. 7:14	C35	A6/A19/B21/C1
33rd Sunday	The Day of the Lord	Mal. 3:19	C36	A31/A42/B22

Lent

1st Sunday	Temptation	Luke 4:1	C37	A15/A38/B19/C26
2nd Sunday	Discerning God's will	Gen. 15:8	C38	A41/B11/B47/C39
3rd Sunday	Doing God's will	Exod. 3:14	C39	A41/B11/B47/C38
4th Sunday	Reconciliation	2 Cor. 5:18	C40	A26/A27/B16/C14
5th Sunday	Starting afresh	Phil. 3:14	C41	A25/B14/C1

Eastertide

Easter Sunday	The Risen Lord	Acts 10:40	C42	A44/C43/C45/C47
2nd Sunday	The Living One	John 20:29	C43	A44/C42/C45/C47
3rd Sunday	Feed my sheep	John 21:17	C44	A21/B52
4th Sunday	The Divinity of Christ	John 10:29-30	C45	A37/A44/B4/B8/B46
5th Sunday	Loving kindness	John 13:35	C46	A17/A33/B41/C18
6th Sunday	The indwelling spirit	John 14:23	C47	B44/B51/C48/C49
7th Sunday	One in us	John 17:21	C48	B44/B51/C47/C49
Pentecost	Receive the Holy Spirit	John 20:21-22	C49	A46/A47/C47

APPENDIX THREE

SUNDAY THEMES

For use with the new (1997) three-year Lectionary
of the Church of England

YEAR A	Theme	Text	Section	Related Sections
Advent				
1st Sunday	The value of time	Rom. 13:11	A1	A19/B25/C34
2nd Sunday	Integrity	Isa. 11:5	A2	B19/B20/B26/C23
3rd Sunday	Perseverance	Matt. 11:1-6	A3	A19/B49/C30/C35
4th Sunday	Emmanuel, Mary's Child	Isa. 7:14	A4	A37/B4/B8/B46/C45
Christmas				
Christmas Day				
Sets I & II	A Saviour is born for us	Luke 2:11	B5	A4/B3/C2/C7
Set III	God Incarnate	John 1:14	B5	A4/B3/C2/C7
1st Sunday	God among the			
	marginalised	Matt. 2:18	C28	A21/B15/B38/B50
2nd Sunday	The Word	John 1:1	B8	A4/A37/B4/C45
Epiphany	Revelation	Eph. 3:3	B9	A12/B2/B24/C8/C38
1st Sunday	The baptism of Christ	Matt. 3:13	B10	A38/B36/C26/C47/C49
2nd Sunday	Man for others –			
	unselfishness	Isa. 49:3	A5	A33/B41/B47/C34
3rd Sunday	Light of the world	Ps. 27:1	A6	A37/B4/B8/B46
4th Sunday	God values the humble	1 Cor. 1:27	C34	A5/A18/B20/B33
Presentation	The Lord comes			
of Christ	to his temple	Mal. 3:1	C36	A31/A42/B22
Ordinary Time				
Proper 1	The light of example	Matt. 5:16	A8	A9/A33/B24
Proper 2	Relationships	Matt. 5:37	A9	A33/B6/B30/B52/
				C10/C19
Proper 3	Seeking perfection	Matt. 5:48	A10	A20/A22/B26/C47
2 before Lent	God's loving providence	Matt. 6: 26	A11	A7/A19/B21/C39
1 before Lent	Christ reveals God's glory	2 Peter 1:17	A37	A4/A44/B4/B8
Lent				
1st Sunday	Original sin	Rom. 5:12	A38	A15/B10/C26/C37
2nd Sunday	Grace and faith	Rom. 4:16	B21	A11/A19/B52/C39
3rd Sunday	God saves us in Christ	Rom. 5:7-8	B52	A9/A33/B30/C10
4th Sunday	Spiritual blindness	John 9:26	A41	A22/B49/C26
or Mothering				
Sunday	The equality of women	John 19:25	A40	B34/B44/C33
5th Sunday	Life after death	John 11:25	A42	A31/B22/C35
Palm Sunday	Passion and glory	Phil 2:8-9	B38	B15/B19/B49/C13
Easter				
Easter Day	The risen Lord	Acts 10:40	C42	A44/C43/C45/C47
2nd Sunday	Believing community	John 20:29	A43	B17/B36/C12

3rd Sunday	Meeting Christ in the sacraments	Luke 24:30-31	A44	A37/B4/B46/B51/C45
4th Sunday	The Priesthood	Ps. 23:1	A45	A14/A46/B13
5th Sunday	Priesthood of the laity	1 Pet. 2:9	A46	B10/B44/C49
6th Sunday	The Spirit of Truth	John 14:16-17	A47	B53/C47/C48
7th Sunday	Worship	Acts1:14	A48	B25/B29/C32
Pentecost	Receive the Holy Spirit	John 20:21-22	C49	A46/A47/C47
Trinity Sunday	The Trinity	Matt. 28:19-20	B54	A37/A47/B28/B40/C47
Proper 4	Holy Scripture	Matt. 7:24	A12	B2/B9/B24/C6
Proper 5	The Church is for sinners	Matt. 9:13	A13	B17/C12/C27
Proper 6	The successors of the Apostles	Matt. 10:1	A14	A24/A45/B13
Proper 7	Sin	Rom. 6:2b	A15	A13/A38/C37
Proper 8	The offering of life	Matt. 10:42	B41	A5/C18/C46
Proper 9	Gentleness	Matt. 11:30	A17	A19/B41/C18/C46
Proper 10	God's word bears fruit	Isa. 55:10-11	A12	B2/B9/B24/C6
Proper 11	Patience	Matt. 13:28	A19	A11/B21/C39
Proper 12	The Kingdom of God	Matt. 13:52	A20	A31/B17/B51/C39
Proper 13	Feeding the hungry	Matt. 14:16	A21	A33/B15/C21/C29
Proper 14	Seeking God	1 Kings 19:12	A22	A10/B28/C16/C38
Proper 15	Mercy	Isa. 56:1	A23	A17/C14/C18/C46
Proper 16	Discernment	Rom. 12:2	B19	A2/A10/A34/B45/C47
Proper 17	Courage	Matt. 16:21	A25	B35/C13/C41
Proper 18	Penance	Matt. 18:18	A26	A27/B16/C14/C40
Proper 19	As we forgive those	Matt. 18:22	A27	A26/B16/C14/C40
Proper 20	Work	Matt. 20:8	A28	A1/A18/A36/A39
Proper 21	True obedience	Phil. 2:7	A29	A14/A32/B13/B31/C25
Proper 22	God's sinful people	Isa. 5:4	A30	A15/A34/A38
Proper 23	Heaven	Isa. 25:7	A31	A20/B3/B51/C48
Proper 24	Civic duty	Matt. 22:21	A32	A29/B14/B33/B34
Proper 25	Love your neighbour	Matt. 22:39	A33	A9/B52/C10/C19
Bible Sunday	Holy Scripture	Matt. 24:35	A12	B2/B9/B24/C6

Before Advent

4th Sunday	Hypocrisy and ambition	Micah 3:5	A34	A2/A15/B26/B44
3rd Sunday	Preparing for death	Matt. 25:13	A35	A42/B21/B22/B23/B41
2nd Sunday	Using talents	Matt. 25:15	A36	A1/A28/A39
Last Sunday	Christ the King	Eph. 1:22	A37	A4/A44/B4/B8

YEAR B	*Theme*	*Text*	*Section*	*Related sections*
Advent				
1st Sunday	Waiting on the Lord	Mark 13;35	B1	A1/A22/A35/B21/C36
2nd Sunday	The Good News	Isaiah 40:9	B2	B9/B12/B24/C2
3rd Sunday	Joy in Christ	1 Thess. 5:16	B3	B51/C2/C47
4th Sunday	Mary – Handmaid of God	Luke 1:38	B4	A4/A40/B7

Christmas

Christmas Day	See Year A			
1st Sunday	Mary, Mother of God	Luke 2:16	B7	A4/A40/C7/C45
2nd Sunday	Salvation in Christ	Eph. 1:3	C2	B3/B14/C2

Epiphany

The Epiphany	Revelation	Eph. 3:3	B9	A12/B2/B24/C8/C38
1st Sunday	The Baptism of Christ	Mark 1:8	B10	A38/B36/C26/C47/C49
2nd Sunday	Vocation	1 Sam. 3:10	B11	A10/A22/C16/C38
3rd Sunday	The Church –			
	Bride of Christ	Rev. 19:6-8	B17	A13/B36/C12
4th Sunday	Authority	Mark 1:27	B13	A14/A24/A29/A32/B14
Presentation	The Lord comes			
of Christ	to his temple	Mal. 3:1	C36	A31/A42/B22

Ordinary Time

Proper 1	Freedom to serve	1 Cor. 9:22	B14	B34/B45/C1
Proper 2	Jesus, friend of outcasts	Mark 1:40	B15	A21/A33/B38/C3
Proper 3	Christ heals and forgives	Mark 2:5	B16	A15/A26/A27/C22/
				C27/C40
2 before Lent	Christ, the eternal Son	Col. 1:15-18	C45	A37/A44/B4/B8/B46
1 before Lent	The glory of God	2 Cor. 4:6	A39	A20/B40/C31/C39

Lent

1st Sunday	Forty days of Lent	Mark 1:12	B43	B47/C37/C40/C41
2nd Sunday	True faith	Rom. 4:16	C22	B33/C30
3rd Sunday	The wisdom of God	1 Cor. 1:19	B37	A2/B20/B26
4th Sunday	Christ the sacrament			
	of God	John 3:14	B46	A44/B16/B51
or Mothering				
Sunday	The equality of women	John 19:25	A40	B34/B44/C33
5th Sunday	Dying to self	John 12:24	B47	A5/A7/A10/B26
Palm Sunday	Passion and glory	Phil. 2:8-9	B38	B15/B19/B49/C13

Easter

Easter Day	The risen Lord	Acts 10:40	C42	A44/C43/ C45/C47
2nd Sunday	Christian unity	Acts 4:32	B48	A20/B17/B36/B51
3rd Sunday	Coping with doubt	Luke 24:38	B49	C13/C22/C30/C41
4th Sunday	The Good Shepherd	John 10:11	B50	B15/B38/C44
5th Sunday	God is love	1 John 4:8	B52	A9/A33/B30/C10
6th Sunday	One with Christ	John 15:9-10	B51	B25/C47/C48
7th Sunday	Consecrated in Truth	John 17:19	B53	A47/C11/C23
Pentecost	Receive the Holy Spirit	Acts 2:4	C49	A46/A47/C47
Trinity Sunday	The Trinity	Rom. 8:16-17	B54	A37/A47/B28/B40/C47
Proper 4	Sunday	Mark 2:27	B18	A48/B29
Proper 5	Firm in the faith	2 Cor. 4:13	C30	B33/C22
Proper 6	Growth to maturity	Mark 4:28	B20	A2/A7/A10/B28
Proper 7	Trust in God	Mark 4:40	B21	A11/A19/B52/C39
Proper 8	Death	Wisd. 1:13	B22	A35/A42/B47/C36
Proper 9	Pastoral care of the sick	2 Cor. 12:9	B23	A35/A52/B38
Proper 10	Justice and peace	Eph. 1:14	B34	A24/A40/B44/C1/C33
Proper 11	Quiet – time for prayer	Mark 6:31	B25	A1/A10/C32/C47
Proper 12	The family	Eph. 2:14	B6	A9/B30/C5
Proper 13	Bread from heaven	Ex. 16:4	B27	A21/A44/B29
Proper 14	Community	Eph. 4:32	A9	A33/B6/B30/B52/
				C10/C19

Proper 15	The Eucharist	John 6:55-56	B29	A44/B18/B27
Proper 16	God's faithfulness	Eph 6:10	B40	B30/B54/C27
Proper 17	The commandments of life	Jas. 1:21	B31	A29/C6/C39
Proper 18	The wonders of God	Mark 7:37	B32	A18/B39
Proper 19	A careful tongue	A2	A2	B19/B20/B26/C23
Proper 20	Human rights	Jas. 3:16	B34	A21/A40/B44/C1/C33
Proper 21	The grace of God	Num. 11:25	B35	B51/B52/C55
Proper 22	The family of God	Heb. 2:11	B36	B10/B34/C12/C17/C24
Proper 23	The greatness of God	Heb. 4:16	A39	A20/B40/C31/C39
Proper 24	The suffering servant	Isa. 53:11	B38	B15/B19/B49/C13
Proper 25	God of compassion	Jer. 31:8	C18	A17/A23/A33/C46
Bible Sunday	Holy Scripture	Isa. 55:3	A12	B2/B9/B24/C6

Before Advent

4th Sunday	Love of God and neighbour	Mark 12:29-30	A33	A9/B52/C10/C19
3rd Sunday	Following Jesus	Mark 1:17	C16	A22/B11/B24/C41
2nd Sunday	Signs of the times	Mark 13:7-8	B42	A18/B34/C17
Last Sunday	Christ the King	Rev. 1:7	A37	A4/A44/B4/B8

YEAR C	*Theme*	*Text*	*Section*	*Related Sections*
Advent				
1st Sunday	Liberation from fear	Luke 21:28	C1	B3/B14/C2
2nd Sunday	Joy of salvation	Ba. 5:9	C2	B3/B14/C1
3rd Sunday	Sharing possessions	Luke 3:10	C3	A7/A21/A33/B41
4th Sunday	God incarnate	Micah 5:2	A4	A37/B4/B8/B46/C45

Christmas

Christmas Day	See Year A			
1st Sunday	The family	Eph. 3:13	B6	A9/B30/C5
2nd Sunday	The Word	John 1:1	B8	A4/A37/B4/C45

Epiphany

The Epiphany	Revelation	Eph. 3:3	B9	A12/B2/B24/C8/C38
1st Sunday	The baptism of Christ	Luke 3:16	B10	A38/B36/C26/C47/C49
2nd Sunday	God's gracious covenant	Isa. 62:4	B35	B51/B52/C55
3rd Sunday	The Old Testament law	Psa. 19:8	C6	A29/B4/B31
4th Sunday	The law's fulfilment	1 Cor. 13:1-3	A33	A9/B52/C10/C19
Presentation of Christ	The Lord comes to his temple	Mal. 3:1	C36	A31/A42/B22

Ordinary Time

Proper 1	God's messengers	Isa. 6:8	C8	B2/B9/B24
Proper 2	The Beatitudes	Jer. 17:7	C9	B2/B3/C2
Proper 3	Love your enemies	Luke 6:27	C10	A9/A33/B15/B52
2 before Lent	Lord of creation	Rev. 4:11	B39	A18/B32
1 before Lent	The glory of God	2 Cor. 3:18	A39	A20/B40/C31/C39

Lent

1st Sunday	Temptation	Luke 4:1	C37	A15/A38/B19/C26
2nd Sunday	Discerning God's will	Gen. 15:8	C38	A41/B11/B47/C39

3rd Sunday	Doing God's will	1 Cor. 10:6	C39	A41/B11/B47/C38
4th Sunday	Reconciliation	Luke 15:24	C40	A26/A27/B16/C14
or Mothering				
Sunday	The equality of women	John 19:25	A40	B34/B44/C33
5th Sunday	Starting afresh	Phil. 3:14	C41	A25/B14/C1
Palm Sunday	Passion and glory	Phil. 2:8-9	B38	B15/B19/B49/C13

Easter

Easter Sunday	The risen Lord	Acts 10:40	C42	A44/C43/C45/C47
2nd Sunday	The Living One	John 20:29	C43	A44/C42/C45/C47
3rd Sunday	Feed my sheep	John 21:17	C44	A21/B52
4th Sunday	The divinity of Christ	John 10:29-30	C45	A37/A44/B4/B8/B46
5th Sunday	Loving kindness	John 13:35	C46	A17/A33/B41/C18
6th Sunday	The indwelling Spirit	John 14:23	C47	B44/B51/C48/C49
7th Sunday	One in us	John 17:21	C48	B44/B51/C47/C49
Pentecost	Receive the Holy Spirit	John 14:15-16	C49	A46/A47/C47
Trinity Sunday	The Trinity	John 16:15	B54	A37/A47/B28/B40/C47
Proper 4	The Church for all people	1 Kgs. 8:43	C12	A6/A13/A43/B17
Proper 5	Coping with grief	Luke 7:13	C13	A25/B38/B49/C18
Proper 6	Forgiveness	Luke 7:47	C14	A26/A27/B16/C27/C40
Proper 7	Prejudice	Gal. 3:28	C15	A40/A41/B15/C1
Proper 8	Come, follow me	Luke 9:59-60	C16	A22/B11/B24/C41
Proper 9	International peace	Isa. 66:12	C17	A33/B34/C4/C10
Proper 10	Compassion	Luke 10:33	C18	A17/A23/A33/C46
Proper 11	Friendship	Luke 10:38	C19	A9/A33/B15
Proper 12	Our Father in heaven	Luke 11:12	C20	A22/B28/C27
Proper 13	Rise above materialism	Luke 12:15	C21	A7/A21/C29
Proper 14	The light of faith	Heb. 11:2	C22	B33/C30
Proper 15	Zeal for what is right	Luke 12:49	C23	A2/C8/C39
Proper 16	Humility	Luke 14:11	C25	A2/A7/B10/B20
Proper 17	The human condition	Heb. 13:3	C26	A15/A38/B22/B49/C37
Proper 18	Choosing the good	Deut. 30:15	B19	A2/A10/A34/B45/C47
Proper 19	Saving the lost	Luke 15:7	C27	A26/B28/C20/C41
Proper 20	Lord of the oppressed	Amos 8:4-7	C28	A21/B15/B38/B50
Proper 21	Not through luxury	Amos 6:1	C29	A7/A21/C21
Proper 22	Increase our faith	Luke 17:5	C30	B33/C22
Proper 23	Thanksgiving	Luke 17:15-16	C31	A17/A39/A48/B41
Proper 24	Prayer	Luke 18:7	C32	A22/A48/B25/B29
Proper 25	Equality	Ecclus. 35:12	C33	A9/A40/B34/B44
Bible Sunday	Holy Scripture	Rom. 15:4	A12	B2/B9/B24/C6

Before Advent

4th Sunday	God of justice	Is. 1:17	B33	C22/C30
3rd Sunday	Hope	Job. 19:25-27	C35	A6/A19/B21/C1
2nd Sunday	The day of the Lord	Mal. 4:1-2	C36	A31/A42/B22
Last Sunday	Christ the King	Col. 1:15	A37	A4/A44/B4/B8

APPENDIX FOUR

SCHOOL ASSEMBLY
Theme Index

The Human Condition

Ambition	A34	Original Sin	A38
Balance in nature	A18	Pain	B38
Conscience	B19	Prejudice	C15
Death	A35, B22	Seeking God	A22
Doubt	B49	Signs of the times	B42
God's sinful people	A30	Sin	A15
Grief	C13	Spiritual blindness	A41
Human condition	C26	Temptation	C37
Hypocrisy	A34	Work	A28

Relationships

Family	B6	Love your neighbour	A33
Feeding the hungry	A21	Married love	B30
Friendship	C19	Reconciliation	C40
Human rights	B34	Relationships	A9
Love your enemies	C10	Sharing	C3

God

Creation	B39	Lord who works marvels	B39
Father who draws us to himself	B28	One God	B40
Glory of God	A39	Spirit of Truth	A47
God is Love	B52	Trinity	B54
Indwelling Spirit	C47		

Communication with God

Covenant of God	B4	Prayer	C32
God's will	C38, C39	Providence	A11
Good News	B2	Revelation	B9
Holy Scripture	A12	Vocation	B11
Mission	B12	Worship	A48

Christ

Christ the Covenant of God	B4	Light of the world	A6
Christ the King	A37	Living One	C43
Christ heals and forgives	B16	Lord of all nations	C24
Divinity of Christ	C45	Risen Lord	C42
Emmanuel	A4	Suffering Servant	B38
Humanity of Christ	C7	The Word	B8
Jesus, friend of outcasts	B15		

Subject Index

INDEX OF SOURCES

Blay, Leon C2
Bloom, Anthony B11
Blue, Lionel A30
Bodo, Murray C47
Boehme, Jacob A18, A31, C2
Boethius A11
Bogart, Humphrey C19
Bok, Edward W. A34
Bonard A19
Bonaventure St C32
Bonhoeffer, Dietrich A35, C28
Bonnell, John Sutherland B17
Bonowski, Jacob B26
Boom, Corrie Ten A27
Boreham, F. W. B6
Bormann, Frank B39
Borrow, George B39
Bossuet, Jacques B. A29, C9
Bouquet, J. A. A17
Bovee, Christian A40
Bradstreet, Anne B13
Braithwaite, E. R. C15
Braque, Georges A47
Brault, Robert B30
Braun, David B12
Braunlih, Hermann G. C21
Briand, Aristide C40
Brooks, Phillip A29, A31, A39
Brown, Charles A43
Brown, H. H. B5
Brown, Raymond E. B10, B48
Brown, William Adams C6
Browne, Sir Thomas B44
Browning, Elizabeth Barrett A34
Browning, Robert A47, B26, C36
Brunner, Emil B8
Bruno, Giordano A39
Buber, Martin B32, B39, B40
Bultmann, Rudolf C20
Bunche, Ralph C8
Bunyan, John A31
Burke, Edmund C6
Burkhart, Roy A. A15
Burns, James C42
Burns, Robert B34
Burridge, William A4
Butterfield, Herbert A38, C26
Buttrick, George A. C18, C25
Butzer, Albert A. A37
Buxton, Charles A15

C
Calvin, John A13
Camara, Helder A21, A22, C12
Campbell, Paul A5
Camus, Albert A41, C36
Camus, Jean Pierre C1
Carey, Elwes OSB Columba C25
Carey, George A14, A48, B14, C12, C42
Carigg, N. A40
Carlyle, Thomas A2, A25, A41, B25, B26, B32
Carnegie, Dale C19, C46
Carpenter, Edmund C33
Carretto, Carlo A5, A7, B11, B29, B53, B54, C9, C32, C48
Carroll, Lewis B2
Carswell, Catherine C8
Cartland, Barbara A40, B53
Cary, Alice C46
Cassidy, Sheila B3, B44, C32
Castle A. P. A9, B22, B39, C14, C30
Cather, Willa B32
Catherine of Siena, St A10, C38
Catoir, John B3
Causley, Charles B43
Cavert, Walter D. A12
Cervantes C19
Chaitanya, Sri C46
Chambers, Oswald A2, A29, B3
Chamfort, Nicholas B20
Channing, William E. B19, B47
Chapman, Dom John A25
Chesterton, Gilbert K. A37, A47, B6, B26, B31, B34, C2, C12, C25
Christophers, The B30
Chrysostom, St John A8, B17, B27
Churchill, Sir Winston A3, A25, A32, A37, B40
Cicero, C10, C31
Clark, Frank C22
Clark, Glen C32
Clarke W. H. A20
Claudel, Paul A16, B15
Claverie of Oban, Bishop A47
Clement, John B39
Clement of Alexandria, St A4, B16, B36, C42
Clifford, D. B22
Clodd, Edward B19
Clough A. H. C43
Coggan, Lord Donald A15, B24, B39, C12, C32

Herrick, Robert B4
Heschel, Abraham Joshua B39, C18
Heywood Thomas B41
Hickman, Franke S. C8
Hietgsche, Friedrick C10
Hildegard of Bingen C8
Hiles, D. T. C42
Hillel, Rabbi C19
Hilton, Walter C3
Hippolytus St A4
Hindu Saying A28
Hobbes Thomas A41
Hodge, Charles B9
Hodgson, Bernard A19
Holland, Josiah A5
Holmes, Oliver Wendell A40, C20, C30
Holtby, Winifred A28
Hooft, Wisser't W. A43
Hooker, Richard C6
Hoover, Herbert C17
Hopkins, Gerard Manley A39, A42
Hopko, Thomas C41
Horace C44
Houghton, William A12, C43
Housman, Lawrence B5
How, Bishop Walsham A1, B35
Howard, St Philip B38
Hugo, Victor B3, B24, C13, C22
Huddleston, Trevor B44
Hume, Cardinal Basil A16, B30, B44
Hunt, Cecil A47
Hunt, Leigh A33
Hunter, Allan A. C3
Huvelin, Abbe A45
Huxley, Aldous C14

I

Ibsen, Henrik C21
Ignatius of Antioch, St A6, A8, A14, C47
Ilich, Ivan A21, B14
Inge, William A42, B20
Ingelow, Jean A28
Irenaeus St C12
Israel of Rizhym, Rabbi C18
Ivins, Molly A18

J

Jacks, L. P. B47, C26
Jackson, Holbrook B49
James, Eric A48
James, William B37, C15

James I, King A17
Jarratt, B. de C13
Jefferies, Richard A9
Jefferson, Thomas B34
Jerome, St A12
Jewel, John A14
Jewish legend A40, C22
Johanan, Rabbi B36
John Chrysostom, St A8, A19, B27, B29, B48, C21, C34, C49
John of Damascus, St A11, A15, B5, B9, B36
John Fr C44
John of the Cross, St A10, C26
John Paul I, Pope A26, A31, B2, B11, C41
John Paul II, Pope A7, A15, A21, A24, A28, A37, A38, A43, A46, B1, B4, B6, B8, B9, B11, B13, B15, B19, B23, B30, B42, B43, B44, B50, B52, C5, C12, C16, C17, C20, C27, C29, C32, C35, C39, C40, C44
John XXIII, Pope A8, A34, B4, B8, C33
John Ruysholch A48, B28, B54, C25
Johnson, C. C14, C36
Johnson, Larry A47
Johnson, Paul A47
Johnson, Samuel A3, B45, C44, C46
Johnson, William B37
Jones, Franklin C11
Jones, Mary B22
Jones, E. Stanley B38
Jowett, Benjamin B49, C8
Julian of Norwich C2

K

Kant Immanuel A12
Kasper, Walter C6
Kauter, Kurt C17
Kavanagh, Aidan C49
Kazantzakis, Nikos B19
Keble, John C34
Keim, Theodor B8
Keller, Helen B3, C20, C30, C35
Kelman, John C23
Kempis Thomas à A10, A19, B1, B19, B35, C1, C3, C31, C43
Ken, Thomas B17, B20
Kendrick, G. B5
Kennedy, John F. A21, A25, B40, C17
Kent, Bruce C17
Kierkegaard, Soren B12, B28, B31, B39, B40, C22, C27, C38

ACKNOWLEDGEMENTS

The compiler and publishers would like to thank the following authors, publishers and copyright holders for permission to reproduce material of which they hold the copyright.

The Catholic Herald for an extract from David Torkington's article on *Repentance*.

D.M. Duncan for extracts from *Through the Year with William Barclay*, edited by Denis Duncan.

Hodder-Headlines Ltd for an extract from *Fear No Evil* by David Watson and material from *The Hiding Place* by Corrie Ten Boom, jointly controlled with Evelyn Singer Literary Agency of New York.

Dimension Books Inc of Denville, New Jersey for extracts from *Invaded by God* by George A. Maloney SJ.

Editions du Seuil, 27 Rue Jacob, 75261, Paris for the extract from *Le Milieu Divin* by Teilhard de Chardin, © Editions du Seuil 1957.

Hamish Hamilton for extracts from *Six Doctors* by J.G. Crowther, published in 1957.

Fr William Burridge WF for his Christmas Story of Shaka.

Basil Blackwell Ltd for extracts from *Day to Day* by Rowland Purton.

Darton Longman and Todd Ltd for material taken from *Letters from the Desert* by Carlo Carretto, published and copyright 1972.

News from Africa Watch for an extract.

The Tablet, London, for material by Fr John Medcalf and Fr Jon Sobrino and other material that has appeared in *The Tablet*.

The Abbot of the Stravropegic Monastery of St John the Baptist, Maldon, Essex, for extracts from *Saint Silouan, the Athonite* by Archimandrite Sophrony 1991, and three extracts from *We shall See Him As He Is* by Archimandrite Sophrony 1988.

Fowler Wright Books Ltd, Gracewing House, 2 Southern Avenue, Leominster, Herefordshire HR6 0QF, for the extract from *The Empire of the Heart* by John F.X. Harriott, published by Gracewing, 1990.

HarperCollins Publishers, 10 East 53rd Street, New York, NY 10022-5299, USA, for the extract from *Instrument of Thy Peace* by Alan Paton. Copyright © 1968, 1982 by the Seabury Press Inc.

HarperCollins Publishers, 77-85 Fulham Palace Road, London W6 8JB, for the extracts from *The Puzzle of Evil* by Peter Vardy, published by Fount Press 1992, and material from *Illustrissimi* by Pope John Paul I, published by Collins.

Hodder Headline Plc, 338 Euston Road, London NW1 3BH for the extract from *Bolts from the Blue* by Rabbi Lionel Blue, published by Coronet Books, 1987.

Oxford University Press, Oxford, for the extract from *The Catholic Faith* by Roderick Strange, published by Oxford University Press 1986.

William Neil-Hall Ltd, 53 Effingham Road, Long Ditton, Surbiton, Surrey KT6 5LA for the extract from *Fear No Evil* by David Watson.

Reverend Prior Provincial of The Order of Preachers (Dominicans), St Dominic's Priory, London NW5 4LB, for extracts from the writing of Father Vincent McNabb OP.

Mrs Nicholl for extracts from *Holiness* and *The Testing of Hearts* both by Donald Nicholl.

Reverend Father Superior, Order of St Benedict, Collegeville, Minnesota, USA, for material from *Christening* by Mark Searle, published in 1980.

Sheil Land Associates Ltd, 43 Doughty Street, London WC1N 2LF, for the extract from *Audacity to Believe* by Dr Sheila Cassiday © 1977.

Ms Angela Tilby for an extract from an article by her in the *The Tablet*.

Every effort has been made to trace the owners of copyright material and we hope that no copyright has been infringed. Pardon is sought and apology made if the contrary be the case, and a correction will be made in any reprint of this book.